Palgrave Studies in Ec

CW01661278

Series Editor
Kent Deng, London School of Economics, London, UK

Palgrave Studies in Economic History is designed to illuminate and enrich our understanding of economies and economic phenomena of the past. The series covers a vast range of topics including financial history, labour history, development economics, commercialisation, urbanisation, industrialisation, modernisation, globalisation, and changes in world economic orders.

George Hong Jiang

The Imperial Mode of China

An Analytical Reconstruction of Chinese Economic History

palgrave
macmillan

George Hong Jiang
Max Weber Institute of Sociology
Heidelberg University
Heidelberg, Germany

School of Economics
Peking University
Beijing, China

ISSN 2662-6497 ISSN 2662-6500 (electronic)
Palgrave Studies in Economic History
https://doi.org/10.1007/978-3-031-27015-4

Cover illustration: CPA Media Pte Ltd/Alamy Stock Photo

This Palgrave Macmillan imprint is published by the registered company Springer Nature Switzerland AG
The registered company address is: Gewerbestrasse 11, 6330 Cham, Switzerland
(www.springernature.com/mycopy)

For my supervisor, Prof. em. Dr. Dres. h.c. Bertram Schefold

"A teacher affects eternity; He will never know where his influence stops".

—Henry Adams

Foreword by Bertram Schefold

The Imperial Mode of China: An Analytical Reconstruction of Chinese Economic History is an ambitious book that proposes an answer to one of the most fascinating questions of our time: What are the structural reasons behind the persistence of fundamental traits in the governance of China and the continuities in the life of the Chinese people, despite some large and many small upheavals, which have taken place in recent decades and indeed in past millennia? The author carried out his research mainly in Frankfurt am Main and Cambridge. During the first few years of his Ph.D. study, Jiang worked on Marxian economics, the history of economic thought and, in particular, Chinese economic history. Under the influence of a project devised by members of the Department of Sinology and the Faculty of Economics of Goethe University on "European and Chinese Histories of Economic Thought", Jiang gradually turned to the interactions between economic, political and intellectual history in China. An early inspiration was the work of Karl Wittfogel, a prominent social scientist in the last century. While Wittfogel's conclusions are controversial due to inaccurate and even wrong details, his hypothesis that the structure of ancient patrimonial civilisations was largely determined by the need to control water became the springboard for Jiang's analysis. Wittfogel had in his early years been a Marxist historian who tried to extend Marx's historical materialism to Oriental empires, building on the Marxian conception of an Asiatic mode of production. Although Chinese textbooks are full of Marxian doctrines, Jiang, who completed his undergraduate education in Mainland China, felt the need to explore the works of Marx and Engels independently. To use historical materialism as the fundamental approach to re-analyse Chinese economic history thus became a starting point of the book, but it soon became clear that it needed to be complemented.

The evolution that leads from China's imperial past to present communist China turned out to be path dependent not only due to exterior influences such as the incursion of the Western powers and Japan, but also following an internal logic of the evolution of institutions influenced by intellectual turnarounds such as the revival of Confucianism. Hence, the framework, as presented in Chapter 1, is based on the integration of three theoretical approaches, i.e., Marxian historical materialism, Weberian ideal types and institutionalist theories. Marx's tenets about the Asiatic society and undeveloped societies were left unfinished, but once developed, they become instruments for the critique of modern forms of Oriental despotism. Jiang's conceptualisation tries to apply historical materialism to the Chinese case. Different from Europe's path, an imperial structure took shape in the Pre-Qin period and prevailed through the two millennia of Chinese history. While the imperial structure has experienced variations, i.e., the Han and Song variants, it was the predominant social organisational form and continuously impacted China in the last one hundred years. Characterised by a centralised decision-making mechanism and a top-down enforcement apparatus, the imperial structure succeeded in responding to the demand of an agricultural economy but failed to transform itself, when it was confronted with the challenges of a commercial and industrial economy. In this sense, the book also tries to unriddle the Great Divergence. In the last part of his book, Jiang tries to explain why present China continues to be heavily influenced by the imperial structure via path dependence, and it is argued that the future will most likely still be shaped by these same forces.

December 2022

Bertram Schefold
Faculty of Economics
and Business Administration
Goethe University Frankfurt
Frankfurt, Germany

Foreword by Werner Plumpe

The economic history of China is currently the focus of global interest not only because the world economy is now shaped by China's development in many respects, but also because for some time now the question of the future shape of China has once again been quite open. Whether the country will continue to cultivate its own capitalism or whether there is a danger of a relapse into authoritarian and economically non-liberal structures with still unforeseeable consequences for the world economy is currently quite open. To give an answer to this question based solely on short-term political and economic considerations is as tempting as it is uninformative. For as topical as many developments may seem to be, those who are unfamiliar with the historical dimensions of economic policy in East Asia will find it difficult to understand how they are shaped. Rather, the complexity of the Chinese economy and its transformation will only be understood by those who are familiar with its historical paths and, above all, with the long-lasting older traditions that continue to have an impact today. This is the starting point and the great merit of Jiang Hong's study. Hong not only succeeds in reconstructing the last 2500 years of Chinese economic history in a comprehensible way; he also makes clear the specific dialectic of institutional framing and economic performance under the specific geographical conditions of this Asian territorial state. By bringing together Marxist and neoinstitutionalist questions, Hong is able to identify an institutional constellation that has long characterised economic change in China, which he himself describes as an "imperial mode". This "imperial mode" consisted in the specific interplay of central authority, bureaucratic development of the mast, and peasant agriculture, which, albeit in a changing form, was of constitutive importance for the older Chinese economy and made possible the great agricultural and industrial achievements that allowed the Chinese economy to be successful in real terms. This "imperial mode", however, had then also become the decisive barrier through which China's economic modernisation had been blocked since the eighteenth century, because the central authority in conjunction with the Confucian bureaucracy had feared the uncontrollable consequences of economic modernisation and had therefore blocked it in order to safeguard the integrity of the Chinese empire against possible threats. In the background of the widening gap between certain Western economies and China since that time (Great Divergence), Hong therefore sees less a consequence of the violent Western free trade imperialism that reduced China to a semi-colonial status in the nineteenth century. The country did try to assert itself through reforms against the pressure of Western powers, but these more half-hearted attempts were pulverised in the rivalry between modernisation and securing the given structures of rule. Ultimately, the country's economic development in the twentieth century also appears quite understandable in this perspective. While the thoroughly intelligent reforms of the republican period eventually came to a halt under the pressure of Japanese expansion, Maoism made attempts at modernisation possible, but they ignored the country's real economic conditions and thus ultimately had little success. Only the opening of the economy since Deng Xiao Ping opened up a radical innovation by successively enabling free economic action, which is admittedly still integrated into the older institutional framework of a strong, bureaucratically supported authority. It is the dynamics of the change now possible and its potential impact on Chinese society that do not leave this very framework untouched. How the Chinese "experiment" will develop further is thus the open question that stands at the end of Hong's reflections, but through him takes on a clear historical dimension.

Hong's thesis that the "imperial mode" was the appropriate form of institutional framing of the older Chinese agrarian world, but that it did not develop sufficient initiatives for its modernisation, but only attempted reforms under external pressure and ultimately proved to be overtaxed, is readily comprehensible and also fruitful because Hong by no means states a smooth break with the older traditions in the present, but rather considers their specified continuing effects. The following consideration that in modern China a further developing form of the "imperial mode" is effective, which today can be seen as framing the Chinese model, whereby at the same time another variant of capitalism ("Oriental Capitalism") with a quite open future has emerged, is fruitful and fits in well with ongoing debates in economic history about the importance of institutional factors in economic change. Hong shows that it is not simply a matter of certain institutions, but that these must be appropriate to refer to the respective historical situation of a country, i.e., that they can by no means be shaped arbitrarily. Anyone who looks at China will have to reckon with its historical legacy, which goes back a long way.

December 2022

Werner Plumpe
Faculty of Philosophy and History
Goethe University Frankfurt
Frankfurt am Main, Germany

Acknowledgements

This book is mainly the fruit of my doctoral studies in Frankfurt and post-doctoral studies in Cambridge and Heidelberg. As my first monograph, the book integrates what I have learned from economics, sociology, history, etc. Born in China, I have been always obsessed with observing and interpreting China. I have witnessed China's rapid economic growth in the 1990s and 2000s. The remarkable achievements have lifted billions of people out of absolute poverty since the 1980s and rendered over millions of people so wealthy that they can afford to study overseas and buy luxuries in a crazy fashion. Economic reforms have profoundly changed the fate of countless people. I clearly know how China's reforms changed the economy and society, hugely because I grew up in a community of a state-owned enterprise in Shanxi Province which is famous for producing coal and metal resources. My grandparents who almost spend their entire life in the community always tell me all sorts of stories and historical changes that they have experienced. For example, while my grandmother applauds Deng Xiaoping's policies because deregulation in the 1980s gave her opportunities to do private business and make money, my grandfather occasionally sighs at widespread corruption and the increasingly huge gap between the rich and the poor because as a communist veteran he thinks that it is the liberalisation policy that leads to the unsatisfying social reality. This mixed atmosphere permeated my childhood, but it also gave me the first-hand experience about economic and social vicissitudes. When I was a child, I always accompanied my grandmother to do business and in other occasions read monographs of Karl Marx and Mao Zedong in my grandfather's study.

As I study more in the undergraduate and postgraduate stage, I realise that the connections between the past and the present are extremely powerful when analysing the Chinese economy and society even though the nexus is often hidden. If we support civilisational diversity in which different civilisations evolve alongside their own pathways, a question must be asked of where the unique characteristics come from. Karl Marx clearly held the idea that human civilisation should follow the same path from primitive communism to communism in the future, while in his works non-western civilisations were somehow treated differently. The Asiatic Society was used to illustrate a few non-western civilisations, including Russia, the Ottoman Empire, India and China, but he never offered a clear and strictly demarcated definition of it. Nonetheless, I pick up some tools from historical materialism to reconstruct Chinese economic history, in the hope that the reconstruction might relieve the plight of historical materialism in the Chinese case. In contrast to Karl Marx, Max Weber rejected the unilinear pathway of civilisational evolution (this point is still controversial, though). Weber offered potent tools to analyse civilisations' characteristics *per se*. Weber's seminal writings on religions provide enlightening instructions on how to make an anatomy of a certain civilisation. A synergy of Marxian and Weberian approaches forms the fundamental logic of the book.

My deepest gratitude goes to my Ph.D. supervisor in Frankfurt, Prof. Bertram Schefold. While Prof. Schefold once said to me with a jocular tone that this project looks like something that one does only after becoming old, he offers all kinds of intellectual support without any reservation. In late 2016 he generously accepted me as his Ph.D. student in Frankfurt. In the first two years I studied Marxian economics and the history of economic thought. Although my Ph.D. dissertation is hardly a work about it, I benefit a lot from submerging into the grand ideas of Karl Marx, Adam Smith, Thomas Malthus and many other economic thinkers. Prof. Schefold also enthusiastically supported me when I told him that I wanted to turn to research of Chinese economic history in the third year. He introduced me to the work of Karl Wittfogel who graduated at Goethe University Frankfurt as well, and other sinologists who established their reputation in Frankfurt, such as Richard Wilhelm. During the period of writing my Ph.D. dissertation, he did not only provide intellectual guides but also steered me to explore more spheres. When I got my doctoral degree in economics in 2021, he has succeeded in making me so interested in Max Weber that I decided to start a second Ph.D. in sociology. I believe that the most important lessons which Prof. Schefold taught me are never about any specific content of economic theories or theoretical methodology, but about an attitude—how to live an intellectual life in pursuit of self-satisfaction. Whenever I feel depressed about my career, I always recall the occasions when Prof. Schefold passionately read classic German poems in front of his huge bookshelf. I think that my entire life will be supported by such an attitude. This book is dedicated to him.

I also want to thank my second supervisor in Frankfurt, Prof. Werner Plumpe. As a founder of regional communist party in Germany, he has a very thorough and comprehensive understanding of Marxism. As a member of Institute of Social Research (Institut für Sozialforschung) in Frankfurt, he has a unique understanding about relations between capitalism and Marxism. Once Prof. Plumpe asked me, "it seems that you use historical materialism selectively". Although I replied with a very relaxing tone at the time, that question provoked lasting and deep thinking in my mind. How I should treat the toolbag of historical materialism in my work becomes the crux. Historical materialism is a half-product which Marx and Engels presented. Efforts to reconstruct historical materialism *per se* have never stopped. My book is an effort to apply its elements to the Chinese case. I also owe a debt of gratitude to Prof. Dr. Rainer Klump and Prof. Guido Friebel, who as members of the defence committee raised valuable questions during my oral defence.

I would like to express my gratitude to Prof. Christel Lane and Dr. David Lane in Cambridge. They generously accepted me as a postdoctoral fellow at the Department of Sociology, the University of Cambridge. As soon as I received the letter from Cambridge, my supervisor in Frankfurt, Bertram Schefold who spent a few years in the early 1970s in Cambridge, told me that I would enjoy Cambridge immensely. After my career there is temporarily over, I can say now that I did enjoy my time in Cambridge. David Lane is an esteemed expert in communism and sociological study of Eastern Europe and the Soviet Union. Christel Lane has extensive research of applying sociological theories to ex-communist countries. They not only give me specific suggestions on the book but also lead me further to sociological research. The privileges that they give me have made Cambridge a personal sweet memory.

I would also like to thank Prof. Wolfgang Schluchter and Prof. Thomas Schwinn in Heidelberg. Prof. Schluchter is one of the prestigious experts in Weberian sociology and still energetically works at the Max Weber Institute of Sociology. We get to know each other in early 2022 and meet up occasionally at his office where artistic works full of Chinese style reflect his dense interest in China. After reading through my dissertation, he gives me important suggestions about how to use Weberian approaches to integrate the materials that I have collected. In particular, he taught me how to chronologise Chinese history in a more theoretical and concise way. It hugely changed the structure of the book. His teachings about ideal types and suggestions to pay attention to variation of different historical stages fundamentally changed my opinions on Chinese history. I also thank him for recommending me to Prof. Schwinn who accepted me as his doctoral candidate. It was this amazing luck that eventually enabled me to pursue my second doctoral degree in sociology in Heidelberg. Simultaneously Prof. Dr. Matthias Koenig also gives me many enlightening instructions about modernities and comparative historical sociology, which improves my understanding about China's and the West's positions in civilisational evolution.

Furthermore, I want to mention the heartwarming encouragement which I receive from Prof. Dr. Hans-Werner Sinn in Munich. A couple of years ago, I encountered one of his monographs in China, namely *Kaltstart: Volkswirtschaftliche Aspekte der deutschen Vereinigung [The Cold Start: The Macroeconomic Aspects of the German Unification]*, which addresses the political economic issues about how a socialist planned economy was transformed into a market economy with difficulties and how two different economic systems were integrated. It initially instigated my interest in the vicissitudes of a socialist economy and macroeconomic changes. Especially, Prof. Sinn once expressed his hope that the academic exchange between China and Germany should be strengthened while most Chinese students go to the US for higher education. After we met up in 2020 in Frankfurt, he has been encouraging me to focus on China's political economic changes. The chapter about China's modernisation in the book is a result of my thinking on relevant issues.

I want to express my deep gratitude to Prof. Kent Gang Deng who introduced me to the wonderful publisher, Palgrave Macmillan, and included my book in the series that he edits. His passion to help young researchers has touched me. Our regular meeting in London has not only improved my thinking on the manuscript but also helped me get a deeper understanding about the English academic circle. It is quite interesting to see the difference between the English and German academic circle. In addition, Deng's unique opinions on Qing China and social evolutionism refreshed my mind. Deng is truly an enlightening teacher and a good friend.

I know that this work contains huge ambitions that I might not be able to accomplish, but I received selfless help and encouragement from many colleagues and distinguished scholars, without which I would not have completed this work. The list is highly inconclusive: Yaguang Zhang, Jianbo Zhou, Debin Ma, Denggao Long, Jinghua Xing, Zhiwu Chen, Junjie Mei (Shanghai), Chunwen Xiong, Ping He (Renmin Uni), Terry Peach, Richard van den Berg, Iwo Amelung, William G. Clarence-Smith, Austin Gareth, Ruixue Jia, Barry Naughton, Isabella Weber, Hao Chen (Yale), Junhao Cao (Utrecht). I would like to give my special gratitude to Joseph McDermott who very sadly passed away on 31 October 2022. I still remember that Joseph led me to walk through the flowering garden behind St. John's College in the spring of 2022. He taught me in detail how to use the wealthy collections of Chinese literature at the Library of the University of Cambridge. We spent a wonderful afternoon in the cosy town and intended to try a Chinese restaurant in Cambridge next time. It is my eternal regret.

I want to thank Ellie Duncan and Noorjahan Begum for their enthusiastic support in this project. Four anonymous reviewers provided valuable suggestions and thoughtful comments.

Last but not least, I want to thank those friends who have spent time together respectively in Beijing, Hong Kong, Frankfurt am Main, Düsseldorf, Cambridge and London. It is the friendship between us that has supported me to walk so far. In particular, I want to thank Xiaogong Jiao in Yuncheng who is willing to sustain friendship with such a friend lacking in feeling of responsibility and presence. I consistently believe that the most important thing which I hold dearly when I become old will never be any substantive item but the emotional and spiritual connections with others. J. W. Goethe once said famously: "All theory, dear friend, is grey, but the golden tree of actual life springs ever green". Let the tree be evergreen!

Heidelberg, DE, Germany
February 2023

George Hong Jiang

Contents

1 Introduction 1

2 The Empire-Building in the Pre-Qin Era 29

3 Thought Matters 63

4 The First Phase: The Han Variant 97

5 The Second Phase: The Song Variant 133

6 A Historical Pattern: The Imperial Mode 177

7 The Great Divergence I: The West 203

8 The Great Divergence II: China 227

9 Pursuing Modernisation in China 255

10 To Understand China: Past and Future 305

Index 321

About the Author

George Hong Jiang is currently a postdoctoral researcher at the Max Weber Institute of Sociology at Heidelberg University, and concurrently an assistant researcher (2019–) at the Center of Foreign Economic Thought at the School of Economics, Peking University. Jiang's research interests include political economy (with a focus on China), macroeconomics, economic sociology and economic history. Jiang has written and published works on Marxian economics, economic and social history, China's economy and the History of Economic Thought. Jiang's works appear on Chinese, English and German platforms. Jiang got his doctoral degree in economics (2021) at Goethe University Frankfurt and was a postdoctoral fellow (2022) at the Department of Sociology at the University of Cambridge. Jiang is also pursuing his second doctoral degree in sociology (2022–) at Heidelberg University. Jiang has lived and studied in Mainland China, Hong Kong, Germany and the United Kingdom.

Major Periods in China

Shang	c. 1600–c. 1046 BCE
Western Zhou	c. 1046–771 BCE
Eastern Zhou	771–256 BCE
Waring States	403–221 BCE
Qin	221–206 BCE
Western Han	206 BCE–8 AD
Eastern Han	25–220
North-South Disunion	220–589
Northern Wei	386–535
Sui	589–618
Tang	618–907
Northern Song	960–1125
Southern Song	1127–1279
Yuan	1279–1368
Ming	1368–1644
Qing	1644–1912
Republic of China	1912–1949
People's Republic of China	1949–

Chronology of Key People in Chinese History

Guan Zhong	725?–645 BCE
Confucius	c. 551–c. 479 BCE
Mencius	372–289 BCE
Shang Yang	390–338 BCE
Qin Emperor the First	259–210 BCE, r. 221–210 BCE
Gaodi of Han	256–195 BCE, r. 202–195 BCE
Wendi of Han	203–157 BCE, r. 180–157 BCE
Wudi of Han	156–87 BCE, r. 140–87 BCE
Sang Hongyang	152–80 BCE
Guangwudi of Han	5 BCE–57 AD, r. 25–57 AD
Wang Mang	45 BCE–23 AD
Cao Cao	155–220
Xiaowendi of Northern Wei	467–499, r. 471–499
Wendi of Sui	541–604, r. 581–604
Yangdi of Sui	569–618, r. 604–618
Taizong of Tang	598–649, r. 626–649
Empress Wu	624–705, r. 690–705
Yang Yan	727–781
Zhao Kuangyin	927–976, r. 960–976
Wang Anshi	1021–1086
Kublai Khan	1215–1294, r. 1271–1294
Hongwu	1328–1398, r. 1368–1398
Yongle	1360–1424, r. 1402–1424
Zhang Juzheng	1525–1582
Kangxi	1654–1722, r. 1661–1722
Yongzheng	1678–1735, r. 1722–1735

Qianlong	1711–1799, r. 1735–1796
Empress Cixi	1835–1908
Zeng Guofan	1811–1872
Li Hongzhang	1823–1901
Yuan Shikai	1859–1916
Sun Yat-sen	1866–1925
Chiang Kai-Shek	1887–1975
Mao Zedong	1893–1976
Deng Xiaoping	1904–1997
Chen Yun	1905–1995
Jiang Zemin	1926–2022

List of Figures

Chaper 2

Fig. 1 The Hydraulic projects in the Eastern Zhou Dynasty 46
Fig. 2 The cognitive map of contributing factors to the empire-building 59

Chaper 3

Fig. 1 The hypothetical population growth by aristocratic class as population grew generation by generation, the number of the king was nevertheless kept as 1; that of lords and dukes increased slightly; that of lower aristocrats increased remarkably. 67
Fig. 2 The cognitive map of intellectual influences upon the imperial mode 93

Chaper 4

Fig. 1 The Magnate's House in the Han Dynasty (*Source* National Museum of China, originally in Chengdu, Sichuan Province) 115

Chaper 6

Fig. 1 The cognitive map of the imperial mode 197

Chaper 9

Fig. 1 Sketch of China's Liberalisation Process. *In Walter's original graph, the year is 1990. However, I believe that the authentic reverse of the conservative/back-to-planning trends after 1989 happened only after Deng Xiaoping had his southern travel in 1992. Threatened by Deng's power, communist cadres returned to economic reforms, including the General Secretary, Jiang Zemin (*Source* Walter and Howie 2012: 4) 297

Chaper 10

Fig. 1 Relative strength of the imperial mode of China 314

List of Tables

Chaper 6

Table 1	Major dynasties and reasons of dynastic cycles	194

Chaper 8

Table 1	Population and Cultivated Acreage Estimates (1400–1913)	249

Chaper 9

Table 1	China's National Income (1850–1949)	274
Table 2	China's National Income *per capita* (1850–1949)	275
Table 3	*Per capita* Production of Agricultural Products	275

CHAPTER 1

Introduction

For a long time, European people's understanding about ancient China was full of Kafkaesque imagination. In Kafka's concise story, "At the Construction of the Great Wall of China",[1] ancient China was symbolised by a streamlined structure consisting of mighty but naïve emperors, imperious bureaucrats, inapproachable scholars and pristine commoners. As a romantic symbol, the construction of the Great Wall once amazed western observers with its astonishing length and sophisticated engineering techniques. The Great Wall seems to be an epitome of the specific structure of this monolithic empire. It originated from the need to defend against nomadic invaders. Emperors and bureaucrats launched magnificent projects by exploiting commoners. To some degree, such a canvas indeed reflected the operational logic of this empire. From this perspective, Kafka's story was never just a novel but also a parable full of sinological meaning (Zhou 2002). It partly caught the essence of this "immemorial" empire.

It was almost contemporary with ancient Egypt and Mesopotamia when the earliest farmers in China learned how to use tools to cultivate fields made fertile by cyclical flood. For almost two millennia, Chinese farmers have created a splendid agricultural civilisation. The Chinese

[1] The original title was "Beim Bau der Chinesischen Mauer". It was written in 1917 and published in 1930, seven years after Kafka's death.

G. H. Jiang, *The Imperial Mode of China*, Palgrave Studies in Economic History, https://doi.org/10.1007/978-3-031-27015-4_1

empire continued to expand geographically and achieved unparalleled technological progress in the agricultural era. In the Tang (618–907 AD) and Song (960–1279 AD) dynasties, material prosperity reached its peak. In the following Yuan dynasty (1271–1368 AD), Marco Polo described such prosperity with voluminous details and dramatic literal style. Even for those great thinkers in the Enlightenment Movement in France, such as Turgot and Quesnay,[2] the Chinese empire was believed to be the most elegant and fully fledged regime. It was once praised as the model for European countries. However, in the nineteenth century, the backwardness of this empire was soon exposed in front of the overwhelming military and economic power of occidental countries. The relative prosperity of China to its western counterparts diminished significantly in this period. In the twentieth century, China experienced several dramatic political swings. China had become one of the poorest countries in the world until communist statesmen decided to reopen its borders to the international community and to launch economic reforms in the 1980s (Acemoglu and Robinson 2013: 234). For a time, the remarkable speed of economic growth of China has attracted thinkers to delve into every aspect of this "polytope". Some observers believe that China is a heterodoxic civilisational entity which has a totally different pathway from the one on which the West has walked, while others insist that China is an integral component of a globalised wave (see below). The intellectual conflicts which in many cases have apparent pragmatic meaning will long be debated.

The purpose of this book is to explore and analyse China's long-run economic and social transitions, from the beginnings of the Chinese empire to China today. While ancient China was not stagnant at all, some fundamental characteristics have been kept consistently. Before globalisation started in the late Middle Ages,[3] oriental and occidental civilisations

[2] For example, Turgot's best-known work, *Reflections on the Formation and Distribution of Wealth*, was written ostensibly for the benefit of two young Chinese students. Quesnay was fond of Chinese Daoism, and his economic ideas were influenced by Chinese economic thought.

[3] There are debates about when globalisation truly started. For example, Valerie Hansen argues that globalisation began far earlier before the discovery of the New World. Some historians speak highly of the intercontinental trade between East Asia, India, the Arabic World and Europe in the early Middle Ages. Nevertheless, the mainstream opinion is still that globalisation began since Western Europe discovered new routes to the New World and Asia. See: Hansen (2000).

evolved relatively independently. After the rise of Western Europe and especially the Industrial Revolution, economies and societies marched fast towards industrialisation and modernisation. Nonetheless, while the "Occidental Mode" seemed to have an overwhelming potency, "different economies, facing a variety of local circumstances, found their own paths to the twentieth century" (Mokyr 2009: 11). Theoretical universality always encounters empirical specificality. In this sense, China is an appropriate case to be analysed. In other words, China is "a mediate ground between the two" (Anderson 1974: foreword).[4] Marx had already seemed to have paradoxical attitudes towards China's societal nature, in that (1) on the one hand, Marx constructed an evolutionary path which was believed to be inevitable across civilisations; (2) on the other hand, Marx asserted that China, and other Asiatic societies, were never-changing. Taking Marx's particular points aside, historical materialism offers a potent tool for holistic analysis regarding China's long-run transitions. At the same time, Max Weber who proposed ideal types provided analytical examples through his historical-comparative sociology, about how to interpret societal variants between stages within one society and between societies. Moreover, from the micro-level perspective, institutionalist approaches are effective tools for specific structural analysis when we conduct an anatomy on China's individual institutions. This chapter will present three approaches, namely Marxian, Weberian and institutionalist approaches, and show how they are utilised as methodologies in this book.

1 A Marxian Approach: Historical Materialism

"Historical materialism is so central to Marxism", so wrote William Shaw (Bottomore 1991: 238). Historical materialism, or the materialist conception of history, was devised by Marx and Engels and further developed by Engels later (Hollander 2011: 328–336). Its main tenet is that the economic structure, consisting of productive forces which in turn

[4] Anderson's *Lineages of the Absolutist State* (1974) was an excellent application of Marx's historical materialism. While Marx and Engels asserted that Western Europe experienced the transition from feudalism to capitalism, Anderson added a stage, i.e., Absolutism, between them. Anderson's book created an exemplar in which the theoretical courses of Marxists and empirical issues raised by historians were compatible and reinforced mutually.

determine the relations of production, is the real foundation of society. The economic base thereby determines the superstructure, including "all political institutions, especially the state, all organised religion, political associations, laws and customs, and finally human consciousness expressed in ideas about the world, religious beliefs, forms of artistic creation, and the doctrines of law, politics, philosophy, and morality" (Kołakowski 2005: 277). Accordingly, productive forces refer to technology, the whole set of the equipment available to society and the technical division of labour; relations of production refers to property relations and the social division of labour in which products are distributed and exchanged between producers (Kołakowski 2005: 277). In Marx's Preface to *A Contribution to the Critique of Political Economy* (Marx [1859] 1970), Marx emphasised the determining role of economic base:

> In the social production which men carry on they enter into definite relations that are indispensable and independent of their will; these relations of production correspond to a definite stage of development of their material powers of production. The sum total of these relations constitutes the economic structure of society - the real foundation on which rise legal and political superstructures and to which correspond definite forms of social consciousness. The mode of production in material life determines the general character of the social, political and spiritual processes of life. At a certain stage of their development, the material forces of production in society come into conflict with the existing relations of production, or - what is but a legal expression for the same thing - with the property relations within which they had been at work before. From forms of development of the forces of production, these relations turn into their fetters. Then comes the period of social revolution.

In this well-known preface, Marx highlights that particular productive forces call for particular relations of production. They in turn bring about a particular kind of superstructure. As society's productive forces develop, existing relations of production and superstructure tend to clash with developing productive forces. Thus, a social revolution becomes inevitable and necessary, in order to unfetter productive forces. This is the principal meaning of historical materialism. It has been, however, criticised as economic/technical determinism. Historical materialism tends to envisage particular societal phenomena, especially societal types, as a response to the existing level of productive forces. Engels had argued that the Calvinistic theory of predestination was a religious expression of the fact that commercial success or bankruptcy does not depend on the businessman's intentions but on economic forces (Kołakowski 2005: 281). Meanwhile, an outstanding critic and developer on this aspect was Max Weber. Emphasising the role of spirits which certain groups of people hold in influencing societies, Weber believed that such spirits could not be completely explained by materialistic environment or class interests. Weber developed a kind of dualist approach (Bendix 1977: 46–48). In his works on religions, especially Calvinism, he highlighted the mental power of religious tenets upon social development.

Nevertheless, Marx's tenets were never solely monistic determinism. The relations of production can influence the momentum and quantitative direction of the development of productive forces. On some occasions Marx and Engels acknowledged that superstructural phenomena gain independence from the economic base. Many modern Marxists aspire to radically enlarge this perspective with the aim of saving historical materialism from critics who assert that it is nothing more than an abstract law too imprecise to be empirically efficient. However, no such efforts have been particularly fruitful. More importantly, such interpretations contradict Marx's and Engels' works. By all means, nonmaterialistic power is secondary. For Marx and Engels, the primacy of productive forces was unambiguous and undeniable. Although independence of relations of production was acknowledged, it, and even further, the effect of "reacting back", occurs *only within* prescribed limits of productive forces. Simultaneously, Marx relatively underplayed the role of the former (Bottomore 1991: 236). In an early work of Marx, *The Poverty of Philosophy*, he explicitly highlighted the primacy of productive forces:

> The mode of production, the relations in which productive forces are developed, are anything but eternal laws, but … they correspond to a definite development of men and of their productive forces, and … a change in men's productive forces necessarily brings about a change in their relations of production. (Marx [1847] 1910: 122)

On the other hand, the relation between the economic base and the superstructure is not unequivocal. While historical materialism asserts that the superstructure is determined by the economic base, Marx and Engels retreated and spoke of the "relative independence" of the superstructure, the "reciprocal influence" of the base and the superstructure, "zigzags" of historical trends, and the determining role of economic factors "in the last resort" (Kołakowski 2005: 298). But the compromise does not satisfy opponents of the theory. In fact, the lack of a dynamic association between the two has been pinpointed by Otto Hintze.

> Das Marxsche Bild vom Unterbau und Überbau scheint mir nicht glücklich als Ausdruck für diese eigentümliche Verbindung von Interessen und Ideen; ganz abgsehen davon, daß der "Ideologie" dabei leicht alle Realität genommen wird, leidet es an dem Mangel, daß es im Geist der Statik gedacht ist, während es doch zugleich die Dynamik der "Umwälzung" veranschaulichen will. Wo sich ein Unterbau umwälzt, folgt der Überbau nicht nach, indem er sich entsprechend verändert, sondern stürzt mit dem Ganzen zusammen. Passender erscheint mir das Bild von der polaren Zusammenordnung der Interessen und der Ideen. Keines von beiden ist ohne das andere auf die Dauer, im historischen Sinne, lebensfähig; jedes bedarf des andern als seiner Ergänzung (Hintze 1931: 232).
> (Marx's picture of the base and the superstructure does not seem to me to be a relieving expression for this particular association of interests and ideas; Quite apart from the fact that the "ideology" is easily deprived of all reality, it suffers from the lack of being conceived in the spirit of statics, while at the same time it wants to illustrate the dynamics of the "transition". Where one base turns over, the superstructure does not follow by changing correspondingly, but collapses with the whole. The picture of the opposite association of interests and ideas seems more appropriate to me. Neither of the two is viable in the long term, in the historical sense, without the other; each needs the other as its complement.)[5]

More complicatedly, Marx used those terminologies relatively freely. Neither Engels defined these terms accurately. The association and distinction between relations of production, the economic base and the superstructure are not crystal clear. Sometimes they appear to have overlapped in content. In some cases, for example, property relations belong to relations of production which are supposed to be a part of the economic base, while in other cases property relations belong to the superstructure, which include political and legal institutions. Similar difficulties arise in the term, the "mode of production". Marx never used it in any single or consistent sense (Bottomore 1991: 379). Marx seemed to have narrow or broad definitions for it: primarily it refers to the economic base or the economic structure; secondarily it refers to the societal whole

[5] Translated by myself.

composed of the economic structure and of the superstructure (Legros et al. 1979: 243). In a reconstructive effort, G. A. Cohen separated it into (a)the economic mode, (b)the social mode and (c)the mixed mode (Cohen 1978: 79–84). But such a method triggered immense debates. As many reconstructive efforts have not gained universal acknowledgement, it is confirmed that Marx's relevant concepts are not scientifically clear.

To a large degree, Marx mostly spoke of the "mode of production" when he thought of actual historical "supersedure". In their *German Ideology*, Marx and Engels demarcated European history into four stages: first the primitive communal or tribal, second the ancient or classical, based on slavery, third the feudal, and then the capitalist (Bottomore 1991: 514). Indeed, Marx had the ambition to categorise history into "a coherent sequence of models which represent different phases of development and indicate the forces which lead from one stage of development to the next" (Schefold 2014: 14). To some extent he succeeded. From this perspective, Marx "was seeking to identify all possible types of productive system", and "to explain how one had been supplanted by another" (Bottomore 1991: 514). However, Marx's dynamism was subjectively designated for European history. Marx and Engels could rarely find evidence which complied with their theory in other continents. The rest of the world did not in fact evolve in this manner, as many Marxists and historians have recognised. To some extent, Marx himself had already discerned this. Specifically, Marx considered Asia as never-changing and failing to evolve beyond a certain point. This is the "Asiatic mode of production" which has triggered many controversies.

Marx formulated the Asiatic mode of production in order to describe such civilisations outside Western Europe as Russia, India, China and the Middle East. Nevertheless, Marx never provided a definition of this concept or any detail of that mode. Most of his ideas about this mode dispersed in specific comments about the social, political and juridical aspects of particular Asian states rather than their historical development (Brook 1989). This sketchy concept has in fact deep roots in preceding European thought. Most characters attributed to it by Marx, such as the need to construct large hydraulic projects, the communal property of land,[6] etc., could be found in Marx's predecessors, including Montesquieu, Hegel, Adam Smith and Richard Jones (Anderson 1974:

[6] Marx's thought on the communal property of land has a special relation with his ideas on the Asiatic mode of production. See: Thorner (1966).

462–472). In alignment with these predecessors, Marx seemed to believe that Asiatic society was a distinct one from European societies: "In a broad outline, the Asiatic, ancient, feudal and modern bourgeois modes of production may be designated as epochs marking progress in the economic development of society" (Marx [1859] 1910: 21). Marx somehow thought that the Asiatic mode of production could not be perfectly "inserted" in the historical progress as he described, although he tried to place the advent of a capitalist society on the basis of its past (Brook 1989: 5–6). Marx's most observation about historical stages was based on historical details of Europe. Asian history seemed to be an independent and uninfluenced part of Marx's ideas.

Marx's formula posed challenges for Marxists and especially for practical revolutionaries. On the one hand, the formula was standardised by Stalinists in the 1930s, and hence every state was deemed to experience five historical stages: primitive communal mode, ancient or slave mode, feudalism, capitalism and socialism. This standardisation granted socialist revolutions the intellectual potency in every corner of the planet. On the other hand, the Asiatic mode of production seems a "naughty" component of Marxian theory of historical stages. Firstly, the stagnation of Asiatic societies was said to be because of geographical or cultural factors. Then, why was the determining power of technical forces ineffective for such a long time in vast zones of the globe? Secondly, if the stagnation of Asiatic societies had lived for millennia, then it could be very far-fetched to say that human civilisations must follow a uniform pathway. Thirdly, if Asiatic societies had lived in stagnation, then "progress" might not be a necessary or inevitable feature of human history. Therefore, "the Asiatic mode of production appeared contrary to three of the fundamental principles that orthodox Marxists generally attributed to historical materialism: the primary role of productive forces, the uniformity of human evolution in society, and the inevitability of progress" (Kołakowski 2005: 287). Consequently, Stalinists altogether excluded the Asiatic mode of production from the schema of history. On the one hand, this notion brought considerable complication for Marxists. On the other hand, however, in his late years, Marx envisioned the possibility of a direct transition from non-capitalist societies to socialism/communism (see Chapter 9).

Such possibility may narrow the gap between Marx's general theory of historical stages and empirical weaknesses.[7]

For more Marxists, as the Asiatic mode of production is relatively weak in both theoretical and empirical aspects, they gradually learned to abandon this program. In the last twenty years, for instance, Chinese scholars, such as historians and archaeologists, tend to redefine China's historical chronology, rather than to rigidly apply Marx's theories (as discussed below, in the section "The Imperial Mode of China"). One outstanding point is that ancient China did not have a slavery society as defined by Marx and Engels. The notion of the Asiatic mode of production confronted similar fortunes. It distracted largely from the historical facts in China. Anderson once called for a decent burial for this notion which he thought it deserves:

> Asian development cannot in any way be reduced to a uniform residual category, left over after the canons of European evolution have been established. Any serious theoretical exploration of the historical field outside feudal Europe will have to supersede traditional and generic contrasts with it, and proceed to a concrete and accurate typology of social formations and State systems in their own right, which respects their very great differences of structure and development. It is merely in the night of our ignorance that all alien shapes take on the same hue. (Anderson 1974: 548–549)

Later, in an effort to restore Marxism's illustration about non-Western societies, one of the most famous explanations about the Asiatic mode of production was K. A. Wittfogel's "Oriental Despotism".[8] He highlighted the characteristics of so-called "oriental societies". In such an illustration, ancient civilisations, including Egypt, Mesopotamia, China, etc., were built on the organisational demand for large-scale hydraulic projects including irrigation, drainage and flood control. In an agricultural

[7] Why such a "jump" is possible is not entirely clear due to the dearth of Marx's mature considerations. Some Marxists have their own interpretations. As William Shaw wrote, for instance, "nation-states can skip economic stages. Why they are able to do so, however, must be explained in terms of the overall pattern of historical evolution, and the motor for that development is the productive forces". See: Shaw (1978: 80).

[8] In the Foreword to the Vintage Edition, it is quite clear that Wittfogel absorbed much from the concept of the Asiatic mode of production. See: Wittfogel ([1959] 1981: xxii–xlvii).

society, irrigation and flood control were of great importance. This point had been emphasised by Marx himself. For Wittfogel, such hydraulic projects also necessitated despotic regimes which could control resources and cope with transregional collaboration. Therefore, the necessity of hydraulic projects determined the necessity of a despotic regime, which was quite common in ancient "oriental societies". While Wittfogel's logic was straightforward and unambiguous, whether ancient China was such an "Oriental Despotism" stirred up huge debates. Details might lend little support to it. In southern China, most irrigation projects were controlled by small local communities rather than any big despotic regime, because the rice planting only needs small projects and water is quite plentiful there. Even in northern China where the climate is drier, most farmers relied on wells rather than any river to irrigate (Buck 1930). But Wittfogel's logic may be extended to explain the rise of a large-scale and despotic empire in appropriate circumstances. For example, the lasting existence of the Chinese empire may be analysed from the need for public good provision (see Chapter 2).

Finally, "historical materialism is not, strictly speaking, a philosophy; rather, it is best interpreted as an empirical theory" (Bottomore 1991: 235). Marx regarded his theory as a complete account of world history, past and present (Kołakowski 2005: 303). But the explanatory and predictive power of his historical materialism could only be vindicated in a broad line. It is largely a result of Marx's thought that we tend to interpret the historical process as a manifestation of some deeper mechanisms in which the association between the economic base and the superstructure prevails, and for which the mode of production and its supersedure set a reasonable framework. As for the Chinese case, although Marx roughly took it as one "Asiatic mode of production", which has been largely dispelled, historical materialism is still able to offer a framework to analyse the long-term changes in Chinese history.

2 A Weberian Approach: Historical-Comparative Sociology

As a slightly later contemporary, Max Weber shares similar research topics with Karl Marx but offers many diagonally different answers. As Anthony Giddens famously put, Weber fought against the "ghost" of Marx for his entire life (Giddens and Sutton 2021: Chapter 3). Two main differences are in the front. Firstly, while Marx did not reject the potency of superstructure on economic base, he unambiguously emphasises the predominant status of economic base. Material forces are the overwhelming driving forces which facilitate changes of superstructure and then transitions of societies. As mentioned above, however, Weber and other German contemporaries saw the inadequacy of Marx's methodology: it lacks a sort of balanced dynamism and interpretative stability. Weber in particular highlights the power of religious ideas in his religious writings, which belong unquestionably to superstructure in Marx's eyes. In *The Protestant Ethic and the Spirit of Capitalism* ([1904/1905] 1958), Weber called attention to tenets of Protestantism and their influence on followers' behaviours. Weber argued that certain tenets encourage followers to pursue worldly success and live a frugal lifestyle so that profits can be reinvested (see Chapter 7). Through the "patterned action" protestant ethic facilitated the rise of capitalism in Western Europe. Secondly, Weber rejected a sort of unilinear evolutionism when explaining historical stages (Kalberg 2021), although this issue is still full of controversies. Weber agreed with the existence of multiple modernities and diverse pathways of historical evolution (Eisenstadt 2000).

Weber's methodology is excellently symbolised in his historical-comparative sociology. According to Weber, civilisations' characteristics can be revealed through comparisons which can be completed vertically (temporally) and horizontally (geographically). In order to grasp the essence of civilisational comparisons, he devised a unique methodology—ideal types. Just economists who construct abstract (in most cases, mathematical) models, Weber used ideal types to abstract key facts and neglect intentionally unnecessary details. Serving as heuristic tools, ideal types largely extend the interpretative capacity of sociologists. Many targets such as actions, organisations and social forms can be categorised into a variety of ideal types which can be analysed with much higher clarity (Kalberg 2021: 498; Calhoun et al., 2022: Chapter 23). In addition, as ideal types grasp key facts of a social form, chronological demarcation can be properly built, and specific variants can be presented. In this regard, Weber's historical-comparative sociological tools will be used to demarcate history of ancient China. Ancient China presents an ideal type for analyses, namely the Imperial Mode. Under this ideal type, two subtypes (also ideal types), i.e., the Han variant and the Song variant, shared some commonality, while many structural changes occurred, such as the predominant form of land ownership and bureaucratic organisation (Chapters 4 and 5).

Weber himself has a monograph on China's religions, culture and political organisations (Weber 1951). According to Weber's analysis, China is a diagonal comparison to Western rationalism. Different from the West where Christianity has set a salvation path for followers and to some extent rationalism has arisen on that basis since the early modern era, China never has a native salvation religion and therefore produces different rationalities. Under the influence of Confucianism and Daoism, ancestry cult prevailed, and followers concentrated on improving literal capacity (Chapter 3). Confucianism emphasises individual education and personal merits, thus contributing to the formation of the literati class in ancient China. In particular, patrimonial bureaucracy formed relatively early in which personal discretion was restrained and officials were selected and promoted based on merits and performance rather than family backgrounds. Although bureaucratic administration possessed some rationality (Calhoun et al., 2022: Chapters 26 and 27), traditional ethic permeated China's patrimonial bureaucracy (Kalberg 2021: Chapter 10). Consequently, a combination of bureaucracy which is relatively rational and traditionalism which is relatively irrational emerged in China.[9] In a word, Weber's methodology and specific analysis offer enlightening tools for analysing Chinese economic history. This book will make a specific application of them.

3 Institutionalist Approaches

Contemporary to Karl Marx, members of the German historical school had highlighted the role of institutional contexts towards economic growth and societal changes (Tribe 1995: Chapter 4). Max Weber was once a member of the Young Historical School. Gradually, neoclassical economics with its expertise in mathematical methods and modelling, which was absent in the historical school, relatively speaking, prevailed in economic research. Then, institutional factors, including states, organisational contexts and societal elements, were often ignored in economics. Nevertheless, since the rise of new institutional economics, institutional factors gained emphasis and attention again. New institutional economics gives up the standard neoclassical assumptions that individuals have

[9] Here I am grateful for teachings of Wolfgang Schluchter who orally taught me relevant knowledge on 2 September 2022 at his office in Heidelberg.

perfect information and unbounded rationality, and transactions are costless and instantaneous (Menard and Shirley 2005: 1). Accordingly, it introduces more approaches into economic analysis. Such concepts as transaction cost (Coase 1937, 1960; Williamson 1985), state (Barzel 2002; Olson 1982, 2000), institutional efficiency (North 1981, 1990, 2005a; North and Thomas 1973; North et al. 2009; Acemoglu and Robinson 2013, 2019), etc., have strengthened the efficacy of economic analysis and its analytical scope. Menard and Shirley (2005: 1) categorise these approaches as: (i) written rules and agreements that govern contractual relations and corporate governance, (ii) constitutions, laws and rules that govern politics, government, finance and society more broadly and (iii) unwritten codes of conduct, norms of behaviour and beliefs. For research in economic history, institutionalist approaches have been proven to be highly instrumental (Li 2015: xvi). Here we shall have a look at those tools useful for analysing Chinese economic history.

Different from neoclassical economics, institutionalism sets limited rationality as the starting point for analysis. The assumption about rationality has become an essential component in theories of social sciences (Simon 1978). According to the standard economic definition, "the economic rationality principle is based on the postulate that people behave in rational ways and consider options and decisions within logical structures of thought, as opposed to involving emotional, moral, or psychological elements" (DiRita 2014). Basically, it acknowledges that people are driven by self-interests and human nature is self-seeking. In comparison to collective interests, people always prioritise individual interests. This rationality assumption has its part in the occurrence of the free-rider problem and the tragedy of the commons. It also assumes that participants in markets have complete information and transactions are frictionless. Clearly, such an assumption has very high requirements on market mechanisms. There must be a perfectly competitive market. Rejecting this precondition, however, institutionalism holds that rationality is usually undermined by information asymmetry, various attitudes towards risk, moral hazard, etc. The "incompleteness" generates the need for more complex institutions and organisations.

One of the most important tasks of above-individual institutions is to make possible public good provision, through solving conflicts of interest and reducing transaction costs. In mainstream microeconomics textbooks, a public good is given as a good that is both non-excludable and non-rivalrous, in that individuals cannot be excluded from use or could benefit from without paying for it, and where use by one individual does not reduce availability to others or the good can be used simultaneously by more than one person (Varian 1992: 414–415). Due to the nature of public goods, individuals lack the incentive to conduct public good provision since individuals cannot obtain the full benefits from this work. The typical public goods include national defence (in general the largest public good), flood control and an irrigation system, normal public order, etc. In most historical periods, individuals did not have the techniques or intellect to negotiate within a privatised mechanism to achieve public good provision. Under these circumstances, a central power which could extract resources and use them for public good provision was always the most efficient way. A state with forcible apparatus is the typical form to achieve it. Ancient China was especially outstanding in this aspect (see Chapter 2). Many projects, including large-scale hydraulic projects, the Great Wall, the Great Canal, etc., were established under the command of a central authority and were used effectively for public good provision including national defence and hydraulic purposes. The prosperity of Chinese agricultural civilisation relied heavily on those public goods.

However, the mechanism of public good provision induces a couple of problems, two of which are the free-rider problem and the tragedy of the commons. The free-rider problem is a typical market failure that occurs when those who benefit from some goods or services do not pay for them or under-pay. As a result, the good is over-produced, overused or degraded (Baumol 1952). The providers of goods or services do not have the means to collect benefits from others who actually consume the goods or services. In other situations, the collection of entry fees would have too prohibitive costs to be practised. The tragedy of the commons is another problem. It refers to a circumstance in which many users share a common resource to which every user has access; Acting independently according to their own self-interests, every user tries to deplete or spoil the shared resource; The consequence is the overconsumption and the degradation of the shared resource. These two problems always happen in the sphere of public goods. As a result, individuals lack the incentive to provide public goods. Although modern scholars are trying to establish theories which could avoid the collapse of the commons without top-down regulations or through privatisation,[10] they require highly sophisticated mechanisms. In most cases where choices were limited, a central planner is generally simpler and more effective.

Another issue surrounding public goods is externality. The existence of an externality discourages public good provision. In economics, an externality is the cost or benefit that affects a third party who did not choose to incur that cost or benefit (Buchanan and Stubblebine 1962). An externality is either positive or negative. A positive externality occurs always when unrelated third parties enjoy the benefits of one good without paying for it. The examples of a positive externality include social safety, national defence, etc. Due to the lack of sufficient incentive, individuals were not motivated to provide goods or services bearing a positive externality. Correspondingly, a negative externality occurs always when unrelated third parties shoulder the costs of the negative effects of an economic activity. Typical examples of a negative externality include environmental pollution and the widespread effects of a disaster. Especially, a pandemic or famine happening in one place could result in immeasurable negative externalities in other places.[11] In Chinese history, famine caused by natural disasters frequently led to regional disorder and sometimes to rebellions, some of which resulted in dynastic downfalls. For a long time, Chinese emperors had been emphasising the importance of the disaster relief system, such as the granary system. While many economists established theories to "internalise" externalities, practices are still absent. In China, the most frequently used method to deal with an externality, whether positive or negative, was intermediation of a central authority. It was very characteristic to have large-scale projects which produced huge positive externalities and public policies which addressed negative externalities. Even nowadays, the tradition is still powerful in China (see Chapter 9).

[10] For example, Elinor Ostrom's (1990) *Governing the Commons*. It introduced how local communities were able to avoid overconsumption of a common resource through voluntary organisations.

[11] Since 2020, much scholarship has been devoted to issues about a negative externality caused by pandemics. Without any doubt, pandemics bear huge negative externalities. In the COVID crisis, in some regions total lockdown was applied, like Mainland China, while some regions practised partial quarantine in particular districts, like Europe. This crisis was a specific instance in which an activity with huge negative externalities cannot be easily dealt with by individuals.

There are always principal–agent problems when society uses a collective entity to solve the above-mentioned difficulties. As Philip Selznick (1949: 10) said, "the most important thing about [nonmarket] organisations is that, though they are tools, each nevertheless has a life of its own". Since none is omniscient, information asymmetry exists extensively, thus facilitating self-seeking behaviours. Information asymmetry refers to this situation in which one party has more or better information than others in one contract. In modern economics, information asymmetry is an important field, in that it resulted in a contradiction with the assumption of "perfect information" and thus market failures.[12] More problems would ensue, including principal–agent problems and moral hazard. The theory of principal–agent problems is grounded in the study of information asymmetries (Miller 2005: 351). Principal–agent problems occur when one person or entity (the "agent") can make decisions and/or take actions on behalf of, or which impact, another person or entity (the "principal"), but the agent is motivated to behave in their own biggest interests, which is in conflict with the interests of the principal (Eisenhardt 1989). Consequently, the interests of the principal would be harmed by the agent. Usually the principal–agent problem is deemed an example of moral hazard. In economics, moral hazard refers to the situation in which an entity has the incentive to increase its exposure to risk because it does not bear the full costs of that risk (Mas-Colell et al. 1995: 477). Principal–agent problems and moral hazards decrease institutions' competence. In general, incentives, monitoring and cooperation are common solutions.

In the context of public good provision, a transaction cost is a core concept. Kenneth Arrow (1969) had defined transaction costs as the "costs of running the economic system". Roughly speaking, transaction costs are those factors which hobble the "perfect market". Oliver Williamson (1985: 19) described transaction costs as the economic equivalent of "friction" in a physical system. He also categorised transaction costs as *ex ante* and *ex post* types. The *ex ante* type includes costs of drafting, negotiating and safeguarding an agreement. The *ex post* type includes: (1) the maladaptation costs incurred when transactions drift out of alignment; (2) the haggling costs incurred if bilateral efforts are made to correct *ex post* misalignments; (3) the setup and running costs

[12] In 2001, the Nobel Memorial Prize in Economics was awarded to George Akerlof, Michael Spence and Joseph E. Stiglitz for their "analyses of markets with asymmetric information".

associated with the governance structures to which disputes are referred; and (4) the bonding costs of effecting secure commitments (Williamson 1985: 20–22). In most cases, transaction costs are not only extensive but also prohibitively high. Although transaction costs are often difficult to quantify, they are always assessed in a comparative institutional way. If one form of a contract could achieve goals with lower transaction costs, people are prone to choose it. In ancient times, individuals lacked proper means to draft, negotiate or enforce a collective action which was essential for public good provision. For instance, large-scale public projects had massive *ex ante* costs as well as *ex post* costs. A central authority could effectively lower the transaction costs through central planning and enforcement. Institutions able to reduce transaction costs often have higher institutional efficiency.

Aforementioned concepts serve for one aim: to interpret "institutional efficiency". Economists have described it in different latitudes. "Pareto Optimal" replies: no individual's position can be improved without a deterioration in the position of someone else (Eatwell 1994). Some scholars evaluated efficiency through how organisations created, used and amassed human knowledge (Loasby 1991). In the sphere of institutionalism, institutional efficiency is closely related to transaction costs. Those institutions are efficient when they lower transaction costs and then make the market mechanism smoothly function. The judgement could be made from means and ends. Certain institutions can lower transaction costs through means in processes; a retrospective way could be also applied: efficiency of institutions can be calculated by how well they achieve designated goals. In other words, efficiency of institutions relies on whether they encourage economic growth (Borner et al. 2004). As we shall see, in the agricultural era, China's imperial structure could achieve public good provision more efficiently, which was important for agricultural activities. In terms of the second-guessing way, this structure facilitated prosperity of an agricultural economy and lasting economic growth.

To a large degree, nature and quality of institutions strongly influence viability of economic growth and its sustainability (Acemoglu et al. 2001). In interpreting the occurrence of the Industrial Revolution which shaped the modern economic pattern, North (2005b), North et al. (2009) ascribed it to preceding institutional optimisation, including the security of property rights and the founding of open access order. This pathway was further developed by Daron Acemoglu et al. While North emphasises institutions per se and the mechanism of open access order to stimulate economic growth, Acemoglu et al. (2005, 2013) traced the formation of institutions. Nonetheless, they all hold that the political situation is significant for economic institutions. Political processes were always able to determine the nature of economic institutions. If inclusive economic institutions coincide with inclusive political institutions, sustainable economic growth could be achievable; otherwise, crippled juxtaposition, in which either or both political and economic institutions are extractive, would result in either economic stagnation/recession or unsustainable growth. In the process in which institutions arise, history is significant (Acemoglu and Robinson 2013). For the Chinese case, such institutionalist approaches provide potent methods for analysing institutional settings.

4 A Framework: The Imperial Mode of China

Now, three approaches are presented for analysing China's long-run socio-economic changes, i.e., Marxian, Weberian and Institutionalist approaches, have been introduced. Unlike neoclassical economics in combination with developed market economies, all three approaches have certain competence to analyse undeveloped countries, which has been proven by numerous works. The huge difference between the material prosperity of ancient China and its relative demise in the nineteenth and twentieth centuries has once struck many observers as inexplicable. In the early modern time, Western Europe began to catch up very quickly from a relatively neglectable position in the global economy, while most of other regions which were once prosperous and much more advanced than Western Europe began to lag behind very fast. This striking contrast and its reasons consisted of the famous question: the Great Divergence.

Many classical theorists, such as Fairbank and many sinologists in the early twentieth century in the United States, attributed the backwardness of the Chinese empire to its rigid social structure and Confucian culture (see Chapter 8).[13] One outstanding example was Elvin's "High-level Equilibrium Trap" theory.[14] According to him, in the Ming-Qing era, China only achieved quantitative growth but no qualitative changes,

[13] Most articles from Fairbank et al. are dispersed in many books, such as *The Cambridge History of China* (1980), *The United States and China* (1983), etc.

[14] Anderson Perry had a modest criticism about this theory, for it is "too narrow and cursory to be persuasive". See: Anderson (1974: 542), the footnote 64.

which was caused by technological standstill (Elvin 1973: 285–316). For those theorists, the backwardness of traditional China was undeniable. However, they were also criticised due to their "Eurocentrism" because they always took Western Europe as the standard model to point out disadvantages of other regions in Eurasia. More recent revisionists hold that in the early modern time, China, especially the Jiangnan region, was not less developed than Western Europe.[15] For example, factor markets in the Jiangnan region, including the labour market and the land market, were at least equally developed. Commercialisation, urbanisation and international trade also developed fast in the Jiangnan region. In addition, rulers in the Ming (1368–1644 AD) and Qing (1644–1911 AD) dynasties implemented benign governance, such as low taxation, so that the authoritarian regime could not be solely responsible for China's backwardness (Wong 1997: 105–126, 209–251). In short, in the early modern time, China was not so different from Western Europe, as far as material conditions are concerned. But the question ensues: if they were not so different and both stood at the cusp of modernisation, what caused the huge difference thereafter? Some revisionists attributed the rise of Western Europe to the occasional discovery of the New World which brought an enormous amount of precious metal and natural resources, and to the coincidental geographical closeness between industrial zones and coal mines in the British Isles (Pomeranz 2000; Goldstone 2002).

A large proportion of western scholars paid attention to what happened in Western Europe in the early modern time. Scholars present multiple conclusions whose details will be discussed in Chapter 7. Nonetheless, none of the theories could well explain both the prosperity of ancient China and the backwardness of China after the nineteenth century. They often explained one question but presented evidence which would be logically contrary to another question. One truly useful theory should be sufficient to explain both questions (Lin 2011). This book is an effort to answer both questions consistently. The core argument is that China had an imperial structure, i.e., the Imperial Mode of China, which was founded in the Pre-Qin period and lasted until the demise of the Qing dynasty, and it was the root of China's historical changes and the causes

[15] The Jiangnan region was a changeable geographical concept, but in general it consisted of most areas in the Yangtze Delta. After the Tang dynasty, it was constantly the most economically developed region in China.

for prosperity in the agricultural era and backwardness in the commercial and industrial era.

As shown before, in terms of Chinese society, Marx's thoughts are highly reductive, simply referring to the "Asiatic mode of production". With little doubt, the rigid application of historical stages to Chinese history, which Stalinists conducted, is essentially an intellectual deformation (Kołakowski 2005: 298–307). Partly because Marx's analysis was relatively sketchy in specific historical details (Anderson 1974: 23, footnote 12), and the only systematic Marxian treatment of the central problems of the transition is from feudalism to capitalism (Anderson 1974: 21, footnote 10), Marxian approaches should not be applied to other zones rigidly. The Chinese case is especially far more complicated. Unlike Western Europe, in fact, China did not experience all the societal sequences as Marx had conceived. Whether China had slavery has already been deemed as highly controversial. Most characters of so-called feudalism as Marx described did not exist in China during the epochs contemporary to the Middle Ages in Europe. If this is not too far-fetched, the feudal system in China had its relatively complete configuration in the Zhou (c. 1046–256 BCE) dynasty. Since the collapse of the feudal system in the Pre-Qin period, China had a particular epoch to which the West had no equivalent, i.e., an imperial epoch.

The Imperial Mode originated in the "first economic revolution" in the Pre-Qin period, in which enhancing agricultural productivity necessitated the formation of a new mode of production. The demand for public goods, including national defence, hydraulic projects, etc., necessitated an authoritarian regime. After a couple of reforms in the Warring States period (403–221 BCE), a pyramid structure formed gradually which consisted of the peasant economy at the bottom, the central authority at the top, and the bureaucratic system in the middle. Peasants owned lands and provided economic resources, including agricultural surpluses and labour, while central rulers and bureaucrats conducted specific public good provision. This mode took shape in its first phase (Chapter 4: The Han Variant) in which nonetheless the manorial economy still prevailed, and officials were still selected mainly based on family backgrounds. Then it disintegrated temporarily for around four hundred years. In its second phase, the Imperial Mode became mature when the mode stabilised in the Song (960–1279 AD) dynasty (Chapter 5: The Song Variant) in which aristocracy was fundamentally abolished and the peasant economy became entrenched. As Marx said, a suitable synergy between the economic base and the superstructure facilitated further growth of productive forces. In the Tang (618–907 AD) and Song dynasties, China had its "second economic revolution" in which technical progress was eye-catching and economic growth was no less impressive. The Tang-Song transition had presented many characters similar to those which Western Europe had in the early modern time.[16] However, the post-Song eras witnessed the declining suitability of the Imperial Mode. As Anderson (1974: 540–541) wrote,

> For the growth in the forces of production in Imperial China appears, in effect, to have taken a curiously spiral form after the great socio-economic revolutions of the Song age in the 10-13th centuries. It repeated its motions on ascending levels, without ever twisting away into a new figure altogether, until finally this dynamic recurrence was broken and overwhelmed by forces external to the traditional social formation. The paradox of this peculiar movement of Chinese history in the early modern epoch is that most of the purely technical preconditions for a capitalist industrialisation were achieved far earlier in China than they were in Europe. China possessed a comprehensive and decisive technical lead over the Occident by the later Middle Ages, anticipating by centuries virtually every one of the key inventions in material production whose conjugation was to release the economic dynamism of Renaissance Europe.

The Imperial Mode had succeeded in bringing China to the preparatory stage of a commercial and industrial era, but it failed to transform into a newly suitable form. Obviously, "in this respect, everything points to the Ming epoch as the crux of the Chinese conundrum" (Anderson 1974: 540–541). The causes were multiple. The path dependence was so overwhelming that Ming-Qing China was still seeking to solidify and strengthen the Imperial Mode. When the West sparked the Industrial Revolution, China tried to consolidate the agricultural economy and gradually lagged behind the West. After the West came in with astonishing power, including military strength and economic superiority, China realised the necessity of changes. For the last 180 years, China tried

[16] The details of these characters will be discussed in the chapter about the Tang-Song transition. As a fact, many scholars hold the similar standpoint that Tang-Song China were in the makings of a transition to a commercialised, industrialised and even modernised economy. Representatives include Naitō Torajirō and Ichisada Miyazaki.

many sorts of pathways, including monarchical constitutionalism, republicanism, communism and so on, in order for modernisation to be built on the basis of the Imperial Mode. Until today, China is still seeking a way out of the Imperial Mode (see Chapter 9).

Marxian approaches offer a framework for understanding historical changes of the Imperial Mode as a whole, while institutionalist approaches offered tools to analyse the structure within the Imperial Mode. Let us recall the points which Kafka made in his short story: an almighty emperor sitting on the throne, ruling over millions of bureaucrats and many more peasants. They worked day and night in order to complete a grand project which could become a useful defender of this large empire. The formation of the Imperial Mode originated in the demand for public good provision and the relative efficiency of a centralised unit to lower transaction costs.[17] The central authority, which was usually the emperorship, commanded bureaucrats to implement tasks. Millions of bureaucrats were controlled by the central authority and collected surpluses from peasants. They were also burdened with specific tasks of public good provision. Those peasants conducted agricultural activities autonomously, offered taxes and corvée labour[18], and enjoyed the benefits of public good provision. It was an efficient institutional arrangement for the agricultural economy in ancient China, in that central planning and top-down enforcement could lower transaction costs within public good provision which was

[17] As more recent empirical studies have vindicated, the emergence of an authoritarian regime in ancient China was less accidental. For example, through modern econometrics, Bentzen et al. found out the negative association between the density of irrigation projects and the degree of democracy in a relatively large geographical scope. Fernández-Villaverde et al. used dynamic simulation to compare the potential political unification/fragmentation in Eurasia. According to their simulation, topographical features and the location of productive agricultural land would be necessary and sufficient to account for China's recurring political unification and Europe's persistent political fragmentation. Moreover, Stasavage proposed that farmers living in the Loess Plateau in China became more settled when they gave up slash and burned agriculture much earlier than European farmers, thus making an exit option useless. Scholars also hold that the formation of a unified Chinese empire had its roots in the need for wars. Details will be discussed in next chapter. See: Bentzen et al. (2017), Fernández-Villaverde et al. (2020), Stasavage (2020: 146–148), Chen and Ma (2020), Chiu et al. (2018).

[18] Corvée labour under the Imperial Mode of China was different from that under feudalism. Within feudalism, servitude was *personal* and directly attached to lords. In China, corvée labour, which was calculated on the basis of each household, only served the national government.

paramount for agriculture. Otherwise, the alternative to the structure was without exception anarchy and economic failures.[19]

However, inherent problems existed within the imperial structure. The principal–agent problem was the primary one. As the middle layer, commanded by central rulers, local bureaucrats had to carry out various duties. They collected surpluses from peasants, and hence achieved public good provision. Generally speaking, bureaucracy refers to a political entity in which a body of non-elected officials take up the policymaking process and specific administration. Max Weber had listed characters of a typical bureaucracy: hierarchical organisation; chain of command; rigid division of labour; regular and continuous execution of assigned tasks; all decisions and powers specified and restricted by regulations; officials with expert training in their fields; career promotion dependent on technical qualifications; qualifications evaluated by organisational rules, not individuals (Swedberg and Agevall 2005: 18–21). In fact, Max Weber did take the rise of bureaucracy, in comparison to aristocracy, as the most efficient and rational way of organising human activities and therefore as the key to rational-legal authority, indispensable to the modern world. Bureaucracy is relatively efficient regarding enforcement (Cornell et al. 2020). While in Western Europe bureaucracy roughly emerged in the early modern time,[20] in China a professional bureaucratic system had taken shape since the Qin dynasty and was efficiently consolidated since the Tang dynasty.

Due to information asymmetry, monitoring on the bureaucratic system was always prohibitively expensive. A series of bureaucratic problems, such as corruption, cronyism, etc., could potentially mushroom. Then, the bureaucratic system also has the potential to worsen the quality of institutions. In extreme cases, bureaucrats degraded into interest groups which posed political challenges to the central authority. Many Chinese dynasties were actually overthrown by conspiratorial bureaucrats. Central rulers had the lasting task to tame bureaucrats in order to prevent undue extraction of surpluses from productive forces and simultaneously to guarantee their

[19] This sentence is revised from Balazs' saying: "In a peasant China it was a rule without exception that the alternative to the reign of the bureaucracy was anarchy". See: Balazs (1967: 21).

[20] Great Britain was almost the first one to establish the modern civil service system in the eighteenth century—namely, the modern bureaucratic system. It is believed that the establishment of the civil service system contributed to continuous economic growth in Great Britain and the rationalisation of government's policies. Interestingly, British bureaucracy was inspired by the examination system in imperial China. See: Bodde (2005).

political loyalty. In most cases, central rulers also took part in systemic venality, since central courts always had a luxurious and extremely hedonic lifestyle. The multiplied extraction easily eroded productive sectors in the economy and then made peasants rebellious. The feasible logic was that the cooperation between the central authority and the bureaucratic system must utilise modest extraction and secure public good provision to guarantee viability of agricultural activities, although the bureaucratic system only kept upward accountability. This logic has not changed today (Zhou 2013). In sum, the Imperial Mode must be set on a subtle balance.[21]

Because of inherent nature of the Imperial Mode, a balance was difficult to be sustained. This inherent instability contributed to its cyclical collapse characterised by political fragmentation and warfare, while its advantages in the agricultural era led to its cyclical re-establishment. This pattern predominated for two millennia. In the long run, it contributed not only to the prosperity of the agricultural economy in ancient times, but also to China's decline in the early modern time. Further, the Imperial Mode of China did not just consist of productive forces and relations of production. On it were a series of corresponding ideologies attached, social norms and beliefs. Path-dependence power was highly influential. It functioned not only in political and economic institutions, but also within people's minds. As Marx exclaimed, "the dead holds the living in his grasp!"[22] The aim of this book is to provide a framework, by means of Marxian, Weberian and institutionalist approaches, to understand China's past, present and (possibly) future.

References

Acemoglu, Daron, and James A. Robinson. 2013. *Why Nations Fail: The Origins of Power, Prosperity and Poverty*. London: Profile Books Ltd.

Acemoglu, D., and Robinson, J. A. 2019. *The Narrow Corridor: States, Societies and the Fate of Liberty*. GB: Viking.

Acemoglu, D., S. Johnson, and J.A. Robinson. 2001. The Colonial Origins of Comparative Development: An Empirical Investigation. *The American Economic Review* 91 (5): 1369–1401.

[21] About the subtle balance of China's traditional structure, see: Ma and Rubin (2019).

[22] Marx ([1967] 1990): the Preface. The original sentence was a French sentence: *Le mort saisit le vif!*

Acemoglu, D., S. Johnson, and J.A. Robinson. 2005. The Rise of Europe: Atlantic Trade, Institutional Change, and Economic Growth. *American Economic Review* 95 (3): 546–579.

Anderson, Perry. 1974. *Lineages of the Absolutist State*. Verso.

Arrow, Kenneth J. 1969. The Organisation of Economic Activity: Issues Pertinent to the Choice of Market versus Nonmarket Allocation. *The Analysis and Evaluation of Public Expenditure: The PPB System*, 1: 59–73. Washington, DC: U.S. Government Printing Office.

Balazs, Etienne. 1967. *Chinese Civilization and Bureaucracy*, trans. H. M. Wright. Yale University Press.

Barzel, Yoram. 2002. *A Theory of the State: Economic Rights, Legal Rights, and the Scope of the State*. Cambridge University Press.

Baumol, William. 1952. *Welfare Economics and the Theory of the State*. Harvard University Press.

Bendix, Reinhard. 1977. *Max Weber: An Intellectual Portrait*. University of California Press.

Bentzen, Jeanet Sinding, et al. 2017. Irrigation and Autocracy. *Journal of European Economic Association* 15 (1): 1–53.

Bodde, Derk. 2005. Chinese idea in the West. In *China: A Teaching Workbook*. Asia for Educators, Columbia University.

Borner, S., Bodmer, F., and Kobler, M. 2004. *Institutional Efficiency and its Determinants: The Role of political Factors in Economic Growth*, 53–60. OECD Development Centre's Work on Institutions, Governance and Growth.

Bottomore, Tom, et al. (eds.). 1991. *A Dictionary of Marxist Thought*. Blackwell Publishing.

Brook, Timothy (ed.). 1989. *The Asiatic Mode of Production in China* M. E. Sharpe, Inc.

Buchanan, James M., and Wm. Craig Stubblebine. 1962. Externality. *Economica* 29(116): 371–384.

Buck, John Lossing. 1930. Chinese Rural Economy. *Journal of Farm Economics* 12 (3): 440–456.

Calhoun, Craig, et al. (eds.). 2022. *Classical Sociological Theory*. Wiley Blackwell.

Chen, Shuo, and Debin Ma. 2020. States and Wars: China's Long March towards Unity and Its Consequences, 221 BC – 1911 AD. CAGE Working Paper No. 505.

Chiu, Yu Ku, Mark Koyama, and Tuan-Hwee. Sng. 2018. Unified China and Divided Europe. *International Economic Review* 59 (1): 285–327.

Coase, Ronald H. 1937. The Nature of the Firm. *Economica* 4 (16): 386–405.

Coase, Ronald H. 1960. The Problem of Social Cost. *Journal of Law and Economics* 3 (1): 1–44.

Cohen, Gerald Allan. 1978. *Karl Marx's Theory of History: A Defence*. Princeton University Press.

Cornell, A., C.H. Knutsen, and J. Teorell. 2020. Bureaucracy and Growth. *Comparative Political Studies* 53 (14): 2246–2282.

DiRita, Peter. 2014. Economic Rationality Assumption. In *Encyclopedia of Quality of Life and Well-Being Research*, ed. A.C. Michalos. Dordrecht: Springer.

Eatwell, John. 1994. Institutions, Efficiency, and the Theory of Economic Policy. *Social Research* 61 (1): 35–53.

Eisenhardt, K.M. 1989. Agency Theory: An Assessment and Review. *The Academy of Management Review* 14 (1): 57–74.

Eisenstadt, S.N. 2000. Multiple Modernities. *Daedalus* 129 (1): 1–29.

Elvin, Mark. 1973. *The Pattern of the Chinese Past*. Stanford University Press.

Fairbank, John K. (ed.). 1980. *The Cambridge History of China, Vol. 11: Late Ch'ing, 1800–1911*. Cambridge University Press.

Fairbank, John K. 1983. *The United States and China*. Harvard University Press.

Fernández-Villaverde, Jesús, et al. (2020). Fractured-Land and Political Fragmentation. NEBR Working Paper No. w27774.

Giddens, Anthony, and Philip W. Sutton. 2021. *Sociology*. Oxford: Polity.

Goldstone, Jack A. 2002. Efflorescences and Economic Growth in World History: Rethinking the "Rise of the West" and the Industrial Revolution. *Journal of World History* 13 (2): 323–389.

Hansen, Valerie. 2000. *The Open Empire: A History of China to 1600*. New York & London: W.W. Norton & Company.

Hintze, Otto. 1931. Kalvinismus und Staatsräson in Brandenburg zu Beginn des 17. Jahrhunderts. *Historische Zeitschrift*, Bd. 144, H. 2: 229–286.

Hollander, Samuel. 2011. *Friedrich Engels and Marxian Political Economy*. Cambridge University Press.

Kalberg, Stephen. 2021. *Max Weber's Sociology of Civilizations: A Reconstruction*. Routledge.

Kołakowski, Leszek. 2005. *Main Currents of Marxism: The Founders, the Golden Age and the Breakdown*, trans. P.S. Falla. W. W. Norton & Company.

Legros, Dominique, et al. 1979. Economic Base, Mode of Production, and Social Formation: A Discussion of Marx's Terminology. *Dialectical Anthropology* 4 (3): 243–249.

Li, Bozhong. 2015. The Preface to the Chinese version of *The Long Road to the Industrial Revolution* by Jan Luiten van Zanden. Zhejiang University Press. (in Chinese).

Lin, Justin Yifu. 2011. *Demystifying the Chinese Economy*. Cambridge University Press.

Loasby, Brian J. 1991. Efficient Institutions. *Quaderni di storia dell'economia politica* 9(2/3), Vol. I: Alfred Marshall's "Principles of Economics" 1890–1990 (1991): 115–131.

Ma, Debin, and Jared Rubin. 2019. The Paradox of Power: Principal-agent Problems and Administrative Capacity in Imperial China (and Other Absolutist Regimes). *Journal of Comparative Economics* 47: 277–294.

Marx, Karl. 1847 [1910]. *The Poverty of Philosophy*, trans. Harry Quelch. Chicago: Charles H. Kerr & Co.

Marx, Karl. [1859] 1970. *A Contribution to the Critique of Political Economy*. Moscow: Progress Publishers.

Marx, Karl. [1867] 1990. *Capital*, vol. I. Penguin Classics.

Mas-Colell, A., M. Whinston, and J. Green. 1995. *Microeconomic Theory*. Oxford University Press.

Menard, Claude, and Mary M. Shirley (eds.). 2005. *Handbook of New Institutional Economics*. The Netherlands: Springer.

Miller, Gary J. 2005. Solutions to Principal-Agent Problems in Firms. In *Handbook of New Institutional Economics*, ed. C. Menard and M.M. Shirley, 349–370. The Netherlands: Springer.

Mokyr, Joel. 2009. *The Enlightened Economy: Britain and the Industrial Revolution, 1700–1850*. Penguin Books.

North, Douglass C. 1981. *Structure and Change in Economic History*. New York: W. W. Norton Co.

North, Douglass C. 1990. *Institutions, Institutional Change and Economic Performance*. Cambridge University Press.

North, Douglass C. 2005a. *Understanding the Process of Economic Change*. Princeton University Press.

North, Douglass C. 2005b. Institutions and the Performance of Economics Over Time. In *Handbook of New Institutional Economics*, ed. C. Menard and M.M. Shirley, 21–30. The Netherlands: Springer.

North, Douglass C., and Robert P. Thomas. 1973. *The Rise of the Western World: A New Economic History*. Cambridge University Press.

North, Douglass C., Wallis, John J., and Barry R. Weingast. 2009. *Violence and Social Orders: A Conceptual Framework for Interpreting Recorded Human History*. Cambridge University Press.

Olson, Mancur. 1982. *The Rise of Decline of Nations: Economic growth, Stagflation, and Social Rigidities*. Yale University Press.

Olson, Mancur. 2000. *Power and Prosperity: Outgrowing Communist and Capitalist Dictatorships*. New York: Basic Books.

Ostrom, Elinor. 1990. *Governing the Commons: The Evolution of Institutions for Collective Action*. Cambridge University Press.

Pomeranz, Kenneth. 2000. *The Great Divergence: China, Europe, and the Making of the Modern World Economy*. Princeton University Press.

Schefold, Bertram. 2014. Marx, Sombart, Weber and the Debate about the Genesis of Modern Capitalism. *Journal of Institutional Studies* 6 (2): 10–26.

Selznick, Philip. 1949. *TVA and Grass Roots: A Study in the Sociology of Formal Organisation*. Berkeley: University of California Press.

Shaw, William. 1978. *Marx's Theory of History*. London: Hutchinson & Co Ltd.

Simon, Herbert A. 1978. Rationality as Process and as Product of Thought. *The American Economic Review* 68 (2): 1–16.

Stasavage, David. 2020. *The Decline and Rise of Democracy: A Global History from Antiquity to Today*. Princeton University Press.

Swedberg, Ricahrd, and Ola Agevall. 2005. *The Max Weber Dictionary: Key Words and Central Concepts*. Stanford University Press.

Thorner, Daniel. 1966. Marx on India and the Asiatic Mode of Production. In *Contributions to Indian Sociology*, vol. IX.

Tribe, Keith. 1995. *Strategies of Economic Order: German Economic Discourse 1750–1950*. Cambridge University Press.

Varian, Hal R. 1992. *Microeconomic Analysis*. US: W. W. Norton & Company.

Weber, Max. 1951. *The Religion of China: Confucianism and Taoism*. Glencoe: The Free Press.

Weber, Max. [1904/1905] 1958. *The Protestant Ethic and the Spirit of Capitalism*. New York: Charles Scribner's Sons.

Williamson, Oliver E. 1985. *The Economic Institutions of Capitalism*. Collier Macmillan Publishers: The Free Press.

Wittfogel, Karl A. [1959] 1981. *Oriental Despotism: A Comparative Study of Total Power*. New York: Vintage Books.

Wong, R. Bin. 1997. *China Transformed: Historical Change and the Limits of European Experience*. Cornell University Press.

Zhou, Ning. 2002. Myth of "the Great Wall of China": An Analysis of Kafka's Sinologist Discourse. *Journal of Xiamen University (Art & Social Sciences)* 154(6): 89–97 (in Chinese).

Zhou, Xueguang. 2013. Guojia Zhili Luoji yu Zhongguo Guanliao Tizhi: Yige Weibo Lilun Shijiao [Logic of National Administration and Chinese Bureaucratic System: A Weberian Theoretical Perspective]. *Open Times* 3: 5–28 (in Chinese).

CHAPTER 2

The Empire-Building in the Pre-Qin Era

Marked by its many different dynasties, Chinese history is characterised by recurring rise and downfall of imperial regimes, but it is equally noticeable that the persistence of an imperial structure penetrated the history. Not much later than the Egyptian and Mesopotamian civilisations, sedentary agriculture and then cities started to form in valleys of the Yellow River and the Yangtze River. Since the Xia dynasty, the so-called first dynasty which was legendarily recorded in historical texts, has not been confirmed by archaeological evidence, and the Shang (c. 1600–c. 1046 BCE) dynasty was in effect a tribal state, a strictly defined Chinese civilisation that has existed for around three thousand years, from the Western Zhou dynasty in around 1000 BCE to the downfall of the Qing dynasty in 1911. Although there were several periods which were tagged with political fragmentation and military turmoil, unification after such periods of fragmentation were predominant throughout the history of the empire. During this three-thousand-year period, the deep-layered structure of governance always succeeded in controlling the territory which it possessed and in self-sustaining itself as symbolised by recurring dynastic cycles.

This chapter explores the original formation of the structure, i.e., the Imperial Mode. The formation was a result of multiple factors. Firstly, its formation relied on natural conditions of China in that period. The climate in East Asia was strongly influenced by annual monsoon. The loess

G. H. Jiang, *The Imperial Mode of China*, Palgrave Studies in Economic History, https://doi.org/10.1007/978-3-031-27015-4_2

in the central plain facilitated the development of primitive agriculture. Simultaneously the hydrologic conditions improved the efficiency of irrigation but on the other hand threatened farming when the monsoon was abnormal. These natural conditions necessitated a structure which could accomplish public good provision when agriculture encountered environmental threats, such as flood and drought. Secondly, significant economic transformation happened at the end of the Western Zhou (c. 1046–771 BCE) dynasty and through the Eastern Zhou (771–256 BCE) dynasty. In the process, agricultural productivity improved remarkably because of technological innovations in agricultural tools and usage of cattle, and when the private ownership of land was established. Those advancements had favoured the household-level units of production (von Glahn 2016: 60). For the sake of guaranteeing agricultural production, institutions became essential in surpassing the individual decision-making process and thus lower the transaction costs to coordinate collective projects, such as hydraulic projects and disaster relief systems. Thirdly, because of such changes which the economic transformation triggered and other political events, the Eastern Zhou dynasty was characterised by political fragmentation and fierce territorial annexation. Under intense competition, many legalist reforms emerged and eventually created the institutions which laid the foundation of the Imperial Mode.

1 The Natural Conditions in the Central Plain

The advancement of agriculture in the central plain in China, especially in the loess plain, was noticeably early. Before a unified Chinese empire emerged, a stable and developed agricultural civilisation had emerged in this area. The mature agriculture had necessitated many corresponding conditions among which a stable and cross-state polity was almost the most significant (Fernández-Villaverde et al. 2020). Many historians have proposed that climatic and geographical factors had played an important role. Ray Huang (1988) has proposed that the monsoon raining had resulted in seasonal floods and thus the necessity of constructing dams and prevention projects. Karl A. Wittfogel (1959) has described Chinese ancient institutions as "Oriental Despotism" because the necessity of controlling water facilitated the formation of a despotic regime. While many scholars disparaged those ideas (Zhao 2015; Deng 1999), at least one point is certain that natural conditions strongly influenced the early characteristics of Chinese civilisation.

East Asia is the largest monsoon area in the world. Every year the monsoon comes between May/June and October, which brings precious rain important for irrigation agriculture. Normally other areas which locate at the same latitude on this planet are dominated by arid climate and little rain. The central plain is also characterised to some degree by aridity and frequent drought. But the annual monsoon alleviates the aridity in the central plain (Barker et al. 1985: 23). The special continental monsoonal climate is caused by complex geographical conditions. The summer monsoon coming from the Pacific Ocean brings precipitation which is essential for agricultural cultivation. Blazina et al (2014) show the range and affected regions of the monsoon. In some cases, the rain brought by the summer monsoon is still not sufficient for the demand for agricultural irrigation, especially when farming expanded. It is also clear that the central plain and the loess plateau rely on more monsoonal precipitation in comparison with southern regions which have more rivers and lakes.

However, exactly as the monsoon is affected by the periodic vicissitudes of air pressure on the Pacific Ocean, usually the volume of precipitation is quite unstable, and its timeliness is unpredictable. The agricultural production in the central plain relied heavily on the monsoon conditions since the main agricultural forms in this period were irrigation or raining farming. If the monsoon is too strong or arrives at the central plain too early, the volume of precipitation would be too large and then easily result in flood and the failure of farming. Conversely, if the monsoon is too weak or arrives too late, the volume of precipitation would be not sufficient to satisfy the demand of water for farming and the following drought would result in famine and social disasters. It would be correct to say that the monsoon climate forms have unparalleled advantages despite some potential disadvantages for the agriculture in this area. Subsequently, the agricultural forms were strongly influenced by the climatic pattern. As Ho (1969) stated, the loess plateau, the birthplace of Chinese early civilisations, was the typical area of monsoonal climate.

> The average rainfall of the loess highland is between 250 and 500 millimeters (slightly less than 10 and 20 inches). The average rainfall of the low plains is between 400 and 750 millimeters. The 750-millimeter rainfall line generally marks the southern and eastern boundary of the redeposited loess. An annual rainfall of between 10 and 20 inches, if evenly distributed over the four seasons, should meet the minimal requirements of ordinary

> dry-land farming. But in the loess area much of the rain is concentrated in the summer, when the temperature and rate of evaporation are both very high; there is usually inadequate moisture in winter and spring. All this, together with the fact that much of North China lies on the margins of the two main rain-producing systems of warm-season monsoons and cool-season cyclonic storms, makes the loess area of China a semiarid region.

Another crucial factor closely related to the monsoonal climate is the hydrologic condition in the central plain. Rivers, especially large rivers, are not scarce in the East Asian mainland. Most large rivers flow eastwards from mountains or plateaus to eastern oceans. While parts of their water supply come from the mountains' snow at the source fields and underground water, the main source of their water supply is monsoonal precipitation (Skinner 1977). As a result, flood and drought would happen if monsoon failed to properly arrive especially when antique residents had no advanced technology to cope with natural disasters. The fight against flood was a core issue for ancient China and has also formed a beginning point of China's legends. Yu the Great, the legendary hero who led the fight against the overwhelming flood, became the first king in Chinese history around four thousand years ago.[1] It is not an exaggeration to say that the relation between hydrologic conditions captured great attention from antique residents. The importance of flood-fighting and water-controlling was widespread in antique civilisations, such as Egypt and Mesopotamia.

The hydrologic conditions necessitated a couple of artificial projects. Firstly, it became quite essential to take advantage of the surface water for irrigation, especially when monsoonal climate made aridity worse and when the agricultural productivity improved so much that more demand for irrigation emerged. There were indeed innumerable national, provincial and local hydraulic projects throughout Chinese history. Secondly, hydrologic conditions could relatively easily cause flood and collateral disasters, on the one hand due to instability of monsoonal precipitation and on the other hand due to the idiosyncrasy of soil. While flood could

[1] The records of Yu the Great was mainly archived in Sima Qian's *Records of the Grand Historian: Annals of Xia*. In the 1920s and 1930s, some Chinese scholars had questioned the existence of Yu the Great. They were grouped in the "Doubting Antiquity School" which questioned the authenticity of many antique documents. Members had Gu Jiegang, Qian Xuantong, etc.

be prevalent in most regions in China, it could be especially damaging in the central plain and the loess plateau. The soil there is famously soft and permeable, thus making the land vulnerable to water erosion. Consequently, collective actions for water control became crucial. Thirdly, ubiquitous rivers made the construction of large-scale canals profitable and relatively feasible. The construction of canals reflected the demand for transportation and economic growth. In fact, in various Chinese dynasties, the construction of canals had an important role.

Besides the monsoon and the hydrologic conditions, the soil type in the central plain and the loess plateau was also a deciding factor in the formation of early civilisations. The soil ubiquitous in the birthplace of Chinese civilisation is mostly loess, which is famous for its softness and permeability. The loess deposits in the central plain and the loess plateau had two-folded consequences. On the one hand, the soil offered advantages for farming since it is abundant in nutrients conducive to crop growth and easy to be planted as well. It is a key factor that facilitated the early birth of planting agriculture in the regions.

> Here, not only are the loess deposits unusually thick, but the fine particles that make up the loessic soil are exceptionally homogeneous in texture. ... the loess of the highland area, which is largely of aeolian origin, is texturally uniform, fine, pliable, and porous, and hence offered much less resistance to primitive wooden digging sticks. This may have been one of the reasons why, in spite of more arid climatic conditions, the loess highland area was the cradle of Chinese Neolithic culture. (Ho 1969)

On the other hand, however, the loess deposits were quite vulnerable to water erosion and weathering processes. The soft mixture of soil made the effects of flooding more severe; and the loss of loess would harm farming since the quality of arable land was hugely damaged. However, the areas of loess deposits were the exact birthplaces of Chinese early civilisation which stood up in the process of combating natural challenges. The loess deposits were a double-edged sword for the Chinese early agricultural civilisation. The work of Kidder and Zhuang (2015) clearly shows that the monsoonal climate, hydrologic factors and the soil idiosyncrasy intermingled altogether in the location of loess deposits. As planting agriculture advances and villagers demolish forests in order for heating materials and extensive cultivation, water erosion becomes increasingly severe. Even today, the Yellow River is still famous for its low water quality because its water contains too much soil and sand.

The above presented three elements are the fundamental natural conditions which strongly influenced the origin of Chinese early civilisation whose subsistence way was typical planting agriculture. All of them are double-edged swords. The monsoonal precipitation brought precious raining for farming, but its instability made flood and drought relatively frequent. The hydrologic conditions made feasible irrigation and utilisation of water channels, but as the rivers were ubiquitous, irregularity of monsoonal precipitation made frequently occur drought and flood across China. This necessitated the construction of hydraulic projects for a more stable and controllable water supply. The mass of loess in the plateau and the central plain offered great advantages for planting agriculture, but it made cultivation exposed to dangers of frequent flood. Irrigation also became important because of the soil's permeability. The primordial agricultural economy was established on the basis of coping with these challenges.

2 The Primordial Economy and Social Structure

Ancient Chinese civilisation is said to be among the most ancient civilisations all over the world. According to archaeological evidence available by far, there were already residents in the basin of the Yellow River and the Yangtze River at least seven or eight thousand years ago. Residents in Yangshao, for instance, had been able to plant crops and produced pottery (Zhu 2013). In a sense, they formed some small villages and conducted some cultural activities, such as divine cults and rituals. However, social structure of those civilisations and many details of economic and social life have not been confirmed in the absence of sufficient archaeological evidence. Nonetheless, archaeologists have sufficient evidence to affirm that planting agriculture originated in this area and that Chinese agriculture gradually developed on this basis, which provides sufficient basis for the analysis here.

According to Chinese formal history, the first ancient dynasty was the Xia dynasty, although surrounding it are many debates about whether it truly existed and how to judge its existence. It has been established that by now there have not been any archaeological objects which could prove its existence, nor are the documental records compelling enough. In the 1920s, Gu Jiegang (1893–1980), a Chinese historian, concluded that "the later the time, the longer the legendary period of earlier history... early Chinese history is a tale told and retold for generations, during which new elements were added to the front end" (Lee 2002). The tales of the Xia dynasty are at their best uncertain. But one factor is pertinent. According to folklore and formal documents, the founder of the Xia dynasty, Yu the Great, was promoted because his achievement of leading people to control flood.[2] Whether the story is a historical fact or not, its prevalence signified the importance of water control and collective actions at an early time.

The first dynasty which has been soundly confirmed by archaeological evidence is the Shang dynasty, ranging around from 1600 to 1000 BCE. In fact, it would be far-fetched to define it as a dynasty because the organisational structure of the Shang era was very loose and fragmented, although there has not been a comprehensive understanding about its royal and national organisations. However, one thing is basically clear: Shang was rarely a tightly organised nation; the regions directly controlled by Shang kings were very limited in comparison with territories which the Shang kings claimed. Basically, Shang was only the most powerful tribe among many rival tribes, one of which was the Zhou tribe which replaced Shang in approximately 1000 BCE. Shang court used military conquests to punish those tribes which appeared recalcitrant. Many kings of Shang took advantage of wars and marshalled troops all over the regions which they conquered in order to symbolise Shang's dignity and superiority.[3] Moreover, there has been archaeological evidence and conjectures that Shang court used large-scale human sacrifice to pray, to communicate with gods and to punish antagonistic tribes (Cheung et al. 2017). In one word, the Shang court's rule was quite violent and politically fragmented.

The core area of the Shang court was mainly the junctional areas between the loess plateau and the central plain, where people created the splendid bronze economy. The Shang court built large workhouses and camps for metal manufacturing. Archaeological evidence shows that Shang people had moved its capital over ten times in approximately six hundred years, but without exception all capital was located near copper mines (Yang 1992). The melting of copper and the production of bronze

[2] Sima, Qian, the Annals of Xia.

[3] For the specific details of different tribes and early civilisation, see Lattimore (1940).

vessels possessed a vital position in the Shang era. Just as von Glahn (2016: 11–12) puts it,

> Bronze ritual vessels occupied the central place in the political, social, and cultural order of the earliest Chinese states. The sheer quantity of surviving bronze artifacts from China's Bronze Age is without peer among ancient civilisations. ...The scale of these artifacts also is enormous: one bronze cauldron from 1200 BCE weighs 875 kg.

Shang people had obviously mastered skills to produce large bronze artifacts and necessary skills to exploit mines and transport massive artifacts. However, while the production of bronze artifacts was eye-catching, agriculture was the basis of economy. The location provided abundant loess which is hugely beneficial for the prosperity of planting agriculture. Main crops were a variety of cereals, including millet, wheat, rice and barley and various vegetables (Young 1982). Although some scholars argue about the origin of some of the crops (Deng 1993: 46–47), there is no denying that planting agriculture has been deeply rooted in local economy.[4] Farmers used bone-made and stone-made tools to cultivate fields. Bronze artifacts were mainly used by aristocratic class for rituals and ceremonial functions (Deng 2020: 147–155). Roughly speaking, in terms of technological strength of farming, Shang was in the Neolithic era.

Another eye-catching point of Shang economy apart from the bronze manufacturing was its reliance on commerce and transregional trade. On the basis of the already excavated archaeological evidence, Shang people were able to devise large carts to transport bronze artifacts and other goods. Shang people had been widespread all over the regions to conduct trade so that people called merchants as "Shang" in Chinese.[5] Another proof for the widespread existence of commerce in the Shang era was the use of money. Shang people used shells as monetary general equivalent.

[4] The debates about where those crops germinated are hardly meaningless for discussions of economic history. In fact, they refer to whether ancient China had developed agriculture independently. In a sense, they also refer to those planting inventions, such as plows. For debates around crops, see Yao (2016). For debates around agricultural tools, see Guo (1988).

[5] In Chinese, literally, the word of "merchants" is "Shang people"; the word of "commerce" is "Shang career".

Archaeologists have excavated many shells in tombs which were represented as a symbol of wealth and social status. In many early civilisations, the conduct to use shells as money was quite common. The development of monetary shells conforms to the analysis of value of forms in Marx's *Capital*.[6]

However, in the specific situation of the Shang economy lies a mystery. Researchers argue that the Shang people concentrated on commerce, and they relied on launching robbery wars and tributes from other conquered kingdoms to obtain an agricultural surplus. Shang people hardly cultivated fields and they periodically forced other kingdoms to hand over their agricultural surpluses, including crops and livestock (Deng 2020: 147–155). Among those exploited kingdoms was the Zhou tribe headstrong, the rebellious tribe which eventually succeeded to overthrow Shang's dominance. To some degree, this argument is proposing that Shang was a highly specialised tribe which focused on wars, commerce and bronze manufacturing while relied on exploitation upon its surrenders. Although there is little evidence to prove the idiosyncratic behaviours of Shang, there is sufficient evidence to prove the existence of rapacious exploitation. The oldest son of the Zhou King of Wen, the founder of the Western Zhou dynasty, was killed in a bloody way and then cooked, as a punishment for Zhou.[7]

According to Chinese historical documents, Shang's rapacity and bloodiness triggered rebellions of other tribes led by the Zhou tribe. There were few words about the detailed process of the rebellion, and it seemed that the war was ephemeral, and that Shang's troops collapsed very quickly and suddenly. Zhou replaced Shang as the central ruler, which is described as a key victory of agricultural civilisation (Zhou) against commercial civilisation (Shang). As Deng (2020: 150–155) said, Qin's affection towards agriculture derived directly from its succession of Zhou. It is true that many civilisational characters of China were

[6] Marx formulated a theory of form of value in Volume I of *Capital*. According to this theory, as productivity grows and the barter trade cannot serve well, a "general equivalent" or "money" is necessary for commodity circulation. The "general equivalent" differentiates itself from all other commodities and has ability to measure the value of other commodities. In order to achieve this function, there are some requirements for being a "general equivalent", such as easiness to carry, transport, divide and hoard. At the beginning, the most common "general equivalent" was shells in many early civilisations. See Marx (1867: Chapter 1), de Brunhoff (1973: 19–25) and Goetzmann (2017: 8).

[7] Sima, Qian, the Annals of Zhou.

customised by the Zhou dynasty. The process of "Empire-Building" was based on institutions devised in the Zhou dynasty. However, the institutions had inherent instability, such as loose control of regional polities and succession difficulties, thus later leading to political turmoil and progressive political reforms.

The core elements of Zhou's institutions were "Feng-jian"[8] and the well-field system.[9] "Feng-jian" involved two actions: feng, "to demarcate a boundary"; jian, "to establish" (Li 2008: 47–49). After the military victory of the Zhou tribe against Shang, several kings of the Western Zhou dynasty used this political system to substantiate their dominance. Kings and their top counsellors allocated lands to their relatives, respected heirs of previous rulers (including heirs of Shang) and outstanding generals who contributed to Zhou-against-Shang wars. With the allocation of lands political power and responsibilities also had to be distributed. On the one hand, able to extract agricultural surplus and

[8] This word is quite complicated due to the inadequacy of translation and historical complication. In Chinese history, the political system applied nationally was "Feng-jian(封建, in Chinese)", which literally meant "enfeoffment and establishment". This is in larger degree similar to European feudalism. In late nineteenth century, Japanese scholars translated "feudalism" as "Feng-jian", since Japanese political system and European political systems in the Middle Age were indeed to some degree similar; they were both characterised by decentralised power and relatively separate states. Japanese scholars were strongly influenced by Chinese ancient scripts and found this term in them, "Feng-jian", to represent feudalism. Subsequently, since Chinese scholars and Japanese scholars both literally used some specific Chinese characters, the Japanese translation deeply influenced in turn Chinese scholars' translation. To some degree, "feudalism" and "Feng-jian" were synthesised in Chinese. Because both in Japan and Europe, "feudalism" is the social mode before capitalism, Chinese translators used "feudalism (Feng-jian)" to characterise the periods between the Qin dynasty and the Qing dynasty over almost two thousand years. But this translation results in serious misunderstanding of Chinese chronology. "Feng-jian" was the typical political system in the Western Zhou dynasty, while after the Qin dynasty "Feng-jian" was roughly demolished. See von Glahn (2016: 13).

[9] The term was also suffering from the poor translation. The "well-field system" corresponds to "jing-tian(井田, in Chinese)" in Chinese. This term consists of two words: "jing(井)" literally means "well" and "tian(田)" literally means "field". But this system had nothing to do with "well". It did not point to the hydraulic condition of fields. In fact, "jing(井)" meant the shape of fields. A rectangular land was separated into nine roughly equivalent smaller lands which were then allocated. The shape of the nine equivalent lands was just like the Chinese character, "jing(井)". If the term were to be translated correctly on the basis of its authentic meaning, it should be translated as the "chessboard-like field system". But considering the existent norm, the "well-field system" would be still used. See Deng (2020: 156–158).

to force corvée, lords of those states could independently manage residents in their domain. On the other hand, nominally lords had to kneel to the Zhou king. As obligations, local lords must periodically (annually or discretionarily) pay tributes to the Zhou king, including agricultural surpluses and regionally specialised products. According to the will of kings, lords had to go to the capital to participate in national rituals or to pay a formal visit. More importantly, lords also had to act as generals and march their own troops to follow the king's troops when the king launched wars. To a large extent, kings' authority was very weak and their control over regional dukes and lords was fundamentally personal and conditional.

The "Feng-jian" system was actually a compromise between the emerging Zhou elites and those old elites which had existed in the central plain, in that Zhou's victory against Shang was merely a military result, rather than a completely social transition. There is no denying that Zhou's dominance was in fact weak. This political compromise was the result of both passive acknowledgement and active choice. Significantly, old elites were not totally defeated by Zhou and still clustered in Zhou's territory. Subsequently, some states ruled by old elites were established. For instance, Song's rulers were the heir of Shang royal family. At the same time, the Zhou kings deployed kinship-related dukes and relatives to occupy geographical cruxes. Kings were hoping that those kinship-related lords and dukes could support kings when necessary, as the obligations had prescribed. However, as kinship became increasingly distanced and kings' military capacity declined, lords and dukes did not respond to kings' commands anymore.

Besides the "Feng-jian" system, Zhou had created a special political ideology which would influence Chinese civilisation for millennia. Because Zhou's victory was precarious, Zhou chose not only to establish the "Feng-jian" system, but also to create a new political ideology. Such ideology claimed that the victory of Zhou was because of the fact that the Zhou kings received the "Mandate of Heaven". The Zhou kings were appointed by "Heaven" to take the power of Shang, in that those Shang rulers had lost the favour of "Heaven" due to their fragrant individual behaviours and greedy exploitation. Shang rulers had failed the expectation of "Heaven", so the "Mandate of Heaven" must transfer to Zhou whose kings were virtuous and hardworking. Thus, Zhou had accomplished a logically unified ideology. The downfall of Shang must be attributed to its kings' moral corruption and unconcern about the expectation of "Heaven". This ideology later transformed into Confucianism's main political concern and greatly affected gentry's and peasants' political loyalty. In *Books of Documents* (*Shangshu*), Duke of Zhou had it[10]:

> Heaven had taken away the Mandate from the Shang state and passed it to us,
> ......
> But I cannot count on the Mandate resting with us and will respect the Heavenly Mandate and our people forever.
> It is all contingent upon human conduct whether or not mistakes and evils will occur.
> ......
> Heaven is not immutable.
> Heaven will not take away the Mandate that King Wen had received just as long as we carry on his virtuous conduct.

It can be seen that in this ideology there were strict moral and abstinent requirements for rulers. It was necessary for the sake of legitimising Zhou's domination, since Shang's kings had failed in those requirements. The practice of "Feng-jian" had a following significant effect in that it facilitated gradual changes of political and economic situations. Kings took advantage of a kind of patrimonial methods and patriarchal ideals to rule over regional lords (von Glahn 2016: 14–43). The bondage between central kings and regional lords was sustained through moral feelings, intimacy between lords and kings, and the relative strength of kings. The balance was quite risky, which was proven by the immediate collapse of the patriarchal politics after a couple of generations. Regional powerful lords gradually took power from Zhou's kings and consequently achieved far more stable institutions than Zhou's.

Another fundamental institution was the well-field system.[11] The first literal evidence about this system came from *Mencius* whose writer lived in the Warring State period. Under this system, the ownership and allocation of land were stipulated. All land "under the Heaven" belonged to kings of Zhou, which meant that the kings had ownership. Kings applied

[10] *Book of Documents*, in *Shisan Jing Zhushu*(《十三经注疏》) edited by Yuan Ruan in 1815. Reproduced in 2009 by Zhonghua Book Company.

[11] As I have explained, the "well-field system" is a poor translation, but since this name has become customary, I continue to use it here.

"Feng-jian" to manage the universal land by allocating land to lords and dukes; then dukes and lords could allocate land to subservient ministers and their own relatives. The patrimonial order was copied class by class and generation by generation. Regarding specific arrangement, Mencius praised this system highly:

> A square *li* covers nine squares of land, which nine squares contain nine hundred *mu* (135 acres). The central square is the public field, and eight families, each having its private hundred *mu* (15 acres), cultivate in common the public field. And not till the public work is finished, may they presume to attend to their private affairs.[12]

The characters of the well-field system were clear in this text. Eight households cultivated on eight lands and collected the surplus, while they did not possess ownership. The eight households cultivated collectively on the single communal land in which lords collected their surplus. In the eyes of Mencius, this system represented an appropriate method to organise the economy and was the foundation of a fair society. Although some scholars debated about whether this system truly existed or it was just a dream of those Confucian scholars who designated a utopia because this system was too perfect to be practically applied (Zhu et al. 1965), there is ample evidence to assert that such mode of ownership and allocation existed and was practised on a large scale. In fact, whether lands were divided equally into nine pieces is of trivial sense. The importance lies in the nature of ownership and allocation. After demolishing the communal mode of the well-field system, the most significant mechanism of Chinese imperial economy was established—small peasantry and the private ownership of land which existed for the entire duration of imperial China.

3 The First Economic Revolution

During the Eastern Zhou dynasty, influential economic transformation and political reorganisation happened as technology advanced. Among them was the widespread use of iron tools and ox-drawn plows the most important, which led to revolutionary economic changes. Since there is no ample evidence to figure out why this technological progress happened, such progress is considered by many scholars as exogenous.

[12] *Mencius, Teng Wen Gong I*, translated by James Legge.

In fact, it is unclear why such technological progress happened at such an early time. For the analysis here it is much more meaningful to figure out the subsequent transformation that those technological changes triggered. The progress in technology fostered societal changes and transition of states' functions, which laid down the basis of the Imperial Mode. Since this transformation drove up productivity, completely changed the economy and revolutionised social structures, it is not an exaggeration to describe it as "the first economic revolution" in Chinese economic history.

There has been evidence about the usage of iron tools in the ninth century BCE, while at that time bronze was the commonplace metal. In the fifth century BCE and afterwards, the production of iron tools, including spades, hoes, plows, sickles, knives, axes and chisels, had been quite advanced (von Glahn 2016: 60–61). Techniques for casting iron were already pioneered, while in Europe they came into use only in the later Middle Ages (Anderson 1974: 522). The category of iron tools was colourful, and the quality of iron tools had been improved remarkably because more refined metallurgical technology was mature enough to reduce the amount of carbon and harden the iron over the Spring and Autumn period. Artisans had invented the blast furnace and several other methods of iron production that the Europeans did not master until early modern times (Zhao 2015: 201). Various methods of carbonising steel were also invented (Hua 2008). In a tomb of a lord near the Yangtze Delta, a sword had been excavated and its quality could be matched with that of modern technology.[13] In the Warring States period, regional lords had been able to manufacture iron weapons and armours in large amounts. Massive troops equipped with arrows and armours were documented in many texts and confirmed by archaeological evidence in many tombs. The technology of iron casting had been so advanced that iron agricultural tools were authentically widespread.

Besides expanding usage of iron tools, another important innovation was the usage of ox-drawn plows. Although it is difficult to figure out when ox-drawn plows were introduced for the first time, "plow oxen were frequently mentioned in Qin documents from the third century BCE" (von Glahn 2016: 61). The usage of ox-drawn plows hugely improved efficiency of planting. In addition, livestock's manure was used widespread

[13] The Sword of Goujian, the lord of the Yue state in the fifth century BCE. Although this sword is made mainly from bronze, its quality and resistance to tarnish over two thousand years are unquestionably proof of the outstanding metallurgical technology.

across the lands, which led to great increase of agricultural output (Chi 1936: 49–55). The consequences of technological innovations were both intensive and extensive: farmers took advantage of iron tools and ox-drawn plows to increase the unit output of lands and cultivate more lands which could not be exploited before. The expansion of cultivated lands was encouraged by regional lords in need of more agricultural surplus to feed increasingly massive troops in order to compete with rival lords. Total factor productivity would have increased noticeably although there is a lack of accessible data to support this.

Increasing efficiency in the agricultural sector necessitated collateral infrastructures, especially the construction of hydraulic projects capable of providing water control, including irrigation and measures against flood and drought. Before the agricultural revolution, there was little demand for large-scale hydraulic projects, although there were some small-scale works.[14] After the advent of the agricultural revolution brought out by the widespread usage of iron tools, ox-drawn plows and livestock manure, more demand for water control also emerged because farmers needed to increase factor inputs. In the planting economy, in addition to labour, land and capital, water control was regarded as the fourth factor of production (Kelly 1982). As a result of technological innovations, in sum, there was higher demand for more efficient hydraulic projects in the central plain and the loess plateau.

In general, hydraulic works covered three interlinked categories: irrigation, drainage and flood control (Bray 1994: 68–71). The climatic irregularity, as explained before, is not good for agricultural activities. Especially when productivity in the agricultural sector increased so much, a mechanism became essential against the climatic irregularity which happened relatively frequently due to the changeable monsoon. When the monsoon brings too much precipitation, some methods for drainage and flood control are paramount; when the monsoon brings too little rain, irrigation and distribution of water become vital. A good harvest relies largely on the stability of the water supply. More lands were to be cultivated and as a result more irrigation was to become necessary. The unit output in each land was rising and a bulwark against climatic irregularity

[14] In Chinese historical documents, archaic kings were praised because they led people to construct hydraulic projects and to develop agriculture. Although there were not many details about those projects, it is apparent that the importance of hydraulic projects had been highlighted.

was paramount. Sufficient hydraulic projects used for drainage, irrigation and flood control were essential for this purpose. The drainage of water in newly cultivated lands and in lands damaged by heavy raining was as important as irrigation. There were many practices in ancient China for the sake of the three interlinked functions (Bray 1994: 77–94).

However, since the nature of water is fluid, it is difficult to be handled completely by individual units. Flowing automatically according to the law of gravity, the distribution of water and its movement are uneven on the ground or underground. The specific characters of water supply "creates a technical task which is solved either by mass labour or not at all" (Wittfogel 1959: 15). In addition, water control generally involves a quite large area and involves so many households that the tasks must be negotiated among different people. The *ex ante* negotiation cost would have been too prohibitive to make feasible those large-scale projects. In terms of institutional analysis, transaction costs, one of which is the negotiation cost, can make any attempt at individual water control futile. Hydraulic projects also have positive externalities which leads the free-rider problem. Once hydraulic projects were to be accomplished, there would be no way to drive out other parties. While undertakers of hydraulic projects might disallow outsiders to enjoy the benefits of irrigation, undertakers cannot proscribe outsiders to enjoy the benefits of a less damaging flood. The prohibitive transaction costs and the free-rider problem mean that individual units have little incentive to launch such projects.

Consequently, hydraulic projects can be only launched by some public authorities and collective actions. The public authorities can collect necessary resources, such as human labour and materials, and achieve the collaboration of construction tasks. In fact, some public organisations are the institutionally efficient way to solve the free-rider problem and lower transaction costs. Using corvée labour to carry out the works, only the state had the sufficient resources and authority to organise and finance the dredging of the main rivers (Hamashima 1980). For the case of the Eastern Zhou dynasty, many states launched state-level hydraulic projects. The increasing agricultural productivity resulted in the demand for more water control. For the sake of competing with rivals, lords had the incentive to respond to this demand, in that they needed more agricultural surpluses to further increase and feed their troops, which would be only possible when they made the agricultural sector more prosperous. In fact, local lords launched many hydraulic projects and at least a couple of which were quite large-scale.

The earliest records about large-scale hydraulic projects can be dated back to the sixth and fifth centuries BCE. In the Chu kingdom, a canal was constructed under the command of a minister. The site is constructed near the Yangtze River. According to historical documents, its irrigation covered 40,000-hectare lands (Chi 1936: 59). Other states, such as Qi, Wu, Wei, etc., constructed a couple of large-scale hydraulic projects in their own territory. The Wu state launched the Hangou Canal near the Yangtze Delta. While its primary purpose was to deploy warships so that the Wu state could go northwards to attack rivals, its enduring function was irrigation and transportation. Later the Wu state conducted the widening work of the Heshui Canal so that Wu's warships could penetrate inside Qi's territory (Zhao 2015: 206–207). The most successful constructor was the Qin state, the final unifier. It launched the two largest hydraulic projects at that time. One was the Zhengguo Canal. Its construction started with a conspiracy. Its organiser, Zhengguo, came from the Wei state and worked as a spy. Under the order of the Wei king, he devised the idea that the construction of a large-scale project would suck many resources of the Qin state, which would weaken Qin. This idea had the opposite function. The construction of the Zhengguo Canal made the area around the capital of Qin prosperous because of its irrigational utility. Another was the Dujiangyan Canal which was located near the Yangtze River (more precisely, its branch, the Min River). This region was conquered by the Qin state and then a minister was appointed to manage it.[15] The construction of both canals made the irrigated areas prosper. The material prosperity also laid the foundation for the Qin state to defeat other competitors (Hsu 1980: 99–100). The large-scale hydraulic projects are spotted in Fig. 1.

[15] The minister, Li Bing, and his son launched one of the most venerable hydraulic projects in ancient China—the Dujiangyan Canal. The project was started under the direction of Li Bing in 250 BCE and finished ten years later by his son, Li Ergang. This work had very elaborate designation and high-quality construction. Utilising two separate canals, it works effectively both for irrigation and flood control. Needham calls it "one of the greatest of Chinese engineering operations which, now 2,200 years old, is still in use and makes the deepest impression on all who visit it today. The Guanxian irrigation system made it possible for an area of some 40 by 50 miles to support a population of about five million people, most of them engaged in farming, and free from the dangers of drought and flood. It can be compared only with the ancient works of the Nile". See Needham and Gwei-Djen (1971: 288).

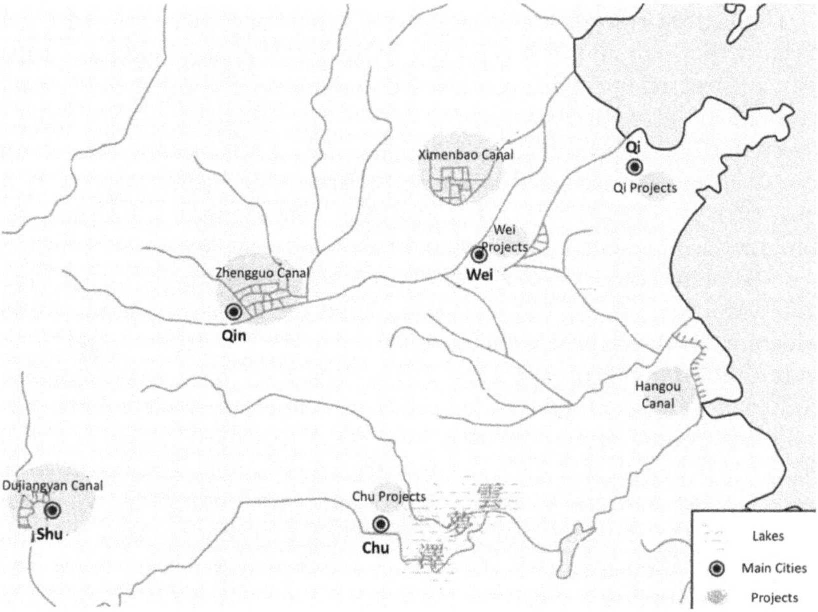

Fig. 1 The Hydraulic projects in the Eastern Zhou Dynasty

The construction of large-scale hydraulic projects necessitated the centralised collection and allocation of necessary resources, such as corvée labour and construction materials. It was only made possible after a centralised regime was accomplished. This process of centralisation was facilitated by the establishment of small peasantry. As shown before, technological progress fostered economic changes, i.e., the great increase of agricultural productivity. Its consequences were both extensive and intensive. Previously unoccupied lands were more greatly cultivated, and farmers concentrated more on their private lands. "People are unwilling to spend their energy on public lands".[16] It is no wonder that people, who were farmers under this circumstance, concentrated more on their private interests, since they were acting rationally from an individual basis. But the tendency was not good for those lords who relied on the surplus

[16] *Chunqiu Gongyang Zhuan Zhushu* (《春秋公羊传注疏》).

from public lands. They collected less and less if they relied only on farmers' voluntary labour on public lands. As lords faced increasingly poor situations, fiscal reforms became necessary.

The first reform happened in the Lu state in the downriver places of the Yellow River. It was recorded that in 594 BCE the Lu state began taxing lands by area, whether public lands or private lands. The policy was recorded in many historical documents, including *Zuo's Commentary* and *Gongyang Zhuan*. In fact, through taxing lands by area, this policy abolished the existence of public lands to complete private ownership and was therefore the most important introduction of property rights in the agricultural era of Imperial China. Such reforms happened also in other states in the Eastern Zhou dynasty. In the Wei state, Li Kui, the premier, advocated economic policies that made the nuclear household the fundamental unit of taxation and services required by the state, in order to generate more income and feed more troops so that the Wei State could compete with other states. According to Li Kui's calculation,

> A typical farming household of five persons cultivated 100 *mu* (15 hectare) of land that yielded a total harvest of 150 *shi* (one *shi* was equivalent to 20 litres) of grain. The state collected a land tax of 10 percent, or 15 *shi*, and the family required 90 *shi* of grain for its own subsistence, leaving a surplus of 45 *shi*. (von Glahn 2016: 62)

It is quite evident that Li Kui had designed his reforms on the total basis of individual households when he started in 422 BCE. Li Kui's reform was quite successful and made the Wei state one hegemon for some time in the Warring States period (403–221 BCE).[17] The most significant reform happened in the Qin state, which was launched by Shang Yang (390–338 BCE). His policies were highly comprehensive, with such reforms making the Qin state the most prosperous and so forth laid the foundation for Qin's unification. His fundamental economic policy was to "abolish the well-field system and cultivate wild fields".[18] Shang Yang's reforms completely abolished the public ownership of land and established the private ownership of land, or so-called household ownership. Its influence became entrenched and universal because of the unification of China by the Qin state. There were also some less influential reforms in other

[17] Sima, Qian, *House of Wei*.

[18] *Ibid., Biography of Lord Shang*.

smaller states, but all those reforms served the same purpose, i.e., to take advantage of improved agricultural productivity and to make individual households the fundamental units of extraction of surpluses.

The small peasantry was established over hundreds of years from approximately 594 BCE to 350 BCE. The private ownership of land was also established at this time and would exist from the Pre-Qin period to 1956 AD, ranging over two thousand years. The technological progress fostered the conditions for corresponding institutional changes. Higher agricultural productivity crippled the well-field system, which made lords try to find other channels to generate income, for the aim of military victory and competitive advantage. These sagacious lords and counsellors reacted actively to the economic changes by acknowledging the private ownership of land and then establishing the small peasantry. The positive association between technological progress and smaller household-level units of production is also supported by modern scholars (von Glahn 2016: 60). However, the peasants had greater demand for large-scale hydraulic projects which could only be organised by some state-level authorities. States were inclined to favour households because corvée labour and agricultural surplus would be easier to collect. The trade-off between the protection of the small peasantry and public good provision had started to form at this period. It is the most fundamental characteristic of Imperial China, and also the basic structure of the Imperial Mode. By placing emphasis on the intensity of technological innovations and the institutional changes which they triggered, one can define it as "the first economic revolution" in the economic history of China.

Apart from the great changes in the agricultural sector, there was huge growth in commerce and transregional trade. Among different states and cities, there was increasingly growing regional specialisation in production of goods such as salt, iron, lacquer and silk (von Glahn 2016: 65). In the Qi state, Guan Zhong, the chancellor there, encouraged the manufacturing of sea salt and lowered the tax when foreign merchants came to do business. The Qi state gradually became wealthier and stronger because salt became very popular and remunerative goods and prosperous commerce generated more income.[19] In the Wu state and the Yue state, silk also became important goods. The legendary merchant, Fan Li,

[19] Sima, Qian, *op. cit., Biography of Guan & Yan*. "Guan Zhong in the Qi state made trade convenient and accumulated wealth, and then made the state rich and troops strong. He designed policies according to what people like and what people do not like".

generated enormous wealth due to selling silk and was iconised as the God of Commerce in ancient China. In the Qin state and the Jin state, some merchants became wealthy due to the sale of livestock. Some merchants became even politically powerful. Lü Buwei, a merchant originally in the Zhao state, even intervened successfully in the royal succession in the Qin state and rumours had it that he was the father of Qin Emperor the First (also known as Qin Shi Huang, 259–210 BCE, r. 221–210 BCE).[20]

The increasing commerce was on the one hand facilitated by growing productivity in agricultural sectors which generated more surplus, and on the other hand made possible by some independent states whose chancellors believe that commerce and trade should be allowed to thrive to bring more income for lords. Because of the political and economic autonomy in regional states, local lords took advantage of local resources to accumulate wealth. For example, as previously mentioned, the Qi state produced and sold sea salt to the interior states of the central plain, which were rich in grain but poor in salt, and reaped a great profit in gold (von Glahn 2016: 65). Lords also had incentives to encourage commerce and trade in order to strengthen themselves so that they could compete with rivals. The prosperous transregional trade facilitated to some degree commercialisation in independent states. In the Warring States period, different states had developed distinctive currency systems of minting and circulation. The Qi state used knife currency and the Qin state used Banliang coins, both of which were highly standardised, and neither of which circulated much beyond the state's border (von Glahn 2016: 63–64). In these main states, different currency types were used which could be only exchanged with difficulties.

Furthermore, some states applied laissez-faire policies towards the economy especially before Legalism became more established. In a popular story, Zichan, an influential minister in the Zheng state, refused an action to get a jade ornament from a merchant through conspiracy and force, because the ruler of the Zheng state had made a pact with the city's merchants under which his government would not intervene in merchants' business.[21] Confucian scholars, especially Mencius, criticised states' intervention in the marketplace and the lords' rapacity when governments deprived merchants of profits and posed heavy taxes upon

[20] Ban Gu, *Book of Han, Treatise on the Five Elements* (班固《汉书·五行志》).

[21] Zuo Qiuming, *Zuo's Commentary: Zhaogong 16th Year* (《左传·昭公16年》).

merchants. Guan Zhong's policy to monopolise the production of salt had triggered serious criticism among scholars. In a dialogue of Yan Ying, a chief minister in the Qi state much after Guan Zhong, "the woods in forest, are guarded by deer; the vegetation in marsh, is guarded by fish; the salt in oceans, is guarded by community's prayer; Crude countrymen invaded into marketplace and robbed profits; Luxurious lifestyle and crazy entertainment are popular in royal palaces. People are suffering and households are cursing".[22]

4 The Empire-Building and Legalist Thinkers' Reforms

In the final years of the Western Zhou dynasty, huge political turmoil had surrounded the Zhou royal court. The politics during these years was characterised by political murder and dramatic events. The theatrical events were just the most visible expressions of disintegration of the institutions which had supported the Zhou royal court, i.e., the "Feng-jian" system and the well-field system. As will be further explained in this final section, the well-field system was crippled by technological progress and subsequent economic changes. The "Feng-jian" system was also invalidated because the kinship-related loyalty had been really weakened after many generations and the Zhou kings had no sufficient power to compel local lords to obey their orders. In a sense, the scenario was just like the western Europe in the Middle Ages. Many regional states in China's heartland rose up and disobeyed the higher kings or emperors (Before the Qin dynasty, there was no literal "emperor"). Some scholars described this circumstance as "city-states" (von Glahn 2016: Chapter 2; Zhao 2015: 55–59).

The inherent weaknesses of the "Feng-jian" system facilitated the collapse of the Western Zhou dynasty. As previously explained, this system was a political compromise between different forces. Technological progress contributed to its collapse. Local lords reacted actively and quite successfully to these technological challenges. The actions which these lords, generals and ministers took served one purpose, i.e., the pursuit of hegemon, although their specific actions varied. The single purpose was to make the state powerful and competitive among states, but what those

[22] *Ibid., Zhaogong 20th Year* (《左传·昭公20年》).

statesmen had accomplished was the establishment of institutions suitable to the demands of an agriculturally based society: the private ownership of land and small peasantry, a bureaucratic state, and the centralisation of political power. It was also these institutions that achieved the empire-building process in the Pre-Qin period. And most statesmen who carried out this process belonged to the Legalist school. It would be no exaggeration to determine that the fundamental structure of the Imperial Mode was accomplished during these periods characterised by political turmoil and groundbreaking reforms.

Historical documents have recorded many reforms which happened during the Eastern Zhou dynasty, and the records about how those reforms were applied are quite detailed. At least in some large states, reforms were thoroughly recorded: Guan Zhong's reform in the Qi state after around 685 BCE; "Chushuimu"[23] in the Lu state in 594 BCE; Li Kui's reform in the Wei state in 422 BCE; the reform of King Wuling of Zhao in the Zhao state in 403 BCE; Wu Qi's reform in the Chu state in about 389 BCE; Shen Buhai's reform in the Han state in 355 BCE; and finally, Shang Yang's reforms in the Qin state in 356 and 350 BCE (Zhao 2015: 195). The reforms focused on military, political/administrative, and economic institutions. Most reforms worked successfully, while Shang Yang's reforms in the Qin state were considered the most comprehensive and the most successful.

The Qi state was the first hegemon in the Spring and Autumn period because Guan Zhong's reforms made the state rapidly grow strong. Guan Zhong was iconised as the first Legalist thinker in the Spring and Autumn period. Confucius had praised him because of his achievements to conserve "Chinese culture".[24] All his achievements were based on his reforms, five of which were the most influential. Firstly, the administrative system was reformed. The capital was divided into 21 districts: six of them merchants, which provided the Qi state's trade revenue, and

[23] "Chushuimu" literally means "initial taxation on cropland on the basis of *mu* (the area)". This reform was the first one to abolish the public ownership of land and acknowledged the private ownership of land, and then the government applied uniform taxation on private lands.

[24] Confucius said: "Guan Zhong acted as prime minister to the duke Huan, made him leader of all the princes, and united and rectified the whole kingdom. Down to the present day, the people enjoy the gifts which he conferred. But for Guan Zhong, we should now be wearing our hair unbound, and the lappets of our coats buttoning on the left side". See: *Analects of Confucius, Xianwen*, translated by James Legge.

fifteen of them attendants, which provided the core of the Qi army. The population outside the capital was organised in the following way: 30 households were formed into one village, 10 villages as one troop, 10 troops as one district, 3 districts as one county, and counties grouped into five regions.[25] And Guan Zhong divided people into four hereditary professions: "shi" (the literal people), farmers, artisans and merchants. All people focused on their own professions and they were not allowed to change the profession. Secondly, another major reform was "to collect taxation according to the quality of croplands". To some degree, the taxation policy confirmed the existence of private ownership of land and took private lands as the mainstream income source. Thirdly, Guan Zhong encouraged merchants to do business in Qi's capital and lower the trade tax on merchants.[26] Fourthly, the state forced a monopoly on salt and iron mines. Private artisans who produced salt by boiling seawater and iron by mining in mountains had to sell all their outputs to the government, and then the government resold refined salt and iron products, with a huge price gap, to all households in the Qi state and some to foreign states. Fifthly, Guan Zhong changed the recruitment policy in the government. Before this reform, positions in the government were hereditary among aristocratic families. Guan Zhong appointed professional bureaucrats as governors and administrators. After all these policies were put into practice, the Qi state gradually grew strong. From the perspective of the efficacy of these five measures, Guan Zhong had not only made Qi the first hegemon in the Spring and Autumn period, but also succeeded in paving the way for successors to build empires.

Another important reform happened in the Wei state under the reign of Li Kui who was also widely recognised as a praised Legalist thinker. Working with Ximen Bao, Li Kui was also an enthusiastic hydraulic engineer. After being appointed as the chancellor in the Wei state, he launched an effective reform which made the Wei state a hegemon, although for a short duration. Zhao (2015: 166–167) has succinctly concluded Li Kui's reform:

> First, he established a full-fledged bureaucracy. More and more officials were selected based on ability and promoted or demoted based on

[25] *Discourses of the States, Discourses of Qi* (《国语·齐语》).

[26] *Guanzi, Bayan*, by Ulrich Theobald, online archive on ChinaKnowledge.de.

> performance. Written records of an official's performance were now kept, regularly reported to higher authority, and evaluated. The privileges and titles were not inheritable. Second, Li established a more comprehensive penal law system. The published penal code attributed to Li Kui had six detailed chapters, on banditry, robbery, gambling, and other activities that were seen by the rulers as disruptive to public order and ethics. Third, agricultural production was promoted. Farmers were required to grow several grains to minimize the damage in the event of a blight on one of them, to grow vegetables and fruit trees in the interstices of grain plantings, and to make the cultivating and harvesting of the crops their first priority. Li Kui also allocated government funds to buy grains in years of good harvests and sell them in bad years. The measure protected the interests of agricultural producers, whom Li Kui saw as vital for the strength of a state. Fourth, he strengthened the army, making military service mandatory for all adult males, and rewarding and promoting warriors based on their military skill and courage. In short, Li Kui's measures were aimed at establishing a strong bureaucratic state that was effectively controlling its population, maximizing agricultural production, and optimizing its army.

The conclusion is quite to the point. Li Kui's reform had prepared the fundamental elements for an empire-building process. The small peasantry was highly valued by officials. Agricultural production was taken as a priority in the task list of officials. The Wei state, located in the central plain, had complex hydrologic and geographical conditions, and thereby large-scale hydraulic projects launched many times not only by Li Kui, but also by his colleagues. The government accepted the growth of the small peasantry and reacted positively by constructing hydraulic projects and appointing able bureaucrats selected by standards of performance, rather than by kinship or hereditariness. Some factors which characterised the Imperial Mode had been formed, such as the emphasis on public order and military defence. Public good provision was of great importance for increasing agricultural production. In order to guarantee the success of these functions, a bureaucratic state was necessary. Li Kui had preliminarily achieved the essential elements of the empire-building process.

The final stage of the empire-building process was taken by Shang Yang's reform. Shang Yang's reform has since been described as the most successful and comprehensive one in the Warring States period, but there is full evidence to believe that parts of measures which he took had been enacted in other states in the central plain (von Glahn 2016: 87).

Nowadays most records about Shang Yang's reform can be seen in the *Book of Lord Shang* and Sima Qian's *Biography of Lord Shang*. Shang Yang's reform was almost the latest one of those Legalist reforms because after his reform the Qin state became much stronger very quickly than other states. No other states had the chance to compete with the Qin state anymore. Very soon Qin Emperor the First accomplished unification of China. For the sake of strengthening Qin's political competence, economic efficacy and military capacity, Shang Yang's reform was clearly effective and successful.

Similar to his predecessors, Shang Yang's reform can be categorised in six main aspects. The first of these, Shang Yang officially abolished the well-field system. Under his order, the government allocated arable lands to peasants and encouraged redundant labour forces to use uncultivated wild lands. The law was officially enacted to acknowledge the private ownership of land and to allow the free transaction of land among peasants. Second, in order to collect tax conveniently and to develop agriculture, Shang Yang launched national household registration. He turned the division of kinship units into households composing of a married couple and their young children. Upon becoming an adult, each child got a share of the family assets and lived separately as an independent household. The nuclear household became the basic unit of providing tax, corvée and military service. Simultaneously, the household registration provided the foundation for land allocation. Moreover, primogeniture once regulated by Zhou's royal law was officially replaced by partible inheritance (Wang 2015). Third, Shang Yang removed powerful aristocrats from government's positions[27] and established a centralised bureaucratic system which was operated by officials selected by standards of their ability and performance, rather than of aristocratic kinship. In addition, for the troops, promotion and awards were based on soldiers' performance on battlefields. When lowly soldiers fought well, they could be promoted to high nobility which before could only be occupied by aristocratic families. Fourth, because Shang Yang had Legalist ideas that commerce was inimical for national strength since merchants were mobile and could not be levied consistently, laws and monetary policies were

[27] Shang Yang punished teachers of the Xiao King of Qin severely, in order to warn other aristocratic members. Shang Yang's bloody death was gruesome because he made those aristocrats furious. Shang Yang was parted alive by five horses which ran towards five different directions. See: Sima, Qian, *op. cit., Biography of Lord Shang*.

enacted to discourage commerce and trade. "Insignificant individuals will occupy themselves with trade, and practise arts and crafts, all in order to avoid agriculture and war. Where the people are given to such teachings, how can the grain be anything but scarce, and the soldiers anything but weak?"[28] Commerce would distract farmers who provided agricultural surpluses and could become soldiers when necessary. As Shang Yang believed, farmers were of great importance for the state's power. Fifth, Shang Yang officially abolished the "Fengjian" system. He divided Qin's territory into forty-one counties and appointed performance-based officials as governors to administer them (Zhao 2015: 196). Those governors did not rely on agricultural surplus offered by tenants like those aristocrats under the "Feng-jian" system. They got an annual salary from the central government. Shang Yang also standardised the system of measurement, including acreage, length, mass. Sixth, Shang Yang established draconian penal codes for all crimes. In order to practise these stringent laws, he established a hostel registration system in order to effectively capture criminals. He also established a collective responsibility system under which five or ten households living nearby were grouped together. If one member in this group committed a crime, the whole group would be punished unless other members in this group reported the criminal. The legal system in the Qin state has been well understood on the basis of documents excavated from a tomb of a Qin clerk at Shuihudi (Lewis 2007: 30).

Shang Yang's reforms were genuinely successful, although he was killed by aristocrats whose interests had been eternally devastated by Shang Yang's reforms. He succeeded to establish a "military-physiocratic state" (von Glahn 2016: Chapter 3). The social and economic frameworks which Shang Yang erected did not only lay the foundation for Qin's final military victory and Qin's unification of China, but also the foundation for the Imperial Mode which endured for almost two thousand years. The private ownership of land was politically and legally established. Agricultural activities were encouraged. Aristocratic politics was largely demolished, and the merit-based and performance-based selection system was applied in the territory. An efficient bureaucratic state was achieved. Under the command of central authorities, the bureaucrats collected agricultural

[28] *Book of Lord Shang: Agriculture and War.*

surpluses to accomplish public good provision, including hydraulic works, warfare activities and construction of large-scale public projects.

Another significant public project was the construction of the Great Wall. It was not originally launched by the Qin state alone. In order to defend their own territory, the construction of high and impregnable walls had been launched by many states in the Warring States period. The Yan states had constructed walls along its southern border in order to protect itself from the Qi state. The Qi state constructed walls on its western border against the Wei state and the Zhao state and on its southern border against the Chu state. The Zhao state and the Qin state also constructed walls in their northern border to keep out nomadic horse riders. Many other states also launched similar projects along their border if they were confronted with dangerous enemies. In one way, the construction of the Great Wall "signified the transformation of the ancient Chinese states from multicity city states into territorial states" (Zhao 2015: 203). It also signified the transition of states' capacity. The large-scale construction was only possible when the government had effective methods to collect surplus products and deploy human labour. The objective conditions were to increase agricultural surpluses and ensure viable technological skills were sufficient as technology advanced (Deng 2020: 304–309). The states managed to extract sufficient resources to achieve public good provision, i.e., the defence against rivals.

The empire-building was successful overall when such reforms succeeded in transforming the states. All leaders of these reforms were unsurprisingly Legalist thinkers, including Guan Zhong, Li Kui, Shang Yang, etc. The specific thoughts that drove Legalist reforms along with other schools of ideas will be presented in Chapter 3. Various thoughts emerged in an era of political turmoil which facilitated intellectual freedom and made social experiments possible. Ensuing reforms changed the fragmented aristocratic states into bureaucratic states ruled by able professional officials. Private ownership of land was acknowledged, and small peasantry was valued in order to keep agriculture prosperous. The central government, as the highest authority, collected resources and accomplished sufficient public good provision, such as hydraulic works, national defence and other large-scale projects. A new empire and social structure emerged.

5 Summary

This chapter has illustrated the empire-building process before Qin unified China. This process had deep-layered mechanisms. Fundamentally the climatic, hydrologic and geographical conditions in the central plain and the loess plateau in China had made a central authority necessary to accomplish irrigation, drainage and flood control. This way the *ex ante* negotiation cost was lowered and then transaction costs made low enough to make public projects happen. Otherwise, prohibitive transaction costs would preclude any effective public projects. A centralised coordination system could overcome the issue of the free-rider problem; it was the most convenient and effective way at that time. In short, a centralised authority could use the benefits of efficiency tied to particular institutions to achieve public good provision, providing peasants with resources that would otherwise not have existed.

When the "first economic revolution" took effect, technological progress had driven agricultural productivity to improve. Pathbreaking economic and social changes ensued. The nature of the whole society was then completely changed. The agricultural sectors with higher productivity called for more efficient "accessory infrastructure", i.e., a centralised negotiation mechanism. The association that improvement in agricultural productivity had led to political unification could be supported by modern computational modelling. Scholars hold that the typographical features and the location of productive agricultural lands are necessary and sufficient to account for China's political unification and also its fragmentation (Fernández-Villaverde et al. 2020). In other words, the productive forces were demanding new relations of production and corresponding superstructure.

But the default mechanisms were the fragmented "Feng-jian" system and the well-field system which was characterised by the public ownership of land. The "Feng-jian" system gave local lords huge independence and economic autonomy, while this system was merely sustained by increasingly distant kinship and the military balance between central kings and local lords. As technological progress happened, i.e., the widespread usage of iron tools and ox-drawn plows, lords could no longer rely on the well-field system to live. The well-field system gradually collapsed, and household-cultivation rose as the predominant practice. Politically, the Zhou royal court was also declining. Local lords competed with each other to pursue hegemony, disregarding the order of Zhou's kings. Wars occurred frequently throughout the Easter Zhou dynasty. In order to satisfy the demand for military rivalry, states also aimed to strengthen their political power and established centralised power. The political and military practices contributed largely to the formation of a unified and totalitarian empire (Chen and Ma 2020; Chiu et al. 2018).

In this process, Legalist thinkers lobbied local lords to conduct reforms, most of which led to the completion of the empire-building process. Ambitious to achieve personal aims and intellectual popularity, Legalist thinkers were enthusiastic intellects to lobby lords. Legalism had a comprehensive blueprint to transform states with the goal of becoming a hegemon. Guan Zhong, Li Kui and Shang Yang had intentionally and successfully made their ideas come true. What they had done acted as "the unconscious tool of history in bringing about that revolution" (Marx 1853). Their reforms had common traits. By implementing the private ownership of land, the small peasantry was established and guaranteed by political actions and legal clauses by abolishing the aristocracy and selecting officials from a universal base of standards on performance and capacity, a merit-based bureaucratic state was established. The central authority was strengthened. Kings deployed bureaucrats to collect agricultural surpluses and to accomplish public good provision, including large-scale hydraulic works, warfare, the Great Wall, etc.

After this period, it was characterised by the private ownership of land, a bureaucratic state controlled by a central authority, and the responsibility of public good provision. This pattern, i.e., the Imperial Mode, would prevail from the first unified empire Qin in 221 BCE to the final decades of the last empire Qing. The links between those factors contributing to its formation were complicated, and in some cases mutual. The causality is not always unidimensional, as seen in Fig. 2. The process was quite comprehensive, so was the interaction between factors. The Imperial Mode was not just passively determined by these factors. It was also the active choice made by rulers and statesmen with an unconscious consideration for institutional efficiency and rational thinking. It facilitated the optimisation of public good provision and thus the continuous growth of agricultural productivity. A bureaucratic state could also provide relatively conducive governance. Roughly speaking, at the dawn of Qin's unification, some factors had already existed which were thought as crucial for the rise of Western Europe since the late Middle

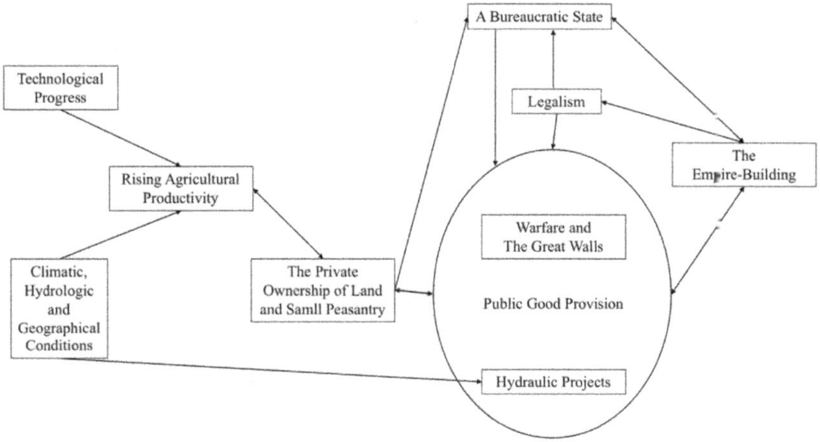

Fig. 2 The cognitive map of contributing factors to the empire-building

Ages.[29] These institutions were quite well suited with Chinese preindustrial society. Those reformers succeeded in responding with requirements presented by the forthcoming agricultural era. In the following millennia, few variations happened until these institutions failed to adjust to those challenges presented by a commercial and industrial era in the early modern time. Anyway, the conclusion in this chapter is concise: driven by economic and political conditions, and moulded by reformatory waves, the Imperial Mode was accomplished regarding its fundamental structure.

References

Anderson, Perry. 1974. *Lineages of the Absolutist State*. Verso.

Barker, R., R.W. Herdt, and B. Rose. 1985. *The Rice Economy of Asia*. Washington, DC: Resources for the Future Inc.

[29] Many economic historians have attributed the economic growth in western Europe after the Middle Age to some institutional factors, including clear-cut property rights, strong fiscal capacity, the rise of a literal bureaucratic system, etc. Many such factors had been existing since Qin unified China. So, it is of questionable value to attribute China's decline in early modern times to the absence of such institutions. See North and Thomas (1973).

Blazina, T., Sun, Y., Voegelin, A. et al. 2014. Terrestrial Selenium Distribution in China is Potentially Linked to Monsoonal Climate. *Nature Communication* 5, 4717.

Bray, Francesca. 1994. *The Rice Economies: Technology & Development in Asian Societies*. University of California Press.

Chen, Shuo, and Debin Ma. 2020. States and Wars: China's Long March towards Unity and Its Consequences, 221 BC–1911 AD. CAGE Working Paper No. 505.

Cheung, C., Z. Jing, J. Tang, et al. 2017. Diets, Social Roles, and Geographical Origins of Sacrificial Victims at the Royal Cemetery at Yinxu, Shang China: New Evidence from Stable Carbon, Nitrogen, and Sulfur Isotope Analysis. *Journal of Anthropological Archaeology* 48: 28–45.

Chi, Ch'ao-ting. 1936. *Key Economic Areas in Chinese History, as Revealed in the Development of Public Works for Water-Control*. London: G. Allen & Unwin, American Council, Institute of Pacific Relations.

Chiu, Yu Ku, Mark Koyama, and Tuan-Hwee Sng, 2018. Unified China and Divided Europe. *International Economic Review*, 59(1): 285–327.

de Brunhoff, Suzanne. 1973. *Marx on Money*. Trans. Goldbloom, Maurice J. London: Verso.

Deng, Kent Gang. 1993. *Development Versus Stagnation: Technological Continuity and Agricultural Progress in Premodern China*. New York: Greenwood.

Deng, Kent Gang. 1999. *The Premodern Chinese Economy: Structural Equilibrium and Capitalist Sterility*. Routledge.

Deng, Kent G. 2020. *The Premodern Chinese Economy: Structural Equilibrium and Capitalist Sterility*. Trans. Yucong Ru et al. Zhejiang University Press.

Fernández-Villaverde, Jesús, Mark Koyama, Youhong Lin, and Tuan-Hwee Sng. 2020. Fractured-Land and Political Fragmentation. NEBR Working Paper No. w27774.

Goetzmann, William N. 2017. *Money Changes Everything: How Finance Made Civilization Possible*. Princeton University Press.

Guo, Wentao (ed.). 1988. *A Brief History of Development of Agricultural Science and Technology in China*. Beijing: China Science and Technology Press. (in Chinese).

Hamashima, Atsutoshi. 1980. The Organisation of Water Control in the Kiangnan Delta in the Ming period. *Acta Asiatica* 38: 69–92.

Ho, Ping-Ti. 1969. The Loess and the Origin of Chinese Agriculture. *The American Historical Review*, 75(1): 1–36.

Hsu, Cho-yun. 1980. *Han Agriculture: The Formation of Early Chinese Agrarian Economy (206 BC–AD 220)*. Seattle: University of Washington Press.

Hua, Jueming. 2008. Metallurgy in Ancient China. In Selin, H. (ed.), *Encyclopaedia of the History of Science, Technology, and Medicine in Non-Western Cultures*. Springer.

Huang, Ray. 2015[1988]. *China: A Macro History*. Routledge.
Kelly, William W. 1982. *Irrigation Management in Japan: A Critical Review of Japanese Social Science Research*. Cornell University East Asian Papers No.30.
Kidder, Tristram R., and Yijie Zhuang. 2015. Anthropocene Archaeology of the Yellow River, China, 5000–2000 BP. *The Holocene* 25 (10): 1627–1639.
Lattimore, Owen. 1940. *Inner Asian Frontiers of China*. Boston: Beacon Press.
Lee, Yun Kuen. 2002. Building the Chronology of Early Chinese History. *Asian Perspectives* 41 (1): 15–42.
Lewis, Mark Edward. 2007. *The Early Chinese Empires: Qin and Han*. The Belknap Press.
Li, Feng. 2008. *Bureaucracy and the State in Early China: Governing the Western Zhou, 1045–771 BC*. Cambridge University Press.
Marx, Karl. 1853. The British Rule in India, in the *New-York Daily Tribune*, June 25, 1853. Online Archive.
Needham, Joseph, and Lu Gwei-Djen (eds.). 1971. *Science and Civilization in China*. Cambridge University Press.
North, Douglass C., and Robert P. Thomas. 1973. *The Rise of the Western World: A New Economic History*. Cambridge University Press.
Skinner, William G. 1977. *The City in Late Imperial China*. Stanford University Press.
von Glahn, Richard. 2016. *The Economic History of China: From Antiquity to the Nineteenth Century*. Cambridge University Press.
Wang, Yuesheng. 2015. *Institution and Population: Based on Chinese History and Reality*. Beijing Book Co. Inc. (in Chinese).
Wittfogel, Karl A. 1981[1959]. *Oriental Despotism: A Comparative Study of Total Power*. New York: Vintage Books.
Yang, Shengnan. 1992. *Shangdai Jingji Shi* [Economic history of the Shang Era]. Guizhou People's Press. (in Chinese).
Yao, Qing. 2016. Re-exploration of the Origin of the Early Agricultural Culture in China—Taking for example the Blending Relationship between the Northern Millet Culture and the Southern Rice Culture. *Journal of Henan University of Technology (social Science Edition)* 01: 11–17 (in Chinese).
Young, L.M. 1982. The Shang of Ancient China. *Current Anthropology* 23 (3): 311–314.
Zhao, Dingxin. 2015. *The Confucian-Legalist State: A New Theory of Chinese History*. Oxford University Press.
Zhu, Yanping. 2013. The Early Neolithic in the Central Yellow River Valley, c.7000–4000 BC. In Underhill, Anne P. (ed.), *A Companion to Chinese Archaeology*, 172–193. John Wiley & Sons.
Zhu, Zhixin, Shi Hu, et al. 1965. *Jingtianzhi Youwu zhi Yanjiu [Research on Whether the Well-field System Existed]*. Hong Kong: Chinese Literature Press (in Chinese).

CHAPTER 3

Thought Matters

Whenever institutions are formed, the role of thought and thinkers cannot be downplayed. As Keynes (1936: 383) told us clearly, “the ideas of economists and political philosophers, both when they are right and when they are wrong, are more powerful than is commonly understood. Indeed, the world is ruled by little else. Practical men, who believe themselves to be quite exempt from any intellectual influences, are usually the slaves of some defunct economist. Madmen in authority, who hear voices in the air, are distilling their frenzy from some academic scribbler of a few years back”. Keynes told the truth. Political thinkers and philosophers in ancient times had come up with some significant ideas which still deeply influence our lives today. It happened in Hellenistic Mediterranean regions. Plato, Aristotle, and many other great philosophers, paved the way for philosophy. At the same time, in the Far East, there were some profound thinkers who moulded the basic way of thinking in Chinese culture. It was in this era that many intellectual schools were established. The constellation included Confucius, Mencius, Laozi, Zhuangzi, Han Fei and many other influential thinkers. What they thought about politics, economy, ethics and philosophy deeply imprinted the imperial structures of ancient China. Their thought had influenced more Asian regions than just China in a geographical sense. Along with Buddha in India and those philosophers in ancient Greece, such shining thinkers characterised this era as the “axial age” (Fairbank and Goldman 2006: 51).

G. H. Jiang, *The Imperial Mode of China*, Palgrave Studies in Economic History, https://doi.org/10.1007/978-3-031-27015-4_3

Pines (2012) suggests that the thought of thinkers in Pre-Qin China played a paramount role in forming the imperial system and contributing to its striking endurance. In particular, the Legalist school of thought directly defined its fundamental characters, including centralisation of political power, the formation of a bureaucratic system in which officials were selected by standards of merits and ability, preference towards agriculture, etc. As partly illustrated in the last chapter, those Legalist thinkers conducted reforms in states in the Warring States period (403–221 BCE), and then the imperial structures were created by those reformatory measures. While Legalism had efficient methods to enable the government to provide sufficient public goods, Legalist measures were sometimes overly stringent and damaging to economy in that they occasionally quelled freedom, extracted too many resources and lacked effective supervision. The negative effect of Legalism was also obvious so that Confucianism and Daoism were always added to the rulers' ways of thinking and acting. Confucianism was established by Confucius, and to some degree, it played as a kind of religion for Chinese people.[1] In those dynasties following the Qin (221–206 BCE) dynasty, Confucianism functioned as a kind of state religion because emperors in the Western Han (206 BCE–9 AD) dynasty took it as official ideology. Especially after the Tang (618–907 AD) dynasty, the teachings of Confucian scholars became the mainstream content of national bureaucratic examinations and the familiarity with Confucian classics became one of the most important standards of promotion and selection. Confucianism always acted as a counterpart to Legalism because Confucianism insisted in the government's benevolence. Daoism also came in especially when wars and turmoil destroyed social order because of its belief in "no acting (Wuwei)". Ideas of Legalism, Confucianism and Daoism all contributed strongly to the formation of the imperial structure.

Chapter 2 has analysed geographical settings, the "first economic revolution" and transformation of relevant institutions. This chapter will present one aspect of the "superstructure"[2] of the Imperial Mode, i.e., those intellects and their thought which contributed to its formation. Those thoughts emerged in chaotic periods when states competed with

[1] Max Weber made this famous in his *Konfuzianismus und Taoismus* (*The Religion of China*). For a detailed analysis about Weber's ideas about Confucianism, see Bendix (1977: Chapter 5) and Kalberg (2021: Chapter 10).

[2] Exactly in the perspective of Marxian theories, namely "Überbau".

each other for hegemony and territorial expansion. Social changes urged scholars to offer alternatives to the unfitting structures. What they offered had a profound influence on the foundation of imperial institutions. Precisely true is the axiom that "the superstructure maintains and shaped the base".[3] The most outstanding illustration was the influence which Legalism posed on the formation of the Imperial Mode. But Legalism was not the only solely important school in imperial China. In dynasties following the Qin dynasty, Confucianism became the state religion. Time to time Daoism was applied as a remedy for crippled economy, too. It is worthwhile figuring out how different schools of thought interacted with the imperial structures in an era characterised by destruction and creation. Ideas that different schools offered impacted strongly imperial institutions, and the influence endured through the whole existence of the imperial system and even beyond.

1 The Background of the Intellectual Boom

The structural changes in the Eastern Zhou (771–256 BCE) dynasty, as analysed in last chapter, resulted in a chaotic society. The "Feng-jian" system characterised by strict stratification and aristocracy was ripped apart. Zhou's kings could not effectively control local lords anymore. Subsequently, local lords rose up to pursue hegemony and tried to stay dominant among states, thus making essential the role of wise consultants. Wise consultants could provide suggestions and wisdom which could make states strong. As universally acknowledged, "a state strengthens with the support of intellects or meets its demise when it loses intellects' support".[4] One of Confucius's pupils, Duanmu Ci, was once appointed as the chancellor of the Lu state and the Wei state. His ability greatly helped the Lu state to avoid the danger of being devastated. As a document commented, "once Duanmu Ci stood up, just for ten years he made Lu protected, Qi chaotic, Wu defeated, Jin kneeled and Yue bowed".[5] In

[3] Engels's letter to J. Bloch; from London to Königsberg, written on September 21, 1890. *Historical Materialism* (Marx, Engels, Lenin), 294–296. Published by Progress Publishers, 1972; first published by Der sozialistische Akademiker, Berlin, October 1, 1895. Translated from German. Online version: marxists.org 1999.

[4] Sima, Qian, *Biography of Comical Characters*.

[5] *Yue Jue Shu* (《越绝书》), a hoary Chinese document, whose writer was not clear. "子贡一出，十年而存鲁、乱齐、破吴、强晋、霸越"。

the Warring States period, those Legalist thinkers conducted comprehensive reforms in different states. Whoever managed to get Legalist policies applied became a hegemon. Without surprise, the final unification was accomplished by the Qin state which was the most successful one to apply Legalist reformatory policies designated by Shang Yang (390–338 BCE).

Therefore, social changes resulted in an emerging class, i.e., *shi*. It is a Chinese word which can only be translated with difficulty. Roughly speaking, it was the lowest rank of aristocratic titles, while it also meant "warriors and intellects". In that aristocratic society, a nobleman must be experienced in military skills, such as aptly using sword and bow, riding horse and manoeuvring cart, and simultaneously must be cerebral and knowledgeable. *Shi* pursued to nurture a perfect personality. However, in the Eastern Zhou dynasty the "Feng-jian" system collapsed, and the practice of partible inheritance produced an unduly large number of low-ranked aristocrats (Zhao 2015: 170). Because such positions as kings and lords were hereditary and thereby the number of hereditary positions was roughly unchangeable (unless kings conducted new "Fengjian"), the number of those top noblemen could not increase by much.[6] However, the number of other members of aristocracy increased remarkably. Taking the assumption of an aristocratic family which bore three children, only one of which could inherit the title, while the number of those who did not get the title would explode just after a few generations. If the population growth rate was presumed as 1%,[7] the number of one-rank-lower aristocrats was times the number of lords after several generations. The simplistic hypothetical circumstance could be seen in Fig. 1. The explosion of the number of lower aristocrats has been confirmed by many historical documents (Zhang 2016). Moreover, the weakening well-field system rendered aristocratic members poorer and poorer; many had to live as commoners. In many cases, they had to earn their life by selling their special skills and statecraft to lords and rich noblemen.

In the final years of the Western Zhou dynasty and the early years of the Eastern Zhou dynasty, a cultural transition also happened which

[6] Most lordships were created at the beginning years of the Western Zhou dynasty. Few new lordships were created in peaceful times of the Western Zhou dynasty. Such scenarios happened sometimes when brothers of kings had to leave from the capital to provincial cities.

[7] The estimate is not unreasonable. See Jiao (2007: 184).

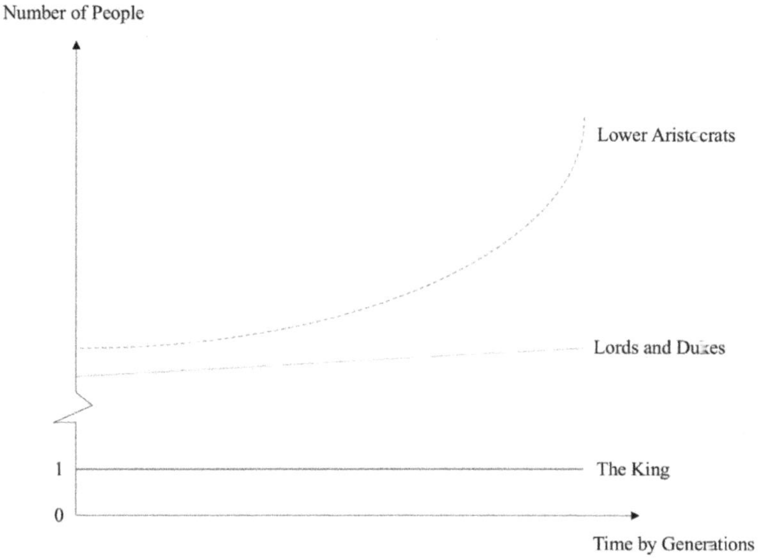

Fig. 1 The hypothetical population growth by aristocratic class as population grew generation by generation, the number of the king was nevertheless kept as 1; that of lords and dukes increased slightly; that of lower aristocrats increased remarkably.

contributed to expansion of the intellects' community. The cultural transition consisted of two aspects: the rise of a private educational system and the textual transformation from an oral to a text-based tradition. In the Western Zhou dynasty, schools founded by the royal court started to educate aristocratic teenagers, in order to serve kings (Creel 1983: 406–409). Aristocratic teenagers had to learn "six arts": rites, music, archery, charioteering, calligraphy and mathematics. While those schools signified the establishment of the formal educational system in Chinese history, they were highly aristocracy-oriented, and the right to be educated was monopolised in the hand of aristocratic families (Xia 2005). However, as the number of aristocratic members increased noticeably along with the gradual collapse of the hierarchical order in the Eastern Zhou dynasty, the formal education sustained by the Zhou royal court was also gradually left desolated. In other words, the central educational system collapsed (Fung 1996: 34–43). Its decline was paralleled by the rise of a decentralised and private educational system. More states competed for intellects whose expertise could help lords to gain advantages over rivals. Those rich men who could attract as many intellects as possible would be praised by people.[8] All these factors contributed to the rise of private education. The enlarging number of lower aristocratic members overlapped with the growing demand of local lords who sought hegemony and competitive advantages. As Hsu asserted, private education had emerged "to meet the demand for training the new administrative experts and strategists" and "opened up a new and lasting path by which any low-born but able young man could gain high office by his own competence" (Hsu 1965: 100–103).

In addition, in the Pre-Qin period, there was a nascent stage of transformation from an oral to a text-based tradition (Nylan 2000). In the Western Zhou dynasty, only a few royal documents were preserved in the royal library, such as *Yi Jing*.[9] Many scholars focused on oral teaching, rather than text-based teaching. In a sense, in the Spring and Autumn period, Confucius also preserved the oral tradition. Just as Confucius told his pupils, "[I am] a transmitter and not a maker, believing in and loving the ancients".[10] But in the Eastern Zhou dynasty, many intellects changed to preserve their ideas in written texts. Many documents at that time were preserved and were iconised as jewels in Chinese culture, including Confucianism's *Analects*, *Mencius*, *Xun Zi*, Daoism's *Dao De Jing* and *Zhuang Zi*, Legalism's *Guan Zi*, *Han Fei Zi* and *Book of Lord Shang*, etc. Unquestionably, the text-based trend contributed to the spread of thought and the prosperity of competing schools.

Besides those changes, some intellectual sources could be traced in the official ideology of the Western Zhou dynasty. As explained in the last chapter, because Zhou's victory against Shang was relatively weak, Zhou's rulers came up with an ideology to legitimise its rule. In the

[8] There were four patrons in the Warring States period who were highly praised because they accommodated thousands of guests: Prince Xinling in the Wei state, Prince Mengchang in the Qi state, Prince Pingyuan in the Zhao state, and Prince Chunshen in the Chu state. For detailed stories about them, see Lewis (1999). Later the chancellor in the Qin state, Lü Buwei, was also famous for accommodating enormous guests. He took those guests to write a book collectively, *Master Lü's Spring and Autumn Annals*. See Sima, Qian. *Op. cit., Biography of Lü Buwei*.

[9] Laozi was once the librarian in Zhou's royal library in the Eastern Zhou dynasty.

[10] *The Analects, Shu Er*, translated by James Legge (《论语·述而》).

official ideology, the worldly order resembled the heavenly cosmic order. When certain stars in the sky had constant positions and regular movement tracks, the people on the ground had the obligation to follow a similar order for the sake of universal harmony. The Zhou's kings, as the sons of Heaven, had the final word on whether the worldly order obeyed harmoniously Heaven's will. The rulers had also the obligation to follow instructions of Heaven, in dint of moral behaviours, industriousness and concern about ordinary people's life. The downfall of Shang, as Zhou announced, was because of the last Shang king's immorality and of his failure to meet Heaven's expectation. This ideology made the existence of a royal court dependent on its moral prestige (Fairbank and Goldman 2006: 46–48). It was also full of animism, conducting ancestry cult and saint cult. "The big deal of a state lies in rites and warfare".[11] Moreover, this ideology had a kind of objective idealism in that it acknowledged the existence and the superiority of a higher power which supervised the land "under Heaven" and in a few cases might meddle with the worldly affairs.[12] Both Confucianism and Daoism had abstracted inspirations from it.

2 Confucianism

It has become quite well known that Confucianism was established by Confucius in the Spring and Autumn period. Confucius (c. 551–c. 479 BCE) was born in a low-ranked aristocratic family which became poor in the disorderly society at that time. Facing the chaotic reality, he meandered among states in order to persuade lords to practise his ideas, but his tour became a blunt embarrassment. After loathly confessing his inability in politics, Confucius became famous for being a headmaster of a private school in the Lu state. His belief in indiscriminatory education had deeply influenced Chinese people so that he was venerated as the highest teacher in Chinese history. When he was still alive, many of his pupils became statemen, businessmen and scholars, among whom 72 people were the most famous (Chin 2007). Regarding Confucius' philosophy, his own

[11] Zuo Qiuming. *Zuo's Commentary, Chenggong 16th Year*(《左传·成公13年》). "国之大事，在祀与戎".

[12] Some important and interesting analysis about Chinese philosophies can be seen at G. W. F. Hegel's *Vorlesungen über die Philosophie der Weltgeschichte*. The English version, i.e., *The Philosophy of History,* was translated by John Sibree in 1956.

thought was quite innocent and uncomplicated in comparison with what had been added to him by Confucians living in subsequent dynasties.

As he believed enthusiastically in the advantages of institutions in the Western Zhou dynasty, Confucius dreamed of restoring those institutions as the remedy for the chaos of his time. In his ideals, the "Feng-jian" system had put everyone at the position which one deserved and unchangeability of social status would tranquilise everyone and thus stabilise the society.[13] The succession of power was also definite since there was crystal clear regulation about who should get the positions. It was determined by bloodline and kinship. Since there was no way to change the bloodline or the relative position of kinship, the predetermined system was quite stable and constant. Thus, Confucius praised the orderly stability in the Western Zhou dynasty. He thought that after the social relationships in a hierarchical system became ambiguous or devastated, social conflict intensified, and turmoil and chaos ensued (Zhao 2015: 180). For Confucius, the best way to cure the ill society was to restore the institutions which once brought peace and social order before. Furthermore, Confucius extended this logic to family life. The harmoniously orderly relationship should be also copied between family members, like the relationship between different social groups. Fathers, mothers, sons, brothers, relatives, etc., had their fixed relative positions and corresponding duties. By fulfilling duties, the harmony within a family was achieved. In sum, Confucius' political philosophy was basically the belief that a stratified system in which everyone kept own positions and fulfilled own duties would create a harmonious society. Here the shadow of the official ideology of the Western Zhou dynasty upon Confucius' thought could be discerned.

Obsessed in restoring previous institutions and instilling his own utopian ideas, Confucius had concrete imagination about what an ideal society looks like. In an article canonised by Confucians, the ideal of "Great Harmony" was painted in detail:

> When the Grand Course was pursued, a public and common spirit ruled all under the sky; they chose men of talents, virtue, and ability; their words were sincere, and what they cultivated was harmony. Thus men did not love

[13] In such a society, patriarchy was totally predominant in which women had no position. Their main (or only) role was to be a subservient wife. Only men could have a higher position in the social hierarchy.

> their parents only, nor treat as children only their own sons. A competent provision was secured for the aged till their death, employment for the able-bodied, and the means of growing up to the young. They showed kindness and compassion to widows, orphans, childless men, and those who were disabled by disease, so that they were all sufficiently maintained. Males had their proper work, and females had their homes. (They accumulated) articles (of value), disliking that they should be thrown away upon the ground, but not wishing to keep them for their own gratification. (They laboured) with their strength, disliking that it should not be exerted, but not exerting it (only) with a view to their own advantage. In this way (selfish) schemings were repressed and found no development. Robbers, filchers, and rebellious traitors did not show themselves, and hence the outer doors remained open, and were not shut. This was (the period of) what we call the Grand Harmony.[14]

Confucius' enthusiasm in a harmonious society was entrenched. In order to achieve that, another important aspect was also valued: personal virtue and merit. Confucians were always prepared for this: "if poor [and lowly], they attended to their own virtue in solitude; if advanced to dignity, they made the whole kingdom virtuous as well".[15] Confucius valued a merit named "ren" very dearly, which included extensive meanings, such as "benevolence", "humaneness", "kindness" and "human excellence" (Zhao 2015: 180). It was the highest personality which one could achieve, while there was no clear standard about what constituted "ren" or what did not. Confucius hoped that one person could spend the whole life to achieve "ren", which in Confucius' eyes was an inaccessible ideal for ordinary people. If everyone was in the pursuit of "ren", a moral social order would be also achieved. In Max Weber's famous *The Religion of China: Confucianism and Daoism*, he asserted that.

> Für den einzelnen war die Ausgestaltung des eigenen Selbst zu einer allseitig harmonisch ausbalancierten Persönlichkeit, einem Mikrokosmos in diesem Sinne, das entsprechende Ideal. »Anmut und Würde« des konfuzianischen Idealmenschen: des Gentleman, äußerte sich in der Erfüllung der überlieferten Pflichten. (Weber 1986, Band 1: 513)
> (For the individual, the development of their own self into a harmoniously balanced personality on all sides, a microcosm in this sense, was

[14] *Li Ji, Li Yun*, translated by James Legge (《礼记·礼运》).

[15] *Meng Zi, Jin Xin I*, translated by James Legge (《孟子·尽心章上》).

the corresponding ideal. "Grace and dignity" of the Confucian ideal man: the gentleman, expressed himself in the fulfilment of the traditional duties.)

In the eyes of Confucius, the best way to pursue "ren" was to be educated, to forever stay humble, to continue learning and to conduct an appropriate lifestyle. Confucius' particular practice of establishing private schools was a good expression of his beliefs. Everyone should try their best to fulfil the duties which the relative positions posed upon their shoulders. The kings had also the necessity to fulfil their duties to build a good society for the common people. Confucius' emphasis on education and personal duties contributed hugely to the formation of the literati class in ancient China and its characteristics. Although Confucius did not speak out expressly what the consequences were if the kings seriously failed to fulfil their duties, his successor, Mencius, pointed out more details of the duties.

Mencius (372–289 BCE) was a pupil of one of Confucius' heirs. Mencius lived in the Warring States period when the competition among states became unprecedentedly fierce and the wars were involved more and more with territorial expansion and annexation. In a period when Legalists were recruited by lords and dukes by dint of their effective but draconian strategies, Mencius enthusiastically persuaded lords to practise more peaceful strategies to make states strong, like Confucius himself. In a sense, Mencius' emphasis on public order, which was an important public good, was quite outstanding at that time. For instance, Mencius talked about the rudimentary disaster relief system.

> King Hui of Liang said, "Small as my virtue is, in the government of my kingdom, I do indeed exert my mind to the utmost. If the year be bad on the inside of the river, I remove as many of the people as I can to the east of the river, and convey grain to the country in the inside. When the year is bad on the east of the river, I act on the same plan. On examining the government of the neighboring kingdoms, I do not find that there is any prince who exerts his mind as I do".[16]

Apparently, the public disaster relief system had already been emphasised by Mencius in the Warring States period. In this following dialogue, although King Hui of Liang thought that he had done much better

[16] *Meng Zi, Liang Hui Wang I*, translated by James Legge (《孟子·梁惠王上》).

than other lords, Mencius was not satisfied with his policies. Mencius commented,

> If the seasons of husbandry be not interfered with, the grain will be more than can be eaten. If close nets are not allowed to enter the pools and ponds, the fishes and turtles will be more than can be consumed. If the axes and bills enter the hills and forests only at the proper time, the wood will be more than can be used. When the grain and fish and turtles are more than can be eaten, and there is more wood than can be used, this enables the people to nourish their living and mourn for their dead, without any feeling against any. This condition, in which the people nourish their living and bury their dead without any feeling against any, is the first step of royal government. Let mulberry trees be planted about the homesteads with their five *mu*, and persons of fifty years may be clothed with silk. In keeping fowls, pigs, dogs, and swine, let not their times of breeding be neglected, and persons of seventy years may eat flesh. Let there not be taken away the time that is proper for the cultivation of the farm with its hundred *mu*, and the family of several mouths that is supported by it shall not suffer from hunger. Let careful attention be paid to education in schools, inculcating in it especially the filial and fraternal duties, and grey-haired men will not be seen upon the roads, carrying burdens on their backs or on their heads. It never has been that the ruler of a State, where such results were seen - persons of seventy wearing silk and eating flesh, and the black-haired people suffering neither from hunger nor cold - did not attain to the royal dignity.[17]

The value of public order was communicated clearly. In the dialogue, Mencius emphasised the importance of acting according to the seasonal requirements of agricultural activities, of the kings' benevolence, and of the educational system. For Mencius, who lived in a period of total transformation towards more advanced agriculture, it was natural to highlight those conditions which were crucial for the agricultural economy to prosper. In other words, Mencius clearly held the value of public good provision as important. Given that agricultural activities were often interrupted by natural disasters, a larger public entity which was institutionally efficient could utilise more resources to cope with regional disaster. It is no wonder that in the Western Han dynasty, Confucianism was chosen as the dominant ideology, which was described as "Imperial Confucianism"

[17] *Loc. cit.*

by Fairbank (Fairbank and Goldman 2006: 62–63). For agricultural activities, public good provision, such as public order, as illustrated in the last chapter, were paramount. Mencius also pointed out explicitly the fact that kings had duties to accomplish them. But Mencius went further than the kings expected. In a dialogue, Mencius said expressly that the common people were more valuable than kings themselves:

> The people are the most important element in a nation; the spirits of the land and grain are the next; the sovereign is the lightest. Therefore, to gain the peasantry is the way to become sovereign; to gain the sovereign is the way to become a prince of a State; to gain the prince of a State is the way to become a great officer. When a prince endangers the altars of the spirits of the land and grain, he is changed, and another appointed in his place. When the sacrificial victims have been perfect, the millet in its vessels all pure, and the sacrifices offered at their proper seasons, if yet there ensues drought, or the waters overflow, the spirits of the land and grain are changed, and others appointed in their place.[18]

Despite respecting official ideology of the Western Zhou dynasty, Mencius's attitudes to downplay kingship were detested by autocratic emperors. The official ideology acknowledged that the fate of kingship depended on kings' fulfilment of their duties. Mencius' teaching pointed out the specific demands of the growing agricultural economy. Whoever failed to fulfil the duties should be overthrown by the people and others who could meet those demands should be promoted to kingship. Mencius explicitly said, "the people are the most crucial and important, next is the state, least is the king".[19] Clearly, the fact that Mencius was more detailed in this aspect than Confucius, was related with the social changes in which technological progress facilitated new economic forms. Mencius' tenets were an active response to contemporary social demand. As illustrated before, Mencius insisted on the duties of kings to sustain public relief system and improving people's living level through governmental measures. They highlighted the significance of public good provision.

While Xunzi was the third influential Confucian thinker after Confucius and Mencius in the Eastern Zhou dynasty, Xunzi respected Confucius but criticised Mencius. Xunzi lived already towards the end of the Warring

[18] *Meng Zi, Jin Xin II*, translated by James Legge (《孟子·尽心章下》).

[19] *Loc. cit.*

States period when territorial annexation was already overwhelming and autocratic states gradually formed. The starting point of Xunzi's philosophy was his judgement about human nature: Xunzi believed that human nature was evil inborn. While Mencius thought that goodness was innate and required only enculturation, Xunzi asserted that selfishness and greed were basic to human nature and thus required strict control (Zhao 2015: 181–182). At this point, Xunzi criticised Mencius vehemently. Xunzi asserted that the evil human nature could be confirmed by biological phenomena, such as the invariably physical needs and the desires for an increasingly better living (Hu and Guo 2011). Despite this, Xunzi believed that goodness could be nurtured through self-learning, education and instruction from virtuous models, such as those moral and noble ancient kings, which was also the tenet of Confucius himself. Then, Xunzi esteemed Confucius and bragged himself as the true successor of Confucius, while he downplayed Mencius in the belief that Mencius had distorted Confucius' teachings (Schwartz 1985: 326).

In order to curb evilness in human nature, Xunzi believed that people must learn moral doctrines and instructions of moral models, which were ancient sages (Pines 2009: 163). The core of Confucius' thought, i.e., "ren", must be highlighted and the holistic institutions to maintain "ren" should be established. A moral system proposed by Confucius himself, thus, was also preached by Xunzi. Such a system could effectively restrain the evilness of human nature and render society into order (Sato 2016: 364). But Xunzi elaborated this process further than Confucius. In order to curb chaos and potential disorder, strict laws and powerful lordship were necessary. Xunzi even proposed to extinguish other schools of thought, in order that people's hearts would not be disturbed by wrong thoughts and colourful ideas (Xiao 1961: 81). Facing a chaotic period, Xunzi came up some proto-Legalist ideas to cope with certain sociopolitical situations (Pines 2004). In this aspect, Xunzi was quite similar to Legalists. It is no surprise that his two pupils, Han Fei and Li Si, were two salient Legalists of that era. Some scholars categorised Xunzi as a genuine Legalist thinker (Xiao 1961: 81). Indeed, Xunzi devised some proto-Legalist doctrines about how a stringent bureaucratic state should function. Mote described Xunzi as the first one to come up with "an imperial structure" (Mote 1971: 59). Through combing ideas of Confucianism and Legalism, Xunzi's thought presaged the ideology of an imperial structure.

In the Pre-Qin period, Confucianism was never more than merely an ordinary school which competed with other schools for the affection of lords. Neither Confucius nor Mencius ever had practical influence upon public policies or concrete projects. But by dint of emphasising social order and public good provision, Confucian tenets matched well with the need for a unified large empire. Hundreds of years later, Emperor Wudi of Han in the Western Han dynasty, elevated Confucianism as the official ideology. After the Tang dynasty, Confucian canons became the content of national examinations and the conformity to Confucian doctrines became the standards of bureaucratic promotion. Reiterating Confucian texts became the most significant lesson for the literati class. As Kissinger said,

> Compiled into a central collection of Confucius's sayings (*the Analects*) and subsequent books of learned commentary, the Confucian canon would evolve into something akin to China's Bible and its Constitution combined. Expertise in these texts became the central qualification for service in China's imperial bureaucracy – a priesthood of literary scholar-officials selected by nationwide competitive examinations and charged with maintaining harmony in the Emperor's vast realms. (Kissinger 2012: 14)

Through the bureaucratic system, Confucianism significantly influenced imperial China. As the pillar of the Imperial Mode, bureaucrats needed to practise emperors' will and achieve the task of public good provision; they had to collect sufficient resources from small peasants and other sources, such as through the national monopoly on salt and iron, etc. When bureaucrats failed to achieve their tasks well, the Imperial Mode became unbalanced. The principal–agent problem would emerge and transaction costs within the operation of the imperial structure increased remarkably. Therefore, the importance of those bureaucrats educated under Confucianism could never be downplayed. The truly important question is, as Schefold wrote, how those Confucian bureaucrats could achieve their tasks, i.e., to create economically useful institutions for ancient China.

> [In China] ist der wirtschaftliche Prozess nie als autonom angesehen worden, sondern er wurde stets als in Wechselwirkung mit dem Staat stehend betrachtet. Es war deshalb selbstverständlich zu fragen, welche Auswirkungen eine konfuzianische oder legalistische Staatsphilosophie auf die Entwicklung hatte oder inwieweit die literarisch ausgebildeten

Mandarine der Wirtschaft nützliche Institutionen zu schaffen imstande waren. (Schefold 2020)

(In China, the economic process has never been seen as autonomous, but has always been seen as interacting with the state. It was therefore natural to ask what effects a Confucian or Legalist state philosophy had on development or to what extent the literary mandarins of the economy were able to create useful institutions.)

3 Daoism

For decades, Daoism was famous among some Chinese economic scholars because of its seemingly close relationship with French Physiocracy, Smith's "invisible hand" and Hayek's "spontaneous order", etc. (Tan 1992). It is true that several physiocratic thinkers were influenced by Daoism which was transmitted to France in the seventeenth and eighteenth centuries. Quesnay's laissez-faire was said to originate in his understanding on Daoism (Bodde 2005). It is widely known that Turgot's best-known work, *Reflections on the Formation and Distribution of Wealth*, was written for two young Chinese students. Daoism did come up with some subtle and unparalleled ideas in such an early period. But a holistic analysis on Daoism is impossible here. The scope would be limited to the influence of Daoism upon Chinese thought and the imperial structure. Unlike Confucianism or Legalism, Daoism did not get an outstanding status in the imperial bureaucratic structure. However, Daoism had a higher practical and intellectual position than it ostensibly had. Practically, Daoism was always the emperors' elixir soon after wars had harmed the economy. Theoretically, with some similarity with Physiocracy and Classical economics, Daoism had much deeper thinking about society and the economy than Confucianism and Legalism.

As a school of thought, Daoism emerged later than Confucianism (Zhao 2015: 182). Against Sima Qian's records, Daoism was not established by Laozi in that the identity of Laozi was never clear.[20] Yang Zhu

[20] In Sima Qian's *Biography of Laozi and Han Fei*, Laozi lived a little earlier than Confucius and Confucius once paid a personal visit to Laozi. While Sima Qian wrote about Laozi's birthplace, a few activities and his work (*Dao De Jing*), Sima Qian frankly acknowledged that he cannot figure out who Laozi truly was. He provided three potential figures who could be Laozi. Nowadays, scholars generally agree with this idea that Laozi lived in the Warring States period and so later than Confucius. And *Dao De Jing* was not written by one person.

was generally believed to be the first influential Daoist thinker. Yang Zhu lived approximately contemporarily with Mencius, but his own writings were totally lost. Few of his sentences could be seen in *Lie Zi* and *Meng Zi*. However, from a couple of his sentences, a radical Daoist could be drawn out. The most prominent idea of Yang Zhu was his concentration on "self". Yang Zhu believed that the "self" was of higher existence than any other collective concept. In *Meng Zi*, "the principle of the philosopher Yang [Zhu] was 'each one for himself'. Though he might have benefited the whole kingdom by plucking out a single hair, he would not have done it".[21] Yang Zhu would not sacrifice himself a little bit even though the sacrifice could benefit the kingdom. Generally, Yang Zhu was criticised because of this extreme selfishness. But Yang Zhu had much more complicated thinking on it. In *Lie Zi*,

> If the ancients by injuring a single hair could have rendered a service to the world, they would not have done it; and had the universe been offered to a single person, he would not have accepted it.
>
> As nobody would damage even a hair, and nobody would do a favour to the world, the world was in a perfect state.[22]

Yang Zhu put every single person at the core of his thinking and rejected altruism. He insisted that the benefit of a kingdom should not be obtained through sacrificing any individual interests. A society consisted of every single "self". If no one was sacrificed for the benefit of others, and no one would give benefits to others, the society would be in harmony. Therefore, Yang Zhu was in the diagonal contrast of a strong state. He thought that the government was just symbolic. Any action of the government should not harm individual interests or freedom. But Yang Zhu was not proposing anarchy (Actually Laozi was proposing anarchy). He was opposing the robbery on individual interests. Comprehensively speaking, Yang Zhu was almost the most radical and also the most confusing scholar in the Pre-Qin period. Preaching self-interest, he opposed altruism; but he was preaching that everyone must be self-interested. Perfect was a society where no one needed to sacrifice for others (Yang, 2011). Judging from these points, Yang Zhu thought about some ideas similar to Pareto's "Optimality": A better situation cannot be obtained through

[21] *Meng Zi, Jin Xin I*, translated by James Legge (《孟子·尽心章上》).

[22] *Lie Zi, Yang Zhu*, translated by Anton Forke (2011) (《列子·杨朱》).

the reduction of any individual's benefit. And his ideas about the government had something in common with modern liberalism. However deep Yang Zhu's thoughts were, they were not so self-evident or straightforward especially when a forthcoming agrarian economy was requesting for collective actions. None of his own writings were left. He was also criticised vehemently by later Confucians and was in effect erased from the official academy.

Laozi was the most famous Daoist thinker, but around him were numerous myths. Sima Qian, who lived a few hundreds of years later, could not figure out who Laozi was or who was the authentic writer of *Dao De Jing*.[23] Now among scholars it is generally believed that this work, *Dao De Jing*, was not the product of a single writer, but a collection of contributions by a number of persons living from the end of the Spring and Autumn period to the middle of the Warring States period (Hu 2009: 209). Specifically, this work dates from before the end of the fourth century BCE (Zhao 2015: 182). Sima Qian's story about the meeting between Laozi and Confucius was also uncertain: at least, scholars are prone to negate that the person who met Confucius was the writer of *Dao De Jing*.[24] Even the name of this tersely written book is not one hundred percent certain.[25]

[23] In Sima Qian's *Biography of Laozi and Han Fei*, Laozi was born in the Chu state and later became a librarian in Zhou's royal archive house in the Zhou's capital. Confucius once went to visit Laozi in pursuit of knowledge about Zhou's rituals and institutions, but it seemed that Laozi could not agree with Confucius' idea to restore Zhou's system. After witnessing the weakening of Zhou royal court, Laozi decided to leave and go westward. When he arrived at a military gate, a general requested him to write something to bestow. Thus, Laozi wrote *Dao De Jing* which consisted of five thousand Chinese characters. Then, Laozi continued and disappeared.

[24] In Chinese, the second character of the book's name, "De", literally meant "morality" or "virtue", which was basically what Confucius himself preached enthusiastically. But in *Dao De Jing*, "De" was criticised vehemently and expressly. From this perspective, one book cannot criticise something which had not existed before itself. "De" had become a negative counterpart to "Dao" which was what Daoist thinkers preached. Therefore, *Dao De Jing* should be at least later than when Confucius himself lived. See: Yi (2009: Chapter 3).

[25] In the early 1970s, the oldest extant text of this book was found in a tomb in Mawangdui. But this version was named only as "Lao Zi", rather than "Dao De Jing". In addition, the internal sequence of this book was also different from "Dao De Jing". It was "De Dao Jing", because the Chapter "De" was before the Chapter "Dao". The difference was never trivial. It was related to *Laozi*'s content: after criticising "De(morality)", he preached his own "Dao".

Laozi's most prominent idea was "dao". It could be translated literally as "way" or "road". But Laozi never gave it an accurate definition. Just as Laozi himself said, "the Dao that can be trodden is not the enduring and unchanging Dao. The name that can be named is not the enduring and unchanging name".[26] According to Laozi's description, "dao" encompassed a range of different concepts, from right behaviour and proper social relations to logic, law, the nature of things, the forces propelling things or events, the right way of doing things, a mysterious power that surrounds us and so on (Zhao 2015: 183). Basically Laozi referred to a highly abstract "law" which regulated everything. Nature had its own "dao": the law of physical movement, the law of biographical metabolism, the law of colourful natural phenomena, etc. Society also had its own "dao": the law of social mechanism, the law of interpersonal relations, the law of economic activities, etc. In other words, "dao" was the pertinent "way" of how things went on. Then, "dao" was the fundamental concept for Laozi to construct his whole framework. It was because of the existence of "dao" that everyone must follow the requirements of "dao". Especially rulers must follow "dao", rather than rule over a state arbitrarily.

"Dao" was a common concept shared by Confucianism and early Daoism. Because "dao" was a widely used concept in Zhou's archives, Confucius spoke highly of "dao" and took it as the great harmony of a society. Confucius said, "'dao' makes no way. I will get upon a raft, and float about on the sea".[27] Also, Confucius took "dao" as the ideal condition of a society.

> When [there is "dao"], ceremonies, music, and punitive military expeditions proceed from the son of Heaven. When [there is no "dao"], ceremonies, music, and punitive military expeditions proceed from the [lords]. When these things proceed from the [lords], as a rule, the cases will be few in which they do not lose their power in ten generations. When they proceed from the great officers of the [lords], as a rule, the case will be few in which they do not lose their power in five generations. When

[26] *Dao De Jing*, translated by James Legge. (道可道, 非常道)

[27] *The Analects, Gong Ye Chang* (《论语·公冶长》). Here Confucius felt pitiful the fact that his doctrines cannot prevail even though he believed that they were perfect. If "dao" cannot prevail, Confucius would take a boat on the sea in order to keep remote from the disappointing world.

the subsidiary ministers of the great officers hold in their grasp the orders of the state, as a rule, the cases will be few in which they do not lose their power in three generations. When [there is "dao"], government will not be in the hands of the great officers. When [there is "dao"], there will be no discussions among the common people.[28]

Both Confucius and Laozi accepted some philosophical inheritance from Zhou's ideology.[29] "Dao" referred to an objective law higher than man's will. On the basis of "dao", Laozi got his advice on "Wuwei", i.e., "no acting" or "do nothing". "Wuwei" was the external expression of following "dao". It was the best thing which a ruler should do. So, Laozi preached,

I will do nothing (of purpose), and the people will be transformed of themselves;
I will be fond of keeping still, and the people will of themselves become correct;
I will take no trouble about it, and the people will of themselves become rich;
I will manifest no ambition, and the people will of themselves attain to the primitive simplicity.[30]

Laozi believed that the best way to do things was to keep them simple and let all beings follow their own natural courses. Then, the result must be good through self-development. Criticising governmental interventions in modern economies, Hayek spoke highly of Laozi's teaching and shared a lot with Laozi in common. In his speech in 1966, Hayek thought that his principles of liberalism had been explained clearly by Laozi.

Is this all so very different from what Lao-Tzu says
In his fifty-seventh poem?
If I keep from meddling with people, they take care of themselves,
If I keep from commanding people, they behave themselves,

[28] *The Analects, Ji Shi*, translated by James Legge, partly revised by myself (《论语·季氏》). Confucius was very disappointed about the condition that lords superseded Zhou's kings and subsequently great officers of lords superseded lords themselves. So, he described this disorder as no "dao".

[29] See Sect. 2 in Chapter 2.

[30] *Dao De Jing*, translated by James Legge (我无为,而民自化).

> If I keep from imposing on people, they become themselves. (Hayek 1966)

However, it would be wrong to conjecture that Laozi took a quite passive or negative attitude towards the world. Laozi's "Wuwei" was based on his dialectics. The purpose of "no acting" was that "nothing cannot be done".[31] In Laozi's dialectics, the opposite forces could always transform into each other. "The softest can overcome the hardest", in that the softest can survive but the hardest can be easily damaged.[32] Therefore, if rulers did nothing, the best result could ensue; if rulers intended to do everything, the worst result would ensue. Because rulers did not follow "dao" but practise their own desires, the natural order would be harmed by intentional actions. The intention to "act" should be eliminated from politics. Laozi had very strong belief in people's "spontaneous order" (Rothbard 2005). Some scholars had long believed that Daoist thought devised by Laozi had much in common with Classical economics (McCormick 1999). Distrusting purposeful actions, Laozi had great influence upon later Legalist thinkers. When the objective and ubiquitous "dao" ruled over, according to Legalist thought, the "dao" should be expressed as fixed laws formulated by wise statesmen. Roughly speaking, Legalist logic was sourced from Daoist philosophy.[33]

Zhuangzi was the successor of Laozi in the Warring States period. For a long time, Zhuangzi had been one of the favourites of Chinese philosophers, poets and writers. In comparison to his influence upon politics, Zhuangzi's influence was much bigger in literature, arts and poetry (Fairbank and Goldman 2006: 49–50). Basically, Zhuangzi took a more negative and passive attitude to the chaos in the Warring States period than Laozi. Zhuangzi criticised vehemently warfare and territorial expansion among states. Subsequently he criticised other schools, including Confucianism which wanted to "rescue" the society, and Legalism which

[31] "Having arrived at this point of non-action, there is nothing which he does not do". *Dao De Jing*, translated by James Legge.

[32] It is famous that when they met, Laozi and Confucius had this interesting conversation. Laozi asked Confucius a question: "can you see my teeth?" Confucius answered no. Laozi continued to ask: "can you see my tongue?" Confucius answered yes. Then Laozi said: "the universal law is here". Confucius said: "the soft survives while the hard dies".

[33] Sima Qian put Laozi, the Daoist representative, and Han Fei, the Legalist representative, under one same chapter, i.e., *Biography of Laozi and Han Fei*. It had been long acknowledged that Laozi and Han Fei had cerebral similarity.

helped lords to enlarge control and strengthen the government's capacity. Zhuangzi took a more radical position towards "Wuwei". While Laozi admonished lords to apply "Wuwei" in order to get a better society as he envisioned, Zhuangzi insisted on completely giving up any action for nothing. The best situation should be an animal world: "A sage would be ashamed (of such a thing). In the age of perfect virtue, they attached no value to wisdom, nor employed men of ability. Superiors were (but) as the higher branches of a tree; and the people were like the deer of the wild".[34] Living independently and undisturbedly, a tree and the deer below composed the ideal condition of which Zhuangzi dreamed. In addition, Zhuangzi's thought even contained pieces of anti-intellectualism inclination. He opposed the pursuit for knowledge and technological progress. In Zhuangzi's vision, a primitive society where every single person lived alone, ignorantly and simplistically, was the best society, for progress meant more desires but more desires/greed resulted in showing more of the dark sides of human nature. At this point, Zhuangzi became the most popular figure among unworldly philosophers. Zhuangzi's writing was also full of beautiful sentences and the wildest imagination. For two thousand years, Zhuangzi had inspired a number of writers and poets.

Basically put, all representatives of Daoism had concepts of "natural order", "no acting", and thus anti-interventionist inclination. Except a few short periods where Daoism did obtain the status of official ideology, like Confucianism and Legalism, the ideas of Daoism had great potential influence ordinarily at the beginnings of most dynasties whose administrative capacity was more or less crippled (Peach 2019). Especially during the reign of the first several emperors of the Western Han dynasty, Huang-Lao thought posed predominant effects upon rulers. Besides prominent announcements of Daoism's predominance in few periods, the liberalist ideas penetrated the Confucian doctrines in a sense. Specific expressions were that rulers should intervene little with peasants' activities, pose light burdens (material taxation and corvée) upon peasants, and respect provincial and local order. As Long (2012) had said, liberalism had been relatively strong in local communities in imperial China. The private ownership of land and the free transaction of lands had been maintained for most periods; the government respected local customs; labour forces

[34] *Zhuang Zi, Heaven and Earth*, translated by James Legge (《庄子·天地》).

could relatively freely conduct productive activities, in terms of farming, handicraft or commerce; the higher government left the local administration to local gentry and elites; taxation was consciously restrained; local markets and small commercial towns could mushroom relatively freely (Long 2012). Although scholars contend that there was little evidence to prove that the policies adopted by emperors were inspired by any certain school of thought (Peach 2019), Daoism played a role of sustaining the peasant economy and the liberalist tradition of the economy in ancient China.

4 Legalism

The specific policies of Legalism which were practised in the Warring States period have been analysed in the last chapter with forensic detail. It has been shown that the formation of a tightly controlled regime was facilitated by Legalist ideas. In this section, a more theoretical analysis will be presented, with concentration on the cerebral aspects of Legalist thinkers. In Legalists' eyes, pragmaticism was much more important than cerebral depth. Legalists once ironised Confucians' naivety and simplicity.[35] What had driven Legalists was the overriding desire to make states powerful militarily.

Guan Zhong (725?–645 BCE) was canonised as the first Legalist thinker in the Spring and Autumn period. However, when Guan Zhong was alive, there was no such Legalist school. The book, *Guan Zi*, which was said to keep Guan Zhong's thought about economic growth and national administration, was in fact compiled by a couple of scholars who belonged to the official academy of the Qi state (Rickett 1993). Even some material was added after *Han Fei Zi* (Hansen 2000: 357). Guan Zhong's specific measures which he took in order to make the Qi state strong were very realist and also efficient. The spirit of *Guan Zi* was basically interventionist. It proposed the government to engage directly in the business of farmers, merchants and artisans. A typical proposal in *Guan Zi* was that the government should pay close attention to the price fluctuations of goods needed by peasants in busy seasons, and it should adopt a

[35] There were numerous examples in the Warring States period that Legalists criticised Confucians and other schools. Even in the Qin state, some Legalists advised to banish other schools so that citizens and lords would not be disturbed by those pedants. See: Sima, Qian, *Biography of Li Si*.

price policy to cut off all opportunities for annexation by the rich (Hu 2009: 114). The aim of *Guan Zi* was to protect small peasants from bankruptcy or being weakened by natural disasters or merchants' exploitation. This idea had been explicitly practised by Li Kui in the Wei state.[36] Another typical policy of interventionism was the policy of monopoly by the government on salt, iron and other natural resources. While *Guan Zi* warned against direct management by the government of iron mines (von Glahn 2016: 65), nominally all kinds of natural resources belonged to the government. When citizens were allowed to utilise those resources for production, the government must get benefits from them. For salt, the transaction was limited so that the government could get tremendous profits; for iron mines, mountain and water surface (for fishery), individuals were permitted to use these goods at the price of a certain amount of rent (Hu 2009: 157–159).

What made *Guan Zi* more outstanding was that it contained some ideas similar to modern economic thought. Along with the proposal to stabilise commodities' prices, *Guan Zi* opposed the frugality of the rich. *Guan Zi* proposed to construct projects in order to stimulate production and employ more people.

> In a year of drought or waterlogging, when people lose their farm-work, efforts should be to construct palaces, houses, terraces and arbours, in order to employ those people who possess at home neither dogs nor pigs. In doing so, the aim is not to enjoy the luxuries, but to practice the policy of the state.[37]

Even Guan Zhong himself developed an alluring propaganda to encourage consumption: "to paint the egg before it is about to be boiled and to carve the firewood before it is about to be burned".[38] *Guan Zi* proposed to use consumption and construction as methods to stimulate production. Modern economists, such as John Keynes, would not feel estranged to such thought, but *Guan Zi* was compiled in at latest fourth

[36] Li Kui had proposed such a policy as "ping di", a policy to stabilise grain prices. According to this policy, the government should purchase and store grain in harvest years in order to stop grain prices to decline, while sell grain in bad years in order to stop grain prices to ratchet up. The fundamental goal was to sustain peasants' motivation.

[37] *Guan Zi, Cheng Ma Shu* (《管子·乘马数》).

[38] *Guan Zi, Chi Mi* (《管子·侈靡》).

century BCE. *Guan Zi* also formed some ideas that follow the quantity theory of money.

> When nine tenths of the money are recalled to the top [the treasury of the state] and only one tenth of it remains below [in circulation], money will get "heavy" and things in general will get "light". At this conjuncture, money in the treasury of the state should be used to purchase things in general. Then money goes into circulation again and things in general are kept by the state. Consequently, things in general will become ten times "heavier" than before.[39]

Here the *Guan Zi* scholars had realised the association between inflation and the quantity of money in circulation. The book also suggested that the government should intervene in the circulation of money, in order to control the market. It is quite clear that the ideas in *Guan Zi* were full of dense interventionism. There is no denying that its economic thought was superior to that of all other thinkers in the whole Pre-Qin period (Hu 2009: 159). Practically, Guan Zhong's practices paved a way for later Legalists who conducted reforms in a couple of states, among whom Shang Yang was the most successful. In terms of more profound effects, the interventionist ideology and its specific practices which statesmen could implement in *Guan Zi*, became part of lessons for imperial bureaucrats. Managing the economy became a taken-for-granted responsibility for imperial bureaucrats, which was hugely different from the occidental world.

Most Legalist thought came from pragmatic considerations, but they also had spiritual sources. Daoism had an obvious influence upon the formation of Legalist ideas (Creel 1970: 48). Firstly, Daoism expressly confessed people's self-interest and self-motivation. Daoist thinkers always claimed that Confucianism overly emphasised social ethics and individual austerity, and therefore ignored human nature. A wise ruler should acknowledge that and efficiently take advantage of that. The Daoist solution was to "let it be" and then everything would go on well by itself. But Legalism thought otherwise. The proposed means of achieving rulers' goals should be a variety of carrot-and-stick policies that would both incentivise people to pursue the rulers' goals and make it impossible for them to do otherwise (Peach 2019: 10). Secondly, Daoism

[39] *Guan Zi, Shan Guo Gui* (《管子·山国轨》).

opposed rulers' intentional interventions because "dao" would do everything necessary for an optimal society. However, "dao" was invisible and unsensible. In a sense, Daoism resorted to agnosticism. For Legalism, the regulations which statesmen designed would function like the invisible and unsensible "dao".[40] Those regulations were not intentionally interventionist, but they were there to prescribe what should be done and proscribe what cannot be done. Thirdly, the obvious intellectual intimacy between Laozi and Han Fei was expressed by Han Fei's teaching on realpolitik and trickery. As presented before, Laozi's "no acting" contained much hypocrisy because the goal was to "do everything". Han Fei proposed to use all possible trickery and tactics to deceive rivals and he suggested that rulers should utilise hypocritical means to dupe subordinates and ordinary people. Indeed, Sima Qian had full reason to put Laozi and Han Fei in the same biography (*Biography of Laozi and Han Fei*).

Han Fei was the last Legalist thinker in the Warring States period and also the most profound and comprehensive one. He studied under Xunzi, the last Confucian thinker at that time. Ironically, Xunzi succeeded in nurturing two big figures of Legalism, Han Fei, and Li Si, the chancellor of the Qin state who helped Qin Emperor the First to annex other rivals and to finally unify China.[41] As shown before, Xunzi believed that human nature was evil and the evilness must be changed with externally objective forces and internally subjective self-education. Obviously, Han Fei had got this firmly. He assumed that all relations between people were based solely on people's self-seeking (Hu 2009: 197). Even the relation between parents and children was built on self-seeking. Han Fei argued:

> When a baby boy is born, people mutually congratulate each other, but when a baby girl is born, they kill her. Now, both of them are born out

[40] I do not use "laws" or "legal system" to describe those clauses which Legalists established, because the spirits of Legalists were distinctly different from modern laws.

[41] Although being classmates, Li Si was responsible for Han Fei's early death. A little older than Han Fei, Li Si went to the Qin state earlier after finishing studying under Xunzi and succeeded to become the chancellor of Qin. Years later, Han Fei also went to the Qin state and got the great favour of the Qin king who was later the First Emperor of Qin. But Li Si was afraid that Han Fei would threaten his political status because he knew that Han Fei was more talented and versatile. Then Li Si fabricated some crimes of Han Fei and put him into prison. Soon Han Fei was poisoned dead under the command of Li Si. See: Sima, Qian, *Biography of Laozi and Han Fei, Biography of Li Si.*

> of the parents' bodies, yet a baby boy receives congratulations while a baby girl is killed. Why? Because considerations of future expediency and thought of long-term advantages advise such courses of action. So, the relation between parents and children is still calculated with self-seeking. What can we hope for a relation without parent-and-children benefits?[42]

On the basis of this murky consideration, Han Fei proposed to use very realist and stringent actions to treat people. For ordinary people, draconian penal clauses should be applied to intimidate them; for subordinates and bureaucratic officials, rulers should use Machiavellian strategies to keep them loyal and feared by rulers. But the rulers themselves were not subject to those legal clauses (Zhao 2015: 185). In Han Fei's envisioned world, everything lived in a wild world to which the law of the jungle was applied. The draconian nature of Legalism was quite common among Legalist thinkers and practices. Without exception, Li Kui in the Wei State, Shen Buhai in the Han State and Shang Yang in the Qin state, used fiercely stringent means to treat officials and ordinary citizens. The penalty was very harsh and bloody. Shen Buhai taught kings to use trickery to keep officials loyal and people feared. Shang Yang conducted holistic reforms in order to render people orderly, deferential and loyal. In order to expand resource bases necessary for military victory, Shang Yang practised many detailed reforms to transform people into peasants and soldiers, as illustrated in Chapter 2. Han Fei developed the pro-agriculture and anti-commerce idea to its zenith.

Han Fei criticised certain classes as the "vermin of society", including merchants, traders, artisans and "wandering philosophers", because merchants specialised in "non-essential" production and "wandering philosophers" earned their life by performing a "useless" function and filling the heads of ordinary people with seditious ideas (Peach 2019: 10–11). Rulers should render people "stupid" and "simple-minded" in order that people could act under the command of rulers.[43] Therefore, people

[42] *Hanfeizi, Liu Fan* (《韩非子·六反》).

[43] Here the association between Daoism and Han Fei can be discerned again. Daoism objected complexity. Laozi dreamed of a small village as the best model where tiny households were fundamental units and interpersonal relationships did not exist. Also, Daoism attributed evilness and chaos to the greed and desires of people. For Daoists, knowing more meant more greed. The pursuit of knowledge made people complicated and too difficult to be administered. Thus, a wise ruler should keep people "stupid" and "ignorant".

must not be allured to conduct commerce due to its easiness of profits. People must be fixed on cropland.

> When office and rank can be bought, then none will despise merchants and artisans. When ill-gotten wealth and stocks of commodities fetch a good price in the marketplace, there will be no shortage of tradesmen When jobbers and forestallers earn twice as much as farmers and enjoy greater esteem than soldiers or plowmen, then men of conscience and fortitude will be few and merchants and tradesmen will multiply.[44]

In order to minimise the attraction of commerce, the role of merchants must be downplayed. Shang Yang asserted that "the security of the state depends on agriculture and war".[45] The anti-commerce attitudes served to Legalists' goals, i.e., to expand the base of military capacity. Agricultural surpluses and the number of soldiers were the key factors for military success. Legalist reforms succeeded in achieving such goals. Through the reforms in states and the final unification of Qin, Legalism was practised all over China, as illustrated in the previous chapter.

Legalists, as they self-admit, established an autocratic regime. Von Glahn (2016: 84–85) described the Legalist regime as "a military-physiocratic state that fused a system of social ranking and obligation derived from military organisation with an agrarian economic base". The agriculture was encouraged, and the peasant economy was established with the consideration to provide surpluses and soldiers. Draconian and detailed clauses were implemented to keep people deferential. The bureaucratic system was ruled by a leader who used Machiavellian strategies to keep officials loyal and in fear. There is no denying that Legalism was the most influential school in the formation of an imperial structure.

5 Summary

In this chapter, different schools of thought and their impacts have been analysed. The intellectual boom was caused by the comprehensive social changes happening in this chaotic era. A large number of low-ranked aristocratic people who were literate and ambitious wandered around the different states in order to earn a reputation. Trained with essential skills

[44] *Han Fei Zi, Wu Du* (《韩非子·五蠹》).

[45] *Book of Lord Shang, Nong Zhan* (《商君书·农战》).

and knowledge, those people were well-prepared for an era of change. Simultaneously, the fierce competition among states drove lords to resort to the assistance of talented and skilful people. Their ideas could pose a great influence upon whether lords would enjoy military victory and domestic prosperity. In addition, the official ideology of the Western Zhou dynasty also laid the intellectual foundation for Confucianism and Daoism. The dream for an orderly society, and the association between the behaviours of kings and the will of gods ("Heaven"), were bequeathed to later thinkers.

To a large extent, Confucianism was the official ideology in ancient China, although it was incessantly transformed. With its fundamental thought, Confucianism was the most suitable school for shaping the imperial structure. Confucius preached an orderly and stratified society; he propagandised the benefits of domestic peace and social order. Those rituals which Confucius wanted to restore were used to keep the stratified society stable and orderly. Social order was a significant public good which an imperial regime could provide, and it was also the key to an agrarian economy in that agriculture could not survive with warfare and frequent chaos. In Confucius' eyes, peace and social order (with a hierarchy) were crucial for a society. After the Western Han dynasty, Confucianism was gradually transformed into an ideology which valued unification and the central authority. Later Mencius did not only amplify standard Confucius' teaching, but also talked about more about wealth distribution and lords' responsibility. Mencius envisioned a public disaster relief system, and he said that rulers had the obligation to aid the helpless and destitute, and to distribute grain in times of drought and famine (Peach 2019: 13). Mencius' ideas were typically the reactions to natural disasters which happened frequently in the central plain and were pertinent to an agrarian economy when people lacked sufficient methods to prevent natural disasters. Thus, Mencius' ideas were also pertinent in order to sustain the peasant economy. Xunzi highlighted the importance of learning and other forces to curb the evil of human nature. He had presaged a bureaucracy full of officials who were selected by strict criteria and implemented strict legal clauses to supervise people. Hundreds of years later, the familiarity with the content of Confucianism became the main standard in the national examination and promotion system. Thus, Confucianism became the key force to maintain the bureaucratic system.

Daoism hardly obtained the official status like Confucianism,[46] but it was always unconsciously applied in the beginning years of a new dynasty. Daoists emphasised the value of "natural order", "no acting" and self-interest. As long as rulers followed the recipe of Daoism, according to Daoists, the optimum would ensue naturally. Daoist ideas were often simplified into low taxation, no warfare, austere lifestyle of the royal members and other non-interventionist policies. Although to some degree, Daoist policies could be seen as desperate attempts to raise revenue and resources in desperate times after wars had destroyed the domestic economy (Peach 2019: 18–19), Daoism still worked as a relieving medicine with the aim of restoring an agrarian economy characterised by small households and peasant economy. When the ideas slowly penetrated official ideology, the liberalist tradition was basically sustained in ancient civil society in China. The Daoist/liberalist tradition enabled imperial China to operate with relatively low costs for quite a long time (Long 2018: 170–171). Nowadays scholars highlighted the similarity between Laozi and Adam Smith's "invisible hand", Hayek's "spontaneous order" and some Classical economists. It is true that they share some common ideas in certain intellectual aspects. It is also true that Daoism once inspired some physiocratic economists. In practice, Daoist did create prosperity which Adam Smith had anticipated (Zhao 2015: 184). However, analysing Daoism with modern economics would be a false proposition: it is of questionable value because Laozi had meditated about something totally different.

Legalism was the most successful school in terms of practical value. It completely stared into the needs of a state which saw military victory above all other things. Legalism succeeded in forming the imperial structure with efficient measures. Firstly, the peasant economy was established and protected by legal clauses. Partible inheritance was required in Legalist reforms.[47] Individual peasants became the basic units of taxation, military service and corvée. Secondly, many officials were selected

[46] The two apparent exceptions were "Huang-Lao" thought in the Western Han dynasty and the official canonisation in the Tang dynasty. "Huang-Lao" thought will be analysed in detail in Chapter 4. The royal family of the Tang dynasty had the surname "Li", and it was said that Laozi, the founder of Daoism, had also the same surname. Then emperors in the Tang dynasty took Laozi as their ancestor (Nobody knew whether the bloodline was true). But in the Tang dynasty, Daoism was never applied seriously.

[47] For example, Shang Yang had prescribed that the family would be punished if parents had adult children living together.

from ordinary people, rather than from aristocratic families. Local administrators became professional bureaucrats who relied on salary from the central government and got promoted or demoted by administrative performance. The bureaucratic system was the pillar to maintain the relationship between the central government and millions of individual households. Thirdly, according to Legalism, the central rulers took advantage of various strategies to rule over bureaucrats and ordinary individuals. Sitting on the highest position, rulers resorted to colourful tactics to keep subordinates loyal and feared. Therefore, on the basis of designation of Legalism, a nuanced equilibrium formed among the central authority, the bureaucratic system and the peasant economy.

Modern scholarship doubts the separation of different schools, since it is difficult to judge who belonged to which school because those scholars took varying positions and far different tenets (Zhao 2015: 178). It is also true that conflicting ideas were advocated by members of the same school, while the same policies would be advocated by different schools, and in some cases self-proclaimed "Confucians" would be castigated as apostates in another (Peach 2019: 20). However, when talking about their influence upon the formation of the imperial structure, the demarcation becomes trivial. Those thought in different schools contributed to the final formation of the Imperial Mode and its subsequent variations in different dynasties. In detail, as illustrated in Fig. 2, responsibility of the central authority and the bureaucratic system was public good provision stipulated by Confucianism and Legalism. The central authority must sustain social order for the whole society through external defence and domestic peace. Extracting economic surplus and providing public goods, such as public projects and a disaster relief system, the bureaucracy should interact with the peasant economy benignly. According to Confucianist teaching, individuals should self-educate and behave properly to be a gentleman. Then, an orderly society would guarantee prosperity and social harmony automatically. Daoism influenced rulers' attitudes towards the agricultural economy and civil administration. To some degree, liberalist measures were left within civil society and the countryside. Legalism destroyed previous aristocracy and eventually established concrete institutions of the Imperial Mode. In sum, a range of certain ideas from the three schools contributed to the formation of a subtle structure which satisfied the demand of an emerging agrarian economy and subsequently facilitated its further growth.

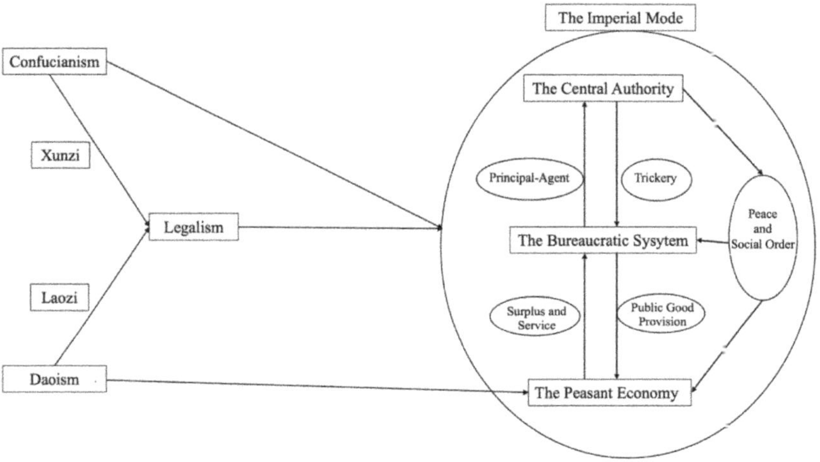

Fig. 2 The cognitive map of intellectual influences upon the imperial mode

References

Bendix, Reinhard. 1977. *Max Weber: An Intellectual Portrait*. University of California Press.

Bodde, Derk. 2005. Chinese Idea in the West. In *China: A Teaching Workbook*, Asia for Educators, Columbia University.

Chin, Annping. 2007. *The Authentic Confucius: A Life of Thought and Politics*. NY: Scribner.

Creel, Herrlee G. 1970. *What is Taoism? And Other Studies in Chinese Cultural History*. University of Chicago Press.

Creel, Herrlee G. 1983. *The Origins of Statecraft in China: The Western Chou Empire*. University of Chicago Press.

Fairbank, John K., and Goldman, M. 2006. *China: A New History*. The Belknap Press of Harvard University Press.

Fung, Yu-Lan. 1996. *A Brief History of Chinese Philosophy*. Peking University Press. (in Chinese).

Hansen, Chad. 2000. *A Daoist Theory of Chinese Thought: A Philosophical Interpretation*. Oxford University Press.

Hayek, Friedrich A. 1966. The Principles of a Liberal Social Order. *Il Politico* 31 (4): 601–618.

Hegel, G. W. F. 1956. *The Philosophy of History*. Trans. Sibree, J. et al. Dover Publications.

Hsu, Cho-yun. 1965. *Ancient China in Transition: An Analysis of Social Mobility, 722–222 B.C.* Stanford University Press.

Hu, Jichuang. 2009. *A Concise History of Chinese Economic Thought*. Beijing: Foreign Languages Press.

Hu, Xiajun, and Jing Guo. 2011. Evil Human Nature: From the Perspectives of St. Augustine and Hsun Tzu. *Open Journal of Philosophy*, 01(2): 61–66.

Jiao, Peimin. 2007. *The General History of Chinese Population: Volume of the Pre-Qin Period*. Beijing: People's Publishing House. (in Chinese).

Kalberg, Stephen. 2021. *Max Weber's Sociology of Civilizations: A Reconstruction*. Routledge.

Keynes, John Maynard. 1936. *The General Theory of Employment, Interest and Money*. London: Macmillan.

Kissinger, Henry. 2012. *On China*. Penguin Books.

Long, Denggao. 2012. The Tradition of Pristine Liberalism in Civil Economy in Ancient China. *Thinking* 38 (3): 84–91. (in Chinese).

Long, Denggao. 2018. *The Evolution of Traditional Institutions of Land Property Rights in China*. Beijing: China Social Sciences Press. (in Chinese).

McCormick, Ken. 1999. The Tao of Laissez-Faire. *Eastern Economic Journal* 25 (3): 331–341.

Mote, Frederick W. 1971. *Intellectual Foundations of China*. New York: Knopf.

Nylan, Michael. 2000. Textual Authority in Pre-Han and Han. *Early China* 25: 205–258.

Peach, Terry. 2019. The Political Economy of the Han. In *The Political Economy of the Han Dynasty and its Legacy*, ed. Lin, Cheng, & Terry Peach, et al., 1–30. Routledge.

Pines, Yuri. 2004. Merging Old and New: Xunzi's Reinterpretation of Chunqiu Intellectual Tradition. *The National Chengchi University Philosophical Journal* 11: 137–184. (in Chinese).

Pines, Yuri. 2009. *Envisioning Eternal Empire: Chinese Political Thought of the Warring States Era*. Honolulu: University of Hawaii Press.

Pines, Yuri. 2012. *The Everlasting Empire: The Political Culture of Ancient China and its Imperial Legacy*. Oxford: Princeton University Press.

Rickett, W. Allyn. 1993. Kuan tzu. In *Early Chinese Texts: A Bibliographical Guide*, ed. Michael Loewe, 244–251. Berkeley: Society for the Study of Early China; Institute of East Asian Studies, University of California Berkeley.

Rothbard, Murray. 2005. The Ancient Chinese Libertarian Tradition, *Mises Daily*, (5 December 2005).

Sato, Masayuki. 2016. *The Confucian Quest for Order: The Origin and Formation of the Political Thought of Xun Zi*. Taipei: National Taiwan University Press. (in Chinese).

Schefold, Bertram. 2020. Zwei Monate am Institute of Humanities and Social Sciences der Peking University. *UniReport* in Geothe University Frankfurt, Page 19, Nr.1, 6. February 2020.
Schwartz, B.I. 1985. *The World of Thought in Ancient China*. Harvard University Press.
Tan, Min. 1992. Zhongnong Xuepai Jingji Xueshuo De Zhongguo Yuanyuan [The Chinese Foundations of Physiocratic Economic Theory]. *Selected Works of PhD Dissertations in Shanghai University of Finance and Economics*, 66–76.
von Glahn, Richard. 2016. *The Economic History of China: From Antiquity to the Nineteenth Century*. Cambridge University Press.
Weber, Max. 1986. *Max Weber: Gesammelte Aufsätze zur Religionssoziologie*. Tübingen. (in German).
Xia, Wei. 2005. Jianxi Xizhou Guanxue Jiaoyu Tizhi Jiqi Tedian [To Briefly Analyze the Governmental Educational System and Its Characters]. *Journal of Changchun Teachers College* 01: 37–39. (in Chinese).
Xiao, Gongquan. 1961. *A History of Chinese Political Thought*. Taipei: Zhonghua Wenhua Chuban Shiye Weiyuanhui. (in Chinese).
Yang, Chu. Trans. Forke, Anton. 2011. *Yang Chu's Garden of Pleasure*. CreateSpace Independent Publishing Platform.
Yi, Zhongtian. 2009. *The Hundred Schools of Thought Before the Qin Dynasty*. Shanghai: Shanghai Literature and Art Publishing House. (in Chinese).
Zhang, Liqiong. 2016. The Expansion of Retainers? Power and the Evolution of the Patriarchal Clan System in the Spring and Autumn Period. *Social Science of Beijing* 10: 46–53.
Zhao, Dingxin. 2015. *The Confucian-Legalist State: A New Theory of Chinese History*. Oxford University Press.

CHAPTER 4

The First Phase: The Han Variant

This chapter will present the trajectory of the first phase of the Imperial Mode: the Han Variant. While the imperial structure formed in waves of reforms in the Warring States period (403–221 BCE), and the Qin (221–206 BCE) dynasty was the first to carry it out in a national scale, it was the Han dynasty that signified main characteristics of its first phase. The Qin dynasty only lasted for over one decade, which left administrative lessons for followers. In the Han variant, three components of the Imperial Mode started to form but had not become entrenched yet. Regarding the peasant economy, while peasants cultivated farmland and many of them had ownership, wealthy landlords and aristocrats still possessed a big share of land at the national level and the manorial economy existed as self-sustainable economic units. The bureaucratic system was dominated to a large degree by aristocratic families and royal kinship, although emperors enjoyed huge authority upon selection and promotion of officials. The central authority was thus weakened by the recurring emergence of powerful aristocratic families. In the Han variant, the main characteristics of the Imperial Mode emerged in a premature fashion. The chapter gives an overview and analysis of this trajectory.

After brutal warfare in the Eastern Zhou dynasty (771–256 BCE), the Qin state succeeded in establishing despotic rule over the territories occupied previously by regional lords. Believing in the efficacy of Legalist policies, the Emperor of Qin the First (259–210 BCE, r. 221–210 BCE)

G. H. Jiang, *The Imperial Mode of China*, Palgrave Studies in Economic History, https://doi.org/10.1007/978-3-031-27015-4_4

adopted them in all areas which he conquered. He was so ambitious that many large-scale projects were started immediately, including the construction of the Great Wall and his extravagant palaces in the capital, external wars against northern nomadic tribes and southern aboriginal tribes, etc. Economic surpluses were extracted for military activities and the luxurious lifestyle of royal members, and a massive populace was driven to battlefields and construction sites. Extraction was so fierce that only after fifteen years the Qin court was overthrown by farmers' rebellions due to overly heavy exploitation. The ephemerality of Qin illustrated both advantages and disadvantages of the Imperial Mode—in the Qin case, the central authority was so arbitrary that the costs of public good provision outnumbered much the capacity of an agricultural economy, while Qin rendered impressive its military performance and ability to mobilise resources.

The rulers of the Western Han (206 BCE–9 AD) dynasty learned lessons from the fall of Qin, and hence in the first fifty years the Huang-Lao philosophy was revered, a transformed type of Daoism. The peasant economy then prospered under the laissez-faire policies. However, Emperor Gaodi of Han (256–195 BCE, r. 202–195 BCE), the founder of the Western Han dynasty, established a political structure in which the central government directly controlled adjacent provinces near the capital and half-independent lordship existed simultaneously. Although regional political independence was eradicated after a few emperors took measures to weaken those dukes and lords, the central court could not stop the rise of local aristocratic clans and magnates. More seriously, the bureaucratic selection system was gradually controlled by aristocratic clans during the Han dynasty. Those aristocratic clans also established a self-sufficient manorial economy in local provinces and counties. Autonomous entities mushroomed everywhere. All these decentralising factors grew strong gradually so that the Imperial Mode was disintegrated, which was symbolised by the de facto demise of the Eastern Han (25–220 AD) dynasty. Hereafter, disintegration lasted for approximately four hundred years until the Sui (589–618 AD) dynasty destroyed regional regimes. While the Imperial Mode formed in the Qin-Han era, it was precocious in that few measures succeeded in keeping a subtle balance between all components. In other words, in its adolescence, the revival of aristocracy decomposed the Imperial Mode. The principal–agent problems between the central authority and the bureaucratic system worsened, as the bureaucratic system degenerated into aristocracy again. But one cultural change in the Western Han dynasty began to pose increasingly huge impacts. It was under the reign of Emperor Wudi of Han (156–87 BCE, r. 140–87 BCE) that Confucianism was established as the official ideology.

During the entire Han era, the central court was always plagued by the recurring emergence of local magnates and consort kinsmen. In the beginning years of the Western Han dynasty, the principal–agent problem existed already, and it became worse in the Eastern Han dynasty. Throughout the entire Eastern Han dynasty, except the founder, there were few emperors who could exert authority over the bureaucratic system. More severely, the bureaucratic system itself was eroded by the rising power of local magnates and consort kinsmen who wanted to keep political power in the hands of their own families through generational inheritance. Bureaucracy degraded into aristocracy which had been roughly smashed in the Qin dynasty. With the central authority unable to control those aristocratic clans and local magnates, China fell apart and different interest groups stood up to chase the crown. Wars and political coups happened frequently. Few regimes could last for a lone time during the period between 189 AD when the Eastern Han dynasty de facto collapsed and 589 AD when Emperor Wendi of Sui (541–604, r. 581–604) eventually unified China, a period which was characterised by political fragmentation, frequent wars and territorial scramble. During this period, the Imperial Mode was basically disintegrated in that the bureaucratic system was replaced by the aristocracy, and the peasant economy was replaced by the manorial economy controlled by magnates, and the central authority existed nowhere.

Failing to organise the society efficiently, public good provision was almost absent. National defence became ineffective and neighbouring nomadic tribes invaded the central plain. Many people chose to run away and moved to the southern territories especially to the Yangtze Delta. The Yangtze Delta was for the first time intensively explored and it paved the way for subsequent economic heyday in the Tang and Song dynasties. In the northern territories, after gradual Sinicisation, those nomadic tribes brought crucial elements which were proven detrimental to aristocracy. During the reign of Emperor Xiaowendi of the Northern Wei dynasty (467–499, r. 471–499), the small peasantry was preliminarily restored with the introduction of the equal-field system, although the private ownership of land was not recovered until the Tang (618–907) dynasty. At the same time, much harsher actions were taken to suppress the power of aristocratic clans over the appointment of officialdom. In the Northern Zhou dynasty, interest groups based on military achievements rose and surpassed the status of previous aristocrats. Later in the Sui dynasty, the state examination system was officially introduced, and hence aristocratic clans slowly lost their voice over the appointment of officialdom. After Emperor Wendi of Sui reunified China in the sixth century, the Imperial Mode was preliminarily re-established. The Age of Disunion was finally ended. The suitability of the Imperial Mode to China's agricultural society was illustrated again by this rebound.

1 The Short-Lived Dominance of Qin

After Shang Yang's reforms, very soon the Qin state gained unparalleled military power and economic growth. Encouraged by Legalist consultants, kings of the Qin state continuously launched large-scale wars against rivals. According to Zhao's calculation, the purposes of wars varied during the Eastern Zhou dynasty. The percent of wars for territory expansion was only 12.9% in the first two hundred years, while the figure became 66.9% in the final two hundred years. Especially in the final one hundred years when Qin arose to supremacy between 363 and 221 BCE, the figure rose to 77.5% (Zhao 2015: 244–245). Although the statistics includes the number of wars between all states, it is quite clear that the process of annexation was hastening. In 221 BCE, the Emperor of Qin the First eventually extinguished all rival lords and accomplished nationwide political unification.

Following suggestions of his top chancellor, i.e., Li Si, the Emperor of Qin the First practised Legalist policies all over the conquered territories.[1] Previous local lordship was abolished, and all regions were under the direct control of the central government. The administrative responsibility laid on the burden of professional bureaucrats who were selected by standards of ability and performance. Bureaucrats were deployed from

[1] In order to extinguish disagreement, the First Emperor ordered to execute hundreds of intellects and to burn documents and records which said anything different from Legalist policies. Although this flagrant action was accused by enormous number of historians, it is debated how large the movement was.

the Qin region to prefectures and counties to administer.[2] Local aristocratic clans were also suppressed. One outstanding example was that the Emperor of Qin the First forced local rich and aristocratic families to immigrate to the capital so that their local influence could be uprooted, and the central government could supervise them easily. According to historical documents, migrating families amounted to almost 120,000 households.[3] In order to strengthen legitimacy and superiority of the Qin court, the Emperor of Qin the First made several inspection tours all over the territories. Quite surprisingly, he died halfway through the last tour. After his death, the Qin court was plagued by intrigues and assassinations. The succession problem brought much death of princes and princesses. Eventually, a young prince succeeded the throne with the help of Li Si and a serpentine eunuch. It is fair to say that the Emperor of Qin the First efficiently established bureaucracy in newly conquered territories, and he successfully controlled the bureaucratic system through Legalist ideas. It has been proven by history that the causes of Qin's quick fall lied not in its inability to control bureaucracy.

Able to manipulate the bureaucratic system, the Qin court was highly efficient to accomplish public good provision, although the provision was superfluous. After the unification, the Qin court destroyed the walls surrounding the capitals of regional regimes and linked those walls to the northern borders. Then, under the command of the Emperor bureaucrats ordered massive labour service to build the Great Wall along the northern borders. At the same time, the Emperor expanded and standardised the highway system all over the empire. The previously existent roads were extended and standardised by the same breadth so that transportation could become easy. The total length of the newly built highways amounted to 4000 miles, as many as in the Roman Empire (Fairbank and Goldman 2006: 56). National postal system was also established along the highways. Existent canals were extended, and a new canal was constructed in the south. The Lingqu Canal connected the Yangtze River and the Zhujiang River for the sake of the transportation of soldiers and personnel. The widespread transportation system became a key factor to sustain the vast empire (van Leeuwen and van Zanden 2018). Moreover,

[2] The details of Qin's administrative system were decoded by many archaeologists. See Liu (2020).

[3] Sima, Qian, *Annals of Qin Shi Huang*.

the Emperor continued his military actions. After eradicating internal rivals, he deployed 300,000 soldiers to attack northern nomadic tribes and simultaneously a large number of troops to tame southern aboriginal tribes.[4] Basically, these military actions were successful and expanded Qin's territory southwards and northwards.

The Emperor of Qin the First went further beyond the abovementioned political and military actions. In culture, he standardised the unit of measurement, including length and weight. The writing system was also unified after different writing style was legislatively abandoned. As a symbol of supreme power and personal vanity, the Emperor ordered to construct of hundreds of luxurious palaces along the river nearby the capital.[5] And he ordered to construct his own spectacular mausoleum in which a large number of precious jewels and artifacts were buried, and a large number of terracotta soldiers were manufactured to be displayed. There is no denying that those large-scale projects made the Emperor one of the most eye-catching emperors in Chinese history, but it would be also difficult to imagine how much manpower and resources were sucked. According to conservative calculation, at least 15% of the entire population was conscripted to work on those large-scale projects, let alone large-scale military actions (Lin 1981: 393). The productive capacity of the peasant economy was hugely jeopardised by these activities.

Basically, the Emperor of Qin the First applied economic measures of Shang Yang' reforms to the entire population, including household registration, the private ownership of land and corvée labour, etc. On the national scale, the government conducted household registration and forced kinship to be divided into small households composed of a couple and their non-adult children. When children became adults, the principle of equal inheritance was applied, and the property was equally divided among all male heirs. At the same time, each small household was the basic unit for national land allocation. Lands were allocated to individual

[4] Historians were curious about the reasons why the Qin's strong army could defeat those regional states in a short time but was defeated by farmers after just fifteen years. Some argues that Qin's professional army was sent to northern and southern borders so the defeat of Qin in the central plain was quick.

[5] For poets of following dynasties, the luxury of Qin's palaces became a highlighted inspiration and was criticised limitless times. They correctly attributed the fall of Qin to the "crazy" construction of those large-scale projects.

households, and then individual households held the duty to provide taxation, corvée and military service. Indeed, the legislative basis of the small peasantry was strengthened in the Qin dynasty.[6] Moreover, the Qin court still announced the public ownership of natural resources, such as mines, forests and water surface, etc. The government leased chartered rights to private merchants and charged merchants certain fees (von Glahn 2016: 95–99). This practice was typical in Legalist economic suggestions, as illustrated in Shang Yang's reforms.

Although the Qin dynasty successfully established the imperial structure all over the territory, the emperors indeed failed to sustain the balance between different components. Those large-scale projects harmed seriously the peasant economy. The first rebellion was launched by a team of farmers who were conscripted to build a large-scale project. The severe penalty terrified both bureaucrats and conscripted peasants who failed to accomplish specific assignments. Bureaucrats were controlled strictly by draconian legal clauses, and if they failed to accomplish tasks, the punishment would be also horrible.[7] After the first one, rebellions mushroomed everywhere. The founder of the Western Han dynasty, Liu Bang, was a lowly bureaucrat, and when he failed to send conscripted peasants to the destination, he had to choose either serious punishment or rebellion. He chose a rebellion almost unhesitatingly. Eventually, Liu Bang, along with many other insurrectionists and warlords, succeeded in overthrowing the Qin court. The central court per se had been inflicted by palace conspiracies before it was overthrown. The sons of the First Emperor competed for succession because of the sudden death of the First Emperor. Massacres also happened upon higher chancellors due to struggles for power.

The Qin dynasty offered key insights into the operation of the Imperial Mode. The relations between the three components were exposed clearly. The central authority drove the bureaucratic system to extract agricultural surplus from the small peasantry and to accomplish the public good provision. The public goods included national defence and maintenance

[6] For more detailed analysis on the peasant economy in the Qin dynasty, see von Glahn (2016: 87–95).

[7] Documents excavated from the Shuihudi Tomb indicated the details of Qin's laws. From the specific regulations, it is clear that even tiny errors could be punished seriously. The strictness of punishment matched the Legalist ideal which preached that everything must operate precisely within laws.

of social order, large-scale public projects such as irrigation and canal systems, and cultural unification, etc. The success of the whole system relied on how relations between different components and within components were harmoniously sustained. In the Qin case, the central authority was so powerful and arbitrary that the relations became completely unbalanced. For the central authority itself, there were also havoc with the succession issue. The failure of the Qin dynasty was so sensational that the following emperors absorbed lessons from it and few of them dared to announce Legalism as the official ideology anymore.

2 The Political Structure in the Han Dynasty

Qin was fast overthrown by many insurrectionists, among whom Liu Bang was not the most powerful one, though. Liu Bang's success relied on his efforts to unite other forces to defeat his main enemy. As a result, while he became the founder and the first emperor of the Western Han dynasty, he did not have sufficient power to wipe out other regional warlords. Then he made a compromise between absolutism and feudalism. In the beginning years, warlords were appointed as kings in half-independent states in eastern territories. The western territories which were divided into tens of commanderies were under the direct control of the central court. It was called "Juxtaposition of Commandery and State". In states, kings had authoritarian power over local affairs, including taxation and administration,[8] and they kept their independent troops. The affiliation was only nominal. In commanderies, the central court appointed professional bureaucrats to administrate. For Liu Bang, there were a few reasons why he chose this structure. Firstly, he took advantage of local warlords' power to obtain military victory, and he had no sufficient power to make those warlords completely bowed. He had to acknowledge their special status. Secondly, many close advisors of Liu Bang believed that the quick downfall of Qin was because Qin lacked the help of kingly relatives who owned troops. According to those advisors, in order to protect the central court when dangers emerged, there should be some "moat", which were regional states. The "Juxtaposition of Commandery and State" persisted for hundreds of years, and later its

[8] As a principle, local kings could appoint their own bureaucrats to rule over their territories. The central government only appoint one bureaucrat for local kings, i.e., top chancellors.

variants facilitated the rise of local aristocratic families although emperors tried to partition and then undermine the half-independent states. This political structure played a leading role for gradual disintegration of the Imperial Mode during the Han era and subsequent eras.

Anxious about those potentially threatening warlords, Liu Bang soon used diverse strategies to wipe out them and let his own relatives to replace them. Consequently, those warlords were only supplanted by members of the Liu clan. The political structure kept the same. In just thirty years, those relatives launched a large-scale war against the central government. The grandson of Liu Bang, Emperor Jingdi (188–141 BCE, r. 157–141 BCE), tried his best to defeat those distant relatives. Although the central government punished those antagonistic relatives (even executed several leading dukes) and reduced their territories, Emperor Jingdi basically kept the structure unchanged. Later, Emperor Wudi (156–87 BCE, r. 140–87 BCE) implemented a judicious strategy to control the regional states: the central government forced lords to use the principle of equal inheritance for kingly succession, while in the past the throne was solely inherited by the eldest son.[9] For example, if the older lord had five sons, his state must be divided into five parts so that every son could inherit one part. Hence, the size and power of regional states were exponentially reduced generation by generation. However, although thereafter regional lords rarely rebelled, the "Juxtaposition of Commandery and State" existed for a quite long time and it greatly weakened the central authority. Local magnates grew strong without direct political intervention from the central court.

Not only the members of the Liu clan, but also relatives of empresses obtained privileges during the entire Han era. The wife of Liu Bang, the Empress Lü (?–180 BCE), was a cunning and brave woman. When Liu Bang was alive, she helped him to wipe out intransigent warlords; After Liu Bang died, she greatly strengthened her own power and her families'. She once succeeded to control three emperors in the early Han years. She had de facto control over the empire. Although all family members of Empress Lü were brutally executed after she died, she erected a lasting model for subsequent political practices. The mother and wife of Emperor

[9] In fact, this strategy has been earlier suggested by Jia Yi in his *Zhi An Ce*, when Emperor Wendi was on the throne. Emperor Jingdi also (unconsciously) practised this idea upon a few states. The policy was not commonly implemented until Emperor Wudi consciously restricted the power of regional lords.

Wendi (203–157 BCE, r. 180–157 BCE) and the wife of Emperor Jingdi had a huge influence upon politics. The wife of Emperor Wendi could even publicly intervene in the policymaking process. Although Emperor Wudi hugely clamped down on the power of consort kinsmen, they persisted to hold control over local affairs and revived after Emperor Wudi died. The downfall of the Western Han dynasty was directly caused by a powerful relative of an empress, Wang Mang (45 BCE–23 AD), in 9 AD. Even in the Eastern Han dynasty, the power of consort kin was greatly strengthened because most emperors were young and naïve so their mothers gained huge power, and consort kinsmen gained the opportunity to exert influence. It was no coincidence that the downfall of the Eastern Han dynasty was caused again directly by a relative of an empress, He Jin, in 189 AD. The power of consort kin grew gradually beyond the control of emperors during the Han era. It was noticeable that most emperors in the Han eras failed to control the bureaucratic system.

The exception was Emperor Wudi who made numerous efforts to achieve political centralisation and to weaken the power of the Liu clan and consort kin. Emperor Wudi was famous for his unprecedented military actions against northern nomadic Xiongnu, unsatiable desire for political power and controversial economic policies. At the beginning years of his reign, Emperor Wudi was restricted by his grandmother, his mother, the Liu clan and consort kin, like his father and grandfather. But quickly he used clever strategies to dislodge those powerful figures from the central government. On the one hand, he took advantage of interest conflicts among those powerful figures to respectively weaken them. On the other hand, he bravely appointed young men and newly selected bureaucrats as his close advisors. Emperor Wudi established the "Inner Court" consisting of young and close secretaries so that he could eschew those older bureaucrats and issue edicts independently. As a pungent reaction, he appointed Legalist scholars as criminal judges, in order to punish members of the Liu clan and consort kinsmen. During the reign of Emperor Wudi, most rich and powerful families were silenced, although they were never completely eradicated. After Emperor Wudi died who in his final years was regretful for his harsh and brutal behaviours towards his relatives and powerful families,[10] however, no emperor afterwards could exert equal control upon the bureaucratic system. Later the bureaucracy itself was even gradually disintegrated by a trend towards aristocracy.

During the reign of Emperor Wudi, he began to use a new system to select bureaucrats, i.e., the "Cha-Ju system". Before this system, children of high-level officials had been always the main source of selecting bureaucrats (Miyazaki 1956: 57–67). In 134 BCE, Emperor Wudi issued an edict to order local officials to recommend "excellent figures" annually. The selection standards were familiarity with Confucian classics and conformity with Confucian moral principles. According to differences in specific standards, titles varied, such as "knowing the classics", "sincere and upright", "capable and good", etc. (Liao 2005: 53). After the recommendation of local officials, those "excellent figures" also had to pass examinations held in the central court. If qualified, they would get appointed to different departments. Basically, this system was the first systematic institution to select bureaucrats through merits and knowledge and thus it signified the start of a sociopolitical pattern in Chinese history (Zhao 2015: 289–292). However, while this system served Emperor Wudi well with the aim to weaken older powerful families, it had a natural tendency towards aristocracy. Zhao Dingxin (2015: 292) has summarised its inherent weaknesses as follows:

> Firstly, the officials who had the authority to make recommendations used it to extend their nepotistic networks, and the individuals who received recommendations regarded their recommenders as patrons. This made for strong patron-client networks, and attendant corruption.
>
> Secondly, the members of a politically powerful family had bigger chances to be recommended since the central government could not supervise the specific process. Many such families grew even more powerful.
>
> Thirdly, heirs and pupils of teachers with powerful political connections were mostly likely to be recommended. In some cases, thousands of pupils registered under one teacher. It further encouraged the dominance of big and powerful families.

As a lasting institution, the "Cha-Ju system" contributed greatly to the rise of a strongly aristocratic trend (Chü 1972). As illustrated before,

[10] Emperor Wudi once executed his oldest son and wives. Furthermore, the battles against the nomadic tribes and the draconian economic policies put unacceptable burden upon people. In 89 BCE, Emperor Wudi issued an edict to regret his "mistakes".

emperors in the Eastern Han dynasty were quite young and naïve, most of whom lacked interest in politics or daily administration. The political power slipped into the hands of powerful clans, including consort kin, local magnates and scholarly families. In a sense, those families were powerful by dint of both economic capacity and intellectual influence. The trend started in the Western Han dynasty, but in the Eastern Han dynasty, it grew to a degree that non-inheritable bureaucracy was mostly replaced by de facto inheritable aristocracy (Miyazaki 1956: 69–70). The principal–agent problem became increasingly worse off. The changes in the political structure in the Han era contributed to the disintegration of the Imperial Mode during the following Northern-Southern dynasties. The aristocratic factors persisted for almost one millennium until they were completely decomposed in the Northern Song dynasty.

3 From the Peasant Economy to the Manorial Economy

The economic sectors also experienced ups and downs in the Han era and eventually became disadvantageous for the Imperial Mode. The economic base changed gradually from the peasant economy to the estate economy during the Han era. The Qin dynasty established small peasantry over the whole nation after it unified China, as it had done in the Qin state. But peasants were harmed severely due to Qin's abysmal extraction. Learning the lesson of the quick downfall of the Qin dynasty, Emperor Gaodi of Han basically inherited Qin's institutional framework except for Qin's draconian criminal laws. The small peasantry and the private ownership of land was acknowledged and protected. Self-sufficient peasant households formed the basic units of taxation and other conscriptions in the Western Han dynasty. Especially in the first fifty years of the Western Han dynasty, a kind of laissez-faire policy was revered and implemented, which led to a prosperous period.

The laissez-faire policy originated from the Huang-Lao philosophy which was a transformed type of Daoism. In the early years of the Western Han dynasty, the Huang-Lao philosophy was so influential that in a sense it was the official ideology before Emperor Wudi repudiated it and made Confucianism the official ideology. The Huang-Lao philosophy preached that the behaviours of human beings must conform to the universal law, which was the natural harmony.[11] As Daoism taught, rulers must adopt a frugal lifestyle, minimal taxation and minimal intervention in people's lives. The Daoist philosophy was generation by generation esteemed by several emperors, empresses and top chancellors. In the beginning years, Emperor Gaodi might have had no alternative but to adopt the Huang-Lao philosophy because the economy was devastated due to years of wars. Much agricultural cultivation was abandoned. The population in the early Han around 200 BCE was estimated to be roughly 15–18 million, which was less than half of the peak population (estimated from 25 to 40 million) when the Qin dynasty was established (Ge 2000: 16–25). Even the emperor could not find four horses with the same colour for his royal carriage.[12] Those founders of the Western Han dynasty could only hope to restore the economy through the lassez-faire policies. While Emperor Gaodi had no alternative, subsequent emperors, empresses and chancellors worshipped the Huang-Lao philosophy out of true heart. A story could illustrate it. The second chancellor of the Western Han dynasty, Cao Can, was inquired by Emperor Huidi about why he did nothing all day, unlike the first chancellor, Xiao He who was very laborious and busy.

> Cao Can replied to the Emperor Huidi: "Who do you think is wiser and more judicious between you and your father (the Emperor Gaodi)?" The Emperor Huidi answered: "How dare I to be compared with my father!"
>
> Cao Can continued to ask: "Who do you think is wiser and more judicious between me and the Chancellor Xiao?" The Emperor Huidi answered: "It seems that you are not a match for Chancellor Xiao."
>
> Then Cao Can said: "Your Majesty is absolutely right. The Emperor Gaodi and Chancellor Xiao have paved the way for us. All laws have been formulated and they are complete. What we need to do is just to follow their regulations. It is quite appropriate to stand on our positions and make no mistake."[13]

[11] The Huang-Lao philosophy was a combination of Laozi's philosophy and a medical book written allegedly very early. The medical book was *Huang Di Nei Jing*, and until today it still offers the methodological foundation for Chinese pharmacy and medicine science. The medical book believes that all illness come from wrong lifestyle and inconformity with the natural law which is the balance between Yin and Yang. Scholars in the Western Han dynasty deduced that rulers must also obey this preaching.

[12] Sima, Qian, *Treatise of Equalisation*.

[13] *Ibid., House of Chancellor Cao*. Translated myself.

Chancellors and emperors witnessed the benefits of the Huang-Lao philosophy and its efficacy to improve people's well-beings.[14] The laissez-faire policies were implemented for almost fifty years. The taxation rate was reduced to 1/15 when Emperor Huidi (211–188 BCE, r. 195–188 BCE) was on the throne and finally to 1/30 in 168 BCE when Emperor Wendi was in the throne.[15] Simultaneously, emperors and royal members lived a frugal lifestyle. According to historical documents written by Sima Qian and Ban Gu, in order to reduce public expenditures, several emperors in the early Han rarely enlarged their palaces or constructed new projects. Especially Emperor Wendi forbode any expansion or construction of royal palaces, and he issued an edict in person to minimise the expenditure on his mausoleum. Most members of the royal family and consort kinsmen were also asked to follow the Huang-Lao philosophy. Furthermore, rulers intentionally avoided wars with the northern nomadic Xiongnu. As a compromise, the royal family sent young girls as brides of Xiongnu's leaders.[16] In order to avoid military expense which would be a heavy fiscal burden for the government and hence peasants, emperors had to take this strategy.

[14] For Emperor Wendi and his mother, the Huang-Lao philosophy to some degree saved their lives and helped them to win the royal succession. As presented in the section "Daoism" in last chapter, Daoism taught people a kind of dialectics of contradiction: the weak could defeat the strong, and the low could transform to the high one day. It preaches that reputation brings bad luck and fortune brings disasters, so people should be humble and invisible. This is the best way for survival. Emperor Wendi's mother, Bo Ji, was just a lowly concubine of the First Emperor. According to Sima Qian, Bo Ji did not get much favour from the First Emperor and they just had one-night relationship. Then Bo Ji was forgotten. After the First Emperor died, his empress Lü was jealous and furious with those concubines. The Empress Lü brutally executed those concubines but Bo Ji in that Bo Ji did not get attention from the First Emperor. Bo Ji was allowed to go to a kingly state with her son and survived there. After the Empress Lü died, those powerful chancellors debated about whom should be chosen to succeed the throne. The powerful chancellors wanted to choose a puppet so that they could continue to exert great political influence. Bo Ji's son pretended to be humble, ignorant and naïve so he got the chance. However, after he became the emperor, he changed his face. It is clear in this history that the survival and victory ofEmperor Wendi was to a large degree because of the Daoist philosophy. They had full psychological reasons to esteem the Daoist philosophy.

[15] Ban, Gu, *Book of Han, Treatise on Food and Money* (《汉书·食货志》).

[16] Although Han emperors announced that those girls were members of royal family, few of them actually came from the royal family. Except a sister of Emperor Wudi, none was a royal member before. In the Easter Han dynasty when the marriage with Xiongnu was no longer a so painful career, more authentically royal girls were sent to Xiongnu.

Another outstanding laissez-faire policy was free coinage adopted by Emperor Wendi in 175 BCE. The Han dynasty inherited Qin's copper coins at first but the government failed to control its private minting and subsequent undervaluation problem, which resulted in rampant inflation. Empress Lü once took legal actions to standardise the coinage and announced the exclusive rights of the government of minting, but the policy failed to curb counterfeiting (von Glahn 2016: 106–108). Emperor Wendi implemented more liberal economic policies. He allowed legally not only private minting in which private coiners paid license fees to the government, but also private exploitation of mineral resources, such as metal and salt. During the reign of Emperor Wendi and Jingdi, the two biggest provisioners of coins were the Duke of Wu, a nephew of Emperor Gaodi, and Deng Tong, a chartered merchant.[17] Most circulating coins were manufactured by them, and the duke's coins were advantageous due to large amounts while Deng Tong's coins were famous for their good quality. In a sense, the free coinage in the early Han achieved what Hayek called "denationalisation of money" in which the competition between different currencies would contribute to the stability of money supply and the disappearance of government-induced inflation.

The economic policies influenced by the Huang-Lao philosophy brought great material prosperity so that the reign of Emperor Wendi and Jingdi was praised as a golden age, "Rule of Wen and Jing". The wheat accumulated in granaries was not consumed and hence perished after years of hoarding, and the coins in the capital were not expended so the ropes putting coins on also perished.[18] In the first fifty years of the Han dynasty, the peasant economy was greatly restored, and the well-being of ordinary people was also improved. However, when Emperor Wudi came to obtain inviolable power, he started many courageous actions, including many external wars and internal political reforms. His aim was not only to repudiate the Huang-Lao philosophy which he thought was not useful enough for an ambitious nation but also to establish a Confucian-Legalist nation in which the

[17] According to historical documents, Deng Tong was a homosexual toy-boy of Emperor Wendi. Out of affection, the emperor bestowed several copper mountains to Deng Tong so that he could issue money and be wealthy. Later in Chinese culture, "Deng" became the synonym of a very rich person.

[18] Sima, Qian, *Treatise of Equalisation.*

central authority had insurmountable power. Out of personal hatred[19] and ambitions for a greater empire, Emperor Wudi launched several large-scale wars against the northern nomadic Xiongnu and southern aboriginal tribes.

Although Wudi's military actions succeeded in defeating Xiongnu and driving them northwards and westwards,[20] which basically eliminated external threats, and the southern military march extended the territory farther, the fiscal burden became increasingly heavy. Advisors surrounding Emperor Wudi devised a series of fiscal policies to solve fiscal difficulty (von Glahn 2016: 113–120). Firstly, the taxation base was broadened to include all commercial activities, including commerce, moneylending and artistry. The taxation target was not operational income but assets. Every 2000 coins of assets would be taxed with 120 coins (von Glahn 2016: 114). Later, a policy that encouraged secret report was practised. An informant would get half of the fortune of the reported family. Secondly, the monopoly in lucrative industries was introduced step by step: the monopoly of salt and iron in 117 BCE; the monopoly of alcohol in 98 BCE (later abolished in 80 BCE); the monopoly of minting since 113 BCE (Schefold 2019). This was a significant watershed in Chinese economic history, in that after this the monopoly of salt and iron was never given up by a centralised government. Thirdly, in 118 BCE the government issued a new bronze coin, the Wuzhu coin, to replace former private coins in circulation. The new coins were proven successful and they would endure for centuries. Fourthly, Sang Hongyang established the system of equitable distribution and price equalisation with the aim to improve the efficiency of the entire fiscal system. Government agents

[19] A sister of Emperor Wudi was sent to Xiongnu as a bride, who had deep emotion with him.

[20] It is fundamentally acknowledged that Wudi's military actions were reactions towards Xiongnu's continuous intrusions and robbery in Han's territories. Many scholars hold that Xiongnu's southward intrusions were heavily affected by climatic factors. But there are two different explanations. Some scholars suggest that due to temperature cooling which resulted in fewer products of livestock northern nomadic tribes tended to invade warmer Chinese territories more frequently. See Zhang et al. (2010). However, an opposite answer also exists. Wang (2022: 35) suggests that warmer climate which enhanced agricultural products in Chinese territories made the central plain a more attractive target for northern nomadic tribes, thus improving the probability of external intrusions from northern nomadic tribes. Both explanations have empirical support. The two theses make the explanatory framework more complicated in which climate is integrated into history as a key variable.

sold products in markets in order to smooth changes in prices and simultaneously earn money for the government. Through this system, as Sang Hongyang envisioned, the interests of peasants could be protected, and the financial income of the government would be heightened, and merchants' opportunistic behaviours could be clamped down.

The economic reforms which reversed previous liberal policies indeed strengthened the fiscal base of the central government and guaranteed financial support for the military actions of Emperor Wudi. As Sima Qian said, "taxes on the people had not been increased, yet revenues sufficed to meet the imperial government's expenses."[21] However, the policies harmed the economy: the extension of taxation drove many households to bankruptcy and commercial monopoly harmed the merchant class. External wars extracted too many surpluses from productive sectors, including grains and human labour.[22] At the final years of Emperor Wudi, he was also inflicted by the tension with family members. Influential statemen were also frequently executed due to the emperor's sensitivity and suspicion. As historians marked, the final years of the reign of Emperor Wudi were just like the final years of the Qin dynasty.[23] After the death of Emperor Wudi, those economic policies were called into question by many scholars and officials. Sang Hongyang (152–80 BCE) stood out to defend the legitimacy and the necessity of those policies. The debate was recorded as *Yantie Lun*, or *Debate on Salt and Iron*.[24] Scholars attacked Sang Hongyang with moral reasons and classical tenets, while Sang Hongyang reacted with pragmatist reasons and sometimes also with classics. The result of the debate kept blurred, but these policies endured as long as the imperial centralised government persisted. It has been proven that these policies were again and again adopted and strengthened once the imperial government encountered fiscal problems.

The debate between Sang Hongyang and those scholars had more than just ideological meaning. After the death of Emperor Wudi, those Legalist practices to which Wudi's policies and Qin's policies were ascribed, were condemned by Confucian scholars. And they expressed a strong favour

21 Sima, Qian, *Treatise of Equalisation*.

22 The Han system did not clearly differentiate military conscription from labour service obligations. See von Glahn (2016: 103).

23 For example, *Zhuzi Yulei*, Li Dai II (《朱子语类·历代二》).

24 Schefold (2019) presents a detailed analysis with the western perspective on *Yantie Lun*. It includes a comparison between *Yantie Lun* and the Hellenistic economic thought.

towards classical Confucian tenets. Politically they described emperors as just moral paragons and the symbol of governance, which made emperors' authority surrender to powerful officials. Economically they rejected those policies issued by Emperor Wudi and any extra forms beyond the peasant economy, i.e., the market economy and monetary exchange.[25] Retreats of the central government happened in both political and economic spheres. Powerful clans were no longer repressed once Emperor Wudi died. Accordingly, the concentration of landownership and wealth increased hugely during the years thereafter, which contributed to the rise of "magnate clans". Magnates became gradually the most important force in the Han era. Many peasants became tenants under the name of local magnates. Local magnates built fortresses and estates within which many productive activities, such as milling, brewery and weaving, etc., were conducted by tenants (see Fig. 1). The peasant economy slowly turned into the manorial economy during the Han era, as peasants lost their economic independence and became tenants on the land owned by magnates. In the central court, political power was grasped by influential officials who came always from magnate clans and consort kin. The central authority fell apart when magnate clans possessed more political power. The Han society was gradually controlled by magnate clans both economically and politically.

4 Imperial Confucianism: Official Ideology

In the Western Han dynasty, Confucianism formally started to become the official ideology. At the beginning years of the Western Han dynasty, Legalism was cursed because scholars believed that the draconian policies of Legalism led to the quick downfall of the Qin dynasty. Hence, as illustrated before, the Huang-Lao philosophy, a transformed type of Daoism, was predominant in policymaking. Although the "Rule of Wen and Jing" created great material prosperity, the efficacy of Daoism could not satisfy an ambitious emperor since it preached "no acting". When Emperor Wudi

[25] In 44 BCE, Gong Yu, a Confucian minister, advocated restoration of a barter economy by abolishing metallic money altogether. Although it was not finally enacted, the trend was clear. See Chiu and Kwan (2019).

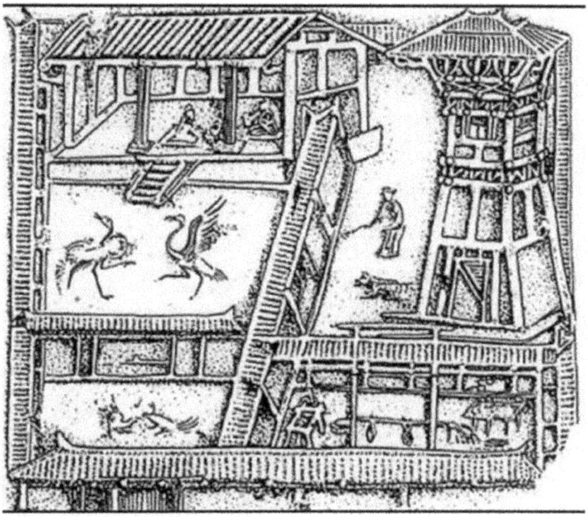

Fig. 1 The Magnate's House in the Han Dynasty (*Source* National Museum of China, originally in Chengdu, Sichuan Province)

obtained totalitarian control over politics after his grandmother died,[26] he started to employ young scholars and talented figures with the aim to strengthen his authority. He succeeded to employ many Confucian young scholars who also wanted to make some difference. The most outstanding figure among those scholars was Dong Zhongshu (179–104 BCE), who contributed much to the birth of a kind of "Imperial Confucianism" (Zhao 2015: 274–279).

The "Imperial Confucianism" consisted of classical spirits of Confucianism and doctrines of other schools, such as Mohism, Legalism and ancient cosmological concepts. The predominant aspect was its belief that human beings are a part of the entire universe (in his words, heaven). The duty of an emperor was to follow the instructions of Heaven, and at the same time, the power of an emperor was bestowed and authorised by Heaven. From this perspective, the power of an emperor was instilled with sacredness. Secondly, like the natural hierarchy between Heaven and

[26] Empress Dou was the wife of Emperor Wendi, and the mother of Emperor Jingdi. She was the staunchest proponent of the Huang-Lao philosophy and wiped out any effort of Emperor Wudi to change the dominance of Daoism.

Earth, such hierarchy existed in interpersonal relationships, too. People must obey this order: the ruler directs ministers; the father directs the son; the husband directs the wife. Hereafter, Confucius's support for a hierarchical order was transformed into a specific social rule. Thirdly, while an emperor should act like a moral paragon who follows Confucian ethic rules and promotes Confucian education, everyone else should also try their best to learn Confucian tenets and practise them in daily life. The best situation would be harmony between the individual and Heaven. When necessary, laws and punishment would be useful to sustain the Confucian order.

This version of Confucianism offered by Dong Zhongshu had great attraction for Emperor Wudi who was looking for some tools in order to strengthen his authority and to efficiently steer the society. It provided the ideological advantages to the emperor because Dong Zhongshu emphasised the ultimate authority of Heaven and thus the absolute authority of the emperor, the son of Heaven. The emperor had the final words over the social hierarchy since Heaven, in most cases, had no word.[27] Moreover, this ideology opened the door for cooperation between elite scholars and the central government. Rulers should emphasise the importance of Confucian ethics, encourage education and take familiarity and conformity with Confucian doctrines as the standard of selecting and promoting officials. Therefore, this ideology served Emperor Wudi well. From a broader perspective, the transformed Confucianism contributed to the strengthening of the imperial structure. It encouraged the balance between different components, including the central authority which should rule benignly, the professional meritocracy and small peasants who did their duty and followed social rules. It facilitated the formation of a bureaucratic state (Stasavage 2020: 152–153). Hereafter, the "Imperial Confucianism" predominated until the demise of the Qing dynasty and was still time to time revived by purposeful rulers.

In the final years of the Western Han dynasty, political power was firmly grasped by a consort kinsman, Wang Mang. He aimed to reform society with classical Confucian tenets. But his program was very hasty, in that in a short time he launched massive policies, including reorganising the bureaucratic system in order to strengthen the control of the

[27] Nevertheless, Dong Zhongshu left a gap: Heaven grants mandates only to good rulers, and when ordinary people are unsatisfied, so is Heaven. Like Mencius's belief, "Heaven observes via people".

central government, prohibiting transactions of land and nationalising the ownership of land, and cancelling hereditary privileges of aristocratic clans. Wang Mang also tried to expand the government's control over commerce and money. However, jeopardising the vested interests of magnate clans, Wang Mang's policies stung them even though he was a prominent member of consort kin. Unable to enact his ideas, Wang Mang triggered social chaos and insurrections. Finally, this so-called Confucian idol was killed in an imperial palace. Later the Eastern Han dynasty was established by a distant kinsman of the Liu clan. The status of magnate clans was continuously strengthened and no emperor in the Eastern Han dynasty could ever change their dominance. The central court finally collapsed under the pressure of consort kin and magnate clans.

5 The Rise and Decline of Aristocracy

In the Eastern Han dynasty, few emperors could be described as individually powerful. Even the founder of this dynasty, Liu Xiu (5 BCE–57 AD, r. 25–57 AD), could not exert his will in an authoritarian way since he was surrounded by powerful consort kinsmen.[28] Although during the first half of this dynasty, the empire enjoyed stability and peace, and international trade with the Middle Asia and Rome developed fast, political power was gradually obtained by eunuchs and consort kinsmen at the central court and by local magnates in provincial administration (Hansen 2000: 136). Especially during the second half of this dynasty, most emperors succeeded the crown when they were just little children. Nominally their mothers or grandmothers gained the highest authority, but in fact they relied on eunuchs and their relatives, i.e., consort kinsmen, to operate this vast empire (Hinsch 2002: 25). As a result, the central court was full of violent political struggles and brutal coups. Eventually, the struggle became so severe that a consort kinsman invited an intransigent and notorious warlord to help to extirpate the eunuch group. However, this action led unsurprisingly to the actual demise of the Han royal court. Hereafter, the Imperial Mode was formally disintegrated.

[28] The clan of Liu Xiu's wife, the Empress Yin, for example, owned a large number of land and also more than a thousand retainers. Liu Xiu was famous for his amiability, but this attitude contributed to the continuous rise of consort kin.

The subsequent disorder was called “the Three Kingdoms period” where three main kingdoms formed out of the vehement military struggles. Among those warlords was Cao Cao (155–220 AD) the most outstanding. He was an extreme pragmatist and took advantage of Legalist ideas to control the territories which he occupied. Facing the shortage of crops and fiscal resources, Cao Cao ordered to enact the “tun-tian” system in which soldiers on distant expeditions were ordered to cultivate the conquered lands, in order to provide crops for the army and to strengthen their existence in distant territories (Elvin 1973: 37). In a sense, the system satisfied the demand of army for crops and restored the economy. On the other hand, Cao Cao practised Machiavellian skills to control those powerful officials and local magnates. Under his reign, many representative figures of aristocratic clans were depressed and even tortured physically and psychologically. Basically, in dint of typical Legalist strategies, Cao Cao’s endeavours would have contributed to the restoration of the bureaucratic system and the peasant economy. However, the aristocracy had been so entrenched that soon after Cao Cao’s death it was institutionally guaranteed.

During “the Three Kingdoms period” the political situation in this land was just like that in the Sacred Roman Empire in which one highest emperor existed but regional warlords acted independently regardless of the central authority. Cao Cao respected (hijacked in fact) the last emperor of the Eastern Han dynasty but did not dare to replace him. After Cao Cao’s death, his son, Cao Pi (187–226 AD, r. 220–226 AD), immediately asked the last emperor to abdicate and made himself the emperor of a new dynasty, the Wei (220–266 AD) dynasty. Without executing the previous officials of the Eastern Han dynasty, Cao Pi issued an edict to double check the qualifications of those officials. Hence, the nine-rank system was officially enacted over the territories that the Wei dynasty controlled. In the nine-rank system, provincial officials needed to evaluate comprehensively outstanding figures in their administrative regions with standards of merits, talent and reputation, etc., and listed them from one to nine rank. On the basis of the rank which those figures got, they would get candidacy for different administrative positions. In practice, those family members of local magnates and heirs of high officials always received a higher evaluation, and hence got a bigger chance to get appointed to higher positions. The common rule was that the political status of a father had lots of influence on the evaluation of a son (Wang 2010). Contrary to the original idea of Cao Pi who wanted to centralise the power of selecting officials into the central court and to clamp down on the aristocracy, the nine-rank system degraded to the convenient tool of local magnates, which made their advantages stable and inheritable.[29] The nine-rank system enabled the aristocracy to systematically replace bureaucracy, and solidified aristocracy for hundreds of years until Emperor Wendi of Sui established the state examination system.

Just after decades, the royal court of the Wei dynasty could not nominate any adult successor since two emperors continuously died young. But the Cao family was alert of close relatives who were politically ambitious and arrogant (Miyazaki 1956: 91). They could not rely on adult relatives to help with the baby emperors. As a result of this emotion, political power was grasped again by aristocratic groups and magnates, among whom the Sima family was the most outstanding. After years of surreptitious actions, the Sima family finally replaced the Cao family and established a new dynasty, the Western Jin (266–316 AD) dynasty. Soon the Sima family eventually ended "the Three Kingdoms period" and temporarily unified China. However, unlike the Cao family who consciously pressed the power and influence of aristocratic groups, the Sima family did not only acknowledge their existing prerogatives but also strengthen the power of royal members. Many kinsmen of the Sima family were crowned as kings with a semi-independent army, independent taxation and territories free of direct control by the central court. The political situation at the beginning of the Western Jin dynasty was just like that of the Western Han dynasty, which was characterised by the "Juxtaposition of Commandery and State". The Sima family also took advantage of marriages with magnates to strengthen its legitimacy. However, as a member of aristocratic groups, the Sima family did not at all recognise the harm which aristocracy could have on the central authority. The political situation soon derailed since the second emperor was lunatic and naïve. Semi-independent kings of the Sima family fought against each other in order to compete for the throne. Subsequently, the internal warfare weakened national defence. Northern and western nomadic tribes invaded the central plain.

[29] Miyazaki (1956: 73–146) conducted detailed research on the origin of the nine-rank system and its historical changes.

The political structure of the Western Jin dynasty was hardly an efficient tool. It could not drive those officials efficiently,[30] and the population declined enormously due to decades of warfare.[31] Too many peasants became tenants and retainers of local magnates. The whole structure could not fulfil its task on public good provision, especially social order and national defence. In the final years of the Western Jin dynasty, neighbouring nomadic tribes launched wars against the Jin court and immigrated into the central plain. On the one hand, it started the ethnic synthesis which lasted for hundreds of years until the Tang dynasty. On the other hand, the warfare drove many native residents to flee to southern territories. Many people emigrated to the Yangtze Delta and hence they brought advanced agricultural technology and more labour power. It facilitated economic exploration in this region (von Glahn 2016: 160–166). After the demise of the Western Jin dynasty, the replacement of royal courts happened frequently. Few regimes could last for over fifty years. No ruler could exert exclusive power upon officials or generals. Every regime was plagued by frequent coups and rebellions of magnates and warlords. The political chaos was so serious and lasting that this period was described as the "Age of Disunion".

While in the southern regimes old aristocratic groups convened again after refuging, in the northern territories most regimes were established by nomadic and sinicised semi-nomadic tribes, including Xiongnu and Xianbei. In comparison with those rulers in southern regimes, the Xiangnu and Xianbei rulers had little hesitation to destroy aristocracy since it indeed impeded rulers' authority. Partly because of individuality, many nomadic rulers in northern regimes were ruthless and brutal. Many aristocratic clans were heavily clamped down. The de-aristocracy process reached a small peak in the Northern Wei dynasty established by a Xianbei

[30] As I define "bureaucrats" as those officials who get promoted and appointed by standards of individual merits and ability rather than inheritance, most officials in the Wei and Jin dynasty could be hardly called "bureaucrats" in that they were selected through the nine-rank system. This was a very aristocratic system in which the political ranks of ancestors and the father were the determining factor. I use "bureaucracy" as the antonym of "aristocracy".

[31] Cao Cao had a famous poem to describe the tragic situation during this period: "While armour and surcoats lie bloody and wormy, wars raging, people are dying. Ungathered bones strew the whilderness. For thousands of miles, not a rooster to be heard. One tenth of the populace may have ever survived. What a heart-breaking disaster." *Haoli Xing*, translated by Zhu Chunshen.

tribe.[32] The most significant event was the reform of Emperor Xiaowendi of the Northern Wei. Consciously depressing the power of local magnates and aristocratic groups, he conducted a comprehensive reform. On the appointment of officials, he tried to reestablish the "Cha-Ju" system which was once practised in the Han era. The nomination of officials was based on recommendations and also results of examinations and interviews. Hence, to some degree, the monopoly of aristocratic families on officialdom was broken apart. Moreover, the regular inspection and examination of existing officials were scrupulously implemented. If failed the inspection, officials would get punished and really demoted. Obviously, Emperor Xiaowendi had the intention to restore the bureaucratic system which was under the direct control of the central authority.[33]

However, the reform did not have enough time to achieve all its goals. The Northern Wei court was soon devastated by coups of military warlords. Another Xianbei group grasped the power and established the Northern Zhou (557–581 AD) dynasty. Unlike those emperors of the Northern Wei dynasty, rulers of the Northern Zhou dynasty expressed huge hatred towards sinicisation and retained their nomadic traditions (von Glahn 2016: 179–181). Aristocracy was dropped down, and the status of officials was based on military achievements. Officialdom was mostly possessed by military personnel and generals. "Officials in the (Northern) Zhou dynasty were mostly military generals".[34] Rulers of the Northern Zhou dynasty did not rely on officials coming originally from aristocratic clans to rule over the conquered territories. In contrast, they established their own special aristocracy. Xianbei-based generals formed special interest groups and replaced former old aristocrats. Both founders of the Sui and Tang dynasty came from those Xianbei-based military groups. These were so-called "Guan-Long aristocratic groups" (Chen 1942).

Soon the power at the central court of the Northern Zhou dynasty was grasped by a consort kinsman, Yang Jian. He was also a head of those warlords of the "Guan-Long aristocratic groups". He established

[32] For the intentional efforts to establish absolutist rule in the Northern Wei dynasty, see Pearce (2019: 71–78).

[33] For more details about the changes of officialdom in the Northern Wei dynasty, see Miyazaki (1956: 301–372).

[34] *Book of Sui, Biography of Zhang Jiong* (《隋书·张熲传》).

the Sui dynasty to replace the Northern Zhou dynasty and then successfully destroyed southern regimes. Yang Jian took more aggressive actions than the Emperor of Xiaowendi of the Northern Wei dynasty to depress old aristocrats. Firstly, he issued an edict to abolish the administrative level of "commandery". In the past, as the biggest regional administrative unit, commandery was the stronghold of old aristocrats in that the appointment of local officials was firmly controlled by local magnates. Through abolishing the "commandery", the power to appoint local officials was controlled again by the central court. Secondly, Yang Jian started to consciously introduce the state examination system in order to select officials because there would be many positions in provincial entities to be filled. Theoretically, the appointment relied completely on the results of examinations. Thereafter, the central authority firmly controlled power to select officials. Except for those "Guan-Long aristocratic groups", aristocracy was nominally destroyed. The establishment of the state examination system was an earthshaking point because bureaucracy stood firmly hereafter, and aristocracy would have no chance to revive again. By means of the state examination system which would be continuously improved in the following dynasties, the bureaucratic system became a self-reinforced and self-reproducing mechanism under the control of the central authority. It was a key self-strengthening factor of the Imperial Mode. The principal–agent problem was partly relieved.

6 The Revival of the Peasant Economy

As illustrated before, during the Han era, especially the Eastern Han dynasty, the manorial economy grew fast and undermined the peasant economy severely. Magnates kept politically powerful, and their estates were legally tax-exempt. Subsequently, the tax burden upon small peasants became increasingly heavy so they were compelled either to become tenants/retainers of magnates or to become "landless" (Lin 2003: 928). Simultaneously, those magnates would feel delighted to "buy" more lands to enlarge their estates in order to become richer. However, it led to serious social problems. Firstly, many "landless" people had no choice but to become bandits or insurrectionists, which resulted in frequent rebellions. Uprisings continued to create social disorder and weaken the central authority. Secondly, magnates became more powerful not only politically but also economically. The rising manorial economy undermined the peasant economy. The central court further lost its control over peasants and thus necessary economic resources, which weakened its capacity in public good provision. Then, disintegration of the Imperial Mode during the "Age of Disunion" was systematic, including decomposition of the peasant economy, degradation of bureaucracy into aristocracy and the absence of a central authority.

Because most emperors in the final years of the Eastern Han dynasty were just puppets of magnates and warlords, it became increasingly difficult for the central court to sustain the imperial structures. During the "Age of Disunion", the disorder was so severe that the population declined enormously. The registered population fell from 60 million in the Eastern Han dynasty to about 15 million by the end of the Western Jin dynasty (Ge 2002: 424, 464, 473). Upon the demise of the Western Jin dynasty, the registered population in the northern territories amounted to only five to six million (Tan 1934). Although obviously, the registration could not be complete partly because many households ran away, at least it also reflected the state's weakening capacity to conduct an accurate statistical investigation. Moreover, magnates and monasteries hid the number of their tenants so that accurate population registration was not viable, neither was the taxation (He 1995: 411–416). Since warfare destroyed the economy, regional warlords also encountered fiscal problems.

Cao Cao devised a system to bypass those magnates in order to provide his armies with crops and other resources. Unable to extract sufficient agricultural surpluses, Cao Cao took suggestions of close advisors to order soldiers and refugees to cultivate ownerless lands. This was the so-called "tun-tian" system.[35] He also established official positions to organise the cultivation. In essence, the "tun-tian" system was a kind of public ownership of land. The government allocated lands to refugees and soldiers, and both the government and cultivators participated in the distribution of the agricultural harvest. But the system partly restored the autarkic method of peasantry since cultivators were not subject to magnates' estate economy. This system was efficient to provide economic resources for Cao Cao's

[35] The "tun-tian" system was not originally devised by Cao Cao. In the Qin and the Western Han dynasty, this system was practiced mainly in frontier lands to northern steppe. In order to reduce the costs of transporting crops from the central plain to frontier lands, armies were ordered to cultivate lands by themselves. However, this system was not practiced in a large scale until Cao Cao enlarged it in the central plain.

armies and to some degree restored the economy in the northern territories. However, after Cao Cao's death, the system was quickly eroded by magnates. They privatised those allocated lands since Cao Cao's successors routinely granted magnates with lands and tenants who worked on these lands (Gao 1986: 109–120). The "tun-tian" system degraded into a tool that served the estate economy.

In the Western Jin dynasty, an edict named "zhan-tian ke-tian" was issued. The practice of this policy was not very clear. According to historical records, an adult man was deemed capable of cultivating 50 *mu*, and higher officials could possess more lands. Against previous scholarship which thought that "zhan-tian ke-tian" was a system of allocating lands (Balazs 1967: 101–112), this policy was just setting the maximum area of lands that one could own. Households with lands less than the maximum could continue to cultivate more. The government just *acknowledged* the possession of those lands. Accordingly, the government organised taxation (Jiang 2005: 140–149). It had nothing to do with the allocation of lands. However, the policy was to a large degree flawed since it had no forceful regulation if someone possessed lands more than the maximum. Clearly, it could not curtail the prerogatives of magnates in effect (von Glahn 2016: 159). To some degree, the power and hereditary prerogatives were even strengthened in the Western Jin dynasty. Especially in the Eastern Jin regime which was established by a distant relative of the Sima family in the Yangtze Delta after nomadic and semi-nomadic tribes occupied the northern territories, the supremacy of magnates reached its zenith (von Glahn 2016: 159).

As illustrated before, the northern territories were under the control of regimes established by nomadic and semi-nomadic tribes. They met fewer restraints of magnates since many magnates fled southwards and also had less emotional burdens. Equally importantly, the economic depression forced rulers to think about solutions. In the Northern Wei dynasty, Emperor Xiaowendi issued edicts to reorganise agricultural activities. The policies consisted mainly of the equal-field ("jun-tian") system, the three-elders ("san-zhang") system and the regional headquarters ("fu-bing") system. Firstly, the overwhelming land-allocating system, i.e., the equal-field system, was enacted. Unlike predecessors, the equal-field system involved authentically the allocation of lands which was conducted by the government. As far as ownerless lands were concerned, each household was allocated arable lands, oxen and tools. Adult females were also allocated lands in order to support textile production. But sales of those allocated lands were legally forbidden. Lands would be reverted to the government upon death. So, it was obviously a kind of public ownership of land.[36] Meanwhile, "the central purposes of the system were to extend agrarian cultivation and to check the formation of large private estates by aristocratic landowners" (Anderson 1974: 522–523). Secondly, as a complementary effort, the three-elder system was put into practice. It was greatly similar to the household registration in the Qin and Han dynasties. Three-level communal officials were appointed to control rural villages. It facilitated the accurate investigation and registration of population. On the basis of the equal-field system and the three-elder system, a taxation system was also introduced, i.e., the hu-diao system. In this taxation system, "the amounts of grains, cloth, and labour service owed to the state were directly proportional to the land allocation the household received" (von Glahn 2016: 173). Thirdly, on the basis of the new fiscal system, the regional headquarters system was introduced. Those farmers who were allocated state-owned lands should provide military conscription in return for a certain period of each year. The identity of soldiers was not hereditary. It was bonded with the rights of being allocated with lands. This new military system broke down the monopoly of warlords on armies and "helped the state to absorb the private armies into the state military" (Zhao 2015: 309). Emperor Xiaowendi's policies had profound effects. The immediate result was that more lands were cultivated, and the fiscal and military capacity were heightened. More importantly, they facilitated the re-establishment of the small peasantry in the northern territories and laid the foundation for the reunification of China (Zhao 2015: 303).

While northern China was suffering from frequent warfare and political chaos, the economy in the Yangtze Delta was explored intensively with more immigrants who brought more advanced agricultural technology. Immigrating magnates and native magnates transformed the vast wilderness into fertile rice paddies. Irrigation was greatly enhanced in this area. Reservoirs were constructed to provide irrigation to lower-lying rice fields. Many small-scale hydraulic projects were constructed nearby mountain streams and lakes (Li 2009). The agricultural conditions were greatly improved. Simultaneously, commerce and the artisanry industry also developed. Artisanry centres mushroomed in the Yangtze Delta, such

[36] For more details about the equal-field system, see Yang (2003).

as the paper industry in Shaoxing and shipbuilding in Yangzhou. Several canals were constructed to connect those commercial centres and the capital, Jiankang. The most populous city, Jiankang, became the centre of regional and even international trade in the fifth and sixth centuries (von Glahn 2016: 163). The natural conditions in the Yangtze Delta were more advantageous than in the northern territories because the hydrologic, climatic and geographic conditions were all more conducive to agricultural and commercial activities. During this period, the Yangtze Delta was for the first time intensively explored and it contributed to the rise of the so-called Jiangnan economy. During the following millennium, the Jiangnan economy "began its inexorable rise as the new economic heartland of the Chinese world" (von Glahn 2016: 130).

7 Cultural Trends During Political Chaos

During the "Age of Disunion", Confucianism possessed no longer the favour of magnates and ordinary people since it had no pragmatical value for the imminent disorder. The impact of Confucianism waned significantly. Conversely, the influence of other cultural beliefs was on the rise. One important philosophy was "Xuanxue". It was a combination of Daoist philosophy and Confucian education. Facing the fact that Confucians could not fix those social problems, the educated retreated to the unworldly philosophy of Daoism. Those scholars of "Xuanxue", many of whom became high officials in the central court, loved talk salons and social gatherings in order to show off their unworldly lifestyle. Moreover, as this philosophy fitted well with aristocratic aesthetic views, members of aristocratic families were fond of this ethereal culture. As a result, the mastery of "Xuanxue" and hence the fame of being skilful at "Xuanxue" became the standard of the nine-rank system, i.e., the qualification to be recommended as officials. The aristocracy was closely connected with the spread of "Xuanxue" during the disorderly era. Although it had no lasting impact on Chinese history, it temporarily undermined Confucianism (Zhao 2015: 300).

The most striking cultural event during this era was the rise of Buddhism in the core area of China. Originating in ancient Nepal, Buddhism entered into the eyes of Chinese people around the first century AD. Before that, Buddhism propagated mainly in Middle Asia and the western territories of the Han empire. Overcoming many linguistic and Sinification problems, Buddhism started to propagate in core areas of China.[37] In this process, early Buddhist monks also encountered similar problems which early Christian priests encountered when they preached in Northern Africa and Eastern Europe, such as Cyril. Eventually, Buddhist monks succeeded to get favour of some influential magnates and high officials. Disappointed with Confucianism and their own inability, many émigré aristocrats in southern territories found solace and religious salvation in Buddhism. For a time Buddhism undermined Confucianism's social popularity among the populace and its cultural influence (Greif and Tabellini 2010). In the sixth century AD, Buddhism became so popular that the first emperor of the Liang dynasty, a southern regional regime, from time to time abdicated and became a monk in a monastery.[38]

The popularity of Buddhism fostered the monastery economy. In the Liang (502–557 AD) dynasty, "there are over five hundred monasteries in the capital which are extremely luxurious and grand. The number of monks and nuns is over one hundred thousand and their wealth is massive".[39] The bestowments to monasteries were so generous that they depleted the treasury of the Liang dynasty. Monasteries became economically influential. Whatever in northern and southern territories, monasteries possessed a vast number of lands and tenants. In some areas, monasteries even became market centres.[40] Like magnates, monasteries had economic privileges, including tax exemption. High monks hid the number of tenants belonging to monasteries. Monasteries even developed a financial system in which monasteries lent money to all kinds of borrowers and charged high interest (Zhou et al. 2018). Along with the estate economy controlled by aristocratic magnates, the monastery economy undermined economic power of the central authority. The two forms of economy impeded the direct control over peasants by the central authority. In the later years of the "Age of Disunion" and the Tang dynasty, several emperors took action to destroy the power of monasteries. In those anti-Buddhism movements, a large number of monks

[37] Fairbank and Goldman (2006: 73–76) had a detailed exploration at the Sinification problems which Buddhism met when it entered into Chinese territories.

[38] This emperor abdicated and came back several times. The official treasury spent a lot "buying" him back from the monastery.

[39] *The History of South Dynasty, Biography of Guo Zushen* (《南史·郭祖深传》). Translated by myself.

[40] About the prosperity of the monastery economy, see Zhou et al. (2017).

were forced to rebecome farmers, and the fortune of monasteries were confiscated. After the mid-Tang dynasty, restricted by the government's policies, the monastery economy was only sustained at the subsistence level.[41] Clearly, the central authority aimed to destroy the intermediate economic forces, including the estate economy and the monastery economy, in order to reestablish direct control over the economic base.

8 Summary

This chapter illustrates the first phase of the Imperial Mode—the Han variant where the fundamental characters have been explicitly specified. The Qin court successfully established the bureaucratic system, maneuvered it efficiently and achieved public good provision via wars and large-scale projects. But it failed to sustain the subtle balance between the central authority and the small peasantry. Excessive agricultural surpluses were extracted, and the populace were plagued by incessant corvée labour. The Qin court was overthrown by peasants' rebellions soon after its founding. The first rulers of the Western Han dynasty paid much attention to the maintenance of the peasant economy and adopted the Huang-Lao philosophy to restore agriculture, which created material prosperity. Later when Emperor Wudi obtained power, policies were changed to strengthen state control. More interventionist policies were introduced into economic sectors and a more stringent ideology, the "Imperial Confucianism", was erected as the official ideology. The ideological, political and economic policies of Emperor Wudi paved the way for subsequent imperial practices. However, after Emperor Wudi, the estate economy rose strongly, and the peasant economy gradually decomposed.

At the beginning of the Western Han dynasty, the central court was plagued by local warlords. Although there were clear efforts to strengthen the central authority and the peasant economy as principles, the principal–agent problem gradually eroded the imperial structures. Except during Emperor Wudi's reign, local magnate clans and consort kin were very influential. The whole structure during most periods of the Qin and Han dynasties was deeply imprinted by this character, and it contributed to the

[41] Zhou et al. (2017) explained that the fall of the monastery economy was because of technological advancements and thus disintegration of the estate economy. Such explanations are in line with the standard Marxian historical materialism.

disintegration of the Imperial Mode since the bureaucracy was replaced by hereditary aristocracy, and a large number of small peasants became tenants of magnate clans, and the central authority was almost silenced by powerful consort kinsmen and magnates. In a word, during the Qin-Han era, the Imperial Mode showed its fundamental operational characters, while the disintegration proved its precocity. The balance between the three components, and their respective statuses, have not been kept firm. The gradual disintegration of the Imperial Mode also elicited the weakening of its fundamental functions, i.e., public good provision. Very soon, devastating social disorder exploded internally and externally.

The themes that this chapter contains are of special value for the understanding of the Imperial Mode. Characterised by political fragmentation and disruption, this period was seemingly different from most Chinese historical periods. But it is exactly the "abnormality" that highlights the nature of the Imperial Mode. This model was successfully established in the Qin dynasty. Why did the Imperial Mode disintegrate in the final years of the Eastern Han dynasty? As illustrated before, it consisted of the central authority, the bureaucratic system and the peasant economy. All of them were undermined during the Han era, and none of them was kept during the "Age of Disunion". The frequent replacements of royal courts just epitomised the fact that the central authority had no power to control those aristocratic groups and those groups were competing fiercely with each other. The bureaucratic system was replaced by aristocracy. The nine-rank system selected officials according to candidates' family background and hence most officialdom was hereditary. Population hugely declined due to warfare, and peasants surviving warfare degraded into tenants and retainers of magnates. As Miyazaki (1956: 57) wrote, rulers in the Han era had little experience about how to rule over vast territories and an enormous population. Unlike Qin's emperors who took advantage of draconian Legalist strategies, few Han's rulers consciously clamped down on those aristocratic groups. In other words, failing to maintain the essential components of a peasantry society, Han's rulers did not recognise the nature of the society which they administered.

Then, why was the Imperial Mode re-established during the ensuing Sui and Tang dynasties? Obviously, it was not a coincidence that the Sui dynasty finally accomplished reunification. When the neighbouring nomadic tribes established dominance in the central plain, they had no other choice but to imitate the Imperial Mode in that it was the most efficient mechanism to administer this land. They had to establish the bureaucratic system and the small peasantry. They also aimed to restore the central authority. Simultaneously, warfare drove many aristocratic families away, and hence nomadic and semi-nomadic rulers found much fewer obstacles when they adopted reforms than southern rulers (if they would have tried to do so). The re-establishment of the Imperial Mode in this period just proved its institutional efficiency in agricultural China. The Northern Wei dynasty succeeded to restore the peasant economy and replaced old aristocratic groups with military groups, which paved the way for Sui's reunification. Further, the state examination system established in the Sui and Tang dynasties would step by step destroy the base of aristocracy.

The ups and downs of the Imperial Mode during these hundreds of years highlighted not only its characters, but also the historical pattern. Besides the Warring States period, the "Age of Disunion" was most similar to the feudal system in Medieval Europe. Although this period was characterised by political fragmentation and military competition, China was eventually unified again and continued on a track different from Western Europe. While there must be roles of cultural traditions,[42] institutional efficiency was the dominant factor. It was an efficient mechanism to organise the agricultural society in ancient China. After the precocity in the Qin-Han era and the "Age of Disunion", the Imperial Mode would have its heyday in the Tang-Song era. The maturity of this mode would be accompanied by a great economic transformation, which will be the theme of the next chapter.

References

Anderson, Perry. 1974. *Lineages of the Absolutist State*. Verso.

Balazs, Etienne. 1967. *Chinese Civilization and Bureaucracy*. Trans. Wright H. M: Yale University Press.

Chen, Yinque. (1942). *A Brief Introduction to the Political History of Tang Dynasty*. The Commercial Press (in Chinese).

Chiu, Gavin S.H., and S.C. Kwan. 2019. Monetary Thought in the Han Dynasty and Three Kingdoms Period. In *The Political Economy of the Han Dynasty and Its Legacy*, ed. Peach, Terry et al., 86–100. Routledge.

Chü, Tung-tsu. 1972. *Han Social Structure*. University of Washington Press.

[42] Confucianism was said to have positive influence on this reunification. See Pearce et al. (2001: 3).

Elvin, Mark. 1973. *The Pattern of the Chinese Past*. Stanford University Press.
Fairbank, John K., and M. Goldman. 2006. *China: A New History*. The Belknap Press of Harvard University Press.
Gao, Min. 1986. *Qinhan Weijin Nanbeichao Tudi Zhidu Yanjiu* [Studies on the Land System in the Qin, Han, Wei, Jin, and the Northern and Southern Dynasty]. Zhongzhou Classics Press (in Chinese).
Ge, Jianxiong. 2000. *Ge Jianxiong Zixuanji* [Self-Selected Works of Ge Jianxiong]. Guangxi Normal University Press (in Chinese).
Ge, Jianxiong. 2002. *Zhongguo Renkou Shi* [A Demographic History of China]. Fudan University Press (in Chinese).
Greif, Avner, and Guido Tabellini. 2010. Cultural and Institutional Bifurcations: China and Europe Compared. *American Economic Review: Papers & Proceedings 100* (May): 135–140.
Hansen, Valerie. 2000. *The Open Empire: A History of China to 1600*. New York & London: W.W. Norton & Company.
He, Ziquan (ed.). 1995. *Zhongguo Tongshi: Sanguo Liangjin Nanbeichao* [A General History of China: The Three Kingdoms, the Two Jins, and the Northern and Southern Dynasties]. Shanghai Renmin Press (in Chinese).
Hinsch, Bret. 2002. *Women in Imperial China*. Lanham: Rowman & Littlefield Publishers.
Jiang, Fuya. 2005. *Weijin Nanbeichao Shehui Jingji Shi* [The Socio-Economic History of the Wei, Jin, and the Northern and Southern Dynasty]. Tianjin Classics Press (in Chinese).
Li, Bozhong. 2009. *Agricultural Development in Jiangnan in the Tang Dynasty*. Peking University Press (in Chinese).
Liao, Boyuan. 2005. *Bamboo-slip Writings and Institutions: A Study of Bamboo-slip Writings in Yinwan Han Dynasty Tomb*. Guangxi Normal University Press (in Chinese).
Lin, Jianming. 1981. *Qin Shi Gao* [*Draft History of Qin*]. Shanghai Renmin Press (in Chinese).
Lin, Jianming. 2003. *Qinhanshi* [History of Qin and Han]. Shanghai Renmin Press (in Chinese).
Liu, Sanjie. 2020. *Qinzhuan* [Qin Bricks]. Beijing Joint Publishing Company (in Chinese).
Miyazaki, Ichisada. 2020[1956]. *Jiupin Guanrenfa Yanjiu* [Studies on the Nine-Rank System], trans. Dan Wang. The Elephant Press. (in Chinese).
Pearce, Scott. 2019. Northern Wei. In *Cambridge History of China*, ed. Albert E. Dien and Keith N. Knapp, vol. 2: The Six Dynasties, 220–589. Cambridge University Press.
Pearce, Scott and Audrey Spiro, et al. 2001. *Culture and Power in the Reconstitution of the Chinese Realm, 200–600*. Harvard University Press.

Schefold, Bertram. 2019. A Western Perspective on the Yantie Lun. In *The Political Economy of the Han Dynasty and Its Legacy*, ed. T. Peach, et al., 153–174. Routledge.

Stasavage, David. 2020. *The Decline and Rise of Democracy: A Global History from Antiquity to Today*. Princeton University Press.

Tan, Qixiang. 1934. Jin Yongjia Sangluan Hou Zhi MinZu Qianxi [*Mass Ethnic Migration After the Turbulence in the Yongjia Reign of the Jin*]. *Journal of Yanjing University* 15: 51–76 (in Chinese).

van Leeuwen, Bas, and Jan Luiten van Zanden. 2018. China as a Nation. In *China in the Local and Global Economy*, ed. Steven Brakman and Charles van Marrewijk, et al., 1–17. London: Routledge.

von Glahn, Richard. 2016. *The Economic History of China: From Antiquity to the Nineteenth Century*. Cambridge University Press.

Wang, Xiaoyi. 2010. Reconsideration of the Historical Truth of the Nine-Grade System in the Cao-Wei Period. *Journal of Literature, History & Philosophy* 2: 118–129 (in Chinese).

Wang, Yuhua. 2022. *The Rise of Fall of Imperial China: The Social Origins of State Development*. Princeton University Press.

Yang, Jiping. 2003. *A New Probe into the Juntian System in the Northern Dynasties and Sui-Tang Dynasties*. Yuelu Shushe (in Chinese).

Zhang, Zhibin, Huidong Tian, et al. 2010. Periodic Climate Cooling Enhanced Natural Disasters and Wars in China during AD 10–1900. *Proceedings of the Royal Society* 277: 3745–3753.

Zhao, Dingxin. 2015. *The Confucian-Legalist State: A New Theory of Chinese History*. Oxford University Press.

Zhou, Jianbo, Shengmin Sun, et al. 2018. Buddhist Faith, Business Credits and Institutional Change: The Vicissitude of Temple Finance in China's Medieval Ages from a New Institutional Economics Perspective. *Economic Research Journal* 6: 186–198 (in Chinese).

Zhou, Jianbo, and Bo Zhang, et al. 2017. An Economic Analysis of the Rise and Fall of the Buddhism Economy in China's Mediaeval Ages. *China Economic Quarterly* 3: 1219–1236 (in Chinese).

CHAPTER 5

The Second Phase: The Song Variant

After the "Age of Disunion", the Imperial Mode stepped into its second phase—the Song variant. From the Sui (589–618 AD) dynasty, China not only accomplished territorial reunification but also began a slow process of political centralisation. As older aristocratic groups succumbed to newly military groups prospering in the process of the Sui-Tang military conquest, the bureaucratic system was gradually re-established with the introduction of the state examination system. Although military aristocratic groups still possessed great influence in the early Tang dynasty, their power waned gradually. However, at the late Tang dynasty, the central authority failed to control the warlords who arose in the An Lushan Rebellion (755–763 AD), and the central court per se was plagued by conflicts between eunuchs and literati factionalism. The Tang court was finally buried by regional warlordism. After relatively short interregnum, the Song (960–1279 AD) dynasty established dominance over the core area of China. In the Song dynasty, the relationship between the central authority and the bureaucratic system grew mature since more efficient institutions were adopted to control the bureaucratic system. The most outstanding institution was the state examination system which was greatly optimised on the Sui-Tang basis. The principal–agent problem was to a large degree reduced. Furthermore, the official ideology, i.e., Confucianism, was transformed into Neo-Confucianism during this era. The ideological support for the Imperial Mode was also strengthened.

G. H. Jiang, *The Imperial Mode of China*, Palgrave Studies in Economic History, https://doi.org/10.1007/978-3-031-27015-4_5

More importantly, during this era, many economic breakthroughs happened as a result of technological progress. In the early Tang dynasty, social order and international trade brought benefits to the domestic economy. The Yangtze Delta was intensively explored so that this region became the chief source of revenue and economic lifeblood (Fairbank and Goldman 2006: 86). During the Song dynasty, progress in farming techniques, handicrafts, proto-industrial innovations, credit system, market structure and waterway networks, etc., led to unprecedented material prosperity.[1] Commerce enjoyed huge freedom and convenience in the Song dynasty. Simultaneously, the peasant economy was strengthened. As farming techniques advanced, agricultural productivity improved. After the collapse of the equal-field system in the mid-Tang dynasty in which public ownership of land was the rule, private ownership of land started to dominate rural areas. Especially in the Song dynasty, many institutional innovations contributed to the reinforcement of private ownership of land. Multi-layered mechanisms emerged to protect peasants from landlords' annexation (Long 2018: 80–107). In sum, the economic changes were so profound that the period was called the Tang-Song transition.[2] It brought a revolutionary chance that a new economic mode could have merged as the replacement of the Imperial Mode. In terms of Marxian historical materialism, the economic base and the superstructure within the Imperial Mode matched with each other during the Tang-Song transition. Whatever in political, or economic spheres, the interaction grew ripe, and the productive forces developed to the zenith which the superstructure could hold. The superstructure succeeded to push the productive forces to the entrance of a new stage. New economic elements emerged, and they could have brought a new society.

In the Song variant, the main characteristics of the Imperial Mode became mature and entrenched. The peasant economy became dominant as private ownership of peasants was protected by laws and complex transaction systems. The bureaucracy system was self-sustainable with the introduction of the state examination system. The central authority

[1] Elvin (1973: 113–199) has listed the technical revolutions in the Song dynasty.

[2] Naitō Kōnan in the early twentieth century argued that the changes in the Tang-Song era marked a crucial turning point in Chinese history and also the beginning of a precocious "modern age" in China. Japanese scholars in Chinese history widely accepted the concept of the "Tang-Song transition". Miyazaki (2018) made an analogy that the changes in the Song dynasty could be described as the Renaissance in China.

fundamentally gained absolute control over political issues. Nonetheless, inherent problems of the Imperial Mode still existed. In the Song dynasty, the court was always plagued by embarrassing failures on battlefields against northern nomadic or semi-nomadic empires which were Khitan and Jurchen firstly, and Mongol later. Unable to defeat the nomadic cavalry, the Song court was conquered by the Mongol tribes and its territories were annexed into a much larger Mongol universal empire. The Yuan dynasty established by the Mongol tribes lasted for almost one hundred years. It became famous in the West partly because of Marco Polo's travelling records and Mongolians' incredible military success in the Islamic world and Eastern Europe. While international trade prospered during the Yuan (1279–1368 AD) dynasty, the policies which the government adopted were always frustrating largely because they were often made complicated due to ethnic disputes. Later the Ming (1368–1644 AD) and Qing (1644–1911 AD) dynasties extremely strengthened the imperial structure. The bureaucratic system was further saddled and restricted by institutional arrangements. The monarchy enjoyed limitless power, which was unprecedented before. However, the principal–agent problem between the bureaucratic system and the peasant economy worsened. The frequent fiscal reforms through the Ming and Qing dynasties did not eliminate fiscal crises. In the nineteenth century, the Qing court could not collect sufficient resources to cope with internal and external threats. As a result, regional warlordism and fragmentation emerged and finally took the Qing empire apart.

During the Ming-Qing era, the Imperial Mode had exposed its reactionary aspects: the *Produktionsverhältnisse* (relations of production) fitted no longer with the productive forces. As illustrated before, in the Song dynasty, new economic trends could have contributed to the birth of a new economy that was characterised by commercial and proto-industrial elements, but this process was interrupted by the Mongol conquest and pro-agriculture policies in the Ming and Qing dynasties. The first emperor of the Ming dynasty, Hongwu (1328–1398 AD, r. 1368–1398 AD), enacted comprehensive policies to pull the empire back to a primitive and simplistic agricultural society. The institutional arrangements were highly purposeful to streamline the imperial structure: a highly powerful emperor ruled over millions of peasants with the help of humble bureaucrats. Other classes, especially the merchant class, were seriously repressed with well-designed policies. One specific example was the stringent practice of the sea-ban policy. Path dependence made emperors insist on the Imperial Mode. As Liu (2015a) suggested, the politics in the early Ming dynasty changed China in that it diverted the economy towards a command economy. While during the Ming and Qing dynasties, China was also involved in international trade, the imperial structure appeared increasingly anti-commercial. Although the population grew astronomically and urbanisation in the Jiangnan region developed remarkably, there was nothing that could be described as "qualitative growth". Conversely, the economy started to drop into "a high-level equilibrium trap".[3] Consequently, they could not adopt to the advent of a new economic era, an era characterised by commerce, market economy and industrial growth. The Imperial Mode did not loosen its control on Chinese society until Western nations knocked on the door after the mid-nineteenth century.

1 Strengthening Control Over Bureaucracy

With the military victory of Emperor Wendi of Sui (541–604 AD, r. 581–604 AD), old aristocratic clans were severely undermined. They were replaced by military aristocratic groups, namely "Guan-Long aristocratic groups". As explained before, their rise was a result of political reforms in the Northern Zhou dynasty. As a close relative of an empress in the Northern Zhou dynasty, Emperor Wendi himself was an outstanding member/head of these groups. In essence, the founders either of the Sui dynasty or the Tang dynasty were merely powerful members of these groups. Wang (2022: Chapter 3) suggests that emperors in the Sui and Tang dynasties established oligarchical rule, rather than absolutist rule because the royal families were just a few of the powerful aristocratic groups. In addition, the military aristocratic groups were ethnically semi-nomadic races. On the other hand, however, the military aristocratic groups were not purely aristocratic. In a sense, they were more *bureaucratic* than aristocratic (Miyazaki 1987: 11), because they were weapons of emperors to obtain military victory. More importantly, Emperor Wendi abolished the administrative level of "commandery" and established a primary version of the state examination system. From the beginning of

[3] Elvin (1973: 285–316) described the development in the Ming and Qing dynasties as "quantitative growth, qualitative standstill". The gross number in most economic indicators continued to increase, while there were little qualitative breakthroughs. The economy dropped into "a high-level equilibrium trap". Elvin argues about several possible causes for this phenomenon.

the Sui dynasty, he began to adopt policies in order to efficiently control the bureaucratic system.

Emperor Wendi was a pragmatic and frugal emperor. His rule once brought precious but brief domestic peace and material prosperity. The population increased enormously, and agricultural activities revived. While in 589 AD the number of registered households was only 4.1 million, in 609 AD the amount rebounded to 9 million and the number of persons was 46 million (Liang 1980: 38, 69). It reflected not only economic recovery but also the strengthening capacity to conduct household registration. However, after he died, his second son succeeded, i.e., Emperor Yangdi of Sui (569–618 AD, r. 604–618 AD). He was infamous in Chinese history for his extravagant lifestyle and abysmal expenditure on large-scale projects and military expeditions in the Korean Peninsula. During his reign, the Great Canal connecting the Yangtze Delta and the loess plain was launched. With the Great Canal, crops could be transported from the Yangtze Delta to the capital region. In addition, the construction of a new capital, i.e., Luoyang, and an equally ambitious program of road and bridge construction were started under his command (von Glahn 2016: 184). On the one hand, the infrastructure facilitated the transportation of products and laid the foundation for interregional trade in subsequent dynasties; On the other hand, the construction of large-scale projects and military expeditions sucked too many resources from agricultural sectors. Corvée labour put a heavy burden upon ordinary people. Furthermore, the anti-aristocracy policies implemented by Emperor Wendi and Yangdi made aristocratic groups restive who had not yet been completely extirpated (Miyazaki 1956: 412–414). The Sui court was soon devoured by farmers' and aristocrats' rebellions.

The brief prosperity and fast downfall of the Sui dynasty proved compellingly the mechanism of the Imperial Mode. The empire offered essential public goods for agricultural activities, including domestic peace and large-scale projects, which contributed to economic growth. However, if the central authority failed to sustain a balance between different components within this structure, the disorder could come and the structure itself could quickly collapse. In the Sui dynasty, specific misbehaviours included rulers' extravagance and discretionary extraction of resources from productive sectors. Many Chinese historians have compared the Sui dynasty with the Qin dynasty, both of which collapsed very quickly when the second emperor was on the throne, who eroded the balance with an exaggerated speed. The results of policies adopted by Sui and Qin were similar in that they stirred up huge dissatisfaction of peasants and aristocrats/bureaucrats. The subtle balance within the Imperial Mode was broken down by extremely arbitrary policies of the central authority.

After the end of the Sui dynasty, another clan of the "Guan-Long aristocratic groups" took the throne, namely the Li family. The founder of the Tang dynasty, Li Yuan (566–635 AD, r. 618–626 AD), was a cousin of the Emperor Yangdi of Sui. The fact meant that the influence of military aristocratic groups could not be easily eradicated. Indeed, these military aristocratic clans and the old aristocratic clans who had thriven in the "Age of Disunion" both held a strong influence upon politics in the early Tang dynasty. Even the central court organised literati to compose official lists of the great clans' genealogies in order to highlight the special status of those aristocrats.[4] In 659 AD an officially sponsored list of the genealogy was published. It was 200 chapters long and contained 2287 families from 235 clans (Fairbank and Goldman 2006: 84). It was a combination of the "Guan-Long aristocratic groups" and older aristocratic groups. Marriage between members of those clans was encouraged; marriage between one aristocrat and one ordinary person would be despised. Especially the marriage of the royal family, i.e., the Li family, must be carried out among members of those upper-class aristocrats. The consorts of the first, second, third and fourth emperors in the Tang dynasty all came continuously from influential aristocratic clans. In a sense, although aristocracy was vehemently attacked in the Sui dynasty, it still kept alive and energetic in the early Tang dynasty.

The real demise of aristocracy was accompanied by the enhancing practice of the state examination system. As presented before, the state examination system was established by the Emperor Wendi of Sui. In the Tang dynasty, the state examination system was more optimised and systematised than in the Sui dynasty. The content of examinations was separated into classics, practical policies, and literature, etc. The state examination was organised regularly by central ministries and was in the charge of high chiefs. The Ministry of Rites and the Ministry of Personnel were normally responsible for carrying out the examinations. When Empress Wu, the wife of the third emperor of the Tang dynasty,

[4] IT was *Shi Zu Zhi* [Records of Clans]. Its edition went through decades under the direct command of emperors.

took de facto control of political affairs, she introduced a palace examination in which she would in person interview those candidates selected by her officials, and a military examination in which candidates could get selected by dint of military capability and fighting skills. In the early Tang dynasty, the state examination system was perfected and institutionalised. However, its role should not be overrated in that the number of personnel selected from the state examination system was quite small in the Tang dynasty. The number was on average around two dozen per year. In contrast, the number of officials recommended by aristocratic clans and promoted through achievements in battlefields was at least tenfold (Miyazaki 1987: 5). In total, during the early Tang dynasty the proportion of aristocrats in officialdom was more than half and later three fifths (Fairbank and Goldman 2006: 83). It was until the Song dynasty that the state examination system played a significant role in the bureaucratic system.

The burial of the "Guan-Long aristocratic groups" and old aristocratic clans was conducted by the Empress Wu who came from a middle- or even lower-class aristocratic clan. She was first a concubine of the third emperor of the Tang dynasty, Emperor Gaozong (628–683 AD, r. 649–683 AD).[5] But she was a very ambitious, courageous, and skilful woman. During her life, she took advantage of spectacular strategies to attack aristocratic clans. Through assassinations and military repressions, she executed many members of the Li family. By promoting officials with humble origins and improving the state examination system, she suppressed the influence of aristocratic clans. Even her four sons and daughter became her political tools to play political games. After decades of de facto control behind the scene, Empress Wu (624–705 AD, r. 690–705 AD) stepped on the stage. Although her political life was controversial in Chinese history, her actions of clamping down aristocracy laid the foundation for the true maturity of the bureaucratic system. As Twitchett (1979) suggests, "the Tang thus began the transition from rule by aristocratic families, in which the imperial house was merely *primus*

[5] In fact, Empress Wu was chosen at first as a concubine of Emperor Taizong, i.e. the father of Emperor Gaozong, but they did not have intimacy when the Emperor Taizong was at his final years of life. After Emperor Gaozong took the throne, he married Wu as a concubine. Through complicated palace intrigues, she executed other concubines and became the empress. To some degree, it was those brutal palace intrigues that made Empress Wu notorious in Chinese history.

inter pares, to rule of China by a trained bureaucracy selected by merit partly through the examinations".

After the natural death of Empress Wu, the Li family came back to take the throne. Under the reign of Emperor Xuanzong (685–762 AD, r. 712–756 AD), the Tang dynasty reached its climax of material prosperity and military power. However, the equal-field system in which the public ownership of land was the rule and the government was in charge of land allocation could not persist any longer in that "population growth and the pressure it placed on the land also hindered full application of land allocations" (von Glahn 2016: 185–186). The government did not have sufficient lands to allocate. Those peasants would neither like to lose the lands in which they had invested much after their death. A shift towards de facto private ownership of land was happening (Twitchett 1963). As a result of the disintegration of the equal-field system, the regional headquarters ("fu-bing") system could not be sustained in which farmers with allocated lands had to offer military conscription to regional military headquarters. In addition, the fiscal burden, as a result of the territorial overexpansion of Tang armies, further contributed to the birth of a new military system. Generals in frontier regions were authorised to recruit private armies. The new military system, i.e., the "mu-bing" system, formed and gradually controlled the main military power of the empire.

Those generals were very powerful in that they "possessed the land, the populace, the armed troops and also the fiscal revenue".[6] The situation began to severely worsen in the later years of Emperor Xuanzong. Emperor Xuanzong in his old age fell in love with a concubine and let the political affairs deteriorate. The central court was plagued by fierce bureaucratic factionalism. A sino-barbarian general, An Lushan, gained much power and grew ambitious to replace the Li family. In 755 AD he launched a destructive rebellion, which was so devastating that the Tang's power never recovered although the rebellion was eventually extinguished. The An Lushan Rebellion had a lasting influence. The economy in the central plain and the loess plateau was undermined hugely in which the main battlefields happened. Many people emigrated to the southern territories, especially the Jiangnan region. In the second half of the Tang dynasty, the capital region and frontier regions had to rely

[6] *New Book of Tang*, Vol. 50, Treatise 40: Military. (《新唐书》卷五十, 志第四十: 兵).

on revenues extracted there (von Glahn 2016: 188). Emperors in the capital were desperate for ships transporting crops on the Great Canal from the Jiangnan region. The changes contributed further to the rise of the Jiangnan economy. Moreover, the defeat of An Lushan was basically accomplished by other generals in frontier regions. They per se controlled a large number of private troops. Their military victory made the central court more reliant on their loyalty than before. In other words, the repression of the An Lushan Rebellion made warlordism ironically more serious than before. Few emperors in the later Tang dynasty could exert influence upon those semi-independent generals. What made the situation worse was that in the central court, conflicts between eunuchs and different factions of bureaucrats almost paralysed any meaningful actions

In the final years of the Tang dynasty, the safety of the central court had to rely on the mercy of warlords. In 907 the Li family was overthrown by a hypocritical warlord who originally pretended to be loyal. Then, warlords started to compete for the throne and an interregnum came. The to-and-fro of regional regimes left China almost into anarchy (Fairbank and Goldman 2006: 86). Eventually Zhao Kuangyin (927–976 AD, r. 960–976 AD), a general, stood out and skilfully eradicated other regional regimes. In 960 the Northern Song dynasty was established. In comparison with the Age of Disunion between the Eastern Han dynasty and the Sui dynasty, the interregnum after the Tang dynasty was relatively brief. Partial reasons lay in the personality and skills of Zhao Kuangyin. However, more importantly, as the pillar of fragmentation, aristocracy was fundamentally weakened during the Tang dynasty. Warlords were just powerful individuals. Institutional foundations of aristocracy which could endanger the central authority had been undermined. Furthermore, with technological progress, the peasant economy gradually grew mature, and it needed one unified regime. The economic foundation of a magnate society disappeared. In sum, the structure of the Imperial Mode was greatly strengthened in the Tang dynasty. The anti-aristocracy trend and the growth of the small peasantry continued in the Song dynasty. It was exactly in the Song dynasty that both the peasant economy and the bureaucratic system controlled by the central authority became entrenched.

Zhao Kuangyin was no more than a powerful general before he took the throne from a baby emperor. After the founding of the Song dynasty, he took systematic actions to undermine the power of other generals and to demolish the economic and political foundation of regional fragmentation. In a romanticised story, he used soft but efficient skills to dismantle the generalship of other powerful generals (You 2020: 9–12). In order to eliminate the possibility of warlordism, Zhao Kuangyin further set new administrative positions to control fiscal revenues and civil affairs in local prefectures. New officials needed to guarantee that fiscal revenues must be transported to the capital, and then the central treasury was responsible for the redistribution. In addition, officials were sent from the central court to prefectures to supervise local civil affairs. In the central court, new positions were also set in order to make checks and balances between different bureaucrats. For example, professional generals were forbidden to lead troops. Imperial troops must be led by literati for the sake of preventing warlordism.

The most successful action was the optimisation of the state examination system in the Northern Song dynasty. Several emperors took very nuanced and efficient steps to reform the selection procedures. Such details as the format of examination papers and the position of examinees' names were officially set. Examinees' names must be blocked so that examiners had no chance to give unfair scores due to personal relationships. Furthermore, in the palace examination emperors must in person interview those candidates selected through examinations and determine the ranking of those candidates.[7] The palace examination became routine in the Song dynasty. By dint of the palace examination, emperors directly controlled the power of selecting new officials. Those candidates succeeding in the palace examinations became direct beneficiaries of emperors themselves. During the Northern Song dynasty, the number of selected candidates increased gradually and hugely. When Zhao Kuangyin was on the throne, in average the number of selected candidates in the subject of "jin-shi" was nine per year; During the reign of the second emperor, the number rose to fifty per year; During the reign of the third emperor, the number continued to increase to seventy-eight per year; During the reign of the fourth emperor, the number leaped to one hundred thirty-one per year (Miyazaki 1987: 25). With the expanding size of the selection, the state examination system gradually became mature and efficient. Hence, "a lettered bureaucracy came

[7] The palace examination was not originally devised in the Song dynasty. The Empress Wu came up with this form of examination. However, its practice was relatively rare in the Tang dynasty.

to be the permanent hallmark of the Chinese imperial state" (Anderson 1974: 524).

The political maturity in the Song dynasty was the result of a series of changes since the Sui-Tang era (Deng 2014: 198). Aristocracy was eliminated, and bureaucracy gained irreversibly predominant status. After the Song dynasty, aristocracy never emerged again in Chinese history. The relationship between the bureaucratic system and the central authority was reset so that the former was more easily controlled by the latter. Powerful generals or chancellors could not violate flagrantly the authority of emperors like before. In a sense, from the perspective of driving the bureaucratic system efficiently, the principal–agent problem was mitigated by the subtle political structure in the Song dynasty. The bureaucratic system was so efficiently saddled that hereafter it truly became an easily tamed tool. After the Song dynasty, the interregnums during dynastic replacements were very brief. Another piece of evidence comes from the low homicide rate of emperors and the low rate of coup d'état after the Song dynasty because central rulership rendered bureaucratic groups localised and weak in national affairs (Wang 2022: Chapter 4). "Accordingly, China was almost continuously unified for approximately a millennium" (Zhao 2015: 313).

2 The Second Economic Revolution

Chinese history witnessed its "second economic revolution" in the Tang-Song era after the "first economic revolution" in the Eastern Zhou dynasty. Technical progress led to increasing productivity in agricultural sectors and others. Private ownership of land was strengthened and thereafter became the predominant norm. Complex transaction systems of land property rights in a large degree guaranteed the mobile status of peasants. Interregional trade thrived with the expanding transportation network. Market expansion and innovations in credit system hugely transformed the Chinese economy and society. Commerce and trade contributed to the rise of a mercantile state in the Song dynasty (Liu 2015a: 8). Even proto-industrialisation developed fast with the stimulation of commercial profits and technological progress. New economic factors mushroomed so vibrantly that new possibilities emerged already on the horizon.

The most significant technological boom since the iron age in Chinese history happened in the Tang-Song era. During the Tang dynasty, farming technology gained huge progress. Irrigation projects were constructed nationwide, especially in the Jiangnan region. The construction techniques of hydraulic projects were also more advanced than before. The high efficiency of hydraulic projects provided a solid foundation for agricultural growth. Moreover, new metallurgical technology provided more efficient farming tools. New plows were also devised and applied widespread. Manure and pesticides were utilised more efficiently with new methods. Especially in the Jiangnan region, a new planting system was applied so that the efficiency of lands was heightened. For example, the tea industry and the silk industry prospered because of more appropriate utilisation of lands, timing and space. In sum, the technical progress happening in the Tang dynasty was unprecedented since the iron age and contributed to skyrocketing agricultural productivity. It could be called "an agricultural technological revolution".[8] After the An Lushan Rebellion, as more people immigrated to the southern territories, the Jiangnan region further arose to the most economically developed region in the empire. The Jiangnan economy started its glorious days which would last for the next millennium.

The re-establishment and entrenchment of private ownership of land happened during the Tang-Song transition. As illustrated before, the equal-field system collapsed gradually after the mid-Tang dynasty, resulting from population growth. Slowly the public ownership of land became defunct. In the late eighth century, Yang Yan, a chancellor, adopted a new taxation system to acknowledge the demise of the equal-field system. In his plan, as the previous complicated taxation system was abolished, the amount of tax was levied on the number of persons in one household and the area of lands the household possessed. The household tax was collected in late summer and the land tax was collected after the autumn harvest. This was the so-called two-tax system (the "liang-shui fa"). The taxation system was standardised and simplified. The corvée labour owed to the central government was also eliminated. The implementation of the two-tax system marked an important change in Chinese economic history. Thereafter private ownership of land became the norm, and the central government would never interfere seriously in peasants' landholding until the communist party launched rural revolutions in the 1950s (von Glahn 2016: 213).

[8] Li (2009: 55–96) has listed in detail the important technical progress in the Tang dynasty.

In the Song dynasty, private ownership of land became unprecedentedly sophisticated and nuanced. Peasants' ownership of land was not only protected by legal clauses, but also guaranteed by a sophisticated land transaction system. When peasants went bankrupt unfortunately due to natural disasters or financial incaution, peasants usually chose to sell their lands to landowners. In Chinese history, such behaviours usually resulted in land annexation and hence social unrest. However, as Long (2018) suggested, from the Song dynasty the land transaction system began to become sophisticated towards the direction of guaranteeing peasants' ownership of land. Gradually, when peasants had to sell their lands, they could choose various forms of transaction. They could pawn the lands and then borrow money at the price of interest. A popular method was that peasants pawned the ownership of one land and continued to cultivate on this land, thus making peasants become tenants. Tenants could purchase back the ownership of this land and become peasants again. Furthermore, the relation between landowners and tenants became very sophisticated. Tenants were not at a disadvantageous status. For example, as tenants had to invest in the land, such as manure, ploughing and so on, tenants could have a louder voice when negotiating with landowners. More flexible and complicated financial methods were also developed to satisfy the demand of peasants, with lands as collateral. Starting from the late Tang dynasty to the Qing dynasty, forms of private ownership of land became increasingly sophisticated (Han 2013). In sum, the land transaction system guaranteed the predominant status of the peasant economy. To some degree, peasants were protected from dramatic bankruptcy. Since the Song dynasty, the area of lands owned by peasant households was always above 70% of the total cultivated area.[9] "Henceforward, private agrarian property, although subject to certain important restrictions, was to characterise Chinese imperial society down to the end", and this "property rights, may have altered comparatively little after the Song epoch" (Anderson 1974: 527, 539).

Besides agricultural sectors, progress in a waterway transportation system and commercial organisations facilitated market expansion. As

[9] Long has detailed and accurate analysis about the development of the private ownership of land from the Song dynasty to the Qing dynasty. See Long (2018: 80–107). About the estimates on the overall rate of tenancy from the eleventh to the nineteenth century, see Perkins (1969: 98–102).

illustrated before, Emperor Yangdi of Sui launched ambitious construction programs in order to build new canal networks and to link old water networks. In the Tang and Song dynasties, the canal and water networks continued to be renovated and widened. As the Jiang economy developed, the existence of the central court in North China relied increasingly on the transportation network through which revenues and crops could be transported to the capital. In addition, technical progress in shipbuilding and sailing led to improved efficiency of the transportation system. The dredging of rivers and the upgrading of inland waterway networks also contributed to the optimisation of a nationwide waterway system. Diverse commercial organisations, such as shipping brokers, made the transaction costs of transportation lower. Goods could circulate at lower prices. As Liu (2015a: 88) suggested, the shipping costs had experienced an astonishing decrease in this period. In most transportation networks, the shipping costs in the Song dynasty were just one-fifth of that in the Tang dynasty. With these advantages, the nationwide economy was gradually integrated into a whole, thus contributing to the division of labour and the market expansion (Elvin 1973: 131–145).

Equally importantly, institutional innovations regarding commercial organisations contributed to thriving commerce and trade. The form of partnership emerged at this time and began to become popular in ocean and canal shipping. Investments became separated from ownership. Some modern business forms, such as bookkeeping and contracts, were gradually applied in dividing profits, delivering goods, and hiring sailors and labourers (Shiba 1970: 56–70, 72–106, 109–129). In transactions, brokerage mushroomed to facilitate business. Not only the domestic market but also international trade was hugely improved. Especially in the Southern Song dynasty, its lifeblood lied in the revenues both from commercial taxes and international trade (von Glahn 2016: 247–252). The popular goods included porcelains, iron goods, rice, books, and silks (Elvin 1973: 171–172). Such cities as Hangzhou and Quanzhou became prosperous because of international trade. Simultaneously, rural economy was increasingly linked with the market mechanism. Many towns in the Jiangnan region became handicraft centres, and the proportion of commercial crops was rising. In addition, urbanisation developed quickly in the Song dynasty. The capital cities, Kaifeng in the Northern Song dynasty and Hangzhou in the Southern Song dynasty, was densely populated. In the twelfth century, there were seven prefectures with over 200,000 households, two in the north and five in the south

(Elvin 1973: 176). The demand for economic products in the urbanisation process drove further the commercialisation process in the rural economy. In sum, the economy in the Song dynasty experienced energetic internationalisation, marketisation and urbanisation.

The rapid development of commerce and trade was accompanied by innovations in the money and credit system. During the Tang-Song era, the earliest forms of paper money emerged in world history. As the tea trade grew fast, in the eighth century the Tang government developed a transaction system based on paper money which was called "flying cash". This practice was for the convenience of interregional trade, thus making merchants avoid the risk of carrying lots of copper coins. After the adoption of the two-tax system in which taxes were paid with copper coins, the quantitative deficiency of copper coins became increasingly serious. In the Northern Song dynasty, merchants in Sichuan region developed a kind of private promissory notes, i.e., "jiao-zi", for the sake of convenience and circulation.[10] In the Southern Song dynasty, the government started to issue quasi-fiat paper money to facilitate commerce and to solve fiscal problems. The issuing of the quasi-fiat paper money, "hui-zi", once stirred up heated discussion in the central court. From time to time, officials debated the benefits and potential harms that it could bring to the economy and the state (He 2019: 122–158).

Alongside the boom of commercial activities, the Song government evolved gradually into a fiscal state. Facing tremendous fiscal pressure from sustaining a huge number of professionalised soldiers and offering tributes annually to northern nomadic empires, the Song government devised diverse methods to enlarge revenues without unduly harming productive sectors, including expanding excise taxes and issuing bonds, etc. (Liu and Guan 2021). "The result was that for the first time in history, agriculture ceased to provide the bulk of State revenues in China. Imperial income from commercial taxes and monopolies was already equal in volume to that from land taxes in the eleventh century; in the Southern Song State of the later twelfth and thirteenth centuries,

[10] The specific history was far more complicated. In Sichuan region in which copper mines were scarce, once iron coins replaced copper coins in circulation. In the early Northern Song dynasty, Sichuan region was a blackhole of copper coins. The government once implemented ban on bringing copper coins into Sichuan. The monetary policies changed several times and once triggered economic disasters. Eventually, the government allowed sixteen chartered merchants to issue officially recognised notes and they must take responsibility of the notes. See von Glahn (2016: 156–159).

commercial revenues greatly exceeded agrarian revenue" (Anderson 1974: 530). From multiple perspectives, the Song central government had implemented mercantile policies and developed in a sense into a fiscal state (Liu 2015b).

The zenith of a fiscal state was the Wang Anshi's reform in the Northern Song dynasty. From a retrospective view, Wang Anshi's reform was a combination of an adjustment to the fast-growing commercial economy and a traditional Legalist practice with the purpose to solve the fiscal crisis of the government. As illustrated before, in order to eliminate the possibility of warlordism, the Song central government weakened the power of prefectures and concentrate its armies on the capital. The enlarging teams of bureaucrats and the costs of supporting massive armies inflicted the Song government. In the late eleventh century, Wang Anshi (1021–1086 AD) was appointed as a chief minister. He immediately launched comprehensive reforms and implemented many innovative policies. Wang Anshi's reform could be understood from two aspects. First and foremost, it was an updated version of Sang Hongyang's policies. With the aim to increase the government's revenues and to reduce the government's fiscal burden, Wang Anshi streamlined the taxation system by reducing or eliminating in-kind payments and corvée labour. He also extracted more income from the monopoly of specific commodities and foreign trade, such as tea. Secondly, Wang Anshi organised new institutes to interfere deeply in commercial activities. Bureaucrats were sent nationwide to do business in markets by buying commodities when the prices were low and selling them when the prices were high. An innovative method which was known as the "Green Sprouts" ("qing-miao") program was also applied. According to this program, low-interest loans were lent to peasants by the government when peasants had the demand. Its original purpose was to protect peasants from the exploitation of private lenders.[11] Wang Anshi's policies had multifaceted consequences: while these policies successfully relieved the fiscal burden of the Song government, its interventionism stirred up huge unsatisfaction of merchants and Confucian scholars. The bureaucrats whom Wang Anshi deployed were also charged with corruption and opportunistic behaviours. Following the death of Wang Anshi, his policies experienced

[11] The content of Wang Anshi's reform consisted of both conventional methods of Chinese Legalism and new ideas which responded to growing commercial activities. About the specific content of Wang Anshi's reform, see von Glahn (2016: 236–242).

vicissitudes and were finally repudiated. However, it is clear that his policies were a reflection of a growing market economy and could have possibly contributed to the rise of a fiscal state.

Based on the aforementioned trends, obviously China was experiencing an economic revolution during the Tang-Song era. The technical progress in agricultural sectors and handicrafts industry, the national waterway networks, and the organisational innovations contributed to the rapid monetarisation, marketisation and urbanisation. The small peasantry was entrenched. Productivity in agricultural sectors improved hugely. Market expansion developed quickly due to the enhancement of the transportation system. Interregional and international trade prospered. Urbanisation also developed quickly. Paper money emerged, and the credit system grew gradually mature. New organisations with the function to lower transaction costs were devised and became popular in commercial activities. As Perry Anderson (1974: 531) states, "the Chinese Empire of the Song epoch was unquestionably the wealthiest and most advanced economy on the globe in the eleventh and twelfth centuries, and its florescence was based far more securely on the diversified production of its agriculture and industry, rather than mainly on the exchange transactions of international trade". Even a fiscal state seemed to emerge on the horizon. Among economic historians, it was widely acknowledged that the rise of a fiscal state and the organisational innovation such as partnerships contributed to the economic boom in early modern Europe.[12] Plainly speaking, most economic elements which were significant for the economic boom in early modern Europe had also emerged and developed energetically in the Tang-Song transition. Similar trends could be observed especially in the Song dynasty. Since the "first economic revolution" in the Warring States period in Chinese history, in the Tang-Song eras, China was experiencing the "second economic revolution".

3 Neo-Confucianism: Ideological Maturity

During the Tang dynasty, the influence of aristocratic clans was in decline. Along with the practice of the state examination system, Confucianism was revived because the main content of examinations gradually concentrated on those Confucian classics. Especially in the Song dynasty, with

[12] About the role of a fiscal state, see Epstein (2006) and Tilly (1992). About the role of organisational innovations, see de Vries and van der Woude (1997).

the perfection and the enlargement of the state examination system came the whole revival of Confucianism. In the Northern Song dynasty, a new school of Confucianism, "Li-Xue", was established. It was a transformed philosophy of Confucianism.[13] The most significant scholars of "Li-Xue" were Cheng Yi, Cheng Hao and Zhu Xi. Zhu Xi (1130–1200 AD) became later the representative of Neo-Confucianism for the next millennium.

The academic relation between Confucius's Confucianism and Neo-Confucianism was relatively weak in that Neo-Confucian scholars have added many more new spices into Confucian tenets. The biggest common point could be that both emphasised social responsibility and the feeling of social mission (Wei 2003: 28–38). Confucians believed that a society could be improved by people's moral efforts and Confucians should lead the moral campaign. Similarly, Neo-Confucians emphasised the role of learning Confucian classics. However, the texts they used were quite different from those in previous dynasties. They focused on four books: *The Analects* ("Lun-Yu"), *Mencius*, *Great Learning* ("Da-Xue"), and *Doctrine of the Mean* ("Zhong-Yong"). Moreover, Zhu Xi added his own understanding of the four books and set his own understanding as the standard explanation of those texts. Young Confucian scholars must learn and recite Zhu Xi's explanations which later became the standard answers in the state examinations. Furthermore, Neo-Confucians began to delve into metaphysical speculation which was uncommon in old Confucians. Confucius himself did not want to think about supernatural or metaphysical conjecture. Confucius said: "To give one's self earnestly to the duties due to men, and, while respecting spiritual beings, to keep aloof from them, may be called wisdom".[14] But Neo-Confucians integrated Buddhist concepts about the universe into their new tenets (Zhao 2015: 332–334). In the Song dynasty, Cheng Yi came up with the concept "Li" (Principle) as the final purpose of the universe. It could be understood as a similar concept to Hegel's "absolute spirit". Neo-Confucians believed that "Li" manifested itself everywhere and scholars must "observe, sense and experience" it in all aspects of the natural and human worlds.

[13] About the relation between Neo-Confucianism and old Confucianism, see Munro (1988).

[14] *The Analects*, Yong Ye. (《论语·雍也》).

The role of Neo-Confucianism was multifaceted. Firstly, it was a conducive complement to the state examination system. As the state examination system became entrenched in the Song dynasty, private schools mushroomed. The rise of Neo-Confucianism offered the standard textbooks for the educational system and set the content of examinations. Its doctrines limited the spiritual scope of scholars and directed most intellects to social duties and services to the government. Secondly, Neo-Confucianism had specific principles about daily life. It penetrated local society and people's individual life. To some degree, the appearance of a gentry society in local communities was the result of this penetration. Thirdly, Neo-Confucianism could be easily transformed into an official ideology with the purpose to protect the legitimacy of a central authority. Loyalty and obeyance were doctrines of Neo-Confucianism. And scholars were taught to focus on academics rather than practical affairs. Neo-Confucianism succeeded to sustain the Imperial Mode until it began to fall apart in the late nineteenth century when the occidental modernisation came in.

4 The Role of Mongolians' Reign

To some degree, the Song dynasty was rather infamous for its military weakness in Chinese history when compared with other dynasties regarding military victories against northern nomadic tribes. In the early Northern Song dynasty, the Song court was embarrassed by continuous failures with the nomadic empire, Liao (Khitan tribes) in the northern prairie, and the semi-nomadic Tangut tribes in the northwest. The northern borders were always under the threat of nomadic armies. Later a new power rose and took part in the game. Jurchen tribes set out from the heartland of Manchuria and moved southwards. After decades, they succeeded to defeat the Khitan empire and the Northern Song dynasty and established a dynasty known as "Jin" in north China.[15] The Song court fled to the Jiangnan region and established in the twelfth century an

[15] The Jin dynasty was quite successful in adopting Sinicization, changing from a hunter-gatherer civilisation to a regime which can establish professionalised bureaucratic system to rule over a sedentary agricultural society. In hundreds of years, the Qing dynasty was founded by the Jurchen (Manchurian) people, too. Interestingly, the Qing court was even far more successful in terms of reproducing tactics used to rule over a large empire than its own ancestors.

émigré regime, the Southern Song dynasty. However, none of the above-mentioned players enjoyed lasting peace. A far more powerful empire was rising in the Mongol plateau. Genghis Khan annexed most Mongol tribes and started his large-scale expeditions in Eurasia. He and his heirs succeeded to destroy other regimes, including the Southern Song regime and the Jin regime. They continued to conquer lands that are known today as Russia, Caucasus and Iran, etc. Though for a short time, the topsy-turvy in this vast area was ended eventually by the Mongol universal empire.

The military inability of the Song dynasty was usually interpreted as the consequence of a complicated political structure.[16] Wary of warlordism, emperors of the Northern Song dynasty intended to weaken the capacity of regional armies, including those nearby borderlines. The political status of generals was suppressed; the leadership of imperial armies was transferred to literati lacking in basic military training or know-how about wartime tactics. At least half of the national armies were deployed at the capital in case of regional rebellions. Generals did not have discretionary power even when wars were imminent. They must wait for commands from emperors or higher literati, which were sent out of the capital. Lacking in flexibility and wholehearted support to military units, this complicated political structure undermined the military capacity of armies. Nonetheless, this explanation does not tell the whole story, though it is correct. It is not righteous to be unduly censorious towards the Song court. Indeed, few emperors in the Song dynasty had big ambitions for territory expansion.[17] Most military actions were self-defensive against nomadic invasions. Except for saddling bureaucrats, emperors in the Song dynasty had little interest in forceful interventionism. They did not pay much attention to territorial expansion or external wars as those ambitious emperors did in previous dynasties. This was also one of the reasons why commerce and market economy could prosper in the Song dynasty. Moreover, enemies of the Song dynasty were several strong nomadic empires, which rose in the northern plateau in a continuous

[16] In the PRC, many Marxian historians, such as Jian Bozan and Fan Wenlan, held this kind of view, and such view were taught as the standard answer.

[17] For the whole Song dynasty, the Beijing region was always in hands of northern nomadic empires. First several emperors of the Northern Song dynasty aimed to "reclaim" this territory. However, their endeavours all failed. Thereafter, no emperor continued this military expedition.

manner. The incessant rise of nomadic empires was rare even in world history. The Song court had to sequentially and continuously encounter Khitan, Tangut, Jurchen and Mongol empires in northern borders. As Miyazaki (1956: 388) suggests, Chinese history always contained questions that cannot be interpreted by internal factors, and it is necessary to understand Chinese history in dint of external factors. At that time, the Mongol empire found almost no counterpart over Eurasia. It is hardly convincing to overrate the military weakness of the Song dynasty.

The Mongol empire destroyed other regimes in this land and established the Yuan dynasty in 1271. It was the first Chinese dynasty led by non-Han rulers. From every angle, the Yuan dynasty was not a typical Chinese empire. Its administrative manner in China was a combination of Mongolians' feudalism and Han's despotism. To a large degree, "the administration was almost like colonial governments because of the oil-and-water mixture of Chinese and tribal ways" (Fairbank and Goldman 2006: 123). In Mongolians' concepts, the lands they conquered and the people on the lands were their properties, and these properties were subject to feudalistic allocation. In north China, in the first place some Mongol rulers indeed wanted to forbid planting agriculture and transform China completely into a big pasture (although it was not practised eventually).[18] Throughout the entire Yuan dynasty, it was consistently a dual empire consisting of Mongol's and Han's elements. In many cases, rulers, including emperors and courtiers, struggled to find a way in which both elements can be balanced. For instance, the state examination system was not restored until 1315 after they gradually recognised the value of Chinese imperial mechanisms. But they hardly find a feasible way to fit in the dualism.

One important character of the Yuan society was its wholesale discrimination system. Residents were classified into four classes, first of which was Mongolians, second the residents with colourful eyes (mainly from Middle Asia and foreigners), third the northern Chinese, and fourth the southern Chinese. Residents previously under the rule of the Southern Song dynasty were especially discriminated. This system entailed comprehensive regulations in taxes, juridic rights, qualifications in government recruitment and various privileges in civil affairs (Mote 1994). For example, in the state examination system, quotas were generously

[18] The story was widely known in Chinese history. The main figure was Yelü Chucai who successfully persuaded the emperor to give up that policy.

reserved for Mongol examinees who were mostly less literate than Han examinees and requirements for Mongol examinees were very low. An apparent result was that officialdom was full of corrupted Mongol bureaucrats. In fact, corruption was serious not only in local offices but also in the central court. Mongol bureaucrats could exploit farmers and merchants discretionarily, and top courtiers took the empire as their own properties. Furthermore, these discriminatory regulations were highly rigid and hierarchical identities were hereditary. In principle no Han Chinese, at least 90% of the whole population could shun this system and corresponding policies.

Another result of the dualism was that the succession of the throne was highly instable. The central court was always inflicted with flagrant coups. Civil wars happened to surround the throne succession. Although Kublai Khan (1215–1294 AD, r. 1402–1424 AD) tried to establish *de jure* primogeniture in throne succession, the peaceful transfer of political power was rare through the Yuan dynasty. For one thing, tribal heads were always competing for the throne because it was a Mongol tradition to share political power among all legitimate heirs. For another, the empire was torn between nomadic forces and "sedentary" forces. Top bureaucrats also gathered around different ideologies and supported different candidates. As a result, only Kublai Khan himself, the founder of the Yuan dynasty, had a peaceful reign. All subsequent emperors either succeeded the throne by violent means or were sidelined by imperious courtiers. A further consequence was that top bureaucrats were frequently purged after antagonistic factions took power. Conflicts surrounding the throne succession were highly severe in the Yuan dynasty (Xiao 1983; Fletcher 1979/1980).

Economic activities in the Yuan dynasty never reached that height in the Song dynasty, although international trade continued to develop partly because of the vast geographical space which Mongolians controlled. The population did neither reach the level of the Song dynasty (Mote 1994). The central court was constantly plagued by fiscal crises because of emperors' extravagant lifestyle and their large-scale and frequent largess to relatives and entourages. Top bureaucrats from time to time heightened taxes and expanded monopoly in order to raise revenues, but most fiscal efforts were aborted due to factionalism and political purges. In the late Yuan dynasty, the government hugely relied on printing paper money without reserves to pay bills relating to hydraulic projects and other purposes (von Glahn 2016: 283–284). Subsequently, inflation became sprawling and stirred up unrest in the countryside. Widespread farmers' rebellions finally overthrew the Mongol empire. The last emperor of the Yuan dynasty escaped to the northern prairie from which they set out to conquer Eurasia one hundred years ago.

The legacy of Mongolians in China was mixed. On the one hand, by dint of its unprecedentedly large geographical scope, interregional and international trade continued to grow during the Yuan dynasty. As Mongolians controlled inner Asia, trade routes in the continent extended to the far west, in which Uighurs became active merchants and agents. As for sea trade, in ports on south-eastern shores merchants of different races exported such products as porcelains and silk alongside the South China Sea and Indian Ocean to Arabic World and other places. On the other hand, nonetheless, Mongol rulers inherited much pastoral tradition which emphasised control of people. The social discrimination system, as described earlier, posed negative effects on China. More severely, the essence of such a system was copied by Hongwu, the founder of the Ming dynasty, in order to depress destabilising factors and control the society. In general, Mongol rulers either had no interest to adopt Chinese imperial mechanisms or just launched the Sinicisation process half-heartedly. Its rule was far less successful than the next non-Han empire, the Qing dynasty. Perry Anderson (1974: 531) once described the negative sides of Mongol rulers:

> Industrial innovation largely halted; the most notable technical advance of the Mongol epoch seems, perhaps suggestively, to have been the casting of metal-barrel cannon. The tax-burden on the rural and urban masses increased, while hereditary registration of their occupations was introduced, to immobilise the class structure of the country. Rents and interest rates remained high, and peasant indebtedness steadily rose. Although the Southern landlords had rallied to the invading Mongol armies, the Yuan dynasty showed little trust in the Chinese mandarinate. The examination system was abolished, central imperial authority was strengthened, provincial administration reorganised, and fiscal collection farmed to foreign corporations of Uighurs, on whom the Mongol rulers relied heavily for administrative and business skills.

To a large degree, as a political-economic structure, the Imperial Mode became ripe as the agriculture economy got developed in the Tang-Song transition. As demonstrated before, triggered by technological progress, proto-industrialisation, marketisation and commercialisation which developed intensively and extensively during this era could have gradually demolished corresponding superstructure, if relations of production adjusted itself in response to changes of productive forces. But the Mongol invasion to some extent changed the trajectory. Mongolians' institutions reinforced systems aiming to control people and strengthen despotism, while its vast territory and extensive foreign relations expanded the maritime and continental network of international trade. It has been always argued that Mongolians' occupation of Russia has similar effects on Russian societal structure (Rüstow 1957). The trends of strengthening despotism and curbing non-agricultural elements in the economy prevented an exit from the Imperial Mode. The trends continued and became more institutionalised and systemised in the Ming and Qing dynasties.

5 The Zenith of Authoritarian Monarchy

The Mongol rulers were expelled by a farmer insurrectionist, Hongwu. In 1368 he established the Ming dynasty and enacted comprehensive policies to strengthen the imperial mechanisms. The political structure was changed profoundly with the purpose to heighten the central authority. Firstly, he abolished some official positions, such as prime ministership, in order to strengthen his own supremacy. Hongwu launched a series of beheading on those powerful officials, including prominent generals and prestigious chancellors. After executing Hu Weiyong, a prime minister who was accused of a coup, he refused to appoint a new one and issued an edict to eternally abolish this position. Secondly, he set up new supervisory institutes to control bureaucrats. The most important one was the "Embroidered Uniform Guard" ("jin-yi-wei") which was reorganised in 1369 as secret police on the base of Hongwu's personal bodyguards. They could bypass judicial procedures to prosecute bureaucrats directly under the command of emperors themselves. Hongwu used this institute to establish the spy rule. Thirdly, he issued detailed legal clauses in which light dereliction could be punished harshly. During the reign of Hongwu, officials were often asked to witness the bloody execution scenes in which colleagues or chiefs would be tortured or executed. Fourthly, the state examination system was further institutionalised and simultaneously rigidified. The content of examinations was restricted to standard textbooks, and answers were basically fixed, which were explanations of previous sages. Through comprehensive policies, Hongwu improved the central authority institutionally. The harshness of the political rule in the Ming dynasty was astonishing. Frederick Mote (1988: 44–57) argued that many peculiarities of Ming rule stemmed from the personal characteristics of this strange and powerful man, i.e., Hongwu himself.

Hongwu's obsession with personal control over politics was quite remarkable. The secret police and surveillance system was much more ruthless and extremely extensive than before (Anderson 1974: 532). Hongwu's efforts to reorganise bureaucracy succeeded in establishing an absolute monarchy and maintaining the status quo: he wanted to keep the state apparatus minimally functional and exclude any possibility to trigger changes (Wang 2022: Chapter 6). While he squeezed the space of bureaucracy, he prepared luxurious gifts for his heirs. Influenced by his own memory of famine and hunger, Hongwu issued edicts to give prerogatives to his heirs. Every heir could have certain stipends of rice and cash after birth. The amount was determined on the basis of the relative closeness to the emperors' lineage.[19] The prerogatives would last from "womb to tomb". The prerogatives of royal families put a heavy fiscal burden upon the taxation system. Lands free of taxation were also often bestowed to royal members. In the late Ming dynasty, the number of royal members was over 220,000 and they sucked a great percentage of fiscal revenues (Li 2016). Royal members also occupied massive arable lands. Hongwu's endeavours to guarantee heirs' happiness left bitter legacies for the Ming court. After he died, his grandson, the appointed successor, was overthrown by one of his younger sons, Yongle.

Yongle (1360–1424 AD, r. 1402–1424 AD) was quite like his father. Obsessed in historic fame, Yongle ambitiously launched external wars against northern nomadic Mongolians and aboriginal tribes in Burma and Vietnam. He also sent one eunuch, Zheng He (1371–1433 AD), to conduct large-scale voyages in the West Pacific Ocean and the Indian Ocean. In domestic affairs, Yongle continued the path of his father to strengthen the absolute authority of emperorship. As more supervisory institutes were established, political power was further amassed to emperorship. However, the power brought assignments. Both Hongwu and Yongle had to deal with many routine affairs every day. For example, in an eight-day period, Hongwu received 1600 dispatches of which

[19] *History of Ming*, Vol. 82, Treatise 58. (《明史》, 志第五十八食货六).

3391 issues were presented.[20] During the reign of Yongle, some close advisors were allowed to participate in the policymaking process, while intimate eunuchs also gained power in the political process. They became emperors' secretariats. However, this heavy burden of political tasks still terrified subsequent successors. After the mid-Ming dynasty, emperors continuously eschewed politics and submersed themselves into personal hobbies. Few emperors paid attention to politics. As a result, those close advisors and eunuchs gained huge power. But the conflicts between bureaucrats and eunuchs impeded normal political operations. After the mid-Ming dynasty, the central court was plagued with palace intrigues and factionalism.[21]

In the late Ming dynasty, topsy-turvy prevailed in the central court and local governments. The Ming court frequently conducted wars against the Japanese in the Korean Peninsula and the rising Jurchen tribes in Manchuria. The fiscal problems worsened due to huge expenditures on battlefields. At the same, none of the emperors in the late Ming dynasty were industrious or thrifty. Astronomical money was spent on palaces and their personal hobbies. Moreover, the principal–agent problem became eye-catchingly serious in local governments. The corruption of local bureaucrats was widespread and astonishing. In order to guarantee the fiscal revenues necessary for external wars, the Ming government had no other choice but to increase taxes upon peasants. But this action unquestionably stirred up unrest in rural areas, and the unrest was further heightened due to more opportunistic behaviours of local bureaucrats. Agricultural productivity was also crippled by heavy taxes (Wang 1936). Soon farmers' rebellions swept the Ming empire. In 1644 the last emperor suicided in Beijing, and the Ming dynasty was formally overthrown by farmer insurrectionists. The fall of the Ming dynasty vividly illustrated the dark sides of the Imperial Mode. The central authority, which was arbitrary and despotic, failed to solve the principal–agent problem of the bureaucratic system, and both of them extracted excessive surpluses from the peasant economy. When the balance was destroyed, the dynastic cycles began again.

[20] Hucker (1966) had a vivid description on how the administrative system operated in the early Ming dynasty.

[21] Huang (1981) offered a case study of how a lazy emperor, arrogant eunuchs and powerful ministers influenced politics of the Ming empire. Politics was obviously deteriorating especially in the late Ming dynasty.

However, the farmer insurrectionists did not succeed to establish a national dynasty. The Jurchen conquerors took the chance to replace the Ming dynasty and established the Qing dynasty, which was the last imperial dynasty in Chinese history. Ancestors of Manchus once succeeded defeating the Song dynasty and establishing the Jin dynasty in north China, but they were quickly devoured by Mongolians. In the seventeenth century, Manchus annexed Inner Mongolia and further occupied the territories of the Ming dynasty. In the first half of the Qing dynasty, it enjoyed glorious days. Three emperors ruled for almost one and a half centuries: the Emperors Kangxi (1654–1722 AD, r. 1661–1722 AD), Yongzheng (1678–1735 AD, r. 1722–1735 AD) and Qianlong (1711–1799 AD, r. 1735–1796 AD), from 1662 to around 1796.[22] Kangxi basically achieved domestic peace after he defeated three former Ming generals in south China, the enemy in the Taiwan Island and Mongol Khans in Inner Asia. He also took advantage of soft strategies to control Tibet by subjugating Buddhist Lamas. During the reign of Kangxi, the Qing empire expanded firmly to Mongolia, Inner Asia and Tibet. For nearly one century, from 1680 to 1750s, "Machu rule lowered taxes, checked corruption, maintained internal peace and furthered colonisation" (Anderson 1974: 535).

The military conquests of Manchu rulers were unquestionably successful. Their efforts were equally remarkable to adopt Chinese imperial mechanisms. Compared with Manchus' predecessors, the Jin and Yuan dynasties, the Qing court expressed great interest in Sinicisation. While Manchus tried to keep their own language and cultural characters, they imitated the Ming dynasty to establish imperial administration (Fairbank and Goldman 2006: 143–151). As Anderson (1974: 535) comments, "the new Qing, once installed, was to repeat much the same economic cycles as its predecessor, on a wider scale; politically, its rule was a mixture of Yuan and Ming traditions". The bureaucratic system was soon restored after Manchus established the government, and local elites were encouraged to take office in local governments. Many literati who were once loyal to the Ming dynasty quickly changed their minds and became administrators working for Manchus. The state examination system was very quickly restored once the Manchus established governance in Beijing

[22] Emperor Qianlong nominally abdicated after he took the throne already for sixty years. However, he still de facto controlled the empire while his son officially succeeded the throne.

(Miyazaki 1987: 35–37). Moreover, on the basis of Ming's authoritarian structure, the first several emperors took action to further strengthen their supremacy. Kangxi set up a personal office consisting of several secretariats in his own library, through which he could bypass those influential bureaucrats. He also institutionalised an action known as "zou-zhe" in which memorials of certain local officials could come directly to the emperor and were returned to them with the commands of the emperor himself. Thus, emperors could supervise bureaucrats more efficiently. During the reign of Yongzheng (1722–1736), who was a hard-hearted and assiduous CEO of the large empire, the Grand Council ("jun-ji-chu") was established in which top officials were selected by the emperor himself to participate in the policymaking process. Political power was gradually centralised to the Grand Council, and the emperor held absolute power in its operation. Until the reign of Qianlong, most procedures aiming to strengthen the central authority were accomplished.

During the eighteenth century and the first half of the nineteenth century, the central authority stepped into its zenith. It was a period of totalitarian monarchy. The bureaucratic system was completely subjugated in front of emperorship. High officials became humble servants and retainers of emperors per se. The institutional power of high officials disappeared, and their unique principle was to follow the commands of emperors. Unlike those emperors in the Ming dynasty who lacked interest in politics, few emperors in the Qing dynasty lacked the basic ability of a good CEO. While in the late Ming dynasty, the central court was in a mess because of emperors' laziness and vehement conflicts between eunuchs and literati factionalism, laborious emperors in most periods of the Qing dynasty offered an efficient and strong leadership. Until the second half of the nineteenth century, the Qing court avoided the dominance of eunuchs, empresses or powerful bureaucrats, which was always the fate of previous dynasties. Although the role of individuals is downplayed in Marxian historical materialism, it acknowledges that the function of individuals was enlarged through institutions. In Chinese dynasties, the central authority was always at the heart of the imperial structure. Hence, individual behaviours of emperors posed immeasurable influence upon historical process.

The Qing empire had to face its turning point in the mid-nineteenth century when Western colonists knocked on the door. Thereafter, domestic crises and external threats dragged the empire into the marsh. While Chinese Marxian historians asserted that since 1840s colonialism was the root cause of the tragic fate of Chinese people, those crises were more caused by internal political, economic and social changes which developed already for a long time (Mühlhahn 2019: 23). In the nineteenth century, the Qing empire encountered increasingly serious financial problems due to inability to adjust to monetarisation and commercialisation. During the whole Qing dynasty, rulers had to encounter incessant cycles of deflation and inflation.[23] Agricultural productivity was harmed under frequent economic crises. In the 1850s, a large-scale rebellion, known as the Taiping Rebellion (1851–1864), occupied the richest provinces in south China. Small rebellions led by "Nian" bandits burst out in north China. The northwest territories were also at the centre of unrest: the Shaanxi and Gansu provinces were plagued with Muslim rebellions, and the Uygur region was occupied by invaders from Inner Asia and Russia. Unable to collect sufficient resources to repress those rebellions, the Qing court had to transfer partial power to local governors. Some local figures gained the chartered right to collect taxes and to organise private armies. In the process of repressing rebellions, those governors became gradually governor-lords and gained power in civil affairs (Deng 2012: 60–61). Most outstanding were Zeng Guofan (1811–1872) and Li Hongzhang (1823–1901), etc. Regional entities gradually became mini-states over which the central government lost control. The governor-lords started to practise their will as far as they could exert political influence. The first wave of modernisation in the late Qing dynasty was conducted by them. However, the growth of regional decentralisation in the late nineteenth and early twentieth century contributed to the final downfall of the Qing dynasty.

6 Static Economic Development

For the entire period from the Ming dynasty to the end of the Qing dynasty, the imperial structure had been always unfitting with economic development. The specific reflections were the lasting fiscal problems and the dilemma concerning monetarisation. Another important aspect of the unfitness was the "High-level Equilibrium Trap" as Elvin (1973) suggested. Although the Song dynasty enjoyed great prosperity in commercialisation, monetarisation and urbanisation, such trends were

[23] For a detailed analysis of monetary policy in the early Qing dynasty, see von Glahn (1996: Chapter 7).

interrupted after the thirteenth century. In the Ming dynasty, the trends were completely reversed as Hongwu strengthened the peasant economy and pulled China back to the standard Imperial Mode. "The Chinese resurgence that threw out the Mongol conquerors did not attempt a continuation of the Song but tried in theory back to the models of Han and Tang" (Fairbank and Goldman 2006: 128). While marketisation and monetarisation still developed in certain regions during the Ming-Qing era, the whole system was marching back towards a command economy and the peasant economy.

As illustrated before, international trade prospered in the Song dynasty. Under the rule of the Mongol conquerors, international trade continued to grow because those rulers with the background of one universal empire held quite an open-minded attitude towards foreign trade (von Glahn 2016: 283–284). Ceramics, silk and other goods were exported to Japan, Southeast Asia, the Islamic world and Eastern Africa. The porcelain industry in China was even inspired by an imported pigment from Persia.[24] Accordingly, the level of marketisation and monetarisation in the Song and Yuan dynasties was relatively high, although in the late Yuan dynasty the issuing of paper money once triggered economic disorder (von Glahn 1996: 56–70). However, in the early Ming dynasty, international trade was all but blocked since emperors started to implement the sea-ban policy. Hongwu valued governmental stability and held a very hostile attitude towards commerce and trade. In addition, Japanese samurai robbed coastal provinces from time to time. Chronically while discontinuously through centuries, the Ming court started to implement the sea-ban policy in order to cut off the connection with foreigners. Although during the reign of Yongle grand fleets led by Zheng He arrived in eastern Africa and the Islamic world, the official voyage had little to do with trade or commerce. After Zheng He, the Ming court ceased contact with the maritime world. Even documents about Zheng He's voyages were destroyed (Fairbank and Goldman 2006: 138), and the size of newly built ships was restricted.[25] Until 1567, contact with the maritime world was severely cut off. While the sea-ban policy was occasionally loosened in the late Ming dynasty, China's ability to participate in international

[24] The well-known porcelain was the Yuan blue-white porcelain whose special colour was made possible by a Persian pigment, i.e., "Muslim blue". See Finley (2010: 139–140).

[25] *Records of Yongle*, Volume 27, the Second Year of Yongle (《明太宗实录》卷二十七, 永乐二年正月辛酉).

trade was hugely limited. The ban on overseas trade and connections was inherited almost invariably by the Qing emperors, too. The sea-ban policy through the Ming-Qing era stunted the emergence of international trade just at the time when international trade and the discovery of the New World were fundamentally transforming the institutions of England (Acemoglu & Robinson 2013: 233). As Acemoglu and Robinson (2013: 117–118) comment,

> China was a major naval power and heavily involved in long-distance trade centuries before the Europeans. But it had turned away from the oceans just at the wrong time, when Ming emperors decided in the late fourteenth and early fifteenth centuries that increased long-distance trade and the creative destruction that it might bring would be likely to threaten their rule.

Hongwu's anti-commercialism and preference to an autarky economy dominated the political designation in the early Ming dynasty. Those ideas were also inherited by his successors almost without any change. Hongwu had much hatred for the merchant class and was furious about any power which could threaten his absolute authority. In the Jiangnan region where Hongwu built his capital, the landholdings of big landlords and merchants were confiscated, and they were transferred into governmental assets ("guan-tian") possessed by royal members (Liu 2015a: 160, 200). The anti-commercialism was in line with the efforts to strengthen the peasant economy. Emperors in the early Ming dynasty believed that economic disparity would worsen regional imbalance and hence endanger political unification. Conversely, they tried to strengthen the status of agriculture and it would be simple to sustain the homogeneity of the empire. The rural control system known as "li-jia" was introduced; corvée labour was reintroduced; light taxation rate was implemented (although the burden upon peasants was not relieved because local bureaucrats had to add extra taxes due to the deficiency of local treasury). Supposedly self-sufficient military farms were established all over the directly controlled territories. Economic policies in the early Ming dynasty had a strong tendency to restore the autarky agricultural economy, although the market economy and monetarisation had developed for a while (von Glahn 2016: 285–293).

Emperors in the Ming dynasty insisted on the traditional role of emperorship, which was fancied by Confucians. The outstanding characters of the fiscal system in the Ming dynasty were the light taxation rate upon peasants, the low salary of bureaucrats and the arbitrariness of fiscal budgets. However, the light taxation rate did not bring benefits to peasants. Alongside the fancy of becoming sages, emperors conducted large-scale projects, such as the construction of the Great Wall along the northern borderlines, the dredging and widening of the Great Canal (Cheung 2008), the construction of dams along the Yellow River and luxurious palaces in Beijing and Nanjing (Huang 1974: 403–409). While the central and local governments invested much in those projects, there was no such thing as a budget stipulated by the central or local treasury. The common practice was to use corvée labour and to add nonstatutory fees upon peasants arbitrarily (Huang 1974: 460–461). At the same time, local bureaucrats were plagued by low salaries and deficiency of fiscal support, which inevitably led to corruption and further exploitation on peasants (Fairbank and Goldman 2006: 129). Consequently, not only the fiscal system but also the rural economy was made topsy-turvy.

Another significant aspect of economic degradation in the early Ming dynasty was the demonetarisation. At the beginning of the Ming dynasty, Hongwu was unaware of the catastrophic consequence of unlimited paper money so he kept handing out paper money as awards (Fairbank and Goldman 2006: 134). After inflation devoured the value of paper money, the Ming court completely gave up paper money and retreated to copper coins. However, the government paid no attention to minting new coins. During the whole 276 years, the government minted coins only forty times. According to Huang's estimation, the total production of copper coins during the whole Ming dynasty was only eight billion *wen* (the unit of currency), which was only the amount for two years in the Northern Song dynasty (Huang 1974: 88–104, 462). As a result of the deficiency of coinage, the counterfeit problem was rampant. However, the government not only failed to solve the counterfeit problem but also failed to provide sufficient money in circulation. The use of silver was nevertheless forbidden. The monetarisation was hugely damped. Even in Huizhou, a core area of the Jiangnan economy which was the most economically advanced region in the Ming-Qing area, data revealed that it retreated to a barter economy at the dawn of the fifth century (Liu 2015a: 199). The demonetarisation was slightly mitigated after the sixteenth century since the sea-ban policy was loosened so that the growth of international trade and the import of silver from Latin America and Japan stimulated monetarisation.[26] The fiscal reform in the late Ming dynasty, which was known as the Single Whip ("yi-tiao-bian-fa"), was to some degree a response to the monetarisation. The taxation system was accordingly monetarised. However, the use of silver caused more problems because the government did not have a proper fiscal system which could adjust to this trend.[27] In sum, while in the early Ming dynasty, the government intentionally neglected the need for a proper monetary mechanism, in the late Ming dynasty the government was unable to recast a fiscal system essential for an increasingly monetarised economy. When the economy was thirsty for money, the government refused to develop a minimal mechanism to respond to that request. Emperors were always thinking about their traditional role in an autarky agricultural economy. "The leaders' primary aim was political stability" (Acemoglu and Robinson 2013: 233), and any non-agricultural activities could bring about destabilisation.

The weaknesses of the fiscal system did not change in the Qing dynasty. The Qing court completely inherited the political structure of the Ming court. As semi-nomadic tribes in Manchuria before, the Qing rulers lacked the necessary expertise to rule over China. Subsequently, they employed most former bureaucrats of the Ming court (Miyazaki 1987: 33–35), and they copied its political structure.[28] This simplistic action made the Qing rulers inflicted by similar fiscal problems. On the one hand, the Manchu rulers expressed great homage to traditional social mechanisms. Their Sinicisation was the most successful in Chinese history. In the early Qing dynasty, Emperor Kangxi and Yongzheng encouraged agricultural activities with true heart and conducted taxation reduction (Deng 2021). In 1713 Kangxi declared that the land tax quotas would be permanently frozen at the level of the 1711 assessments. In 1729, the taxation upon persons was formally merged into the

[26] Frank (1998) made groundbreaking work at this point. According to him, in the Ming-Qing era China was not only deeply involved in the global economy but also the winner of international trade in that lots of silver was "deposited" in China.

[27] The parallel of silver and copper created a sort of bimetallic system and it caused economic instability. See von Glahn (1996: 142–161).

[28] The extent of Qing's copying, as Huang suggested, was even unprecedented in Chinese history. No dynasty had ever copied institutions of its predecessor in such a large and comprehensive degree like the Qing dynasty. See Huang (1974: 469–471).

land tax (von Glahn 2016: 314). The scale of these actions was significant. As they were foreigners in terms of ethnic identity, their actions aimed partly to strengthen their rule over the vast population (He 2019: 320–333). On the other hand, the fiscal problems were never relieved at all. As the Qing emperors announced that their governments would not burden peasants much,[29] fiscal revenues were always in shortage. Nominally light taxation forced bureaucrats to collect nonstatutory fees, which inevitably resulted in corruption (Park 1997). The absence of budgets in local entities made the fiscal system topsy-turvy. In the final years of Kangxi, the fiscal problems became so serious that his successor, Emperor Yongzheng, encountered a precarious situation. Throughout the entire reign of Yongzheng who was famous for his hard-hearted style and draconian penalty, he had to fight against corrupted bureaucrats and the problematic fiscal system.[30] Yongzheng launched sophisticated reforms to correct the fiscal problem (Zelin 1992). Nonstatutory fees were formally acknowledged but were claimed by the central treasury. The budget system was also reformed in order to control the expenditure of local entities. However, the reform of Yonzheng went bankrupt due to the inability of technical methods and overly complicated categorisation of nonstatutory fees.[31] Consequently, in the nineteenth century, the problematic fiscal system resulted in the administrative inability of the Qing court. Facing regional rebellions, the central court had to allow local governors to establish an independent fiscal system so that the regional decentralisation took apart the Qing dynasty (see Chapter 9).

[29] Their "kindness" might be caused by embarrassing inability. Firslty, the Qing government hardly completed a national registration of land and population, while it accepted the records of the previous dynasty, i.e., the Ming dynasty. See Wang (2022: 188). Secondly, the Qing government which controlled a large geographical domain and could not pose direct control upon areas far from the capital had to reduce the taxation rate in order to relieve the principal-agent problem. See Sng (2014) and Sng and Moriguchi (2014).

[30] It has been widely acknowledged that the writer of a famous Chinese novel, *Dream of the Red Chamber*, grew up in a highly ranked bureaucratic family which prospered during the reign of Kangxi but was later heavily punished by Yongzheng. The charge was that this family abused government's money and left huge fiscal deficit. This memory gave the writer great inspirations and transformed into this novel. See Spence (1988).

[31] Zelin (1992) has a very thorough work on the fiscal reforms of Yongzheng. The emperor had to saddle the intransigent bureaucrats. Finally, he failed to supress bureaucrats' corruption which had become a tacit norm.

In comparison with former dynasties, an outstanding character of the rural society was the rise of the gentry society during the Ming-Qing era. Especially in south China, the gentry class and clans played a leading role in providing necessary public goods which the government failed to do. Firstly, the rise of the gentry class was facilitated by the increasing sophistication of the private ownership of land. As Long (2018) suggested, the ownership system of land became further sophisticated and multi-layered in the Ming-Qing era. The surface ownership and the base ownership of land were divided, and the expenditure of investment on lands was widely acknowledged when land transactions happened. Land contracts also became formatted.[32] Under this circumstance, the gentry class often took the responsibility to sustain this system and supervise the practice of land contracts. Furthermore, it was a response to the government's absence in certain spheres. After the mid-Ming dynasty, commercialisation and marketisation restarted slightly in the Jiangnan region. Rural economy was again involved into these processes. The handicraft industry grew continuously. Some family workshops transformed into quasi-corporate businesses (von Glahn 2016: 296–306). The organisations in rural areas grew gradually sophisticated while the central government tried to sustain an autarky economy. In the Qing dynasty, the presence of the government was kept minimised. The Qing court tended to let local administrative units be governed by the "case principle" in which public affairs just followed similar precedents (Wen 2021). The government did not want to take active actions. For example, the Qing government did not conduct any land survey and suspended the compilation of yellow registers ("huang-ce") which were the basis of land and labour taxes. In short, the Qing court paid little attention to villages. Then, the gentry class did some work which local bureaucrats failed to do, such as building rural infrastructure and supervising the practice of contracts, etc. As a result, enthusiastic about sustaining commercial networks and providing local public goods, the gentry class acted as quasi-bureaucrats in communities (Long et al. 2018).

In the Ming-Qing era, it was a striking phenomenon that the market economy became gradually mature in the Jiangnan region. Most members

[32] Long (2018) conducted large-scale investigation on land contracts in the Qing dynasty. Tsinghua University collected many paper contracts in ancient China, which were the precious treasure for economic research.

of the California School have asserted that the level of commercial development in the Jiangnan region had reached at least the same level as those contemporary counterparts in Western Europe. Not only the productive forces in the Jiangnan region (Li 2002) but also the economic mechanisms such as business organisations and administrative methods (Wong 1997), developed to a high level. As Pomeranz (2000) suggests, the accidental boom in West Europe was because of its geographical advantages regarding the discovery of the New World and the short distance with coal mines, rather than some unique institutional arrangements or special mechanisms. China also had flexible ownership system, light taxation, a free factor market and emperors' benevolence in the Ming-Qing era. However, most evidence that the California School uses to support the conclusion that Ming-Qing China had also the potential to occupy the zenith of the global economy was not compelling (Ma 2012). In a commercial and industrial era, Ming-Qing China had lost its capacity to adjust to the new demand. The quality of institutions was low, and in some cases essential institutions were absent. The Imperial Mode was not weakened but strengthened. While a rising new economy was demanding different public goods, emperors were satisfied with their traditional role, i.e., subjugating bureaucrats, launching large-scale projects such as hydraulic projects and the disaster relief system, and strengthening the small peasantry. The growth of new economic factors was not so much a harbinger of a new economic era as a fragile continuation of previous trends under the pressure of an inappropriate superstructure. As Elvin (1973) wrote, Ming-Qing China stepped into "quantitative growth and qualitative standstill".

7 Ideological Ossification

As the Imperial Mode became entrenched, its ideological facet also started to become rigidified. Since Zhu Xi's Neo-Confucianism was esteemed in the Southern Song dynasty, it was worshipped during the Yuan, Ming and Qing dynasties. Even Korea and Japan started to be influenced greatly by Zhu Xi's dictums (Masui 2017: 348–350). But Neo-Confucianism started to become dogmatic during the Ming-Qing era. The preaching of Zhu Xi himself became unchangeable doctrines, and Zhu Xi's own understanding of Confucian classics became the standard answers in the state examination system. Furthermore, the content about interpersonal relationships in Neo-Confucianism became ideological tools to repress heterodoxic elements. Bureaucrats must pay homage to the emperorship unconditionally, as sons did to fathers. The part of objective idealism was transformed into a sort of religious cult. Under this circumstance, a new school of Neo-Confucianism emerged, known as "Xin-xue". The main figures, Lu Xiangshan and Wang Yangming, opposed Zhu Xi's dictums in that they emphasised more one's inner power. According to Lu Xiangshan, the knowledge of one's natural surroundings had nothing to do with one's inner conscience. The single source of truth and perfect virtue was one's own mind. One must not cease to examine himself and self-reflect (Li 1971: 223). Compared with Zhu Xi's neo-Confucianism, "Xin-xue" was more a sort of subjective idealism. Although it partially opposed Zhu Xi's dictums, the tension between them was minimal. By emphasising individual compliance with certain metaphysical principles, they succeeded to transform Neo-Confucianism into a sort of state religion.

Mature already in the Song dynasty, the state examination system changed little during the Ming-Qing era. The most significant change happened in the format of examination answers. Since the Ming dynasty, the standard format of answers became highly fixed, known as the eight-legged essay ("ba-gu-wen"). One standard essay consisted of eight parts, including opening, amplification, preliminary exposition, initial argument, central argument, latter argument, final argument and conclusion (Tu 1974). Examinees could not change this structure; otherwise, they must risk losing the qualification to be considered by examiners. Questions on examination papers always came from one sentence or one paragraph in Confucian classics. Examinees must apply the eight-legged essay to answer questions. From the perspective of literature, the eight-legged essay was a beautiful structure for writing an essay for the logic was firm and smooth. However, there are too many rules in this format. Even the number of words in one sentence in a certain position was restricted. The rhyming techniques were also regulated (Suen 2005). Thereafter, creative ideas were restricted and to some degree forbidden (Teele and Ch'en 1962).

Draconian repression characterised literary inquisition ("wen-zi-yu") in the Qing dynasty. Worried about their legitimacy, Manchu rulers implemented stringent supervision on saying, writing and reading of literate people. The answers in state examinations were especially strictly checked. If there were any hints of criticising the Manchu rulers by metaphor, allusion or insinuation, all relevant persons would be prosecuted. Bloody execution ensued. Literary inquisition amounted to 160 or 170 during the Qing dynasty, which was more than the total number of previous dynasties (Zhang 2010). The consequence of the literary inquisition was serious. Many literate people were bodily exterminated. Other people were so terrified that they learned to be careful about their ideas. Orwellian self-censorship prevailed during the Qing dynasty. Political pressure and terrific atmosphere gave rise to cultural ossification. Although the introduction of the state examination system in the Tang-Song era fundamentally eliminated the foundation of aristocracy and lent the central authority a tool to control bureaucracy, it became ossified in the Ming-Qing era, and the practices of the literary inquisition revealed that the Imperial Mode was exerting its negative and reactionary influence upon social spheres.

8 Summary

This chapter focuses on maturation of the Imperial Mode in the Tang-Song era and its ossification in the Ming-Qing era. After the "Age of Disunion", the Imperial Mode was re-established. The central authority was restored, as aristocracy was fundamentally extinguished in China. The bureaucratic system was restored and entrenched, as the state examination system was practised on a large scale to select officials based on merits and performance. Concerning the tension between the central authority and the bureaucratic system, the principal-agent problem was mitigated. From the tenth century, bureaucrats never in effect threatened the central authority until the late Qing dynasty. The private ownership of land was strengthened especially in the Song dynasty. A sophisticated transaction system of land developed so that the small peasantry was further guaranteed. Henceforward, also strengthened by social and cultural norms, the peasant economy became invariably the predominant economic form until the twentieth century (Schurmann 1956). With technical progress, agricultural productivity increased greatly. Simultaneously, new trends, including monetarisation, marketisation and urbanisation, potentially paved the way for a new economy. In the Tang-Song transition, the whole socio-economic system grew mature (Anderson 1974: 531). Fundamentally speaking, in the Song variant, the main characteristics of the Imperial Mode unfolded and presented its mature forms.

The maturity of the Imperial Mode contributed to economic prosperity. It brought the integration of markets and the division of labour. The Smithian growth began to take effect, and the effect went through the whole second millennium, which was especially outstanding in the

Jiangnan region (Kelly 1997; Shiue and Keller 2004). The productive forces of the Imperial Mode were stepping into its climax during the Tang-Song transition. As Karl Marx said, "No social order is ever destroyed before all the productive forces for which it is sufficient have been developed, and new superior relations of production never replace older ones before the material conditions for their existence have matured within the framework of the old society" (Marx 1859: Preface). On the one hand, the productive forces of the Imperial Mode were at its zenith; On the other hand, new forms of productive forces were growing. To some degree, the Tang-Song transition was bearing the possibility of a new society. Changes were so sweeping that Miyazaki (2018) described it as the "Renaissance of the Orient" in the sense that it would have paved the way for modernisation. It would be fair to say that in the Tang-Song transition, the Imperial Mode had made China gain an access to modernisation. The superstructure had released the power of the agricultural economy, and new productive forces would in turn require a correspondingly suitable superstructure. However, unlike the "first economic revolution" in the Warring States period (403–221 BCE) which gave rise to a totally new social structure, the Tang-Song transition did not eventually direct to modernisation.

Reasons why the Tang-Song transition failed in ushering in a new form of society could be traced to the ossification of the Imperial Mode in the Ming-Qing era. At this stage, its inadaptability started to emerge and hence caused heavy costs for economic development. When a vibrant new economy was emerging in China, the government refused to respond to its needs and insisted stubbornly on its traditional role. Emperors in the Ming-Qing era continued to strengthen their authority and weaken the bureaucratic system. As a result, bureaucracy clearly could not threaten the emperorship, but its administrative capacity was also severely undermined. The principal–agent problem was not mitigated but worsened. The fiscal system was kept overly simplistic so that the oversimplicity resulted in topsy-turvy. A plight called a "strong state, weak capacity" inevitably turned out to be detrimental to economic growth (Ma and Rubin 2019). Nevertheless, the government was satisfied with the traditional role, as required in the Imperial Mode, and disregarded the demand of new economic trends. The market economy was rising, and the global trade network was forming. The government ignored those institutional arrangements necessary for qualitative development, such as constitutional constraints on emperorship and legal protection of business, etc.

The growth of the market economy in the Ming-Qing era was to a large degree a quantitative continuation of previous achievements in the Song dynasty. In sum, the ossification of the Imperial Mode, including the political structure and cultural factors, posed negative effects upon new economic trends.

As productive forces had "prepared" to step into a new stage, the superstructure "refused" to quit so that the Imperial Mode started to pose a negative countereffect on the society. Commercial and industrial civilisation requires many prerequisites different from those which agricultural civilisation requires, just as agricultural civilisation engendered different societal structures from those of hunter-gatherer civilisation. The Imperial Mode consists in essence of extractive economic and political institutions, but for new productive forces a synergy of inclusive political and economic institutions is crucial, in which such factors as secure property rights, checks on political power and tolerant cultural norm, etc., can facilitate commercial and industrial economy. The inability of the Ming-Qing governments to develop inclusive institutions was rooted in the basic deficiencies of the imperial system (Acemoglu and Robinson 2019: 225). This theme will be addressed in Chapters 7 and 8 in which a contrast with the West will be also presented.

References

Acemoglu, D., and J.A. Robinson. 2013. *Why Nations Fail: The Origins of Power.* Prosperity and Poverty: Profile Books Ltd.

Acemoglu, D., and J.A. Robinson. 2019. *The Narrow Corridor: States, Societies and the Fate of Liberty*. GB: Viking.

Anderson, Perry. 1974. *Lineages of the Absolutist State*. Verso.

Cheung, Sui-wai. 2008. Construction of the Grand Canal and Improvement in Transportation in Late Imperial China. *Asian Social Science* 4 (6): 11–22.

Deng, Kent Gang. 2012. *China's Political Economy in Modern Times: Changes and Economic Consequences, 1800–2000*. Routledge.

Deng, Kent Gang. 2021. Ultra-low Tax Regime in Imperial China, 1368–1911. LSE Economic History Working Papers, No: 324.

Deng, Xiaonan. 2014. *Invoking Imperial Ancestors' Instructions in Early Northern Song Politics*. SDX Joint Publishing Company (in Chinese).

Elvin, Mark. 1973. *The Pattern of the Chinese Past*. Stanford University Press.

Epstein, Stephan R. 2006. *Freedom and Growth: The Rise of States and Markets in Europe, 1300–1750*. Routledge.

Fairbank, John K., and M. Goldman. 2006. *China: A New History*. The Belknap Press of Harvard University Press.

Finley, Robert. 2010. *The Pilgrim Art: Cultures of Porcelain in World History*. Berkeley: University of California Press.

Fletcher, Joseph. 1979/1980. Turco-Mongolian Monarchie Tradition in the Ottoman Empire. *Harvard Ukrainian Studies* 3–4: 236–251.

Frank, Andre G. 1998. *ReORIENT: Global Economy in the Asian Age*. University of California Press.

Han, Xiao. 2013. Research on Pawning Right of Late Tang and Five Dynasties. *Journal of Henan University of Economics and Law* 01: 165–173 (in Chinese).

He, Ping. 2019. *Currency and Finance of Imperial China*. People's Press (in Chinese).

Huang, Ray. 2015[1974]. *Fiscal Administration during the Ming Dynasty*. SDX Joint Publishing Company (in Chinese).

Huang, Ray. 1981. *1587, a Year of No Significance*. Yale University Press.

Hucker, Charles O. 1966. *The Censorial System of Ming China* Stanford University Press.

Kelly, Morgan. 1997. The Dynamics of Smithian Growth. *Quarterly Journal of Economics* 112 (3): 939–964.

Li, Bozhong. 2002. *Development and Constraint: A Study of Productivity in South China in the Ming and Qing Dynasties*. Taipei: Linking Publishing Company (in Chinese).

Li, Bozhong. 2009. *Agricultural Development in Jiangnan in the Tang Dynasty*. Peking University Press (in Chinese).

Li, Dun J. 1971. *The Ageless Chinese: A History*. New York: Charles Scribner's Sons.

Li, Huarui. 2016. Comparative Research on Scales of Fiscal Dependents Between Song and Ming Dynasties. *Researches in Chinese Economic History* 1: 5–22 (in Chinese).

Liang, Fangzhong. 1980. *Zhongguo Lidai Hukou, Tiandi, Tianfu Tongji* [Statistics on Households, Lands and Land Tax of Chinese Dynasties]. Shanghai Renmin Press (in Chinese).

Liu, William Guanglin. 2015a. *The Chinese Market Economy 1000–1500*. State University of New York Press.

Liu, William Guanglin. 2015b. The Making of a Fiscal State in Song China, 960–1279. *The Economic History Review* 68 (1): 48–78.

Liu, Guanglin, and Qiyun Guan. 2021. Warfare and the Fiscal State during the Tang-Song Transition. *Researches on Chinese Economic History* 2: 39–56 (in Chinese).

Long, Denggao. 2018. *The Evolution of Traditional Institutions of Land Property Rights in China*. Beijing: China Social Sciences Press (in Chinese).

Long, Denggao, Zhenghua Wang, et al. 2018. Traditional Non-government Organization Governance Structure and Institutional Legal Property Right–Focus on the Construction and Management of the Public Facilities in Qing Dynasty. *Economic Research Journal* 10: 175–191 (in Chinese).

Ma, Debin. 2012. Political Institution and Long-run Economic Trajectory: Some Lessons from Two Millennia of Chinese Civilisation. In *Institutions and Comparative Economic Development*, ed. Aoki Masahiko, et al., 78–98. Palgrave Macmillan.

Ma, Debin, and Jared Rubin. 2019. The Paradox of Power: Principal-Agent Problems and Administrative Capacity in Imperial China (and Other Absolutist Regimes). *Journal of Comparative Economics* 47: 277–294.

Marx, Karl. 1970[1859]. *A Contribution to the Critique of Political Economy*. Moscow: Progress Publishers.

Masui, Tsuneo. 2017. *Daqing Diguo* [The Qing Empire], trans. Wenming Cheng. Social Sciences Academic Press (China) (in Chinese).

Miyazaki, Ichisada. 2018. *Dongyang De Jinshi* [*The Modern Age of the Orient: The Renaissance of China*], trans. Xuefeng Zhang et al. CITIC Press Corporation (in Chinese).

Miyazaki, Ichisada. 2020[1956]. *Jiupin Guanrenfa Yanjiu* [Studies on the Nine-Rank System], trans. Dan Wang. The Elephant Press (in Chinese).

Miyazaki, Ichisada. 2020[1987]. *Ke-Ju* [Ke-Ju: The Imperial Examination System], trans. Yunchao Ma. The Elephant Press.

Mote, Frederick W. (ed.). 1988. *The Cambridge History of China*, vol. 7, The Ming Dynasty, 1368–1644. Cambridge University of Press.

Mote, Frederick W. 1994. Chinese Society Under Mongol Rule, 1215–1368. In *The Cambridge History of China*, vol. 6, ed. H. Franke and D.C. Twitchett, 616–664. Cambridge University Press.

Mühlhahn, Klaus. 2019. *Making China Modern: from the great Qing to Xi Jinping*. The Belknap Press of Harvard University Press.

Munro, Donald J. 1988. *Images of Human Nature: A Sung Portrait*. Princeton University Press.

Park, Nacy E. 1997. Corruption in Eighteenth-Century China. *The Journal of Asian Studies* 56 (4): 967–1005.

Pearce, Scott, and Audrey Spiro et al. 2001. *Culture and Power in the Reconstitution of the Chinese Realm, 200–600*. Harvard University Press.

Perkins, Dwight H. 1969. *Agricultural Development in China, 1368–1968*. New York: Aldine Publishing Company.

Pomeranz, Kenneth. 2000. *The Great Divergence: China, Europe, and the Making of the Modern World Economy*. Princeton University Press.

Rüstow, Alexander. 1957. *Ortsbestimmung der Gegenwart. Eine universalgeschichtliche Kulturkritik. Dritter Band, Herrschaft oder Freiheit?* Eugen Rentsch.

Schurmann, H.F. 1956. Traditional Property Concepts in China. *The Far Eastern Quarterly* 15 (4): 507–516.
Shiba, Yoshinobu. 1970. *Commerce and Society in Sung China*. Trans. Mark Elvin: University of Michigan, Centre for Chinese Studies.
Shiue, Carol H., and Wolfgang Keller. 2004. Markets in China and Europe on the Eve of the Industrial Revolution. NBER Working Paper 10778.
Sng, Tuan-Hwee. 2014. Size and Dynastic Decline: The Principal-Agent Problem in Late Imperial China, 1700–1850. *Explorations in Economic History* 54: 107–127.
Sng, Tuan-hwee, and Chiaki Moriguchi. 2014. Asia' Little Divergence: State Capacity in China and Japan Before 1850. *Journal of Economic Growth* 19 (4): 439–470.
Spence, J.D. 1988. *Ts'ao Yin and the K'ang-hsi Emperor: Bondservant and Master*. Yale University Press.
Suen, Hoi K. 2005. The Hidden Cost of Education Fever: Consequences of the Keju-driven Education Fever in Ancient China. In *Education Fever in Korea, Education Fever in the World: Analyses and Policies*, ed. Jong-gak Lee, 299–334, trans. Ki-soo Kim. Seoul: Ha-woo Publishing Co.
Teele, Roy E., and Shou-Yi Ch'en. 1962. Chinese Literature: A Historical Introduction. *Books Abroad* 36 (4): 452.
Tilly, Charles. 1992. *Coercion, Capital, and European States, AD 990–1992*. Blackwell Publishing.
Tu, Ching-I. 1974. The Chinese Examination Essay: Some Literary Considerations. *Monumenta Serica* 31 (1): 393–406.
Twitchett, Denis. 1963. *Financial Administration under the T'ang Dynasty*. Cambridge University Press.
Twitchett, Denis. 1979. Introduction. In *The Cambridge History of China*, ed. D. Twitchett, vol. 3, 1–47. Cambridge University Press.
von Glahn, Richard. 1996. *Fountain of Fortune: Money and Monetary Policy in China, 1000–1700*. University of California Press.
von Glahn, Richard. 2016. *The Economic History of China: From Antiquity to the Nineteenth Century*. Cambridge University Press.
de Vries, Jan, and Ad. van der Woude. 1997. *The First Modern Economy: Success, Failure, and Perseverance of the Dutch Economy, 1500–1815*. Cambridge University Press.
Wang, Yu-Ch'uan. 1936. The Rise of Land Tax and the Fall of Dynasties in Chinese History. *Pacific Affairs*, vol. 9, no. 2, 201–220.
Wang, Yuhua. 2022. *The Rise and Fall of Imperial China: The Social Origins of State Development*. Princeton: Princeton University Press.
Wei, Zhengtong. 2003. *Zhongguo Sixiang Shi* [A History of Chinese Thought]. Shanghai Shudian Press (in Chinese).

Wen, Chunlai. 2021. Case Principle: A Mode of State Governance in Qing Dynasty. *Researches on Chinese Economic History* 2: 57–64 (in Chinese).
Wong, R. Bin. 1997. *China Transformed: Historical Change and the Limits of European Experience*. Cornell University Press.
Xiao, Gongqin. 1983. Lun Yuandai Huangwei Jicheng Wenti [Comments on the Succession Issue of the Crown in the Yuan Dynasty]. *Yuanshi Ji Beifang Minzushi Yanjiu Jikan*[Collected Essays of Research on History of the Yuan dynasty and Northern Races] 7: 22–39 (in Chinese).
You, Biao. 2020. *Zhaosong [Song of the Zhao Family]*. Beijing: Tiandi Press (in Chinese).
Zelin, Madeleine. 1992. *The Magistrate's Tael: Rationalizing Fiscal Reform in Eighteenth-Century Ch'ing China*. University of California Press.
Zhang, Bin. 2010. Literary Inquisition of the Qing Dynasty. *Journal of Northwest Normal University* 5: 55–62 (in Chinese).
Zhao, Dingxin. 2015. *The Confucian-Legalist State: A New Theory of Chinese History*. Oxford University Press.

CHAPTER 6

A Historical Pattern: The Imperial Mode

Although there were many imperial dynasties in Chinese history, a historical pattern and two variants predominated, namely the Imperial Mode and the Han and Song variants. The Imperial Mode was based on sophisticated economic, social and political institutions interacting with each other, and simultaneously they sustained a nuanced equilibrium. While there were some myths in Chinese history which were seemingly beyond the explanatory efficacy of standard economics, economic theories still could produce fruitful consequences when applied to Chinese economic history (Rosenthal and Wong 2011: 1–11). Economists' toolbag can bring theoretical benefits. As presented in Chapter 1, Marxian, Weberian and Institutionalist approaches have offered theories to cope with fundamental structural changes in Chinese economic history. Specifically, the Marxian approach is used to analyse the Imperial Mode as a whole, while the Weberian approach identifies the characteristics of the Imperial Mode and the two variants by the theory of ideal types, and the institutionalist approach is used to analyse internal mechanisms.

Back to the old-fashioned question: how to explain the recurring dynastic cycles in ancient China during the two thousand years? It is of meaning for understanding China's imperial structures (van Leeuwen and van Zanden 2018). The answer is two-sided. On the one hand, an authoritarian unified empire was constantly established in that the

G. H. Jiang, *The Imperial Mode of China*, Palgrave Studies in Economic History, https://doi.org/10.1007/978-3-031-27015-4_6

imperial structure had institutional efficiency when it dealt with challenges that the agricultural economy could encounter. The Imperial Mode consisted of three components: (1) the peasant economy in which small households acted as basic productive units and provided surpluses and labour; (2) the bureaucratic system in which professional officials selected by performance and merits conducted such specific tasks as a collection of economic resources and public good provision; and (3) the central authority in which emperors acted as the autocratic planners and the symbol of unification. As demonstrated in Chapter 2, in ancient China where agricultural activities possessed predominance, public goods, such as national defence, social order and large-scale projects, etc., were essential for subsistence and prosperity. The Imperial Mode tended to reduce transaction costs within the operation of an agricultural society. These mechanisms could achieve public good provision relatively efficiently, and hence they were a bundle of "efficient institutions" that fitted well with the socio-economic demand of the agricultural economy. When this structure was in optimal equilibrium, empires enjoyed prosperity in the agricultural era. Conversely, as long as the dominant economic form was agriculture, this structure had institutional advantages. This was the reason why the Imperial Mode was always repeated time by time after warfare and political fragmentation devastated empires and the imperial system per se temporarily.

On the other hand, however, this structure had its own inborn deficiencies. The three components had inherent tensions with each other. A series of problems, such as the principal–agent problem and moral hazard, could cripple its operation. Taking an analogy, cancer could happen in every part and juncture of the body. Being burdened with too much taxation or corvée labour, peasants and tenants could be exploited bankrupt by corrupt bureaucrats and sybaritic emperors. Peasants always had to encounter excessive exploitation. Moreover, the bureaucratic system could turn inimical to both peasants and emperors. There existed the dual principal–agent problem between bureaucrats, peasants and emperors.[1] Corrupted bureaucrats could conduct opportunistic behaviours to cheat emperors and exploit peasants. Powerful bureaucrats even could turn out to endanger the emperorship. In Chinese history, many royal courts

[1] Ma and Rubin (2019) used different words but similar logic to explain the dual principal-agent problem. In his article, the three components were: emperors, bureaucrats/gentry, and the masses. And there could be multiple principal-agent problem.

were in fact overthrown by powerful bureaucrats or generals. Finally, the central authority per se could undermine the structure. Emperors were given too much power in this structure. For example, ambitious emperors always invested too much in wars against nomadic tribes or the construction of large-scale projects. Despotic emperorship could lead to domestic uprisings and tight control of productive sectors. Consequently, any disequilibrium between the three components could result in the decomposition of the Imperial Mode, which was proven many times in history. Furthermore, when the Imperial Mode decomposed, a dark time often ensue in which social disorder destroyed the economy and the masses' life. The dynastic cycles of imperial China relied on how well the structure was sustained.

According to historical materialism, the superstructure fitted with the base for one time, while it might no longer support further progress of productive forces if productive forces evolve into a higher stage. Under this circumstance, either further progress was strangled, or revolution occurred (Engels 1880). As illustrated in Chapter 2, the establishment of the Imperial Mode was a response to a series of economic changes in the "first economic revolution". The institutions facilitated economic growth by dint of satisfying demand of the agricultural economy. With certain preconditions, the imperial structures were advantageous for the agricultural economy. The outstanding ancient empires, China and Rome, both accomplished agricultural prosperity partly by dint of huge capacity of public good provision (Bang 2008). When new technological and economic changes occurred, new institutions that can accommodate the changes become necessary. In the Han variant, the Imperial Mode strengthened itself and gradually demolished pre-imperial elements (aristocracy and the manorial economy, etc.). In the Song variant, the Imperial Mode became mature and entrenched as the peasant economy predominated and the state examination system destroyed aristocracy fundamentally. However, China failed to cope with new challenges after the Tang-Song transition. The fact that imperial China became a laggard was caused by the inadaptability of the Imperial Mode at the time when Western Europe entered into the industrial and commercial era. This chapter is primarily an anatomy of the Imperial Mode. The imperial system contains institutions that enabled Chinese civilisation to prosper during the agricultural era and inherent drawbacks that caused recurring disintegration.

1 The Peasant Economy

As the base of the Imperial Mode, a vast number of peasants conducted specific productive activities, and hence offered agricultural surpluses, military service and corvée labour. The peasant economy formed the most important productive part of this structure. As presented in Chapters 2 and 3, the peasant economy was established in those Legalist reforms in the Warring States period. Out of thirst for agricultural surpluses, Legalist reformers abolished the well-field system, a kind of communal or public ownership of land, and then established the private ownership of land. The most important characteristics of the Pre-Qin economic reforms was the establishment of the private ownership of land (Chao 1987: 1–3). For peasants, the private ownership of land meant that they could use, manage and sell land according to their own will, with the exclusion of others and exclusion of any control by the government.[2] Under the historical circumstances in the Warring States period, the private ownership of land was efficient in improving agricultural productivity, which was proven by the fact that those states which successfully implemented the private ownership of land enjoyed economic growth and surplus amassment. Shang Yang's reforms in the Qin state expanded the taxation base and enlarged the number of households which were subject to the obligation of military services (Xing 1994). By dint of the military capacity enabled by the private ownership of land, the Qin state succeeded to wipe down other rivals and establish the first imperial dynasty in Chinese history. Thereafter, the private ownership of land as a legal institution, and the peasant economy posed lasting influence.

During the Han dynasty, the peasant economy was temporarily eroded by the rise of the manorial economy. Political power was grasped by aristocratic clans, and their economic capacity expanded in rural areas. As demonstrated before, peasants degraded into magnates' tenants and worked in their private estate ("wu-bao"). Aristocratic clans became potent landlords. The peasant economy disintegrated and was replaced by the estate economy during the "Age of Disunion". It was not restored gradually until the Xiaowendi of the Northern Wei dynasty launched

[2] Here it referred to the legal regulation. Certainly, there were cases in which rich landlords, corrupted bureaucrats and governmental officials thirsty for taxation would intervene into the private ownership of land, especially when the society degraded into disorder.

comprehensive reforms and established the equal-field system.[3] Although in the equal-field system, the ownership of land rested in the hand of the government, farmers gained lifelong tenancy and it formed *de facto* peasantry. Actually, even before the "Age of Disunion", the peasantry operated in a similar way. This restoration of the peasant economy in the Northern Wei dynasty was because it was efficient in agricultural production and essential when a unified empire emerged again. Later, in the Tang dynasty, the equal-field system totally collapsed in that the government could not continue to allocate lands to rising population. Hereafter, the private ownership of land became predominant in following dynasties until the sweeping rural reform in the 1950s. In the Tang and Song dynasties, the specific forms of private ownership of land became gradually mature. In the Song dynasty, the government even occasionally attempted to protect the rights of peasants and tenants against landlords (Perkins 1969: 87). After the Song dynasty, peasants composed almost invariably 70% of the population in China (Anderson 1974: 539). If taking into account half-independent tenants, the number would become bigger.

More importantly, the transaction system of lands grew highly flexible and sophisticated in the direction of protecting the peasant economy since the Song dynasty. It was sustained and strengthened by the complicated system of land transactions. While peasants had the right to sell out their lands, their options were quite diversified. Peasants could choose to "dead-sell ('jue-mai')" the land, which meant that peasants could not buy the land back. This option was understandably unpopular. Alternatively, peasants could keep the right to buy the lands back. Often in transactions peasants kept the right to retrieve the land, namely "live-sale ('huo-mai')". When peasants became tenants of landlords, they still enjoyed relatively sufficient rights to benefit from the cultivation on the cropland. There was even accurate regulation about how to get compensation if tenants made an investment in the cropland which they did not own, such as manure which nurtured the cropland and ploughing work which softened the cropland. Moreover, even the tenancy was often not only lifelong but also hereditary (von Glahn 2016: 324–325). From the Song dynasty to the 1950s, peasants invented a multi-layered and

[3] The equal-field system was supposed to be a sort of the public ownership of lands. However, it distributed lands to landless farmers, and farmers possessed exclusive rights as long as they cultivated on the lands. In fact, the lands were even privately sold. See Twitchett (1963: Chapter 1).

flexible system to deal with transactions of land.[4] The private ownership of land was not only entrenched with guarantee in laws but also flexible economically in transactions. It was characterised by low transaction costs, dividability, replicability and recoverability (Long 2018: Preface). Therefore, the peasant economy was constantly sustained and strengthened.

Henceforward, the private ownership of land became the most fundamental institution in imperial China. Against the conclusion of Chinese Marxian historians, Chinese traditional society was not in the eternal tension between tenants and landlords. The dominant form was petty landowners for most periods in Chinese history (Deng 2020: 60–63). Except in the "Age of Disunion", few large landholdings prevailed.[5] In the eighteenth century, 92% of registered land belonged to individuals, and the rest, i.e., 8% of registered land, belonged to state-owned manors (Feuerwerker 1984). Even in the chaotic periods in 1920s and 1930s, at least 70% of rural households were self-sustained peasants (Tawney 1964: 34). In different regions, while the percentage of lands possessed by peasants varied, the percentage of lands possessed by landlords hardly amounted to 30%. In some southern provinces, lands were in many cases possessed by patriarchal communities, which lowered the percentage of the peasantry (Long 2018: Chapter 5). The communities usually utilised the revenue of communal lands to invest in local public good provision, including schools, roads, irrigation projects and bridges, etc. (Long et al. 2018). It infers that there was no feudal order in China during the two millennia from the Qin to the Qing dynasty. Structural serfdom hardly existed in China, which was the fundamental character of feudalism. Politically independent peasants, who were at least partly economically independent, were typical people in imperial China.

As the economic base of imperial China, the peasant economy had determining effects on the imperial structures. It generated much demand for the superstructure. Although in the peasant economy, the basic unit of production was one household, and the distinguishing characteristic of

[4] Long (2018) provides a thorough analysis about the transaction system of land in ancient China.

[5] Another insignificant exception was the late Ming dynasty when royal members possessed a vast percent of lands over the whole nation. In Ming dynasty, lands of royal members were exempt from taxation, and many royal members conducted large-scale annexation, which seriously harmed the government's fiscal capacity.

peasantry agriculture was self-sufficiency, enormous households were in need of public good provision which could not be achieved by individuals. When the peasant economy became gradually mature, the bureaucratic system and the central authority began to preliminarily form in the Warring States period. Able to largely reduce transaction costs and streamline policymaking process, a centralised despotic regime was efficient in enforcing collective actions. Under the unified central authority, independent regional lordship was abolished; Local governors were appointed by the central authority and supervised rank by rank by higher officials; Officials were selected through a universal base and by the standard of merits and performance; Large-scale projects aiming to provide public goods were accomplished by professional bureaucrats under the command of central planners. It is no exaggeration to say that peasantry was the determinant force to form "traditional China" (Deng, 1999, 2020: 70–72).

Apart from the agricultural sector, other industries, such as the handicraft industry and commerce, never gained equal attention from rulers. They were heterogenous factors for the Imperial Mode. Since the Spring and Autumn period, rulers had been familiar with the standard action to monopolise significant industries, including salt and iron production. In the reform of Guan Zhong in the Qi state, the monopoly on commerce and handicraft industry had been introduced. In following dynasties, the official monopoly was again and again strengthened in order to guarantee the fiscal revenue. For example, Sang Hongyang's reform in the Han dynasty, Liu Yan's in the Tang dynasty and Wang Anshi's in the Song dynasty, expanded the government's intervention within non-agricultural fields. However, rulers never posed positive values upon such productive sectors. Anti-commercialism became one part of standard Confucianism in imperial dynasties (Zhong 2019). Rulers mostly took commerce as a source of fiscal revenues. In order to strengthen the agricultural base of the Imperial Mode, rulers consistently downplayed the value of commerce and other economic sectors. The only exception might be the Song dynasty in which a mercantile state appeared to form.[6] The commercial economy grew constantly in the Jiangnan region since the Song dynasty. Nonetheless, even in the Song dynasty, the nature of extractive institutions never changed (Acemoglu and Robinson 2013: 233–234). In

[6] The Song court started to intentionally use mercantilist ways to support the fiscal system, and Song rulers did not hold much hatred to commerce. See Liu (2015).

the Ming-Qing era, international trade was periodically banned. Though marketisation continued to grow, the governments never valued it. The governments still emphasised the peasant economy as the social base, which was the path dependence of the Imperial Mode.

2 The Bureaucratic System

The peasant economy determined the fundamental nature of the Imperial Mode. The economic demand of the peasant economy entailed a necessary bureaucratic structure. A sufficient number of bureaucrats with professional skills were essential to conduct specific tasks, such as a collection of surpluses and the construction of public projects. For the central authority, bureaucrats must be always subjugated in order to (1) implement central commands so that the demand of the peasant economy could be satisfied; (2) protect emperors' authority so that the whole stability of the imperial structure could be sustained. In order to fulfil the aims, the bureaucratic system in the Imperial Mode had two mechanisms: the static mechanism and the dynamic mechanism. The former concentrates on controlling existing bureaucrats so that the principal–agent problem could be minimised. The latter concentrates on employing new staff in the bureaucratic system. The dynamic mechanism was not stable until the state examination system was introduced in the Sui and Tang dynasties. A smooth operation of the two mechanisms is key to a balance between the central authority and the bureaucratic system.[7]

After Shang Yang's reform established professional bureaucracy, how to rule over the enormous number of bureaucrats became a necessary lesson for following emperors. The static mechanism of the bureaucratic system was related to the dual principal–agent problem. Between the central authority and the bureaucratic system, emperors had to take advantage of diverse strategies to keep bureaucrats' loyalty. Legalist thinkers taught rulers to play various Machiavellian strategies to subjugate bureaucrats. Inside the bureaucratic system, the personnel were always categorised as literati ("wen") and generals ("wu").[8] For literati,

[7] Wang (2022) argues that Chinese rulers faced a fundamental dilemma: a coherent bureaucracy capable of taking collective actions to strengthen the state was also capable of revolting against emperors. The dilemma persisted through most Chinese history.

[8] About the relation between "wen" and "wu", see Fairbank and Goldman (2006: 108–112).

from dynasties to dynasties, there were often ambitious emperors who conducted political reforms to strengthen the emperorship and weaken the prime ministership. In the Western Han dynasty, Emperor Wudi established the "Inner Court" in order to compete for decision-making power with the "Outer Court" consisting of chancellors and ministers. In the Sui and Tang dynasties, the prime ministership was divided into three divisions and six ministries. In the Ming dynasty, the prime ministership was totally abolished. In the second millennium AD, there were few events in which literati could really threaten the emperorship. Another effort of the emperorship was to consistently suppress the power of military generals. In Chinese history, there were often events in which generals launched rebellions or robbed power from emperors. In the Song dynasty, the power of generals was hugely undermined institutionally. After that, no generals could pose real threats to the emperorship until the central court had to give more power to local governors in the late Qing dynasty.

Equally important, the principal–agent problem must be curbed between the bureaucratic system and the peasant economy. It was related mostly with the opportunistic behaviours of local bureaucrats and moral hazard. When the emperorship issued edicts in order to collect agricultural surpluses and use corvée labour, local bureaucrats had relatively arbitrary power considering in ancient times the technical methods constrained the surveillance from the central court. A typical problem was that local bureaucrats always collected more taxes than the central court asked for. They always had incentives to exploit more, because bureaucrats did not need to bear the full of costs of extra taxation. In the Ming dynasty, Hongwu used very draconian laws to punish those corrupted bureaucrats. But the fiscal system was flawed in the Ming and Qing dynasties so that extra taxation became gradually a norm. The Emperor Yongzheng of Qing once launched a comprehensive and courageous reform to change *status quo* but he eventually failed.[9] This is just an illustration of the principal–agent problem existing in local entities. Actually, the principal–agent problem existed throughout the history of the Imperial Mode. Sometimes it could be so serious that farmers' rebellions erupted. Failing to address this problem, the imperial structure could be periled.

[9] Zelin (1992) hast a thorough monograph about this reform. It is a vivid illustration about the principal–agent problem between the bureaucratic system and the small peasantry.

The second mechanism is the dynamic mechanism, i.e., how to employ more staff in the bureaucratic system. In the Imperial Mode, emperors tried to select bureaucrats from a universal base, rather than aristocratic families (Deng 2020: 72–76). Also, selection and promotion should be based on merits and capacity, namely meritocracy. Legalist reforms laid the foundation of such a selection and promotion system in the Pre-Qin period. In the Han dynasty, emperors used a sort of recommendation system to select new bureaucrats, which gradually resulted in the restoration of aristocracy. In the "Age of Disunion", the nine-rank system completely decomposed the bureaucratic system in that it selected bureaucrats from aristocratic clans, which led to the situation that officialdom was monopolised by them. Later in the Sui and Tang dynasties, the adoption of the state examination system ("ke-ju") restored the bureaucratic system. In terms of legal regulations, the scale of bureaucratic selection was hence extended to the masses of the empire. Gradually, in order to sustain fairness in examinations, ministries devised a series of measures, such as covering names and other information of examinees, transcribing by third parties and submitting good papers to be judged by emperors themselves, etc.[10] After becoming qualified scholars in classics, they gained success in examinations and thus were selected and promoted. In the Song dynasty, the state examination system became very mature and efficient. Hereafter, the state examination system became the necessary choice for empires' rulers.

Bureaucrats selected from examinations were equipped with expertise in their respective fields and appointed by the central authority, bureaucrats were distributed in every department to conduct specific tasks. They became the pillars of the Imperial Mode. Balazs (1967: 16–17) had a vivid description:

> All mediating and administrative functions were carried out by the scholar officials. They prepared the calendar, they organised transport and exchange, they supervised the construction of roads, canals, dikes, and dams; they were in charge of all public works, especially those aimed at forestalling droughts and floods; they built up reserves against famine, and encouraged every kind of irrigation project. They social role was at one

[10] The biggest advancement was made in the Northern Song dynasty. In order to get fairness, top officials devised many solutions to forbid cheating. See Miyazaki (1987: 21–29).

> and the same time that of architect, engineer, teacher, administrator, and ruler. Yet these "managers" before their time were firmly against any form of specialisation. There was only one profession they recognised: that of governing.

As the medium within, the bureaucratic system practised emperors' top-down commands and collected resources from peasants on a bottom-up basis. They conducted specific work of public good provision, such as public projects, launching fighting against external enemies, etc. However, the dual principal–agent problem afflicted the relation between the emperorship, the bureaucracy and the peasantry. The emperorship must be always wary of such problems. The bureaucratic system must be sustained properly through the static mechanism and the dynamic mechanism. Any failure to cope with those issues would result in the decomposition of the Imperial Mode. However, on the other hand, it must be recognised that China's bureaucracy was distantly different from the civil bureaucracy which developed in the early modern time in England and was acknowledged as a key catalyst for British modernisation (Cornell et al. 2020). Indeed, China developed professional bureaucracy far earlier than Western Europe, but China's bureaucracy became a pillar of extractive institutions. Its conservativeness and dependence on the central authority determined that its "advantages" would become inimical towards changes which demobilised the imperial structures.

3 The Central Authority

Sitting at the top of the hierarchy, the central authority acted as a despotic planner. In the Imperial Mode, the central authority referred to individuals consisting of emperors and top ministers[11] and simultaneously an abstract central planner. In institutionalism, an abstract authority always has such characteristics (Bolton and Dewatripont 2012: 343):

[11] Whether top ministers belong to the central authority relied on specific conditions. Acting as close advisors, ministers loyal to emperors and practise their will certainly belonged to the central authority. However, sometimes top ministers could grow disloyal and even launched coup against emperors themselves. Under this circumstance, it was described as a failure for emperors to control the bureaucratic system. Thus, the boundary of the central authority was malleable.

1. Authority is a supervisor's power to initiate projects and direct subordinates to take certain actions.
2. Authority also involves the concomitant power to exact obedience.
3. Authority is the power to ratify and approve actions in a predetermined area of competency.
4. Authority also involves the manager's duty to monitor subordinates and her ability to reward them for good performance.

With the aforementioned characters, an authority has advantages for certain projects. As interpreted before, a couple of problems discouraged public good provision which was paramount for agricultural activities of peasants. By dint of lowering transaction costs within the negotiation and enforcement, etc., the central authority could better achieve public good provision, including social order, public projects and national defence; The central planner could overcome such problems as the free-rider problem and externality. In one word, the institutions driven by a central authority were the efficient choice for agricultural growth. In the Chinese case, in the Warring States period, all political units transformed into despotic structures, which epitomised the success of a process in which a decentralised feudal system was replaced by a centralised imperial system (Deng 2020: 71).

Within the relation between the central authority and the subordinate bureaucratic system, the central authority still practised draconian and cunning stratagem to control those bureaucrats. As illustrated in Chapter 3, Legalism taught top rulers to take advantage of tricks and surreptitious conspirations in order to keep subordinates loyal and feared. In Chinese history, the principal–agent problem was partly mitigated by rulers' Legalist tactics. For example, inspired by Legalist predecessors and instructed by his chancellor Li Si, the Emperor of Qin the First succeeded to make bureaucrats and commoners feared of his draconian personality and relentless ruling style. In subsequent dynasties, how to "domesticate" bureaucrats became an essential lesson for emperors-to-be. Taking advantage of the mixture of official honours, rewards and penalties, rulers drove bureaucrats to operate as they pleased. The temperamental carrot-and-stick policies kept bureaucrats tamed. If failing to do so, the central authority would be threatened by the power of bureaucrats. In fact, several dynasties were overthrown due to their failure to control powerful bureaucrats. Besides keeping bureaucrats loyal, emperors had to curb the venality of bureaucrats in case of casing unsatisfaction of the masses. It always happened that emperors had to strike a compromise between bureaucrats' loyalty and integrity.

Another important aspect of the central authority in the Imperial Mode was its cultural authority. It is widely known that in ancient China there was no role for churches or bishops. The similar function of the clergy was burdened by scholarly officials and the literate gentry class. In the very early time of Chinese civilisation, kingship replaced theocracy to rule over the spiritual world (Gao 2018: Chapter 1). Political rulers held the final words over ideological issues. Rulers utilised cultural issues to keep commoners obedient. Formally, rulers chose Confucianism as the official ideology after the Western Han dynasty in that "the virtues preached by Confucianism were exactly suited to the new hierarchical state: respect, humility, docility, obedience, submission, and subordination to elders and betters" (Balazs 1967: 18). In following dynasties, Confucianism was canonised as the content of the state examination system, and during the Song dynasty, Neo-Confucianism was completely transformed into an ideological tool to serve for the central authority. In addition, the central authority launched cultural projects to keep commoners awed, such as those awe-inspiring palaces, complicated and nuanced rituals and grand mausoleums, etc. Without exception, emperors in every dynasty launched grand projects in order to epitomise their superiority and greatness. Although those projects were in part launched because of their individual hedonism, one consideration was apparently essential—to buttress legitimacy of empires. For example, the Emperor of Qin the First ordered to construct grand palaces and his magnificent mausoleum near the capital, led a huge entourage on his conquered territory and conducted holy rituals in coastal locations, in order to announce his superiority (Zhao 2015: 263–269). A sort of charismatic leadership was instilled into the Chinese emperorship.[12]

However, apart from benefits that a central authority could bring, it was always plagued by two typical problems—the succession problem and the effect of emperors' personality—which often dragged a dynasty into a horrible trap. The principle of the bloodline was established very early in the succession issue in Chinese history. The father-son sequence started in the Xia dynasty in documentation, although some historians think it is just a myth. In the Shang dynasty, the most popular situation was that

[12] About Weber's analysis on "Charismatic leadership", see Bendix (1977: Chapter 10) and Kalberg (2021: 75).

the order of succession followed agnatic seniority (Chao 1982: 11–19), like what the royal family is doing in Saudi Arab today. After the Western Zhou dynasty, the primogeniture was formally established in monarchy as a fundamental principle. However, few successions were accomplished peacefully in Chinese history. Sons competed with each other at the price that losers would be banished or executed, or emperors selected one candidate and silenced others. Before the Emperor Yongzheng of Qing, there was no reliable way to guarantee a peaceful succession.[13] And imperial succession always triggered lots of political troubles, especially at the time when an old emperor was yet to die. It became a highly unstable moment. The succession per se could stir up political intrigues and instability. We can also observe that the competition and conspiracy among the eligible always caused huge social costs in every dynasty. The process of succession could bring tremendous dangers to the imperial structures.

More importantly, emperors' personalities could be enlarged through the imperial structure. Holding unassailable power, emperors could easily expose their personalities within the decision-making process. On the one hand, hedonic, naïve and incompetent emperors often failed to exert their influence upon the bureaucratic system. Corruption could worsen in local entities. Top bureaucrats could also grow more powerful so that the authority of the emperorship would be undermined. As a result, the principal–agent problem became much more severe. For example, the demise of the Western Han and the Eastern Han dynasties was in a large degree because of the extremely waning influence of adolescent emperors. On the other hand, courageous emperors could always pursue individual "prestige" and vanity so the peasant economy was posed with a heavy burden. Their will was achieved at the price of ordinary people's pain. For instance, the military expeditions of Emperor Wudi of Han forced Sang Hongyang to take radical fiscal measures in order to satisfy fiscal needs.

[13] In the Qing dynasty, Emperor Yongzheng devised a secret candidacy system. If he made the decision, he wrote the successor's name on two scrolls. Then, he placed one scroll in a sealed box and stored that box behind the stele in the Qianqing Palace. He kept the other scroll probably in his bedroom or just hid it. After his death, top officials would take out the two scrolls and compare the scroll in the box with the scroll which he had kept. If the names on the two scrolls were identical, the person whose name was on the paper would be the new emperor. This system had its advantages because candidates could to some degree avoid fierce competition and the emperor could change his mind at any time secretly. Princes must forever act properly until the old emperor died. See: *Draft History of the Qing*, Volume 9, the Annal of Shizong. (《清史稿》, 卷九, 世宗本纪).

The expensive tours of many emperors were another specific reflection. Emperor Qianlong of Qing spent astronomical fortunes on his extravagant tours in the Jiangnan region.[14] Although Confucianism taught emperors to be frugal and charitable, at most times it was just an illusionary imagination for the emperorship. Both bureaucrats and peasants could fall victims of emperors' inappropriate personality.

4 The Equilibrium

The Imperial Mode consists of three components: the peasant economy as the foundation, the bureaucratic system as the channel that transferred resources and services, and the central authority as the head. Considering their amount of population, hierarchical status and the roles that they played, three components formed a subtle and fundamentally stable pyramid structure. Enormous self-sustained peasants conducted agricultural activities and then provided surpluses, including taxation, military service and corvée labour. The bureaucratic system conducted specific tasks, including collecting surpluses from peasants and implementing assignments distributed from the head. The central authority, which was always emperors and their close ministers, conducted central planning in order to provide public goods. The three components acted as both independent entities and interconnecting organs. As individual components, they played their respective roles as producers, implementers and planners. As a whole, the structure achieved a stable equilibrium under the normal and balanced circumstance.

The most outstanding characteristic of this equilibrium was that it could achieve public good provision efficiently in the agricultural economy. By reducing transaction costs, it could construct large-scale projects and guarantee social order, which were paramount for agricultural activities but could not be achieved by millions of individuals. Thus, when the equilibrium of the Imperial Mode was kept, a dynasty could usually enjoy material prosperity. Furthermore, one huge advantage of the structure was its scale, i.e., its ability to unify transregional economies and achieve the division of labour. It happened frequently in Chinese history that the disaster relief system could work relatively well because the territory of China was big enough to simultaneously take advantage

[14] Zhang (2012: Chapter 5) has an interesting and vivid description about the vanity of the Emperor Qianlong.

of resources in different regions. The most significant examples were the granary system and the pandemic governance (Leung 2020). The Imperial Mode was able to internalise the negative externality through political actions. Furthermore, due to enforced unification and then the extended scale of markets, the division of labour could facilitate economic growth anticipated by the Smithian growth model. Smithian growth usually refers to the effects of increased market (population) size and interaction rates for socio-economic organisation, the diversity of tasks and tools, and productivity (for both individuals and groups) (Ortman and Lobo 2020). Simply put, according to the Smithian growth model, growth could be driven by increased specialisation caused by the geographical expansion of markets (Kelly 1997). In imperial China, economic growth was encouraged by the unification of markets and the increasing homogeneity of the population.

Especially in the Song dynasty and the Ming-Qing era, Smithian growth was quite apparent. In the Song dynasty, economic evolution was spurred by a large, unified and commercialised network, leading to the "Heyday of the Jiangnan Economy".[15] The economic acceleration was partly caused by the creation of a national waterway network (Kelly 1997). Later the trend continued to hasten so that some Chinese Marxian historians recognised the economic growth in the Ming dynasty as "Sprouts of Capitalism".[16] As Wong (1997: 17–20) wrote, "the dynamics of Smithian expansion were present throughout"; market expansion, commercialisation, and the maturity of factor markets were salient in the Yangtze Delta but hardly limited to this vast area. Capable of sustaining political unification and a relatively homogeneous society, the Imperial Mode was conducive to Smithian growth. Public good provisions, such as a national transportation system and the standardisation of nationwide business,[17] functioned positively for the economy. It is not exaggerated

[15] There is consensus among economic historians that in the Song dynasty, the Jiangnan region experienced accelerating economic growth and hence it epitomised the "heyday of the Jiangnan Economy". See von Glahn (2016: 255–294).

[16] This idea was quite influential in the field of Chinese economic history. However, it has been more and more debated in that the quantitative growth in the Yangtze Delta was inherently different from capitalist growth. More historians do not endorse this idea any longer. See Ma (2004).

[17] Though, the standardisation of measurements cannot be overrated in that many scholars have observed that many measurement units, such monetary units, weight, etc., were not in fact the same across different regions.

that in terms of cost minimisation and utility maximisation, the Imperial Mode achieved economies of scale (Deng 2020: 68–70). It had the ability to facilitate agricultural economy and Smithian growth.

However, as illustrated before, there were many difficulties in achieving the equilibrium. The equilibrium relied on a benign interaction between the peasant economy, the bureaucratic system and the central authority, which can only be sustained subtly. Petty peasants were harassed by corrupted bureaucrats and their illegal activities, but there was basically no bottom-up supervisory mechanism to control bureaucrats' behaviours. Inherent tensions between the central authority and the bureaucratic system were never completely eliminated. The worsening principal–agent relations between them led to weakening fiscal capacity and then languishment of public good provision.[18] Social chaos and rebellions always ensued when central powers failed to restrain the opportunistic behaviours of local bureaucrats (Hao 2016). During the final years of every dynasty, rulers were always jeopardised by fiscal crises, and peasants were always harmed by natural disasters or man-made disasters. The dynastic cycles in Chinese history, i.e., the incessant to-and-fro of imperial courts, could be explained well by the malfunction of the Imperial Mode. The malfunction could be categorised into three types: ① firstly, extracting too many surpluses but failing to provide sufficient public goods, the corrupted central authority and bureaucrats stirred up peasants' rebellions; ② secondly, the central authority failed to control the bureaucratic system so that powerful bureaucrats or warlords overthrew the central court; ③ thirdly, the central authority and the bureaucratic system could

[18] Wang (2022) argues that Chinese emperors always faced a dilemma: to strengthen emperors' power tends to weaken bureaucratic elites and thus reduce their administrative capacity, thus leading to declining state capacity, but strong elite groups which can improve administrative capacity tend to weaken emperorship and threaten the survival of emperors. The negative association between emperorship and state capacity is tested by quantitative historical records. The result is partly confirmed by frequency of coup d'état and the homicide rate of emperors before the Song dynasty. In Table 1 it is also clear that before the Song dynasty the direct reason for a dynasty's downfall was mostly disloyal bureaucrats and their coup d'état.

Table 1 Major dynasties and reasons of dynastic cycles

Major dynasty	*Primary reason for its downfall*	*Subsidiary reason(s)*
Qin, 221–206 BCE	①	
Western Han, 206 BCE–8 AD	②	①
Eastern Han, 25–220	②	①
Wei, 220–266	②	
Western Jin, 266–316	②	③
The North–South Disunion	The Zenith of ②	
Sui, 589–618	①	②
Tang, 618–907	②	①
Song (Northern and Southern), 960–1279	③	
Yuan, 1279–1368	①	
Ming, 1368–1644	①	③
Qing, 1644–1912	②	①③

not cope with external threats, which were always northern nomadic invasions.[19] In many cases, they were intertwined together to undermine the imperial structure.

Table 1 lists how the dynastic cycles happened in Chinese history. The disequilibrium of the Imperial Mode resulted in recurring downfall and re-establishment, but even its equilibrium had weaknesses. It had the motivation to curb other heterogenous elements incompatible with the imperial structure, in order to sustain a balance of the structure itself. In the dawn of modern economic growth in Western Europe, three institutions were essential: decentralised administration; protected ownership from authoritarian robbery; markets full of competition (Deng 2020: 144). The combination of the three institutions made huge contributions to economic booms during commercial and industrial periods. But in imperial China, none of such institutions had the chance to survive. Merchants were always depressed because merchants could do little contribution but endanger political stability. Monopoly on profitable business and industry was a lasting institutional choice

[19] The third type is more complex in that it involves some exogenous and causal factors. Northern nomadic invasions played an influential role in Chinese dynastic cycles. In the nineteenth century, the threats from occidental nations acted in a sense like that.

for political rulers. The interests of merchants could be sacrificed as long as rulers pleased. The ownership of commercial property was never protected. The Qing government discretionarily confiscated merchants' assets, for example, when the West had already started to industrialise (Acemoglu and Robinson 2013: 233). As Eric Jones (1990) pointed out, the economy "failed to move from extensive to intensive growth because its political structure did not establish a legal basis for sufficient new economic activity outside agriculture".

After its maturity in the Song dynasty, the Imperial Mode had a very strong inclination to sustain its own constancy. Path dependence impacted rulers and drove them to sustain the structure beneficial for their interests. The Imperial Mode which once facilitated socio-economic progress began to become reactionary. From the perspective of the Imperial Mode, many policies in history could be understood. For example, in the Ming and Qing dynasty, the government forcefully implemented the sea-ban policy ("hai-jin") in order to exclude the influence of overseas trade and external culture. Although scholars debated about its true efficacy,[20] the policy was obviously an effort to clamp down on the power of businessmen and hence to repress heterogenous elements which could be detrimental to the stability of the empire. Like other absolutist rules in other parts of Eurasia, China rejected political pluralism and potential technological innovations which might bring about demobilising effects. The Imperial Mode had already become a monolithic obstacle for modern economic growth.[21]

5 Summary

This chapter presents the structure and the equilibrium of the Imperial Mode. The framework is useful to understand the pathway of Chinese long-run economic changes. From the Han variant to the Song variant, evolutions occurred in political, social and economic spheres. Since the

[20] The California School believes that even in Ming and Qing, China was still deeply involved inside the international trade network and benefited much from international trade. Frank (1998) suggests that the huge trade surplus of China was the sound evidence.

[21] For an in-depth presentation of how the Imperial Mode hindered modern economic growth in Ming-Qing China, see Chapter 8.

imperial structure got ripe in the Song variant, involutions replaced evolutions as the economy stopped growing qualitatively but expanded quantitatively, and political despotism developed rapidly.[22] Applying conceptual tools of Marxian, Weberian and Institutionalist approaches to Chinese history brings new insights. Different from neoclassical economics, they offer suitable tools to analyse premodern and non-western societies. In addition, a part of the legitimacy lies in the inability of existing theories to explain authentic reasons for the Great Divergence (Hao 2016). Scholars attributed the backwardness of China to the absence of conditions paramount for economic growth in Europe. However, scholarship is divided on which conditions were absent and which conditions were paramount. For instance, the absence of secure property rights was once the focus. However, the real situation in ancient China was much more complicated than simply suggesting that secure property rights did not exist. As Chinese scholars demonstrate, the ownership system of land was much more sophisticated and even more mature than we imagined before (Long 2018; Deng 2020). Specific discussion will be presented in Chapters 7 and 8.

As illustrated in Fig. 1, the Imperial Mode was the most fundamental character in the era of agricultural economy. It consisted of complex institutions. Public good provision is important for agricultural activities, including national defence, social order, large-scale public projects, etc. The Imperial Mode could create a larger market so that Smithian growth could happen. It could overcome some weaknesses, including the free-rider problem and problems of externality. Transaction costs could be reduced. Thus, this structure had advantages in the era of the agricultural economy. In other words, it had institutional efficiency. That is the reason why China enjoyed lasting superiority over other civilisations in the first thousand years after the Qin dynasty. It also contributed to the unparalleled durability of China's dynastic cycles, although domestic rebellions which toppled regimes often occurred. The characters of the Imperial Mode may answer the research question: what is the reason for

[22] Here I express my gratitude to Wolfgang Schluchter who teaches me to pay attention to the subtle difference between evolutions and involutions in Chinese history. Weberian sociology provides key insights to conduct anatomy into a civilisation. Evolutions occur when institutional innovations emerge and replace older institutions; Involutions occur when innovations disappear, and existing institutions only develop on a self-sustaining level or expand marginally.

the Chinese recurring dynastic cycles? On the one hand, the structure had institutional efficiency to facilitate agricultural growth. Its incessant restoration was demanded by the agricultural base. On the other hand, the equilibrium of the structure was subtly sustained. Intense tensions existed between the three components. The stability of the structure was easily jeopardised by malfunction between components. A couple of problems surrounded the structure, including the principal–agent problem which resulted extensively in functional inefficiency. Furthermore, the structure per se is a conservative mechanism aiming to sustain stability and thus repel any factors that might lead to structural change.

The next question follows: why did China become much less developed in the late imperial periods while Western Europe began the modern economic boom? Although it has been a very popular issue among economic historians, it might not be the best form of this kind of question. It reflected the "Eurocentric" inclination, which is not good for understanding Chinese economic history (Huang 1991). Scholars tend to think that without external threats from occidental nations, the political and economic institutions of imperial China might persist and evolve automatically (Deng 2020: Preface). Mao Zedong, the founder of the People's Republic of China, also announced once that without foreign

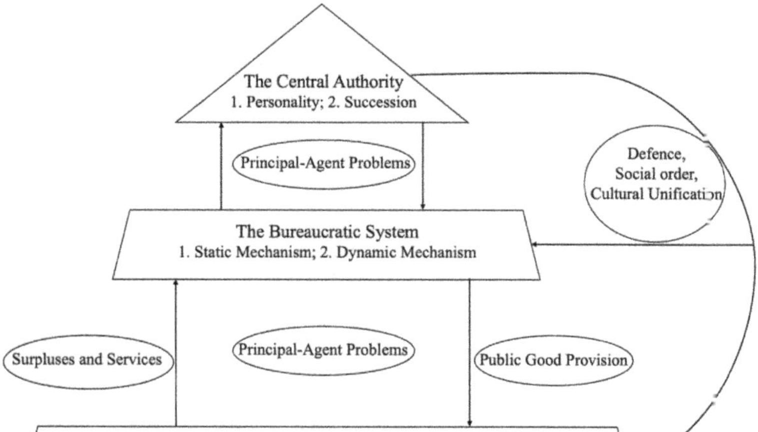

Fig. 1 The cognitive map of the imperial mode

disruptions, capitalism would have grown naturally (Mao 1965: 309). A better form of this question is: why China failed to achieve modern economic growth. Driven by creative destruction which technological innovations bring about, modern economy is mainly commercialised and industrialised economy. It entailed more complex settings of institutions than those of the agricultural economy.

Marxian theories believe in the rights of a higher civilisation over a lower one (Kołakowski 2005: 286). The development of productive forces and relations of production forced history to develop from one stage to next stage. The predominant productive forces would bear seeds which would grow to eventually break down current relations of production. The Imperial Mode was a successful response to the rising agricultural economy in the Pre-Qin period. It also made it possible that the agricultural economy reached its peak and the commercial economy emerged in the Tang-Song transition. However, while some elements closely relating with commercial economy rose, they were repressed later by the Imperial Mode. In other words, the Imperial Mode restrained the structural changes when a new economic form should have emerged. In Marxian language, the Imperial Mode had made the economic base develop to its peak in the era of agricultural economy, and new productive forces began to emerge, but the superstructure refused to exit, even though its inadaptability had been exposed. Presumably, without the connection with the occidental world in the nineteenth century, a probable consequence was that China would have struggled with the Imperial Mode and a new economy would also have come finally out of the ruins of the Imperial Mode, although no one would have known the exact timing. Eventually, whether actively or passively, those actors in the theatre of history acted as "the unconscious tool of history" (Marx 1853).

References

Acemoglu, D., and J.A. Robinson. 2013. *Why Nations Fail: The Origins of Power, Prosperity and Poverty*. Profile Books Ltd.

Anderson, Perry. 1974. *Lineages of the Absolutist State*. Verso.

Balazs, Etienne. 1967. *Chinese Civilization and Bureaucracy*. Trans. H.M. Wright. Yale University Press.

Bang, Peter Fibiger. 2008. *The Roman Bazaar: A Comparative Study of Trade and Markets in a Tributary Empire*. Cambridge University Press.

Bendix, Reinhard. 1977. *Max Weber: An Intellectual Portrait*. University of California Press.

Bolton, Patrick, and Mathias Dewatripont. 2012. Authority in Organizations: A Survey. In *The Handbook of Organizational Economics*, ed. R. Gibbons, and J. Roberts. Princeton University Press.

Chao, Kang. 1987. *Man and Land in Chinese History: An Economic Analysis*. Taipei: Southern Materials Centre Inc.

Chao, Lin. 1982. *The Socio-Political Systems of the Shang Dynasty*. Taipei: Institute of the Three Principles of the People Academia Sinica Monograph Series.

Cornell, A., C.H. Knutsen, and J. Teorell. 2020. Bureaucracy and Growth. *Comparative Political Studies* 53 (14): 2246–2282.

Deng, Kent Gang. 1999. *The Premodern Chinese Economy: Structural Equilibrium and Capitalist Sterility*. Routledge.

Deng, Kent G. 2020[2002]. *The Premodern Chinese Economy: Structural Equilibrium and Capitalist Sterility*. Trans. Yucong Ru et al. Zhejiang University Press (in Chinese).

Engels, Friedrich. 2018[1880]. Socialism: Utopian and Scientific. marxists.org, Marxist Internet Archive, retrieved 6 September 2018.

Fairbank, John K. and M. Goldman. 2006. *China: A New History*. The Belknap Press of Harvard University Press.

Feuerwerker, Albert. 1984. The State and the Economy in Late Imperial China. *Theory and Society* 13: 297–326.

Frank, Andre G. 1998. *ReORIENT: Global Economy in the Asian Age*. University of California Press.

Gao, Xuchen. 2018. *Between Theocracy and Kingship*. China Social Sciences Press (in Chinese).

Hao, Yu. 2016. A Political Economic Framework in Late Imperial China. *Journal of Translation from Foreign Literature of Economics* 3: 49–67 (in Chinese).

Huang, Philip C. C. 1991. The Paradigmatic Crisis in Chinese Studies: Paradoxes in Social and Economic History. *Modern China* 17 (3): 299–341.

Jones, Eric Lionel. 1990. The Real Question about China: Why was the Song Economic Achievement Not Repeated? *Australian Economic History Review* 2: 5–22.

Kalberg, Stephen. 2021. *Max Weber's Sociology of Civilizations: A Reconstruction*. Routledge.

Kelly, Morgan. 1997. The Dynamics of Smithian Growth. *Quarterly Journal of Economics* 112 (3): 939–964.

Kołakowski, Leszek. 2005. *Main Currents of Marxism: The Founders, the Golden Age and the Breakdown*. Trans. P.S. Falla. W. W. Norton & Company.

Leung, Angela Ki Che. 2020. Chinese State and Society in Epidemic Governance: A Historical Perspective. *Centaurus* 62: 257–262.

Liu, William Guanglin. 2015. *The Chinese Market Economy 1000–1500*. State University of New York Press.

Long, Denggao. 2018. *The Evolution of Traditional Institutions of Land Property Rights in China*. Beijing: China Social Sciences Press (in Chinese).

Long, Denggao, Zhenghua Wang, et al. 2018. Traditional Non-government Organization Governance Structure and Institutional Legal Property Right—Focus on the Construction and Management of the Public Facilities in Qing Dynasty. *Economic Research Journal* 10: 175–191 (in Chinese).

Ma, Debin. 2004. Growth, Institutions and Knowledge: A Review and Reflection on the Historiography of 18th–20th Century China. *Australian Economic History Review* 44 (3): 259–277.

Ma, Debin, and Jared Rubin. 2019. The Paradox of Power: Principal-agent Problems and Administrative Capacity in Imperial China (and Other Absolutist Regimes). *Journal of Comparative Economics* 47: 277–294.

Mao, Zedong. 1965. *Selected Works of Mao Tse-Tung*, vol. 2. Oxford: Pergamon Press.

Marx, Karl. 1853. The British Rule in India, in the *New-York Daily Tribune*, June 25, 1853. Online Archive.

Miyazaki, Ichisada. 2020[1987]. *Ke-Ju* [Ke-Ju: The Imperial Examination System]. Trans. Ma, Yunchao. The Elephant Press.

Ortman, Scott and José Lobo. 2020. Smithian Growth in a Nonindustrial Society. *Science Advances* 6(25), [eaba5694].

Perkins, Dwight H. 1969. *Agricultural Development in China, 1368–1968*. New York: Aldine Publishing Company.

Rosenthal, Jean-Laurent and R. Bin Wong. 2011. *Before and Beyond Divergence: The Politics of Economic Change in China and Europe*. Harvard University Press.

Tawney, R.H. 1964. *Life and Labour in China*. New York: Octagon Books.

Twitchett, Denis. 1963. *Financial Administration under the T'ang Dynasty*. Cambridge University Press.

van Leeuwen, Bas and Jan Luiten van Zanden. 2018. China as a Nation. In *China in the Local and Global Economy*, eds. Steven Brakman and Charles van Marrewijk et al. 1–17. London: Routledge.

von Glahn, Richard. 2016. *The Economic History of China: From Antiquity to the Nineteenth Century*. Cambridge University Press.

Wang, Yuhua. 2022. *The Rise and Fall of Imperial China: The Social Origins of State Development*. Princeton University Press.

Wong, R. Bin. 1997. *China Transformed: Historical Change and the Limits of European Experience*. Cornell University Press.

Xing, Tie. 1994. The Issues of Partible Inheritance among Sons in Ancient China. *Journal of Chinese History Studies* 4: 3–15.

Zelin, Madeleine. 1992. *The Magistrate's Tael: Rationalizing Fiscal Reform in Eighteenth-Century Ch'ing China*. University of California Press.

Zhang, Hongjie. 2012. *Jie'e De Shengshi* [The Hungary Prosperity: The Gains and Loss in the Qianlong Era]. Hunan People's Publishing Company (in Chinese).

Zhao, Dingxin. 2015. *The Confucian-Legalist State: A New Theory of Chinese History*. Oxford University Press.

Zhong, Xiangcai. 2019. Dong Zhongshu and Confucian Economic Thought as State Ideology in the Western Han Dynasty. In *The Political Economy of the Han Dynasty and its Legacy*, eds. Cheng Lin and Terry Peach et al. 51–66.

CHAPTER 7

The Great Divergence I: The West

The lasting material prosperity in ancient China has impressed many economic historians. In Maddison's research, China possessed a leading position in the world economy in ancient times (Maddison 1998). However, its backwardness in the industrial era was equally striking, especially in comparison with the progress made by Western Europe since the Industrial Revolution. From the sixteenth century, Western Europe, especially the Netherlands and Great Britain, revolutionised its economic and social institutions. While Ming-Qing China was slowing to an economic standstill in terms of qualitative development, Western Europe was changing its commercial organisations, relations between the government and society, status of citizens and lifestyles of individuals. A comprehensive economic revolution was happening between the sixteenth and nineteenth centuries. The result of such a revolution is that Western Europe enjoys its economic leadership until today. How Western Europe rose above ancient China in the early modern time is still relevant and can help us understand the world today (Ferguson 2011). This chapter will present the trajectories of the first two modern economies, the Netherlands and Great Britain, and the driving forces behind their spectacular economic growth and social changes.

In the sixteenth and seventeenth centuries, the Netherlands became the first economic hegemon in international trade. While restricted by geographical conditions and a fragile international status, it still thrived

G. H. Jiang, *The Imperial Mode of China*, Palgrave Studies in Economic History, https://doi.org/10.1007/978-3-031-27015-4_7

in the commercial era. Great independence which merchants enjoyed gave them huge freedom to do business domestically and overseas. They devised diverse strategies to do business and to invest in commercial activities, such as partnerships and stock companies, etc. Influenced by Calvinism, the Dutch gradually developed a different lifestyle, including more independence for women and later marriage age.[1] The government also participated actively in the protection of the interests of those chartered companies. Similar mechanisms also happened in Great Britain. But Great Britain walked further than the Dutch. For centuries, British people marched step by step to limit the power of the monarchy. With the Magna Carta, the sovereign was declared to be subject to the rule of law, and therefore the liberties held by "freemen" were guaranteed. Up until the Glorious Revolution, the monarchy was seriously weakened, and the parliament held the greatest political power. The authoritarian monarchy ended in Great Britain. From that point, it began to rise to become a lasting economic hegemon over the global economy. More importantly, the scientific revolution led to more progress in technological spheres. One common feature of the stories of the Netherlands and Great Britain is that there was compatibility between the interests of the state apparatus and the interests of a new rising economy. The governments in the Netherlands and Great Britain provided not only constitutional protection for merchants' property but also real encouragement for commercial expansion over the globe.

Contemporarily, most regimes in Eurasia were centralising their power in the early modern time (Goldstone 2008: 119). However, the extent, nature and especially the consequence of such centralisation were not identical. Increasing capacity of states in Western Europe provided important support for economic growth, while strengthening despotism in Ming-Qing China did not provide similar support for economic growth but harmed the potential of the commercial economy. Chinese emperors concentrated on sustaining the stability of imperial mechanisms which were no longer suitable to the new mode of production. The bureaucratic system was strictly controlled, and the peasant economy was enthusiastically encouraged. Merchants' businesses were still treated as a strange part

[1] Coates (2017) has a fascinating book about the unique characters of the Dutch. While it is easy reading, the theme which it reflects is never superficial. It traces the cultural and historical source of those characters.

of this structure. Local bureaucrats did not pay attention to the protection of merchants' property or try to support commerce. Merchants were scared by arbitrary taxation and frequent exploitation by local offices. While the state apparatus of Ming-Qing China was powerful and repressive, its governance was of bad quality. To trace back how Western Europe succeeded sheds light not only on why traditional China failed to modernise, but also on how underdeveloped economies could learn from the lessons of Europe's success.

1 "The First Modern Economy": The Netherlands

The Netherlands could hardly be described as an advantageous place to develop agriculture. Many areas are full of marshes, and many regions are even under sea level. The territory gradually expanded towards the ocean since the Dutch constructed engineering projects to drain water and dredge waterways. Agriculture, the handicraft industry, and commerce slowly developed in regions such as Holland, Utrecht and Leiden. In the fight against Spain, the provinces of the Netherlands gradually joined together and gained political independence. In 1581 the Dutch Republic was founded, and it epitomised the beginning of the "Golden Age" in Dutch history. Different from other contemporary European countries, the Dutch Republic chose republican institutions rather than a monarchy. Refusing foreign monarchs and electing their own, Dutch people organised the government by themselves.[2] This led to a positive result: the Dutch merchants were free from the exploitation of an absolutist monarchy, and the republican government elected mainly by merchants behaved actively to serve those merchants' interests.

The trade network of the Dutch merchants expanded quickly during the "Golden Age". One important reason lay in those novel organisations which the Dutch applied to business. As international trade boomed after the discovery of the New World, the geographical position of the Netherlands became a great advantage, and the Dutch succeeded in catching this opportunity. They invested on a large scale in international business. More efficient institutions to collect investment were invented. Among them, partnerships and stock companies were the most outstanding.

[2] About formation of the Dutch Republic, see Wielenga (2020: Chapter 1).

In 1602, the first securities market was established by the Dutch East India Company in Amsterdam (Braudel 1982: 100–106). Partnerships were also widely practised in naval expeditions. More transparent and efficient property right systems were thus established. Such innovations succeeded at lowering transaction costs in commercial activities (Wielenga 2020: 39). Simultaneously, banking practices became more widespread, and new financial methods further drove commercial activities up. Not only individual merchants but also the republican government popularly utilised financial methods to support their activities (de Vries and van der Woude 1997: 91–147). More capital was leveraged in commercial and public affairs. With innovative commercial organisations, the Dutch quickly became a hegemon in international trade.

An equally important catalyst came from the support of the republican government. The republican government acted not only as a protector of merchants' property rights, but also as an "agitator" for commercial expansion. In 1602 the republican government granted the Dutch East India Company the permission to monopolise Asian trade. It soon became one of the most successful commercial entities in the international trade network. In 1621 the Dutch West India Company was also founded, which was less successful. With private companies and large chartered companies, Dutch merchants succeeded in establishing commercial ports in Africa, America, South Asia, Southeast Asia and East Asia.[3] One outstanding ingredient within the story of the economic rise of the Netherlands is the role of its republican government. Unlike other absolutist regimes which took measures to strengthen control over merchants and commerce, the republican government of the Netherlands became a strong propeller for commercial expansion.

In addition to expanding commerce and trade networks, the economy was experiencing other changes in the Netherlands. It was quite striking that the commercialisation of the agricultural sector and urbanisation were developing quickly during the "Golden Age". Population growth propelled urbanisation and hence increased the demand for agricultural products. The construction of a dense network of canals, particularly in Holland, Utrecht, Friesland and Groningen, further integrated the

[3] Phillips et al. have offered a fascinating story about the rise of those chartered companies in the early modern time. They argue that those chartered companies contributed to the rise of company-states which left enormous institutional legacies to the modern world. See Phillips and Sharman (2020: 22–65).

domestic market (Wielenga 2020: 82–85). A salient example of agricultural commercialisation was the widespread cultivation of tulips. Initially an exquisite item for the rich, within just decades the tulip became a mass-produced product that triggered Tulip Mania and even caused an economic crisis in the 1630s. The commercialised mode of production further fostered mechanisation. In line with commercially prosperous zones, mechanised handicraft industries congregated in the middle and south of the Netherlands. Several commercialised and preliminarily industrialised cities then developed.

Within the process of urbanisation and commercialisation, a slow but profound change was also contributing to the rise of a new economy. The opinions of the Dutch about lifestyle and family experienced distinctive changes during the sixteenth century. As van Zanden wrote, the rights of women in marriage and family life became increasingly respected in the Netherlands because of religious factors and cultural concepts, which led to positive changes in the labour market and capital markets. As more and more women stepped into marriage at a later age, the labour market became more energetic. People began to save for themselves rather than devoting themselves fully to family life, thus making the capital market more vibrant (van Zanden 2009: 101–141). The changes in the marriage pattern and attitudes towards individual life began to form a new kind of citizenship. More equal status between men and women in marriage, greater independence of individual members of a family, and unprecedented concepts about life[4] completely changed how citizens regarded the relationship between individuals and society. During the "Golden Age", independence, individuality and rationality became indispensable characters of the Dutch, thus giving rise to a rationalised, commercialised and urbanised society in which we find familiar activities (de Vries and van der Woude 1997: 165–172).

During the "Golden Age", the Netherlands experienced unparalleled economic progress. All those aforementioned factors propelled the Dutch economy to an eye-catching position in global economic history. The first republican government in world history protected people from the potential exploitation of an absolutist monarchy. Innovative commercial organisations lowered transaction costs and hence helped Dutch merchants to thrive all over the globe. The interests of the government

[4] See Sect. 4.

stood in line with the interests of those merchants and hence the rising economic forms. The government's actions not only set merchants free from the anxiety of despotic exploitation, but also encouraged merchants to gain more profits from thriving international trade. Equally importantly, the cultural conceptions in the Netherlands completely changed the lifestyles of ordinary people, transforming the Dutch into modern citizens and "freemen" in both the political and economic meaning (Prak 2018: Chapter 7). Rationally behaving "freemen" instilled energy in the labour market and the capital market, which made possible a benign economic cycle. All these factors formed an interrelated and self-propelling dynamic to support economic growth. Although the economic hegemony of the Netherlands during the "Golden Age" partly benefited from "the relative weakness of the surrounding countries" (Wielenga 2020: 91), efficient institutions were more determinant mechanisms. As North and Thomas (1973: 145) wrote,

> The Dutch during the early modern period became the economic leaders of Europe. Their centrally located geographical position and their government, which established an efficient economic organisation, account for this growth. ... In point of fact the Netherlands was the first country to achieve sustained economic growth in the sense we have defined it. Moreover, far from declining, they continue to thrive and achieve higher levels of per capita income in successive decades and even centuries. It is simply that the centre of the economic stage shifts to England.

2 The Constitutional Path of Great Britain

From the late seventeenth century, the centre of economic leadership transferred from the Netherlands to Great Britain. A pivotal event was the landing of King William III on England in 1688, which seemingly epitomised the transition of hegemony from the Netherlands to Great Britain. Between the eighteenth and the nineteenth century, Great Britain saw unparalleled economic growth and achieved industrialisation. The scale of commercial expansion was far larger than what the Dutch had achieved in the seventeenth century. Great Britain intentionally established colonies all over the globe, offering support for primitive accumulation and further economic growth. More importantly, the Industrial Revolution swept through eighteenth-century England, laying the foundation for a modern society. How did Great Britain achieve so much so quickly? To understand this, we must look back earlier history when the constitutional path started.

The characteristics of British institutions can be traced back to the Magna Carta, one of the most significant legal documents in British history. In the early thirteenth century, King John of England launched a series of wars against European rivals but confronted embarrassing failures and hence lost many overseas territories. Under this circumstance, King John raised taxes on nobility in order to support his wars (Carpenter 1990: 7). Before that, his arbitrary decisions in politics had already irritated many barons in England (Turner 2009: 139). The tension between the king and barons was increasing, especially after King John was defeated by the French. Barons launched rebellions and forced the king to accept a draft proposing political reforms. In 1215, the formal text was issued, namely the Magna Carta. Although the text was brief and was further revised,[5] the Magna carta became the cornerstone of British institutions. It confirmed a few significant rules: the protection of nobility from the kings' arbitrary judgement, and the limitation of the monarchy to collect taxes. Through the Magna Carta, the monarchy was subject to laws, and to some degree, kings had to rule via the representation of nobility. Subsequently, the property rights of barons were protected from the exploitation of absolutist monarchs and human rights were to be respected unconditionally. The Magna Carta laid a primary foundation for Anglo-Saxon liberalism.

Nonetheless, the Magna Carta did not spark the British economy immediately. But it prepared a key institutional condition. Great Britain had to wait until the advent of a commercial and industrial era to fully realise their economic promise. In the first half of the seventeenth century, the tension between the king and the parliament grew so intense again that a civil war erupted (Cust 2007: 244–358). Subsequently the armies of King Charles I were defeated, and the king was sentenced to execution. Thereafter Great Britain witnessed the rule of Cromwell and the restoration of the monarchy, but political stability was hardly guaranteed. What also irritated nobility was that the monarchs always tried to revive the Catholic church rather than to maintain Protestantism. In 1688 barons

[5] The Magna Carta was reissued with some corrections in 1216, 1217 and 1225.

launched a coup d'état to overthrown James II. His daughter and son-in-law were invited from the Netherlands to claim the throne of England. In 1689 the Bill of Rights was passed. These political events marked the formal end of any possibility to implement an absolute monarchy in Great Britain. In particular, with the passage of the Bill of Rights, the power of the monarchy was hugely restricted: the monarch could not suspend laws, levy taxes, make royal appointments or maintain a standing army during peacetime without the parliament's permission. The Glorious Revolution in 1688 and the following Bill of Rights in 1689 guaranteed a parliamentary government and the security of law and liberties (Dekrey 2008), which made it one of the high points of British history.

How did these political events influence economic growth in the early modern time in Great Britain? As economic historians have elaborated, the protection of property rights and human rights provided huge support for commercial expansion in both the British Isles and overseas trade. Like the Netherlands, England attempted to establish a property rights system and similar institutional arrangements (North and Thomas 1973: 146). The property rights of merchants and ordinary people were respected. A legalised environment is also one of the most profound public services which the government should provide in the commercial and industrial era. Moreover, the British parliament not only provided protection for property rights but also took aggressive actions in international trade like the Netherlands had.[6] The government encouraged the overseas expansion of British business and chartered a few large companies to establish overseas colonies, among which the British East India Company was the most famous.[7] Again, we see that the interests of the government stood in line with the interests of the rising economic forms. When institutions matched with the demand of the developing economy, transaction costs of economic activities could be lowered, and hence economic growth could be encouraged.

At the latest by the eighteenth century, Great Britain had developed a different pathway from the rest of the world. It was characterised by

[6] For example, the Queen Elizabeth I encouraged underhandedly pirating behaviours to rivals. Several British kings competed for market shares intentionally through all kinds of tactics.

[7] The British East India Company even obtained the power to establish armies in colonies. It provided civil governance in colonies, too. From every aspect, it was more like a sovereign government in colonies, rather than a commercial company.

constitutionalism and the common law. Constitutionalism guaranteed the security of absolute property rights and prevented the discretionary power of despots to extract resources, which was vital for the adolescent bourgeoisie and mercantile class to arise. The evolution (rather than revolution) of constitutionalism in the British Isles had a long history: from the Norman Conquest in 1066, to the Glorious Revolution in 1688, and to later history. Another element is the common law. While Continental Europe widely accepted the Roman law after the Renaissance, the British Isles established a unique legal system, namely the common law. As Maitland (1909: 21–22) wrote, the common law in Great Britain was unique and gave British people the legislative basis to guarantee democracy, while Roman Law tended to result in despotism on the continent. Since its juridical decisions are based on preceding cases, customs and so-called conscience, rather than statutory codes, the common law tends to respect individual liberties and limit public powers much better than civil law which was adopted mainly in Continental Europe at the time. In retrospect, as Hayek (1973: 94) asserted, countries that adopted common law had a better economic performance. The societal environment in which inclusive institutions prevailed formed firmly in Great Britain. It provided sufficient incentives to do business, to invest in profitable activities, and thus create an economic boom.

However, commercial expansion did not give Great Britain enough power to outcompete its rivals by much. Many institutional arrangements in Great Britain existed already in the Netherlands. Even the quantity and quality of the labour force experienced similar processes. In Great Britain, in the seventeenth and eighteenth centuries, wages in the labour market tended to increase gradually but constantly. The literacy rate and the standard of living of British workers were rising at remarkable speed. The labour market in the Netherlands and Great Britain possessed some similar characteristics (Allen 2009: 25–56). What really made Great Britain the absolute hegemon in the global economy was the Industrial Revolution which started in the second half of the eighteenth century. Previous handicraft industries swiftly utilised new mechanical methods. The steam engine, devised and innovated by James Watt, was put into production on a large scale. The textile industry became mechanised very fast. Other industries also experienced gradual but sweeping industrialisation. Without a doubt, the Industrial Revolution transformed the British economy from an economy consisting of modest agriculture, thriving commerce and primary mechanisation into a new industrialised economy.

Arguably, the Industrial Revolution eventually shaped most of the characteristics which modern society possesses. Nevertheless, this was the final of a series of fundamental changes which Western Europe had experienced in the prior several centuries.

3 Inclusive Institutions

After reviewing the brief history of the Netherlands and Great Britain in these centuries, we now delve into how those phenomena were related to these countries' economic successes. Apparently, a certain common institutional inclusiveness existed and grew stronger in both the Netherlands and Great Britain. In the Netherlands, the United Provinces achieved self-governance without monarchy, and later the constitutional monarchy of the Orange Dynasty was kept very weak politically. In Great Britain, the monarchy had been largely restricted by some aristocratic assembly, and after the Glorious Revolution, the constitutional monarchy was formally established. Although democracy was definitely not erected by modern standards,[8] political evolution led to increasingly inclusive institutions.[9] Such inclusiveness paved the way for more promising economic possibilities (Acemoglu et al. 2001). As Acemoglu and Robinson (2013: 74–75) assert,

> Inclusive institutions, ... are those that allow and encourage participation by the great mass of people in economic activities that make best use of their talents and skills and that enable individuals to make the choices they wish. To be inclusive, economic institutions must feature secure private property, an unbiased system of law, and a provision of public services that provides a level playing field in which people can exchange and contract; it also must permit the entry of new businesses and allow people to choose their careers. ... Inclusive economic institutions foster economic activity, productivity growth, and economic prosperity. (Acemoglu and Robinson 2013: 74–75)

[8] Acemoglu and Robinson (2019: Chapter 6) traced the evolutionary path of British and European political systems since the early medieval period. They suggest that European democratic path has its roots in tribal tradition and feudalism.

[9] Political institutions have a determining role on the formation of economic institutions. Whether economic institutions can be conducive to economic growth stem from political arrangements and historical path-dependence. See Acemoglu and Robinson (2013: Chapter 1).

What inclusive institutions were there? This issue has been densely explored, especially by neo-institutionalists. More secure property rights were central (North 1981; North and Thomas 1973). In north-western Europe, a strong sense of individual property rights grew. Originally the baronial class resisted the discretionary power of kings and put limits on their ability to extract financial resources. Later the protection of property rights prevailed everywhere. Ordinary people, especially the merchant class and entrepreneurs, enjoyed absolute property rights in the Anglo-Saxon style. After the early modern time, monarchical power was hugely restricted by the constitution and the assembly. As North and Weingast (1989) put it, the principle that Britons would not be taxed unless they agreed to be, embodied in Articles 4 of the Declaration of Rights of 1689, should be regarded as an important step towards constraining one form of rent-seeking which was inimical to "productive" activities. Subsequently, entrepreneurship grew smoothly without worry about unexpected confiscation or arbitrary plundering by the monarchy. It created a benign result: more investment in physical and human capital, and then higher efficiency in their use. An outstanding example is the patent system. When property rights were more securely protected by political institutions, patents could be utilised more broadly and efficiently. As exemplified in Great Britain in the eighteenth century and in the United States in the nineteenth century, an optimised patent system allowed for spearheads in both scientific and technological innovations. As Acemoglu and Robinson (2013: 33) described the relationship between democratic institutions and patents,

> Just as the United States in the nineteenth century was more democratic politically than almost any other nation in the world at the time, it was also more democratic than others when it came to innovation. This was critical to its path to becoming the most economically innovative nation in the world.

Logically and empirically, inclusive institutions fostered economic energy in the markets. More secure property rights encouraged economic growth (Knack and Keefer 1995; Hall and Jones 1999). More democratic political institutions where political power was distributed among a larger mass of people could efficiently curb corruption, and artificial monopoly which are inimical to economic growth (Mauro 1995; Acemoglu and Robinson 2013: 35–36). Furthermore, legal systems functioned to protect human rights and various fundamental rights of those in "productive" activities. While the legal systems in England and continental Europe differed in whether or how much they accepted Roman law, they shared certain universal values in judicial exercises, such as a conception of natural law. Especially the English Revolution paved the way for a series of laws that proved conducive to mercantile and industrial activities.[10] Democratisation of political power and improvements to legal systems induced ever-higher inclusiveness. Inclusive institutions abolished any vested privileges of the monarchy and lowered the entry cost of markets for most people, thus fostering incentives for the majority to work and invest. For example, commercial activities could be operated more widely and more efficiently by people with mercenary incentives. There is little wonder that the gradual evolution towards inclusive institutions in the West set the preconditions for a commercial boom and industrial prosperity.

These inclusive institutions were accompanied by the higher efficiency of the state apparatus in Western Europe. There was a seeming paradox before the Industrial Revolution that European governments were strengthening their centralised political power. Feudal aristocracy and the manorial system were increasingly administered by central governments, resulting in the rise of the "absolutist state" in Western Europe (Anderson 1974: Chapter 1). The central government collected more financial resources and broke up regional barriers. For example, the British government extracted taxes more efficiently (He 2013; Ma and Rubin 2019), and in continental Europe local barons and lords were subjugated by the central authority. To some degree, central rulers possessed more quasi-despotic power than before. However, the centralisation of political power was measured chronologically in a relative degree. Due to the restriction of various democratic institutions, the power of the central authority was never absolutist. While state capacity increased, European monarchs never got rid of those restrictions created by parliament-like organisations. As Perry Anderson (1974: 51) put it,

> No Absolutist State could ever dispose at will of the liberty or landed property of the nobility itself, or the bourgeoisie, in the fashion of the Asian tyrannies coeval with them. Nor did they ever achieve any complete

[10] The seventeenth-century English revolution changed the Anglo-Saxon legal system in which Calvinism played a pivotal role. See Berman (2003: Chapter 11).

> administrative centralisation or juridical unification; corporative particularisms and regional heterogeneities inherited from the medieval epoch marked the Ancien Régime down to their ultimate overthrow. Absolute monarchy in the West was thus, in fact, always doubly limited: by the persistence of traditional political bodies below it and the presence of an overarching moral law above it. In other words, the sway of Absolutism ultimately operated within the necessary bounds of the class whose interests it secured.

Subsequently, the strengthening state apparatus was deeply imprinted by the interests of the bourgeois class. In the eyes of theorists of state capacity, with expanding economic resources, states succeeded in providing public services more efficiently. International competition between European states necessitated increasing state capacity (Tilly 1992; Epstein 2006). In return, this increase helped states become more competitive. The Netherlands as the first, and Great Britain later, took advantage of national strength to conduct colonial expansion. Especially Great Britain conducted primitive accumulation for mercantile and industrial activities through colonialism all over the globe. Inclusive institutions guaranteed that the strengthening state had high compatibility with the interests of the mercantile and manufacturing classes which would play a crucial role in the upcoming capitalist era. This compatibility is again best illustrated by Anderson (1974: 40–41):

> The apparent paradox of Absolutism in Western Europe was that it fundamentally represented an apparatus for the protection of aristocratic property and privileges, yet at the same time the means whereby this protection was promoted could *simultaneously* ensure the basic interests of the nascent mercantile and manufacturing classes. The Absolutist State increasingly centralised political power and worked towards more uniform legal systems: … It did away with a large number of internal barriers to trade, and sponsored external tariffs against foreign competitors. … It provided lucrative if risky investments in public finance for usury capital. … It mobilised rural property by seizure of ecclesiastical lands. … It offered rentier sinecures in the bureaucracy. … It sponsored colonial enterprises and trading companies. … In other words, it accomplished certain partial functions in the primitive accumulation necessary for the eventual triumph of the capitalist mode of production itself. … There was, however, always a potential field of compatibility at this stage between the nature and programme of the Absolutist State and the operations of mercantile and manufacturing capital.

4 The Behavioural Revolution

While scholars were always searching for materialist causes for the rise of Western Europe, some found influences from conceptual and spiritual changes which led to the revolution of human behaviours. Although Marxian theories emphasised the determining role of materialist power, they never refused the counter-power of the superstructure.[11] Concepts, minds and knowledge nurtured people's behavioural patterns, and in sequence, these patterns affected how the economy was organised and driven in a society. It was precisely a behavioural revolution happening in the late medieval period in Western Europe that paved the way for the rise of new socio-economic institutions, i.e., the capitalist mode of production. During the revolution, people's attitudes towards themselves, their families and their relations with society were gradually but drastically changed. Curiously, the subsequent behavioural patterns appeared highly compatible with a capitalist economy. The individual's emancipation from traditionalism, as Max Weber defined, supported the growth of capitalism.

According to Max Weber, a modern capitalist society was not made possible by economic impulse alone (Weber 1927: 355). The association between Calvinism and capitalism was quite intimate. After the Reformation movement since the late medieval period, Protestantism, including Calvinism and other branches, thrived in Western Europe and England. Weber especially probed into the role of Calvinism. Against the supremacy of the Catholic Church, Calvinism rejected the possibility of salvation in the afterlife since God had predestined everything. Therefore, there was no value in buying so-called "indulgences" or ingratiating oneself with the clergy by means of venal methods. Instead, people should act as a tool of God's will and perform positively in society. On the one hand, Calvinism got rid of those supernatural tenets which might render people saved. On the other hand, Calvinism urged people to live industriously and honestly. To be distinguished is the external signal of being predeterminately chosen by God. This atmosphere fostered "the rational spirit, the rationalisation of the conduct of life in general, and a rationalistic economic ethic" (Weber 1927: 354). In the past, people were controlled

[11] Nonetheless, Marxist theories were always criticised due to their light attitudes towards the role of non-materialist factors. On the one hand, Marx and Engels did not explore this theme enough. See Hollander (2011: 332–334). On the other hand, Marx did not establish a convincing dynamic relation between the economic base and the superstructure. See Hintze (1931: 232).

by traditional lifestyles and worldviews dictated by the Church. During the widespread flow of the Reformation movement, people became "disenchanted" and started to view society from a rational standpoint. Rationalism contributed to pragmatic ethic and world-oriented individuals, thus facilitating economic activities (Kalberg 2021: Chapter 18; Schluchter 1979). Weber believed that this disenchantment was somewhat beneficial for the prevalence of experimental science and ascribed it to the uniqueness of Western culture (Bendix 1977: 67–70).

Alongside the rationalisation of the conduct of life in Western Europe, the influence of "economic knowledge" was also omnipresent. Economic change in all periods depends on what people believe and know, and how those beliefs affect their economic behaviour (Mokyr 2009: Introduction). Schefold (2018) highlighted the significance of the propagation of knowledge about economic life on economic growth and increases in welfare. From the late medieval period to the nineteenth century, some economic knowledge that was considered inaccessible before gradually made its way to ordinary people. For example, people had more intellectual power to calculate interest rates and engaged in usury more conveniently.[12] This economisation of human minds was facilitated by intellectual progress happening in Western Europe, including the efforts of philosophers and economists. As a consequence, people could take advantage of more effective intellectual tools and more rationalised minds to act, which lowered the transaction costs of commercial activities and therefore prepared conditions for economic expansion. Being prepared intellectually to conduct more aggressive mercantile activities and emancipated from traditional ethical and moral codes, European people possessed advantages in the process of capitalisation.

Another emancipating factor came from the rise of the "European Marriage Pattern" (EMP). Hajnal (1965, 1982) proposed the EMP to describe demographic changes happening in north-western Europe after the late medieval period. Fostered partly by the Black Death that killed a large part of the population (Belich 2022), such a unique pattern was characterised by a later marriage age, the increasing popularity of nuclear families and more participation of women in the labour market, etc. This contrasted with the relatively restricted status of women in the medieval

[12] In fact, the usury was judged as evil and illegal in the Middle Age by the Church. However, the usury was never eliminated. See Fang (2019: Chapter 5).

period.[13] Women grew more independent both personally and financially. Such a pattern of emancipation first emerged in the Low Countries and in England. In the EMP, women gradually gained a bigger voice in household affairs, including inheritance. More importantly, women gained more independence through stepping into the labour market (van Zanden et al. 2019: 25–37). The EMP exerted a gradual but profound influence on economic growth. It changed demographic patterns and facilitated the labour market, thus leading to the increased accumulation of human capital (van Zanden et al. 2019: Chapter 3). Simultaneously, with women earning more revenues, they saved more, and the capital market gained more reserves to be reinvested (van Zanden et al. 2019: Chapter 4). In a word, marketisation and the rise of capitalism were energised by the emergence of the EMP.[14]

On the other hand, the uniqueness of such a pattern in the late medieval period was played down by Macfarlane (1978). According to Macfarlane, the drastic change of personal attitudes towards household life and property inheritance, which appeared very individualistic, was not real as described by Karl Marx, Max Weber and other historians who argued that before the late medieval period, in Western Europe, the typical peasantry society prevailed not just in the continent but also in England. A peasant society was characterised by common ignorance of individual claims for property rights, which at the time was predominantly land, the immobility of the labour force, and the widespread existence of stem households, etc.[15] They proposed that since the late medieval period, the typical peasantry society in England disintegrated, and the English society transformed into an individualistic one. Macfarlane insisted that English individualism had already been prevalent at least by the twelfth century, according to archives that he collected. While Macfarlane dismantled the classical framework that historians and sociologists had built, in fact, he proved the belief that the West, or at least England, had possessed some institutional elements that other civilisations

[13] About features of the traditional family pattern, see Shorter (1976: Chapters 1 and 2).

[14] The reason why the EMP emerged at that time in those regions was another issue which is weakly related here, so I spare it. For reference, see van Zanden et al. (2019: Chapter 1) and Walter and Schofield (1989).

[15] For Marx's analysis on the peasant society, see Duggett (1975).

did not. It was also those elements rooted deeply in minds of the English that established preconditions for an economic revolution.

Simultaneously, the changes in the labour market were intertwined with the "Industrious Revolution".[16] According to Jan de Vries, before the Industrial Revolution, the consumptive behaviour of households in Western Europe started to change. Stimulated by desire, people purchased more and more variegated consumer goods, including various imported foods and other luxuries (de Vries 2008: Chapter 1). In order to satisfy the demand for greater consumption, people had to obtain more revenues. Subsequently, men lengthened their working hours, and more women and children stepped into the labour market. The increasing revenues fostered a virtuous cycle between consumption and production. A mutually sustaining and strengthening process was activated. Later, this trajectory disseminated out of Western Europe and took root in North America. Gradually, this pattern of consumption and increased working became typical of industrialising societies.

In Robert Allen's work (2009), the cause of the Industrial Revolution lies in the fact that labour wages were increasing in England. After the black death in the Middle Ages, the population decreased dramatically in Western Europe. Subsequently, the wage rate (both nominal and real) in the labour market increased with equally remarkable speed and stabilised at a relatively high level. Under these conditions, a novel method to utilise more capital and less labour would be worth considering for engineers and entrepreneurs. Simultaneously, Allen investigated the price of heating materials in England, including wood and coal. He found that the price of wood increased a lot compared with the relatively cheap cost of coal, as more houses and apartments installed heating stoves. These phenomena, cheap coal and the desire to seek a mechanism that could utilise less labour, coincided (Allen 2009: 25–56). Consequently, the engine of the Industrial Revolution was started.

A behavioural revolution swept Western Europe prior to the Industrial Revolution. It involved the rationalisation of the conduct of life,

[16] This term, the "Industrious Revolution", was originally proposed by a Japanese scholar, Akira Hayami, in 1967. It was used to describe the labour-intensive technologies in Tokugawa Japan. Later, de Vries (2008) expanded this term. While its usage by de Vries has some merits, this term is contested by economic historians. See Liu and Zhang (2012).

the increasing availability of economic knowledge, and changing attitudes towards individualism in household and individual life which led to energised factor markets. People began to treat society, household life, and relations between individuals and the world in a novel way. People started to unchain themselves from the bonds of churches and traditional family life, living a more independent life. In other words, millions of "freemen" in the modern definition began to emerge. The ideas and knowledge that they held completely transformed the labour market and the ways in which people organised their economy. All of this not only propelled a commercial boom before the Industrial Revolution, but also prepared the conditions for the final advent of an industrialised capitalist economy. Apart from the macro-level institutional changes, people's individual ways of life and what was happening in their brains were having profound effects on the building of the "industrialised world" (Mokyr 2009: Introduction). As Robert Lucas (2002: 17–18) said,

> For income growth to occur in a society, a large fraction of people must experience changes in the possible lives they imagine for themselves and their children, and these new visions of possible futures must have enough force to lead them to change the way they behave, the number of children they have, and the hopes they invest in these children: the way they allocate their time. In the words of a more recent title of Naipaul's, economic development requires "a million mutinies".

5 The Enlightenment Movement and Scientific Revolution

The economic background of the Industrial Revolution is worth enormous attention. An equally important question lies in how the engineering innovations of the time were viable, among which the steam engine was the most outstanding. As Joel Mokyr (2002: 29) wrote, "the Industrial Revolution's timing was determined by intellectual developments, and that the true key to the timing of the Industrial Revolution has to be sought in the scientific revolution of the seventeenth century and the Enlightenment movement of the eighteenth century. The key to the Industrial Revolution was technology, and technology is knowledge". Human rights were respected in a relatively tolerant political atmosphere, which contributed to the intellectual activities of free thinkers and theorists. The philosophical methodology brought by the Enlightenment movement in England and Scotland enabled interactions between theories and experiments, which gave rise to the eventual emergence of those engineering innovations.

From the late seventeenth and eighteenth centuries, Western Europe experienced a sweeping boom of modern philosophy and science. During the Enlightenment movement in France, Descartes' rationalism became widespread and dominated intellectual life on the European continent. For proponents of rationalism, the reason is the chief source and test of knowledge. Accordingly, thinkers should take reason as the criterion for the truth and deduce the truth starting from reason. Mathematics and logic are the cornerstones on which we can understand the world. Phenomena in the world can be deduced. Under rationalism, experiments in laboratories became less popular among intellectuals (Goldstone 2008: 154). As a result, continental thinkers gradually immersed themselves in constructing grand and abstract philosophical and scientific systems. In contrast, in the British Isles, thinkers enthusiastically supported empiricism which emphasises experience and positivistic reasoning. Key figures in the Enlightenment movement there, including Francis Bacon, John Locke, and David Hume, established dominance of empiricism. According to empiricism, knowledge comes only or primarily from sensory experience (Psillos and Curd 2010: 129–138). Therefore, empiricism emphasises evidence, particularly evidence discovered in experiments. While there were philosophical debates between British empiricists and continental rationalists,[17] empiricism continued to guide intellectual life in the British Isles. Consequently, scientific exploration thrived in the British Isles. The experiments organised by the Royal Society greatly facilitated people's understanding of physics and engineering. When Isaac Newton took the presidency of the Royal Society, scientific activities reached a peak. Experiments were systematically organised. New instruments were devised to support experiments and engineering innovations. The jobs of artisans and theorists were closely connected. Just as importantly, in the eighteenth century, enthusiasm for empiricism gradually steeped in universities. The most modernised empirical curriculum of that time started to form at the universities of Edinburgh, Glasgow, Aberdeen

[17] The most famous and extreme example was skepticism of David Hume. Continental rationalist once attacked Hume vehemently because his skepticism questioned the certainty of knowledge and the possibility to obtain true knowledge.

and St. Andrews, which offered an inexhaustible source of intellectual support for scientific research and technological innovations (Goldstone 2008: 136–161). It was the scientific revolution happening in the seventeenth and eighteenth centuries in the British Isles that paved the way for the Industrial Revolution.

The thriving intellectual market was facilitated by political fragmentation in Europe. Interstate rivalry unconsciously provided a liberal stage for free thinkers. Since the collapse of the Western Roman Empire, Western Europe had been divided into numerous independent lordships, loose federations, independent cities and small kingdoms, etc. This fragmentation lasted into the early modern times. Edward Gibbon (1823: 504–505) once wrote:

> Europe is now divided into twelve powerful, though unequal, kingdoms, three respectable commonwealths, and a variety of smaller, though independent, states ... The abuses of tyranny are restrained by the mutual influence of fear and shame; republics have acquired order and stability; monarchies have imbibed the principles of freedom, or, at least, of moderation; and some sense of honour and justice is introduced into the most defective constitutions by the general manners of the times. In peace, the progress of knowledge and industry is accelerated by the emulation of so many active rivals.

Political fragmentation was able to contain the state apparatus, in that such an interstate system "constrained the ability of political and religious authorities to control intellectual innovation. If they clamped down on heretical and subversive (that is, original and creative) thought, their smartest citizens would just elsewhere (as many of them, indeed, did)" (Mokyr 2017: 74). René Descartes, and Jean-Jacques Rousseau, for instance, were famous for their exiles in which they produced groundbreaking ideas. Even later, in the nineteenth century, Karl Marx lived in exile in France and England where he produced many of his most important works. A relatively liberal environment was sustained so intellectuals could be "creative and productive". The Enlightenment movement had an immeasurable influence on scientific circles. A scientific revolution ensued. Under the influence of new theories and experimental methods, engineers and scientists found a path on which human beings had never walked. The efficiency of utilising natural resources was enhanced. The scientific revolution equipped the economy with an unprecedented motor, a motor of technological progress and scientific innovations. No one can deny the impact of the Industrial Revolution on human civilisation. As a technology-driven economic revolution, it had been rooted in the Enlightenment movement and the contemporary scientific revolution.

6 Summary

The rise of Western Europe was a milestone for human civilisation. It marked the advent of a new civilisational mode after the hunter-gatherer civilisation and agricultural civilisation. The capitalist mode of production is a new one, different from all predecessors. In this mode, productive forces were commercialised, industrialised and marketised, and the relations of production were capitalised. Its capacity to transform economic, social and cultural spheres has quantitatively outperformed all predecessors. It has also been qualitatively different from all predecessors. The new mode "relies heavily on technical advances, the accumulation of improved capital goods, and new skills and competences that embody and enable innovations" (Mokyr 2009: 4–5). This complex is based on a set of institutions much more sophisticated than those on which its predecessors relied. This was a long-term process, and institutional changes lasted through the late medieval period and the Industrial Revolution.

The Industrial Revolution was undoubtedly a sea change, but it was the consequence of a series of changes that happened prior to it. Preconditions occurred in both micro- and macro-level institutions. There were institutional changes in political and economic systems, which allowed more liberty in productive activities. There were micro-level revolutions in human behaviours, which revolutionised people's attitudes towards their personal lives, and their relations with society and the world. There were pioneering jumps in intellectual fields, which fostered technological progress and scientific innovations. All these streams flowed interactively while parallelly, and they formed a confluence eventually. The confluence arrived at its zenith in the eighteenth and nineteenth centuries when it led to the Industrial Revolution which marked the erection of the capitalist mode of production. While in Western Europe the revolutionary changes hugely facilitated economic growth and paved the way to modernisation, in China the imperial system was strengthened. The reasons why China occupied the lower position in the Great Divergence will be the theme of next chapter.

References

Acemoglu, D., and J.A. Robinson. 2013. *Why Nations Fail: The Origins of Power, Prosperity and Poverty*. Profile Books Ltd.

Acemoglu, D., and J.A. Robinson. 2019. *The Narrow Corridor: States, Societies and the Fate of Liberty*. GB: Viking.

Acemoglu, D., S. Johnson, and J.A. Robinson. 2001. The Colonial Origins of Comparative Development: An Empirical Investigation. *The American Economic Review* 91 (5): 1369–1401.

Allen, Robert C. 2009. *The British Industrial Revolution in Global Perspective*. Cambridge University Press.

Anderson, Perry. 1974. *Lineages of the Absolutist State*. Verso.

Belich, James. 2022. *The World the Plague Made: The Black Death and the Rise of Europe*. Princeton University Press.

Bendix, Reinhard. 1977. *Max Weber: An Intellectual Portrait*. University of California Press.

Berman, Harold J. 2003. *Law and Revolution II: The Impact of the Protestant Reformations on the Western Legal Tradition*. The Belknap Press of Harvard University Press.

Braudel, Fernand. 1982. *The Wheels of Commerce: Civilization & Capitalism 15th–18th Century*, vol. 2. Trans. Sian Reynolds. New York: Harper & Row.

Carpenter, David A. 1990. *The Minority of Henry III*. University of California Press.

Coates, Ben. 2017. *Why the Dutch are Different: A Journey into the Hidden Heart of the Netherlands*. Nicholas Brealey Publishing.

Cust, Richard. 2007. *Charles I: A Political Life*. Pearson Education.

Dekrey, Gary S. 2008. Between Revolutions: Re-appraising the Restoration in Britain. *History Compass* 6 (3): 738–773.

Duggett, Michael. 1975. Marx on Peasants. *The Journal of Peasant Studies* 2 (2): 159–182.

Epstein, Stephan R. 2006. *Freedom and Growth: The Rise of States and Markets in Europe, 1300–1750*. Routledge.

Fang, Qin. 2019. *Institutions with Intentions: The Foundations of Institutional Analysis*. The Commercial Press.

Ferguson, Niall. 2011. *Civilization: The West and the Rest*. Penguin Books.

Gibbon, Edward. 1823. *The History of the Decline and Fall of the Roman Empire*. W. Baynes & Son.

Goldstone, Jack A. 2008. *Why Europe?: Global Change in a Global Context, 1500–1900 AD*. Mcgraw-Hill Higher Education.

Hajnal, John. 1965. European Marriage Patterns in Perspective. In *Population in History: Essays in Historical Demography*, ed. D.V. Glass, et al., 101–140. Chicago: Aldine Publishing.

Hajnal, John. 1982. Two Kinds of Preindustrial Household Formation System. *Population and Development Review* 8 (3): 449–494.

Hall, Robert E., and Charles I. Jones. 1999. Why Do Some Countries Produce So Much More Output per Worker than Others? *The Quarterly Journal of Economics* 114 (1): 83–116.

Hayek, Friedrich A. 1973. *Law, Legislation and Liberty*. London: Routledge and Kegan Paul.

Hollander, Samuel. 2011. *Friedrich Engels and Marxian Political Economy*. Cambridge University Press.

He, Wenkai. 2013. *Paths Toward the Modern Fiscal State: England, Japan, and China*. Cambridge, MA: Harvard University Press.

Hintze, Otto. 1931. Kalvinismus und Staatsräson in Brandenburg zu Beginn des 17. Jahrhunderts. *Historische Zeitschrift*, Bd. 144, H. 2, 229–286.

Kalberg, Stephen. 2021. *Max Weber's Sociology of Civilizations: A Reconstruction*. Routledge.

Knack, Stephen, and Philip Keefer. 1995. Institutions and Economic Performance: Cross-Country Tests Using Alternative Institutional Indicators. *Economics and Politics* 3 (7): 207–228.

Liu, Jinghua, and Songtao Zhang. 2012. To Replace the "Industrial Revolution" with the "Industrious Revolution"—A New Direction of Research on the Industrial Revolution in the West. *Historiography Quarterly* 2: 79–89 (in Chinese).

Lucas, Robert E. 2002. *Lectures on Economic Growth*. Harvard University Press.

Ma, Debin, and Jared Rubin. 2019. The Paradox of Power: Principal-agent Problems and Administrative Capacity in Imperial China (and Other Absolutist Regimes). *Journal of Comparative Economics* 47: 277–294.

Macfarlane, Alan. 1978. *Origins of English Individualism: The Family Property and Social Transition*. Wiley.

Maddison, Angus. 1998. *Chinese Economic Performance in the Long Run, 960–2030 AD*. OECD Publishing.

Maitland, Frederic William. 1961[1909]. *The Constitutional History of England: A Course of Lectures*. Cambridge University Press.

Mauro, Paolo. 1995. Corruption and Growth. *The Quarterly Journal of Economics* 110 (3): 681–712.

Mokyr, Joel. 2002. *The Gifts of Athena: Historical Origins of the Knowledge Economy*. Princeton University Press.

Mokyr, Joel. 2009. *The Enlightened Economy: Britain and the Industrial Revolution, 1700–1850*. Penguin Books.

Mokyr, Joel. 2017. The Persistence of Technological Creativity and the Great Enrichment: Reflections on the "Rise of Europe". In *The Long Economic and Political Shadow of History, Volume I. A Global View*, eds. Stelios

Michalopoulos, and Elias Papaioannou, 73–80. A VoxEU.org Book. CEPR Press.
North, Douglass C. 1981. *Structure and Change in Economic History*. New York: W. W. Norton Co.
North, Douglass C., and Barry R. Weingast. 1989. Constitutions and Commitment: The Evolution of Institutions Governing Public Choice in Seventeenth-Century England. *The Journal of Economic History* 49 (4): 803–832.
North, Douglass C. and Robert P. Thomas. 1973. *The Rise of the Western World: A New Economic History*. Cambridge University Press.
Phillips, Andrew and J.C. Sharman. 2020. *Outsourcing Empire: How Company-states made the Modern World*. Princeton University Press.
Prak, Maarten. 2018. *Citizens without Nations: Urban Citizenship in Europe and the World, c. 1000–1789*. Cambridge University Press.
Psillos, Stathis, and Martin Curd. 2010. *The Routledge Companion to Philosophy of Science*. Routledge.
Schefold, Bertram. 2018. *Die Bedeutung des ökonomischen Wissens für Wohlfahrt und wirtschaftliches Wachstum in der Geschichte*. Franz Steiner Verlag.
Schluchter, Wolfgang. 1979. *Die Entwicklung des okzidentalen Rationalismus: Eine Analyse von Max Webers Gesellschaftsgeschichte*. Mohr Siebeck.
Shorter, Edward. 1976. *The Making of the Modern Family*. London: Collins.
Tilly, Charles. 1992. *Coercion, Capital, and European States, AD 990–1992*. Blackwell Publishing.
Turner, Ralph. 2009. *King John: England's Evil King?* The History Press.
de Vries, Jan. 2008. *The Industrious Revolution: Consumer Behavior and the Household Economy, 1650 to the Present*. Cambridge University Press.
de Vries, Jan and Ad van der Woude. 1997. *The First Modern Economy: Success, Failure, and Perseverance of the Dutch Economy, 1500–1815*. Cambridge University Press.
Walter, John, and Roger Schofield. 1989. Famine, Disease and Crisis Mortality in early Modern Society. In *Famine, Disease and the Social Order in Early Modern Society*, ed. John Walter and Roger Schofield, 01–74. Cambridge University Press.
Weber, Max. 2003[1927]. *General Economic History*. Dover Publications, Inc.
Wielenga, Friso. 2020. *A History of the Netherlands: From the Sixteenth Century to the Present Day*. Bloomsbury Academic.
van Zanden, Jan Luiten. 2009. *The Long Road to the Industrial Revolution: The European Economy in a Global Perspective, 1000–1800*. Leiden: Brill Academic Publisher.
van Zanden, J.L., T. de Moor, et al. 2019. *Capital Women: The European Marriage Pattern, Female Empowerment, and Economic Development in Western Europe, 1300–1800*. Oxford University Press.

CHAPTER 8

The Great Divergence II: China

While groundbreaking changes occurred in England and the Low Countries, China changed much less in the contemporary centuries. As demonstrated in Chapter 5, Ming-Qing China focused on strengthening the imperial system. The central authority was further strengthened to its zenith. While the bureaucratic system no longer posed structural threats to the emperorship, it was weakened to such an extent that the quality of governance declined to a nadir. Villages and towns were left to the gentry class regarding communal affairs. The fiscal system could not adjust to changing economic situations, thus weakening the state capacity of the Ming and Qing governments. All layers of government often had to encounter a dearth of financial resources, which made bureaucrats resort to informal arrangements. The peasant economy was constantly encouraged, while commerce and trade were dissuaded. Before the 1840s, international trade was restricted to the Guangzhou harbour. The ideological authority abolished spiritual freedom, which was achieved by using both cultural despotism and the state examination system. The state examination system drove literate people towards Confucian classics and away from the scientific interest which would have paved the way for a scientific revolution, as in Western Europe (Lin 2018: 48–56). While European states were commercialising and industrialising the economy, the Chinese empire had a static expansion of the agricultural economy in the Ming-Qing era, rather than a qualitative upgrade.

G. H. Jiang, *The Imperial Mode of China*, Palgrave Studies in Economic History, https://doi.org/10.1007/978-3-031-27015-4_8

Why did China lag behind European states? Similar questions form one point of the Great Divergence, which also involves other Asian states in a broader term, while how modern economic growth occurred in Western Europe forms the other point of it, as presented in Chapter 7. Although scholars are still debating about when the Great Divergence began,[1] there are few scholars doubting that ancient China had been backward in comparison with Western Europe at the latest in the early nineteenth century. From some perspectives, the rise of Western Europe in early modern times was a special exception in a static world where the rest of human society was operating on respective conventional tracks. The rest of the world was maintaining a basically static economy, while Western Europe started an economy which relied on innovations and technological breakthroughs. Nevertheless, another aspect of the question is why China could not compete with such an "occidental" model. Why did the imperial system fail to continue to push the economy upwards, especially when European counterparts posed real challenges? If speaking in terms of the stage theory, the question transforms partly into why China failed to step into an industrial and modern society from an agrarian and despotic society. Especially when taking into account the fact that Ming-Qing China had possessed many characteristics which were considered as significant to economic booms in European counterparts, China's failures are highlighted further. This chapter will focus on deep-layered mechanisms of its failures and conclude that the inadaptability that the Imperial Mode caused was the main obstacle.

1 Traditional Interpretations

It had once been popular to interpret the downfall of the Qing empire as the consequence of the "Malthusian Trap". The Malthusian Paradigm has been popularly used to interpret economic pitfalls in the non-modern Western world and the non-Western world (Lee and Feng 2001: 4). Malthus highlighted the persistent tension between population growth and the demand for subsistence resources in his famous monograph, *Essay on Population*. His logic is succinct: (1) Mating behaviours between males

[1] The Californian School, e.g., Goldstone (2002), insists that the Great Divergence between Western Europe and China happened very late—China was not considered backward until the nineteenth century.

and females are unavoidable, and the increase of population is of geometrical manner; (2) The increase of subsistence resources, such as grain, is of arithmetical manner, and it is subject to the law of diminishing returns. These axioms lead to a pessimistic conclusion: subject to limited resources, the population would at last fall into the "Malthusian Trap". People have to either actively choose preventive checks, such as contraceptive strategies, or passively confront positive checks which resulted in passive death among people, such as warfare, famine or pandemic (Blaug 1996: 66–88).[2] These two checks are the sole "exits" for the tension between subsistence resources and population growth.

While "recent empirical work has indeed confirmed that the broad outlines of his theory were correct for Western Europe, and especially England, before the nineteenth century" (Lee and Fang 2001: 13), Malthus's paradigm met many problems when it was applied to ancient China. Chao Kang (1987) had attributed economic stagnation in ancient China to population pressure after the population exploded in the Ming-Qing era, especially after the shrinking man-land ratio. However, the Malthusian application has three main drawbacks in the Chinese case: (1) it neglected technological changes and improvements[3]; (2) the land provision in China was approximately inelastic; (3) it assumes that there were no preventive checks on population in traditional China (Deng 2020: 11–14). None of the three were true in ancient China during the Ming-Qing era. Firstly, although technological advancement was much slower in the Ming-Qing era than in previous eras, the growth of subsistence resources was still notable (Li 1996). While the population exploded due to changes in taxation and the import of new grain species, relative prices remained stable. Price increases were caused by the large import of silver. As von Glahn (2016: 329–330) asserted, "China did not yet face a Malthusian subsistence crisis" until the end of the eighteenth century. In fact, in a more general sense, Malthus's neglect of technological progress has made his theory easily "attacked". Ironically,

[2] Blaug (1996) provided not only a detailed analysis of the Malthusian paradigm but also an accurate supervision on Malthus's logics which he deduced out of his conclusions.

[3] In fact, this criticism is also applicable to Malthus's theory per se. It was technological progress since the Industrial Revolution that took human beings out of the gloomy prediction which the "Malthusian Trap" had made. But Malthus did not take it into account.

as Mokyr (2009: 6) wrote, "Malthus wrote his famous and highly influential *Essays on Population* at just about the time that it became irrelevant". Secondly, exploration and cultivation of new fields were still enthusiastically conducted in southern China. In the Ming-Qing era, for example, massive migration explored many cultivatable fields in the middle Yangtze field. "Irrigated riziculture steadily expanded and improved in the valleys and plains, with the spread of early-ripening strains and double-cropping outwards from the Lower Yangtze to Hubei, Hunan and Fujian; in the South-West, Yunnan was colonised" (Anderson 1974: 533). In the Ming dynasty, people immigrated to the Hunan and Hubei regions from Jiangxi Province on a large scale; In the Qing dynasty, people immigrated further westward to the Sichuan Province (Oh 2020: Chapters 1 and 2). New migrants cultivated previously unoccupied fields in hills and lake banks. Farmers' cultivation in the Hunan Province even resulted in environmental problems including the shrinkage of the Dongting Lake (Perdue 1987). Immigrants' exploration also happened in frontier regions in which the Qing government established dominance, such as Xinjiang and Mongol. Thirdly, the demographic trend in traditional China possessed some characteristics which Malthus thought of as preventive checks.

In Lee and Fang's (2001) research, traditional China was not totally subject to the Malthusian Paradigm. Firstly, there were widespread and numerous practices of so-called preventive checks in ancient China. Due to pressure from a lack of subsistence or preference towards male children, it was common to practice infanticide in China's villages. Adoption was also a widespread practice in China.[4] The fertility rate of Chinese females was distinctly lower than European counterparts. Secondly, while nuptiality and childbirth was a relatively individual matter in Europe (Hajnal 1965), fertility was never an absolutely individual affair in China. Marriage and childbirth were strongly subject to family planning and state intervention. When a family felt stress to raise an extra child, the couple would conduct infanticide or send this baby to others. The government also often brought in demographic planning, either to increase the population or migrate people. The roles of family (clan) and state led to an

[4] While adoption was relatively rare in Europe, the Chinese found it very acceptable to adopt children if a couple could not bear any child in traditional China. The adoption happened often within one bloodline in which male decedents shared the same surname. Adopting (buying) a child from strangers was completely acceptable. See Macfarlane (1978: 150).

extraordinarily complex fertility behaviour in traditional China. In ancient China, it was not uncommon to conduct economical decision-making about demographic issues. In consequence, the Malthusian Paradigm was not strongly associated with traditional China.

Apart from the classical Malthusian theory, Fairbank's socio-economic interpretations once prevailed as standard answers in the last century. Fairbank attributed the failure of China's modernisation to its traditional socio-economic structure.[5] Firstly, the relation between agriculture and population resulted in reliance on labour-intensive agriculture in the Ming-Qing era. This point has something to do with the Malthusian Paradigm. According to Fairbank, abundant population led to cheap labour, which made the economy overly labour-intensive, while there was no motivation to increase capital input or utilise machinery. It resulted in the maximum labour input and the minimum capital input in agriculture, the predominant form of production in ancient China. But such labour input was exceedingly subject to the law of diminishing returns. Under this circumstance, the so-called "involution" happened,[6] a distinctive sort of economic stagnation or even an extended form of recession. As Huang (1990: 308) suggested, "in agriculture, wage labour-based farms could not compete with familised peasant cultivation. In industry, urban workshops could not compete with low-cost home producers".

Another obstacle came from the abnormal merchant-bureaucracy relation. Although commerce and proto-industrialisation grew remarkably since the Song-Yuan era especially in southern China, as illustrated before, China's non-agricultural economy was fundamentally a patronage economy. Merchants' business relied on the will of officials. On the one hand, there was no civil law or other codes to protect merchants' property rights, in that theoretically the emperorship owned everything "under the heaven". The rich had to often face the potential risk of confiscation or nationalisation. Absence of secure property rights and of institutional restraints on the government's power resulted in a kind

[5] Fairbank's interpretations were strewn separately across many monographs, see Fairbank (1983, 1987, 2006).

[6] Geertz (1963) termed "involution" in order to describe the agricultural stagnation in Indonesia. He observed increasing labour intensity in fields without increasing outcome per head. It was a famous example of the law of diminishing returns. Without technological progress or institutional changes, as Geertz suggested, the economy would eventually encounter the law of diminishing returns.

of economy in which only land could be suitable for long-term and passive wealth holding, thus making motivation for reinvestment absent (Mühlhahn 2019: 199). On the other hand, whether merchants' business could prosper would rely on government's decisions by way of monopoly and discretionary regulations. Such a condition led to the highly personal trait of commercial practices, because merchants always had to get licences or monopolistic power from officials, which was often achieved by corruption or nepotism. In consequence, in commercial operations, there were no impersonal financial arrangements or transactions (Faure 2006: 52). Fairbank and Goldman (2006: 181) have a vivid description of commercial practices in traditional China:

> In premodern China, the merchant had an attitude of mind quite different from that of the Western entrepreneur extolled by our classical economists. According to the latter, the economic man can prosper most by producing goods and securing from his increased production whatever profit the market will give him. In old China, however, the economic man would do best by increasing his own share of what had already been produced. The incentive for innovative enterprise, to win a market for new products, had been less than the incentive for monopoly, to control an existing market by paying for an official license to do so. The tradition in China had been not to build a better mousetrap but to get the official mouse monopoly.

Similarly, Elvin (1973: Part Two) had an eclectic and influential interpretation: the High-level Equilibrium Trap. Elvin asserted that ancient China once had great technological achievements in the Tang and Song dynasties. The Chinese made innovative engineering practices in transportation, urban life, hydraulic projects and agricultural tools, etc. Such technological achievements led to the medieval economic revolution which included changes in agriculture, proto-industrialisation, the financial system, urbanisation and science. However, the technological advantages did not last. The turning point came in the fourteenth century. In the Ming-Qing era, China achieved only quantitative growth but no qualitative changes, which was caused by the technological standstill (Elvin 1973: 285–316). Technological stimulation was absent. However, while Elvin's answer pinpointed some key aspects of China's stagnation, it was criticised as a kind of technological determinism (Deng 2020: 16–17) which argues that a society's technology determines the development of a society and its societal structures. To some degree, technological standstill was the consequence or expression of some deeper mechanisms. The puzzle of why this technological standstill ensued has been asked by Joseph Needham and requires an answer.[7]

All aforementioned theories focused on the material aspects of China's economic stagnation. Max Weber provided a canonical and powerful (also controversial) theory. While Weber traced the steps of Karl Marx to describe a revolutionary transition in Western Europe from the medieval societal structures to a modern capitalist society, Weber related such a transition with nonmaterialistic aspects of European societies. In the Weberian paradigm, Western Europe experienced paramount changes in residents' societal concepts and cultural atmosphere. Psychological and ethical changes drove people to treat society with new insights. Residents, most of whom were self-sustained, geographically immobile and disdainful of financial practices in the past,[8] became more open to conduct capital accumulation, investment and other activities which would bring benefits to the growth of capitalism. Such spiritual changes paved the way for commercial and industrial development. Weber asserted that such spiritual changes had a close relation with the Reformation movement. The tenets of Luther in Germany and especially of Calvin had strong compatibility with the spirit of capitalism. Calvinism in particular not only emancipated residents from the chains of conservative concepts of Catholic Christianity, but also encouraged people to conduct "worldly"

[7] Joseph Needham raised the famous question: Why the Industrial Revolution did not happen in China, while China was the spearhead in technological spheres in the medieval era. The Needham Puzzle has been highly similar to the topics surrounding the Great Divergence. Both enquire about the reasons why the West arose while the East declined. See Lin (2008).

[8] Weber defined a series of traits of pre-capitalism as "traditionalism" in his famous *The Protestant Ethic and the Spirit of Capitalism*. Traditionalism was exemplified in laziness of professional works, preference towards leisure, and hatred of novel ideas, etc. Obviously, it was a quite conservative worldview. Weber considered traditionalism as the obstacle to the rise of capitalism. See Weber (1958: 59–67), Bendix (1977: 52) and Schluchter (1979).

affairs positively by means of the doctrine of "Predestination".[9] Thereafter, the spirit of capitalism, which was nurtured by the Reformation movement, became a profound motor for capitalist economic growth.[10]

Weber took China as an opposite when he construed the spirit of capitalism. In his *The Religion of China: Confucianism and Taoism*, Weber contrasted Confucianism with Protestantism, thereby deducing why China did not develop capitalism. Weber's main conclusion was that Confucian doctrines were not conducive to the germination of the spirit of capitalism. Unlike Protestantism which encouraged people to do well in world affairs as the tool of God, Confucianism had no such concept which could be compared with salvation by God or the afterlife. Confucius himself had no interest in supernatural themes. Confucian classics urged people to concentrate on the current world and the harmony of interpersonal relationships. In the eyes of Weber, Confucianism had traits as follows: belief in harmony and vested order; self-control in order for dignity and self-perfection; the dominance of paternal ethic; personal relations as the basis of public relations (Bendix 1977: 140–141). Subsequently, the prevalence of Confucianism engendered widespread norms that loyalty/trustworthiness could only be limited within kinship-based relationships and personal change, while in a commercial and industrial era extensive impersonal change becomes inevitable. The emphasis on clan and acquaintance relationships limited inter-clan cooperation (Greif and Tabellini 2010). None of these traits could be considered as suitable to the rise of capitalism, in striking contrast to Protestantism.

[9] The doctrine of "Predestination" is a key component of Calvinism in the Reformation movement. In the Middle Age, churches monopolised the power to communicate with God, so they monopolised the way to salvation. Churches conducted various profitable activities which were declared to be able to reduce people's sins. In contrast to the possibility of absolving sin, Calvin pronounced that everyone had been predestined by God. Those who had been chosen to get salvation would be predestined to get it, while those who had not been chosen would do nothing to change their pathetic fate. But no one could know who had been chosen. There were only some external symbols, such as success in careers and important responsibility in social affairs, etc. Worldly glory came from predestination. So, Calvinist followers must be loyal, industrious and contemptuous of laziness and indulgence. Apparently, Calvinism had a strong affinity to capitalist ambitions.

[10] About a detailed analysis about the relation between Calvinism and the spirit of capitalism, see Bendix (1977: 49–69) and Macfarlane (1978: 47–49).

The Weberian interpretation of Confucianism complied with Weber's total canvas in which spiritual content had a role in material content.[11] For Weber, the Protestant ethic and the corresponding spirit had paramount effects on the capitalist system, and such ethics and spirit were precisely absent in Confucianism and the areas influenced by Confucianism. While Confucianism which emphasises individual education and moral behaviours of the literati class contributed to an early emergence of bureaucracy in imperial China, it forms an obstacle to rationalism that modernisation requires (Kalberg 2021: Chapter 10). Meanwhile, Weber did not have a pessimistic view on China's development. He asserted in 1919 that "China could not become capitalist (Weber meant capitalism in the modern sense) without eliminating such obstacles, but that the Chinese would be excellent capitalists, once the obstacles were removed"—perhaps one of the best predictions ever made in the social sciences (Schefold 2014: 12).

2 Revisionist Explanations

In recent decades, the California School arose remarkably in the social sciences. It consisted of many scholars in economic history, sociology and anthropology, etc., most of whom worked or had ever worked in the University of California. The California School led a new trend in social sciences in discerning that the orient did not lag behind the occident until the nineteenth century, before which European and Asian regions had much more similarities than differences. While those scholars agreed with the points that Europe had changed a lot in political, societal and economic structures far before the nineteenth century (Goldstone 2002: 326, 329), they found that contemporary China, especially the Jiangnan region, had comparable changes in its economic indicators to Europe (Li and van Zanden 2012). They conducted thorough research in historical statistics and data analysis so as to prove the "advancement" of Ming-Qing China. In the Jiangnan region, the level of the market economy reached a peak in Chinese history. The advancements included thriving marketisation, urbanisation and regional specialisation. The labour market was quite vibrant, after comparing the wage rate

[11] Weber's research on the spirit of capitalism partly contrasted Marx's theory of Überbau and Unterbau (substructure and superstructure). Arguably, the Marxist canvas is not satisfying. See Hintze (1931).

and the migration phenomena respectively in the Jiangnan region and Western Europe (Pomeranz 2000: 69–107). The demographic change did not lead to negative effects for economic growth in Ming-Qing China since Chinese residents took some inhibitory measures to curb population growth (Lee and Fang 2001). The human capital in the Jiangnan region was never too thin to hinder the possibility of industrialisation. Moreover, the factor markets, including the land market and the labour market, were never less developed in the Ming-Qing China than in Europe. The relative levels of marketisation in China and Europe were similar prior to the Industrial Revolution(Shiue and Keller 2004). The Smithian dynamics in which economic growth originated from the enlarging division of labour and the market scale, did not only emerge in China, but also helped China to experience some forms of proto-industrialization (Wong 1997: 33–70).

The research results of the California School could easily lead to such conclusions: While extant research claims that the increases in such economic indicators as labour wages, consumption level and marketisation level, etc., were important for Europe's economic growth, and those increases eventually sparked the Industrial Revolution,[12] there were no definite differences in those economic indicators between Ming-Qing China and Western Europe in the late medieval period and the early modern time; thus, the authentic causes for the Great Divergence must be traced in other aspects except those economic indicators or the mechanisms which produced them; with regard to economic growth, China and Western Europe did not differ too much until the Industrial Revolution; furthermore, the rise of Western Europe was more like a casual incident, thanks to its exploitation in colonies and the invention of the steam engine. As Pomeranz (2000: Chapter 6) suggested, the economic hegemony of England was "beholden" to a geographical bonanza: the geographical closeness to the New World which provided vast natural resources and a huge market. England had one unparalleled advantage: the zones which produced cheap coal were geographically close to main consumption zones, such as London, which made it profitable to innovate machines which consume cheap coal in order to replace expensive human

[12] According to at least some economic historians, for example, changes in the labour market after the Black Death and consumption situations in England were paramount for the germination of the Industrial Revolution. The incentive to save expensive labour and to utilise more capital input which was relatively cheaper "sparked" the Industrial Revolution. See Allen (2009: Chapters 2 and 4).

labour. However, England encountered ecological restraints which would curb its economic growth as before. What made the quasi-Malthusian story different was the discovery of the New World. By discovering new frontiers, the economic exploration there gave England relief, thus making ecological constraints futile. A further deduction is that the Great Divergence could be only ascribed to the revolution of energy available for mechanical work. Only after the widespread application of steam engines in agriculture, transportation, manufacturing and military operations in eighteenth-century England, did economic growth rise at great pace (Goldstone 2002).

Among scholars of the California School and the adjacent circle, there is a common tendency to describe Ming-Qing China as an economy comparable to contemporary Western Europe. They recognised that Ming-Qing China was experiencing some development which Western Europe was also experiencing. Then, Europe's story before the Industrial Revolution was not different from other regions which were considered as backward according to Eurocentrism. As Shiue and Keller (2004) puts it, "higher efficiency in Europe is seen only in the nineteenth century when industrialisation was already underway". It was something unexpected or extraordinary which changed the historical path. Some enumerated the discovery of the New World, the geographical closeness of coal mines and the innovation of steam engines, etc. However, some statistical results cannot support such ideas. With the support of historical records, historians considered it incorrect to think that Western Europe and other regions which were traditionally considered backward were fundamentally equal economically and socially, since "for the last thousand years, Europe (the West) has been the prime mover of development and modernity" (Landes 1998: xxi). Against some revisionists who believed that the Great Divergence was quite late, the difference in GDP *per capita* between Western Europe and China had started to enlarge much earlier before the Industrial Revolution, specifically for the Netherlands in the sixteenth century and for Great Britain in the seventeenth century (Broadberry et al. 2018).[13] The trend fastened in the eighteenth century. Other estimates had similar results: real wages were twice to four times higher in London and Amsterdam than in Leipzig, Beijing and Shanghai in

[13] Partly because the population exploded, China's GDP per capita declined noticeably in the eighteenth century, which proved that China's previous growth was extensive.

the second half of the eighteenth century (Gupta and Ma 2010: 272–273). The statistical comparison between Western Europe and other Asian regions cannot support the narratives of the California School (Studer 2015).

In addition, at least some of revisionists' research focused heavily on the Jiangnan region which was the most economically developed area in Ming-Qing China. It is arguable that the economic and political diversity within the large empire presents so many difficulties that many researchers chose to compare Western Europe just with the Jiangnan region.[14] As illustrated before, we are left with the impression that in approximately 1750 the preindustrial society of the Jiangnan region and Western Europe had much in common; indeed, they probably seemed in appearance to be more like each other than either one was like those occidental states that would emerge transformed by the Industrial Revolution in the nineteenth century. Yet similarities in appearances were superficial. Beneath the surface lay great differences in social structure, culture, and ideas, as the nineteenth century would demonstrate (Fairbank and Goldman 2006: 186). As for the normalised theory of those who saw the rise of the West as the results of a hundreds-of-years-long (if not thousands of) evolution, such as Marx, Sombart and Weber, the California School fundamentally rejected it (Schefold 2014). In other words, the California School saw Western Europe and China before the Industrial Revolution not only as economically comparable, but also as culturally equal.

Failing to recognise cultural influences and therefore the deep-layered structural roots, the adherents of the California School struggle to clarify well the nature of the Ming-Qing governments. The imperial structure posed a comprehensive and overwhelming influence upon all aspects of the society. Confusingly, the California School believed that the Ming-Qing governments simply had pure goodwill to enhance general welfare and to provide necessary public goods for economic growth.[15] For revisionists, this belief helped to explain economic progress which had happened at the time. For example, they maintain that the Qing government practised laissez-faire and thus pro-commerce policies (von Glahn

[14] Such research produced many insightful results and data, see Li (2002).

[15] The Qing state was described as a provisioning state, one dedicated to improving the people's livelihood through, for example, investments in famine relief and flood control. It was said that the Qing government practised laissez-faire policies. See von Glahn (2016: 313) and Wong (1997: Chapter 5).

2016: 312–336). However, revisionists overly believed in official propaganda of the imperial governments so that they ignored its despotic nature (Ma 2012). The extractive nature of China's imperial systems cannot be simply dismissed by saying that the Qing government insisted on sustaining necessary public good provision such as the relief system and the maintenance of hydraulic projects (Pomeranz 2021), since few Chinese dynasties which had failed to do so lasted for any respectable duration. The extractive nature was a huge obstacle to modernised economic growth (Acemoglu and Robinson 2013: 149–151, 441–442). The political and socio-economic structures in Ming-Qing China were remotely different from those in Western Europe. Institutional factors must play a role in forming a divergent economic pathway.

3 State Capacity

In recent years, scholars in Chinese economic history increasingly took meaning from theories of state capacity which were originally proposed to analyse Europe's transition from medieval feudalism to fiscal or absolutist states in the early modern time (Bonney 1999). Scholars introduced Tilly's (1992) and Epstein's (2006) explanations to interpret China's failure in the Ming-Qing era. The international competition in Western Europe forced feudalism to wane and a more centralised regime to form. To provide public goods, such as fighting external wars and sustaining political stability, was conducive to building state capacity (Besley and Persson 2009). In the process, capacity to extract more financial resources was key to the rise of a modernised government which could be more helpful towards economic growth. For example, England relied on various financial tools, such as issuing bonds and extracting more taxes, to provide an advantageous environment for economic booms (He 2013: Chapter 2). This implies that strengthening control of the government in Western Europe provided necessary support to economic expansion. In contrast, the Qing government had never achieved such capacity. In the Qing dynasty the income of the central government was only 10% of the total GDP, while the revenue of the central government in Great Britain in 1789 was 18% of the total GDP (Goldstone 2008: 112). Other statistical research showed lower results.[16] All efforts of the Qing government

[16] For example, at the end of the eighteenth century, the taxation which the Qing government extracted was only 3% to 4% of GDP; In the middle nineteenth century, the

to issue fiat paper money or public bonds failed in the nineteenth century (He 2013: 133–144, 173–179). What made the situation worse was that the lijin system was controlled by local general-governors and the custom revenues were controlled by foreigners.[17] Therefore, scholars concluded that the fiscal capacity of the Qing government was weak, and this weakness resulted in Qing's fragility characterised by domestic uprisings and an inability to overcome foreign intrusions (Zhang 2021).

Positive association between state capacity and economic growth has been attested by economic scholars, mostly in European cases (Dincecco and Katz 2016; Besley and Persson 2010). Certainly, public institutions able to provide effective administration and to achieve beneficial environments promoted economic growth (Johnson and Koyama 2017). It has been widely acknowledged that the administrative capacity of the Qing (and Ming) government was quite weak, almost the lowest in Chinese history (Zhang 2021). Emperors and bureaucrats confined themselves in traditional roles prescribed by institutional and ideological path dependence (Zhang 2019). The governments only took into consideration stability of the society, domestic peace and such large-scale public projects as the canal system and the granary system. The imperial governments had undertaken such tasks for over one millennium since the Qin dynasty. According to records, the Ming and Qing governments spent lots of energy and money in maintenance of the Great Canal (Huang 1988: 462–464). On the one hand, the governments paid full attention to public projects. On the other hand, nonetheless, it has been recorded that the hydraulic infrastructure also deteriorated seriously in the Qing dynasty, thus resulting in frequent flood and other natural disasters. The granary system aiming to relieve famine was also declining (Naughton 2007: 39). In the nineteenth century, even domestic peace and social order could not be guaranteed, as civil uprisings and foreign intrusions prevailed.

More importantly, the governments failed those institutions which became increasingly important for a rising commercial and industrial economy, including supporting an efficient legal system, creating an efficient system for the protection of property rights and building a tolerant environment for innovations, etc. In this aspect, the Ming and Qing

figure became 1.5% to 2%, although the absolute amount did not decline. See Brandt et al. (2014: 67–68).

[17] Details will be discussed in Chapter 9. Fiscal decentralisation and then political decentralisation had complicated background in the late Qing dynasty.

governments were unquestionably unsuccessful. Such institutions were absent anywhere across the empire. Under these circumstances, the gentry class shouldered responsibility in an autonomous way for rural areas and towns. The transaction system of land, for example, had to be supervised by local autonomous entities. Even some public projects, such as the construction of bridges and hydraulic projects, were organised by such entities (Long et al. 2018). In urban areas, the governments not only failed to provide legal protection for commercial activities, but also constantly exploited merchants with arbitrary taxation regulations. A notable example was the arbitrary extraction of money from the salt merchants during the Ming-Qing era. Local bureaucrats always asked for extra "contribution" from salt merchants at irregular times (Zelin 1992: 58–66). Such exploitation was not limited only to the salt industry. Even peasants were inflicted with discretionary decisions of local bureaucrats. The harmful relations between merchants and authorities had a diminishing effect on the economy (De Long and Shleifer 1993).

As illustrated before, the Ming-Qing emperors succeeded to undermine potential threats of bureaucracy, but they also undermined efficacy of governance which bureaucrats could have offered. Although the principal–agent problem was mitigated between the bureaucratic system and the central authority, it became worse between bureaucrats and productive sectors. The Ming and Qing governments insisted stubbornly in the imperial pyramid structure. The principal–agent problem inherent in the pyramid structure became much worse in the bottom layer (between lower bureaucrats and productive units), by means of information asymmetry and indifference of central rulers (Sng and Moriguchi 2014). The emperors even tolerated the venality of bureaucrats in order to keep them domesticated, thus weakening efficacy of governance (Ma and Rubin 2019). In the Ming dynasty, embezzlement by bureaucrats was shockingly enormous. In the Qing dynasty, it had been a popular strategy for central rulers to guarantee bureaucrats' loyalty by allowing them to collect bribes.[18] Consequently, the competence of local bureaucrats greatly declined. Efficacy of governance in the Ming and Qing dynasties was therefore low. In terms of economic growth, what the imperial structure offered was a discouraging environment.

[18] The most highlighting example was Heshen, a top chancellor of the Qianlong Emperor. See Acemoglu and Robinson (2019: 216–217).

From a comprehensive perspective, the meaning of the state capacity theory is limited in the Chinese case (Peng 2021). If the theory pointed to low efficiency of governance, it would be a reasonable explanation. If it pointed to the centralised power of the Qing government, the imperial court surely would not have been able to go further. When the state capacity theory is applied to the European case, it is a priori assumed that extractive and administrative capacities were monitored and balanced by other institutions, such as strictly protected property rights or an independent parliament. For example, in England, the political power to extract taxes had been transferred from monarchs to a publicly organised entity very early, which later became the Parliament. Thus, efficiency of governance was guaranteed when the state capacity was strengthened. However, such conditions did not exist in imperial China. The absolutist power of China's emperorship had reached its zenith in the Ming-Qing era. It was attested by discretionary confiscation and blackmail upon the rich and the bureaucrats. The nature of the Ming-Qing governments would be better described as a plight of "strong state and weak governance" (Ma 2012). Inefficiency of governance was not caused by dearth of capacity but caused by the inadaptability of whole imperial socio-economic structures. The weakening state capacity of the Qing government was an external manifestation of such inadaptability.

4 Inadaptability of the Imperial Mode

The traditional socio-economic structures in China were defined as extractive institutions.[19] As shown before, the Imperial Mode of China was a pyramid structure consisting of the central authority, the bureaucratic system and the peasant economy. The emperorship and bureaucracy extracted surpluses in order to provide public goods and then to sustain the stability of the whole system. The superstructure ("Überbau") matching with the base ("Unterbau") functioned well in the agricultural era. Agricultural growth valued very dearly such goods as water control, disaster prevention, social order and peace, etc., upon which the Imperial Mode did well. There is little doubt that China's agricultural achievements were almost unparalleled. "But it always was and will

[19] Extractive institutions have properties to extract income from a subset of a society. They are the opposite to inclusive institutions as defined in the last chapter. See Acemoglus and Robinson (2013: 73–76).

be an ever-living fire".[20] When the agricultural economy grew ripe and bred new economic forms, the base began to change. A new set of the superstructure was required to adjust to the new base.[21] In the second economic revolution during the Tang-Song era, new economic forms, i.e., commercialisation and proto-industrialisation started to emerge, but the Imperial Mode refused to step out. It was instead reinforced during the Ming-Qing era. In Western Europe, partly due to the absence of a unified and forceful political entity, new factors were able to grow relatively freely, which were eventually proven to be significant for the commercial and industrial economy. New economic modes started to give new driving forces to economy. The economic systems were transformed gradually but profoundly. In contrast, the Imperial Mode of China grew detrimental to such kinds of economic systems.

Without any doubt, a peaceful and orderly environment is the most precious thing which a government can provide (Ma 2004), and the Imperial Mode was successful in this. Through the stable operation of the bureaucratic system and a central authority, the peasant economy thrived, and ancient China possessed a leading position among ancient civilisations for a quite long time. However, the commercial and industrial economy came, for which more sophisticated institutions became essential. Such institutions relied on an efficient and fair legal system, the protection of property rights and a tolerant cultural environment, etc. Recalling classical wisdom of Adam Smith.

> Little else is requisite to carry a state to the highest degree of opulence from the lowest barbarism, but peace, easy taxes, and a tolerable administration of justice.[22]

Smith's saying pointed to the fundamental role which a government should play in economic growth. The three points to which Smith referred to were peace, a fair and easy taxation system, and an efficient and

[20] Cited from Heraclitus.

[21] In fact, Marx's theories about the dynamic relations between the superstructure and the base were not satisfying. It was unstated and unclear how the superstructure could change (evolve or simply collapse alongside the base) when the base changed. See Hintze (1931).

[22] This sentence came from a note. Dugald Stewart had in his possession some notes from lectures which Adam Smith gave in 1755, some 21 years before the appearance of *the Wealth of Nations* (1776).

tolerant legal system. He had recognised the fundamental requirements of a commercial and industrial economy. Except for domestic order which is important for all modes of production, the Imperial Mode of China rarely succeeded in other fields. The roots of its failures lied in the fundamental functions and its structures. When the base turned out to be more capitalistic, the superstructure was kept static and was thus less compatible with new economic factors.

The most striking feature was the despotic and arbitrary political institutions and the casual legal system. When agricultural economy prevailed, the bureaucratic system needed to extract surpluses in order for public good provision. But in Chinese history, the central authority and the bureaucratic system never developed a strictly and definitely regulated extraction system. The extraction system relied on discretionary policies. We have seen that arbitrary taxing and arbitrary confiscation happened relatively frequently in every dynasty, and such a situation never softened in the Ming-Qing era—it even happened more severely.[23] It contrasted distinctively with the situation in Western Europe in which constrained regimes did not have discretionary power to expand financial revenues (Ma and Rubin 2019). While within the Imperial Mode the bureaucratic system always mobilised resources by means of political commands, the commercial and industrial economy could not be sustained under these conditions, as such an economy valued the impregnable security of property rights. Evidently, such institutions could neither support commercial and industrial activities nor supply worthwhile public services (Acemoglu and Robinson 2019: 215–216).

One highly relevant problem was the legal system. In traditional China, the law was never independent; it was a part of the government. The law meant "punishment", rather than any universal ethic. Since the Pre-Qin period, the law was designed for punishing people who did not follow the edicts of the government. Since the Sui dynasty, the juridical system formally became an integral component of the central government, i.e., the "Xing" Ministry. Most legal codes that remained in governmental documents were about how to administer and regulate society, rather than to support the liberty which individuals should have (Acemoglu and Robinson 2019: 215–216). Legal decisions were very easily impacted

[23] Chen et al. (2019) offered a vivid illustration of such confiscation events. The Qing government conducted confiscation frequently not only on bureaucrats but also on the gentry class, which consisted of local rich people.

by higher political wills. Moreover, just like the role of Lutheranism and Calvinism upon western legal systems (Berman 2003), in ancient China juridical decisions were based on Confucian tenets. Confucian tenets were meant to sustain a moral order and a fixed social hierarchy. Legal objectiveness never existed. Juridical decisions could arbitrarily vary based on the social or kinship status. As a result, the law was "a segment of the whole web of friendship, kinship obligations, and personal relations that supported Chinese life" (Fairbank and Goldman 2006: 186). The legal system could not only dampen any effort to change society, but also served the government as a tool to extract surpluses and control potential dissidents.

Subsequently, despotic nature of traditional socio-economic institutions smothered financial and organisational innovations which were crucial for modern economic growth. As demonstrated in the last chapter, organisational innovations were important for the rise of Western Europe. New commercial and industrial organisations improved institutional efficiency. Although financial innovations were not lacking in traditional China, such as the invention of paper money and some transfer systems, the methods to utilise capital investment were never ripe in China (Goetzmann 2017: Chapter 10). Such a disadvantage was on the one hand caused by the absence of strictly protected property rights and on the other hand caused by the absence of entrepreneurship, both of which were crucial at the beginning of capitalism. Individuals were educated to follow the existent order. Under Confucianism, literati and intellectual individuals looked for inner harmony and compliance with the world, rather than looking to change the world. Every decent person should find elegance within the repression of desires, emotions and incentives for any adventure (Bendix 1977: 120–125, 135–141). In contrast to Calvinism which encouraged followers to pursue worldly successes as tools of God, entrepreneurship could not easily emerge in ancient China. Especially in the Ming-Qing era, the socio-economic institutions conducted structural repression on people's liberty. As shown before, the governments monopolised cultural fields and prosecuted liberal thinkers. Women were organizationally devalued (Fairbank and Goldman 2006: 173–176).

Furthermore, in the Ming-Qing era scientific activities were pressed to a nadir. As illustrated before, the scientific revolution and the Enlightenment movement eventually gave rise to the advent of the Industrial Revolution. Technological progress rarely appeared in the Ming-Qing era, although just in the Tang-Song era China experienced unparalleled technological progress. The chronological contrast was striking in that the degradation happened in just a few centuries. Such confusing phenomena led to the famous question—the Needham Puzzle: Why did modern science not develop in Chinese civilisation which in the previous many centuries was much more efficient than the West in applying natural knowledge to practical needs? (Robinson 2004: 1). As some scholars of the California School emphasised, the difference in the ability to develop modern science finally resulted in the Great Divergence in economic growth (Goldstone 2002). China's scientific backwardness could be interpreted by two reasons. Firstly, the nature of technological progress began to change drastically in the early modern time. Technological progress relied more and more on theoretical breakthroughs and experimental activities. Unlike agricultural techniques which relied on the accumulation of experiences and the trial-and-error process, modern science would be based much more on experiments guided by theories. The large size of population in premodern times would have potentially been an asset for experience-based inventions. "However, if this large population is ill equipped with acquired human capital necessary for undertaking modem scientific research and experiment, the likelihood that the economy will contribute to modem technological invention and scientific discovery is small" (Lin 1995). Secondly, the level of human capital in the Ming-Qing China was worsened by the state examination system. Intellectuals were directed to succeed in the state examination system, but the key to success in such examinations was to have good familiarity with Confucian texts. Few people were interested in scientific fields, such as mathematics and experimental science. Even in the preface of a famous technical book in the Ming dynasty, *The Exploitation of the Works of Nature* ("*Tiangong Kaiwu*"), the writer wrote that ambitious people should not read this book because it would be no help for the state examinations (Lin 2018: 52–54). With such a learning atmosphere, it was clear why a scientific revolution could not happen in the Ming-Qing China.

Ultimately, failures of Ming-Qing China can be briefly interpreted. In terms of Marxist historical materialism, while the Imperial Mode of China was an appropriate match to the agricultural economy in the premodern period and succeeded to push China towards the making of a commercial and industrial economy, its failure to adjust to new economic factors resulted in the gradual decline of China's economic performance. Since the Tang-Song transition, the agricultural economy ripened, and rising commerce as well as proto-industrialisation began to unfold new economic possibilities. A new socio-economic structure suitable to a commercial and industrial economy would have been emerging, precisely like the birth of the Imperial Mode in the Pre-Qin era when the first economic revolution was calling upon new institutions to adjust to the emerging economy. But in the second millennium AD, the superstructure did not try to adjust but strengthened itself. The marketisation process was interrupted in the Yuan and Ming dynasties (Liu 2015). The inadaptability of the Imperial Mode was gradually increasing in the Ming-Qing era, especially after the West came in the nineteenth century. Its refusal to change hindered China's transformation at the proper time. In short, the Imperial Mode matched well with the agricultural mode of production, but it was not compatible with the capitalist mode of production which was arising. As Engels (1878: 126) said,

> This mighty revolution in the conditions of the economic life of society was, however, not followed by any immediate corresponding change in its political structure. The political order remained feudal, while society became more and more bourgeois.[24]

5 Summary

As for why China lagged behind the West in the Ming-Qing era, different scholars have offered various and sometimes contradictory answers. In various theories that try to explain China's failures, a core issue is the relation between the government and a liberal society. Traditional scholars focus on negative roles which the government played, while scholars who applied the state capacity theory pay attention to weakening ability of providing public services in the Qing dynasty. The California School, however, repudiated the evolutionary path, insisting that the rise of Western Europe was a surprising story because of some unexpected coincidences, so China's socio-economic institutions should not be blamed. Theoretically, economic growth revolves around the tension between the government and individual parties in economic activities, which is an eternal theme of economic research. Individual parties always have to

[24] Engels was speaking of the historical conditions in Europe. The description in this sentence is not completely suitable for China, as China was not considered feudal before the bourgeois society. Nonetheless, the points about historical materialism are useful here.

transfer partial liberties to a collective entity so that public good provision can be possible, whether that is through economic surpluses, social liberties or legal rights.

In ancient China, by means of extracting economic surpluses and organising collective actions, including warfare and public projects, the Imperial Mode succeeded in responding to the demand of an agricultural economy in need of domestic peace, social order and large-scale projects, while contemporary Europe at least partly failed to do that. The Imperial Mode is advantageous in developing and sustaining an agricultural economy. Much evidence has been shown that Tang-Song China had stood at the entrance of a potential industrial revolution (See Chapter 5). If this process had developed smoothly, the Imperial Mode would have finished its "historical destiny" and China would have stepped into a new economic stage as a pioneer. However, the process was interrupted by events in the second millennium AD. The Imperial Mode was strengthened and posed adverse effects upon new economic factors. Institutions which appeared advanced under specific conditions could become obstacles when conditions changed (Lin 2018: 54). When the commercial and industrial era came, the Imperial Mode failed to exit. The superstructure was no longer suited to a changing base which appeared increasingly commercial, marketised and industrialised. While Western Europe started to have more sophisticated institutions, which encouraged economic expansion in the early modern time, China was stuck in its traditional role.

There is no denying that economy in the early Qing dynasty still prospered in terms of its aggregate output. Economic expansion in Qing China was so notable that many economic historians called it as the "Age of Glory" or "Heyday of China" (Mühlhahn 2019: Chapter 1; Feuerwerker 1984). Interregional trade developed fast as agricultural output grew in various regions and a national transportation system was sustained by the Qing government that controlled unprecedentedly large territory. Marketisation and commercialisation consistently grew in the Yangtze Region where development of the handicraft industry facilitated commerce and trade. However, it was also clear that growth at this stage was mainly extensive and labour-intensive (Jones 1988: Chapter 3). As illustrated before, massive migration explored many cultivatable fields in southern China. Such extensive growth happened westwards in many peripheral regions. China's "Westward Movement" contributed eye-catchingly to noticeable increase of population and agricultural aggregate output. In the first two hundred years of the Qing dynasty, population increased by around 200% (Pomeranz 2021: 24) due to expanding cultivated yields and introduction of new crops that have much higher output per acre, such as sweet potato and maise. The increase in cultivated fields was dramatic in the Ming and Qing dynasties, as illustrated in Table 1. While Western Europe changed to a system in which economic growth increasingly relied on technological and institutional innovations, China embraced traditional economic path which the Imperial Mode accommodated. The prosperity of Qing China was exploiting the potential of the Imperial Mode by expanding territories and population.

The directly controlled territory of the Qing government was unprecedentedly large. The Qing government did achieve domestic peace through large-scale wars, as all neighbouring nomadic tribes were tamed, and rebellious warlords were eradicated. "Manchu military conquests—which for the first time in history brought Mongolia, Xinjiang and Tibet under effective Chinese control—significantly increased the potential territory available for agrarian cultivation and settlement. China's inland frontiers were extended deep into Central Asia by Qing's troops and officials" (Anderson 1974: 536). To a large degree, the economic heyday during this era was still the result of a scale economy which the Imperial Mode brought out. The economic dynamics were still the vested mechanism under the Imperial Mode. The "Age of Glory" relied on increasing input of production factors and was subject to diminishing returns. It lived on borrowed time when considering that a commercial and industrial society in which the capitalist mode of production dominates was going to replace an agricultural society. The superstructure of the Imperial Mode could no longer accommodate the economic

Table 1 Population and Cultivated Acreage Estimates (1400–1913)

Year	*Population (millions)*	*Cultivated acreage (million shih mou)*
1400	65–80	370(±70)
1600	120–200	500(±100)
1770	270(±25)	950(±100)
1850	410(±25)	n.a
1873	350(±25)	1210(±50)
1893	385(±25)	1240(±50)
1913	430(±25)	1360(±50)

Source Perkins (1969: 16)

base in which industrialisation and commercialisation were occurring. When China stagnated in the nineteenth century, the West came in. New contacts between China and the West urged China to pursue modernisation through demolishing or reforming the imperial system. The zigzag path of China's modernisation will be the topic of the next chapter.

References

Acemoglu, D., and J.A. Robinson. 2013. *Why Nations Fail: The Origins of Power, Prosperity and Poverty*. London: Profile Books Ltd.

Acemoglu, D., and Robinson, J. A. 2019. *The Narrow Corridor: States, Societies and the Fate of Liberty*. GB: Viking.

Allen, Robert C. 2009. *The British Industrial Revolution in Global Perspective*. Cambridge: Cambridge University Press.

Anderson, Perry. 1974. *Lineages of the Absolutist State*. New York: Verso.

Bendix, Reinhard. 1977. *Max Weber: An Intellectual Portrait*. California: University of California Press.

Berman, Harold J. 2003. *Law and Revolution II: The Impact of the Protestant Reformations on the Western Legal Tradition*. Cambridge: The Belknap Press of Harvard University Press.

Besley, Timothy, and Torsten Persson. 2009. The Origins of State Capacity: Property Rights, Taxation, and Politics. *American Economic Review* 99 (4): 1218–1244.

Besley, Timothy, and Torsten Persson. 2010. State Capacity, Conflict, and Development. *Econometrica* 78 (1): 01–34.

Blaug, Mark. 1996. *Economic Theory in Retrospect*. Cambridge: Cambridge University Press.

Bonney, Richard. 1999. *The Rise of the Fiscal State in Europe c.1200–1815*. Oxford: Clarendon Press.

Brandt, L., Debin Ma, and T.G. Rawski. 2014. From Divergence to Convergence: Reevaluating the History behind China's Economic Boom. *Journal of Economic Literature* 52 (1): 45–123.

Broadberry, Stephen, Hanhui Guan, et al. 2018. China, Europe, and the Great Divergence: A Study in Historical National Accounting, 980–1850. *The Journal of Economic History* 78 (4): 955–1000.

Chao, Kang. 1987. *Man and Land in Chinese History: An Economic Analysis*. Taipei: Southern Materials Centre Inc.

Chen, Zhiwu, and Lin, Zhan et al. 2019. *Guanshen de Hebao: Qingdai Jingying Jiating Zichan Jiegou Yanjiu* [The Purse of Officials and the Gentry: Research on Asset Structure of the Elite Households in the Qing dynasty]. CITIC Press Corporation. (in Chinese).

De Long, J.B., and Andrei Shleifer. 1993. Princes and Merchants: European City Growth before the Industrial Revolution. *The Journal of Law and Economics* 36 (2): 671–702.

Deng, Kent G. 2020[2002]. *The Premodern Chinese Economy: Structural Equilibrium and Capitalist Sterility* (Trans. Ru, Yucong et al.). Zhejiang: Zhejiang University Press. (in Chinese).

Dincecco, Mark, and Gabriel Katz. 2016. State Capacity and Long-Run Economic Performance. *The Economic Journal* 126 (590): 189–218.

Elvin, Mark. 1973. *The Pattern of the Chinese Past*. Stanford: Stanford University Press.

Engels, Friedrich. 1947[1878]. *Anti-Dühring. Herr Eugen Dühring's Revolution in Science*. Moscow: Progress Publishers.

Epstein, Stephan R. 2006. *Freedom and Growth: The Rise of States and Markets in Europe, 1300–1750*. Routledge.

Fairbank, John K. 1983. *The United States and China*. Harvard University Press.

Fairbank, John K. 1987. *Great Chinese Revolution, 1800–1985*. HarperCollins.

Fairbank, John K., and Goldman, M. 2006. *China: A New History*. Cambridge: The Belknap Press of Harvard University Press.

Faure, David. 2006. *China and Capitalism: A History of Business Enterprise in Modern China*. Hong Kong: Hong Kong University Press.

Feuerwerker, Albert. 1984. The State and the Economy in Late Imperial China. *Theory and Society* 13: 297–326.

Geertz, Clifford. 1963. *Agricultural Involution: The Processes of Ecological Change in Indonesia*. California: University of California Press.

Goldstone, Jack A. 2002. Efflorescences and Economic Growth in World History: Rethinking the "Rise of the West" and the Industrial Revolution. *Journal of World History* 13 (2): 323–389.

Goldstone, Jack, A. 2008. *Why Europe?: Global Change in a Global Context, 1500–1900 AD*. New York: Mcgraw-Hill Higher Education.

Greif, Avner, and Tabellini, Guido. 2010. Cultural and Institutional Bifurcations: China and Europe Compared. *American Economic Review: Papers and Proceedings 100 (May 2010)*, 135–140.

Goetzmann, William N. 2017. *Money Changes Everything: How Finance Made Civilization Possible*. Princeton: Princeton University Press.

Gupta, Bishnupriya, and Debin Ma. 2000. Europe in an Asian Mirror: The Great Divergence. In *The Cambridge Economic History of Modern Europe*, ed. Stephen Broadberry and Kevin H. O'Rourke, 264–285. Cambridge: Cambridge University Press.

Hajnal, John. 1965. European Marriage Patterns in Perspective. In *Population in History: Essays in Historical Demography*, ed. D.V. Glass et al., 101–140. Chicago: Aldine Publishing.

He, Wenkai. 2013. *Paths toward the Modern Fiscal State: England, Japan, and China*. Cambridge, MA: Harvard University Press.

Hintze, Otto. 1931. Kalvinismus und Staatsräson in Brandenburg zu Beginn des 17. Jahrhunderts. *Historische Zeitschrift*, Bd. 144, H. 2, 229–286.

Huang, Philip C. C. 1990. *The Peasant Family and Rural Development in the Yangzi Delta, 1350–1988*. Stanford: Stanford University Press.

Huang, Ray. 2015[1988]. *China: A Macro History*. London: Routledge.

Johnson, Noel D., and Mark Koyama. 2017. States and Economic Growth: Capacity and Constraints. *Explorations in Economic History* 64: 1–20.

Jones, Eric Lionel. 1988. *The European Miracle: Environments, Economies, and Geopolitics in the History of Europe and Asia*. Cambridge: Cambridge University Press.

Kalberg, Stephen. 2021. *Max Weber's Sociology of Civilizations: A Reconstruction*. London: Routledge.

Landes, David S. 1998. *The Wealth and Poverty of Nations: Why Some Are So Rich and Some So Poor*. NY: W. W. Norton and Company.

Lee, James Z. and Feng, Wang. 2001. *One Quarter of Humanity: Malthusian Mythology and Chinese Realities*. Cambridge: Harvard University Press.

Li, Bozhong. 1996. Qingdai Qianzhongqi Jiangnan Renkou de Disu Zengzhang jiqi Yuanyi[The Slow Population Growth in the Jiangnan in the Early and Mid-Qing Dynasty and Its Reasons]. *The Qing History Journal* 2: 10–19. (in Chinese).

Li, Bozhong. 2002. *Development and Constraint: A Study of Productivity in South China in the Ming and Qing Dynasties*. Taipei: Linking Publishing Company. (in Chinese).

Li, Bozhong, Jan van Zanden, and Luiten. 2012. Before the Great Divergence? Comparing the Yangzi Delta and the Netherlands at the Beginning of the Nineteenth Century. *The Journal of Economic History* 72 (4): 956–989.

Lin, Justin Yifu. 1995. The Needham Puzzle: Why the Industrial Revolution Did Not Originate in China. *Economic Development and Cultural Change* 43 (2): 269–292.

Lin, Justin Yifu. 2008. The Needham Puzzle, the Weber Question, and China's Miracle: Long-term Performance since the Sung Dynasty. *China Economic Journal* 1 (1): 63–95.

Lin, Justin Yifu. 2018. *Demystifying the Chinese Economy*. Beijing: Peking University Press. (in Chinese).

Liu, William Guanglin. 2015. *The Chinese Market Economy 1000–1500*. New York: State University of New York Press.

Long, Denggao, Zhenghua Wang, et al. 2018. Traditional Non-government Organization Governance Structure and Institutional Legal Property Right - Focus on the Construction and Management of the Public Facilities in Qing Dynasty. *Economic Research Journal* 10: 175–191. (in Chinese).

Ma, Debin. 2004. Growth, Institutions and Knowledge: A Review and Reflection on the Historiography of 18th–20th Century China. *Australian Economic History Review* 44 (3): 259–277.

Ma, Debin. 2012. Political Institution and Long-run Economic Trajectory: Some Lessons from Two Millennia of Chinese Civilisation. In *Institutions and Comparative Economic Development*, ed. Aoki Masahiko, et al., 78–98. Palgrave Macmillan.

Ma, Debin, and Jared Rubin. 2019. The Paradox of Power: Principal-agent Problems and Administrative Capacity in Imperial China (and Other Absolutist Regimes). *Journal of Comparative Economics* 47: 277–294.

Macfarlane, Alan. 1978. *Origins of English Individualism: The Family Property and Social Transition*. New York: Wiley.

Mokyr, Joel. 2009. *The Enlightened Economy: Britain and the Industrial Revolution, 1700–1850*. Beijing: Penguin Books.

Mühlhahn, Klaus. 2019. *Making China Modern: from the great Qing to Xi Jinping*. Cambridge: The Belknap Press of Harvard University Press.

Naughton, Barry. 2007. *The Chinese Economy: Transitions and Growth*. Cambridge, Massachusetts: The MIT Press.

Oh, Keum-Sung. 2020[2007]. *Guofa Yu Shehui Guanxing* [State Laws and Social Norms]. Trans. Cui, Ronggen. Zhejiang University Press. (in Chinese).

Peng, Kaixiang. 2021. The State in the Economic History of Ming-Qing China: A Conversational Review. *Researches on Chinese Economic History* 2: 91–100.

Perdue, Peter C. 1987. *Exhausting the Earth: State and Peasants in Hunan, 1500–1850*. Cambridge: Harvard University Asia Centre.

Perkins, Dwight H. 1969. *Agricultural Development in China, 1368–1968*. New York: Aldine Publishing Company.

Pomeranz, Kenneth. 2000. *The Great Divergence: China, Europe, and the Making of the Modern World Economy*. Princeton: Princeton University Press.

Pomeranz, Kenneth. 2021. Between Benign Neglect and Heroic Failure: State Capacity and the Qing Economy in Broad Lines. Trans. Zhou. *Lin. Researches in Chinese Economic History* 2: 19–38. (in Chinese).

Robinson, Kenneth G. (Ed.). 2004. *Science and Civilisation in China* (Vol. 7). Cambridge: Cambridge University Press.

Schefold, Bertram. 2014. Marx, Sombart, Weber and the Debate about the Genesis of Modern Capitalism. *Journal of Institutional Studies* 6 (2): 10–26.

Schluchter, Wolfgang. 1979. *Die Entwicklung des okzidentalen Rationalismus: Eine Analyse von Max Webers Gesellschaftsgeschichte*. Mohr Siebeck.

Shiue, Carol H., and Keller, Wolfgang. 2004. Markets in China and Europe on the Eve of the Industrial Revolution. NBER Working Paper 10778.

Sng, Tuan-Hwee., and Chiaki Moriguchi. 2014. Asia's Little Divergence: State Capacity in China and Japan Before 1850. *Journal of Economic Growth* 19 (4): 439–470.

Studer, Roman. 2015. *The Great Divergence Reconsidered: Europe*. India and the Rise to Global Economic Power: Cambridge University Press.

Tilly, Charles. 1992. *Coercion, Capital, and European States, AD 990 – 1992.* Hoboken: Blackwell Publishing.

von Glahn, Richard. 2016. *The Economic History of China: From Antiquity to the Nineteenth Century.* Cambridge: Cambridge University Press.

Weber, Max. 1958. *The Protestant Ethic and the Spirit of Capitalism.* New York: Charles Scribner's Sons.

Wong, R. Bin. 1997. *China Transformed: Historical Change and the Limits of European Experience.* Ithaca: Cornell University Press.

Zelin, Madeleine. 1992. *The Magistrate's Tael: Rationalizing Fiscal Reform in Eighteenth-Century Ch'ing China.* University of California Press.

Zhang, Taisu. 2019. The Ideological Foundations of the Qing Fiscal State (Introduction). https://ssrn.com/abstract=3503063.

Zhang, Taisu. 2021. The Uses and Limitations of Rationalist Explanations for Qing Fiscal Power. *Researches in Chinese Economic History* 1: 40–53. (in Chinese).

CHAPTER 9

Pursuing Modernisation in China

From the late eighteenth century, the Qing government has not been able to sustain the imperial structure efficiently. Corruption of bureaucrats had worsened; Necessary infrastructure, including the granary system and hydraulic projects, were out of maintenance; farmers became impoverished because of monetary problems and diminishing returns of agricultural activities. What made the governance worse was the advent of the western powers. In the early nineteenth century, British companies exported opium to China in order to balance the trade deficit. Subsequently, it drew lots of silver out of China and resulted in widespread demoralisation. The Qing government tried to prohibit opium, but the efforts led to a fierce conflict with Great Britain. Then the Qing government was defeated embarrassingly. In 1842 the Treaty of Nanjing was signed, which signalled the formal opening of China to the West. Western powers started to expand their existence in China. In the second half of the nineteenth century, China lost much of their sovereignty in a series of conflicts with Great Britain, France, the United States, Tsar Russia, and Japan, etc. While China succeeded to avoid becoming a complete colony, Qing's governance fell almost into fragmentation. It was a period characterised by China's declining international status, deteriorating political enforcement and weakening economy.

On the other hand, China was forced to face the fact that the ancient empire had lagged behind the West. Enlightened intellectuals

G. H. Jiang, *The Imperial Mode of China*, Palgrave Studies in Economic History, https://doi.org/10.1007/978-3-031-27015-4_9

and open-minded bureaucrats began the process of industrialisation and modernisation. Since the mid-1850s, in the process of fighting the Taiping Rebellion, some provincial governors, most of whom were Han ethnically, started to welcome western weaponry and advanced machinery. In the approximately four decades until 1894, provincial governors established many industrial factories relating to weaponry, warship, commercial transportation and steel, etc. The efforts to launch industrialisation were glorified as "Tong-Guang Restoration", which Mary Wright (1962) called "the last stand of Chinese conservatism". Meanwhile, individual efforts of certain bureaucrats became a fiasco in the Sino-Japan War in 1894. Yet their efforts heralded an era of fragmentation. During the self-strengthening movement, the Qing government gradually lost its dominance over the vast territory, while provincial officials gained local, political and fiscal authority. In the following years until 1911, the principal–agent problem worsened, as fiscal and military decentralisation facilitated local warlordism. Finally, the Qing government collapsed in the waves of provincial independence.

The imperial dynasty ended in 1912 nominally, when the Republic of China (RC, 1912–1949) was founded by revolutionary forces led by Sun Yet-sen (1866–1925). The RC wanted an America-style regime with the presidency, the representative democracy and other "western" institutions. Sun had a comprehensive blueprint to achieve China's industrialisation, modernisation and internationalisation. However, lacking military power, Sun could not rival Yuan Shikai (1859–1916), who was previously a powerful bureaucrat in the Qing government. Since the founding of the RC, China fell into an era characterised by political fragmentation, local warlordism and economic chaos. Fragile and fragmented governance of the Beiyang government lasted for fifteen years. Then, the nominal unification of China was achieved by the Kuomintang until 1927, while local warlords persisted in territorial peripheries, such as Xinjiang, Sichuan, Yunnan, etc. The Kuomintang launched a series of nation-building movements in the early 1930s, some of which got positive results. However, the second Sino-Japan war erupted. These nation-building efforts led by Chiang Kai-shek (1887–1975) failed. In 1949 the Kuomintang was replaced by the Chinese Communist Party. On the whole, during the RC, the Imperial Mode collapsed, like any historical predecessor. Social order or national defence could not be guaranteed, and this situation harmed economy. Although the Kuomintang had made efforts to modernise

China, it failed to complete the fundamental preconditions required by modernisation.

After 1949, the Chinese Communist Party (CCP) led by Mao Zedong (1893–1976) took over the vast territories of China which were ravaged by persistent wars and excessive exploitation by warlords. As shown in the last chapter, the Kuomintang failed to achieve political unification. Its political fragility made it impossible to fundamentally change China's backwardness. For the CCP, it eliminated those political obstacles through military victories, thus achieving domestic social order which had been lacking for decades in China. Thereafter, the CCP introduced socialist ideals to transform China. The peasant economy was totally discontinued by collectivisation in rural areas. Industrial and commercial enterprises were nationalised and then managed by the communist bureaucratic system. Cadres with communist training were sent to build branches nationwide, even in small villages where former governors of the Kuomintang and the Ming-Qing emperors abandoned direct control.[1] Essentially, the CCP implemented Stalinist policies before 1956. The Imperial Mode of China would have been replaced by Stalinist socialism, if everything had followed the designation of high cadres of the CCP. However, after certain political events, Mao changed his mind and gradually gave up Stalinism. He introduced his own ways to transform China, which bore many imprints of the Imperial Mode. In the 1960s and 1970s, Maoist socialism was much like an enhanced version of the Imperial Mode with some socialist characteristics. However, the economy was always plagued by political turmoil. During the reign of Mao, economic growth was hardly satisfying, although some industries developed noticeably.

In the 1980s, economic reforms were launched by pragmatic cadres who could not implement their ideas during the Mao's era. They started to gradually abandon the planned economy under which the Chinese economy almost collapsed. Leaders in rural areas gradually gave up collectivisation. The entry barriers of certain industries were lowered. The span of state-owned enterprises shrank. Mechanisms of the free market were

[1] Vogel (1969: 41–180) provided a brilliant case study of how communist cadres built a "new order" in Canton which is in the southern part of China. It might be the most extreme example, because in Canton the situation might be the most complicated. People spoke highly differentiated dialects. The power of the gentry class was especially strong, not to mention its geographical closeness to Hong Kong and Macau which were the most well-known colonies of the European countries. The practice in Canton could be a magnifier of the communist takeover.

introduced to stimulate economic growth. A gradual liberalisation process ensued (Huang 2008). In the 1990s, the CCP announced that the goal of economic reforms would be to establish the "socialist market economy".[2] However, this announcement has more to do with political propaganda than with theoretical meaning. It was the expansion of "capitalism" that drove economic reforms. However, few could either agree with the argument that China had become a capitalist nation, in that from many angles it was still an absolutist regime. The CCP relied on a toolbox consisting of capitalism and the Imperial Mode to rule over China. Utilising capitalist and imperial mechanisms, the CCP established a mixed mode—"Oriental Capitalism".[3] Because of China's path dependence and active choices of the CCP, the Imperial Mode will linger on.

Between 1912 and 1949 China tried to imitate western republicanism. After 1949 China walked on a unique communist path. Not only the Maoist practices between 1949 and 1978 but also economic reforms after 1978 have lessons both for scholarly accounts and practical needs. The former was a Chinese version of socialism whose intellectual sources and real practices came primarily from Europe. The latter was similarly a Chinese version of liberalisation whose models are based mostly on Anglo-Saxon countries. From this perspective, the westernisation process in China continued, which had started since the middle nineteenth century. While these practices were influenced by western sources, they revolved around the Imperial Mode, alternating between moving closer to China's traditional methods of rule or trying to move towards a new path. China is still captured by path dependence. Chinese revolutionaries tried to achieve modernisation through introducing westernisation, but none of them could completely escape from social, economic and especially cultural impacts of the Imperial Mode. This chapter will present the efforts of the revolutionaries to modernise China based on the imperial system.

[2] The term was introduced by Jiang Zemin during the 14th National Congress of the Communist Party of China in 1992. It was described by Chinese propaganda as one of the most creative inventions of Marxism in China.

[3] In their propaganda, the CCP announced that the social mode after the 1980s was "socialism with Chinese characteristics". However, Chinese society was becoming very "non-socialist". If imitating the vocabular structure of this term, "Oriental Capitalism" would be "capitalism with Chinese characteristics".

1 The Collapse of the Imperial Mode in Late Qing

As illustrated before, the Qing government had been confronted with many difficulties since the late eighteenth century. Because of the inner paradoxes within the centralised despotic regime, corruption had become rampant especially during the second half of the reign of the Emperor Qianlong (Acemoglu and Robinson 2019: 216–218). Predominantly due to willingness of bureaucrats to engage in bribery and rent-seeking, public services went out of maintenance. The granary system aimed at disaster relief obtained no further supplement (Will and Wong 1991); Large-scale hydraulic networks started to deteriorate (Elvin et al. 1998). Facing these social problems, the Qing government found no solutions. By the early eighteenth century, the Qing government had clearly entered into a period of dynastic decline (Naughton 2007: 39). Under this stage, it had not been able to fulfil those tasks prescribed by the Imperial Mode. More seriously, in the first half of the nineteenth century, China encountered a prolonged deflation because of the scarcity of silver in the domestic economy, which resulted in widespread depression and unemployment (He 2013: 11). The economic depression was on the one hand caused by declining international supply of silver, which came in a large scale from Latin America (Lin 2006: Chapters 2 and 3). On the other hand, the opium trade extracted much of the silver out from China's domestic economy (Mühlhahn 2019: 91).

In the trade between Qing China and Great Britain, British merchants could not sell much to Chinese peasants because their consumption behaviours were not matched with the products that British merchants offered, while Great Britain had to import much of their tea and porcelain from China, which resulted in numerous trade deficits for Great Britain. In order to pay for these Chinese commodities, British merchants found Bengal opium. In the early eighteenth century, opium was increasingly exported to China (Mühlhahn 2019: 91). The trade of opium triggered a series of social problems in China, including rural impoverishment and demoralisation. Officials worried so much about the negative consequences of opium that the central court sent Lin Zexu (1785–1850) to Guangdong Province to launch Anti-opium campaigns. The forceful policies adopted in Guangdong led eventually to military conflicts with Great Britain. In 1840, the war began and lasted for two years. The Qing empire suffered from a disastrous defeat. It was forced to sign the Nanjing Treaty, on the basis of which five coastal ports were made freely open to international trade and allowing British merchants to gain larger access to the Chinese market.[4]

Although many Chinese consider the Nanjing Treaty as a huge shame and the start of China's degradation, it had sophisticated meaning for China. Before the Nanjing Treaty the Qing government treated foreigners as "barbarians" who should show their respect and homage to the Qing empire, and officials considered contact with foreigners unnecessary. Since 1842, China had to seriously take foreign threats into account. More importantly, it signalled "the advent of the West", although foreign priests and merchants had come to China continuously since the Ming dynasty. Some top-ranking bureaucrats in the Qing empire recognised the meaning of the advent. It was a strange societal mechanism different from what the Chinese were familiar with. It was the capitalist market economy. One of the top governors, Li Hongzhang (1823–1901), called the drastic societal change as "a significant change unseen in thousands of years".[5] He was correct. In the final decades of the Qing dynasty, the Chinese witnessed not only the gradual collapse of the Imperial Mode but also the increasingly expanding influence of the "occidental" model.

However, rulers did not have time to observe the West thoroughly. In the 1850s, a domestic rebellion, which might be the most catastrophic one in Chinese history, erupted in southern China—the Taiping Rebellion (1851–1864). In 1851, Hong Xiuquan (1814–1864), a formerly frustrated candidate in the state examination, organised an army to rebel against the Qing dynasty. Because social unrest had been brewing up for decades, the rebellion gained regional victories very quickly. The Taiping army overwhelmed the southern provinces, and in 1853 it occupied Nanjing which Hong Xiuquan declared as the capital of the Taiping Kingdom. Hong utilised a bizarrely deformed Christian ideology to spiritually control his followers, while he used China's traditional utopian

[4] As illustrated before, prior to the Nanjing Treaty, international trade was restricted to Guangzhou and regulations upon foreign merchants were very stringent. After signing the Nanjing Treaty, five ports, including Guangzhou, Fuzhou, Xiamen, Ningbo and Shanghai, were freely open to foreign merchants. This term was the most important one in the Nanjing Treaty, in that it formally opened access to China's domestic market.

[5] This term came from an official plea to the Tongzhi Emperor in 1872. Li Hongzhang requested the purchase of advanced warships and weaponry. Li aimed to demonstrate the necessity of taking action to defend the Qing empire.

ideal to manage the territory which the Taiping army occupied.[6] The civil war between the Taiping Kingdom and the Qing government lasted for a decade and swept the Yangtze Delta, which was the most economically prosperous and populous region in the Qing empire. The rapacious plundering of the Taiping army also caused huge destruction in war-involved regions. Nevertheless, leaders of the Taiping Kingdom, including Hong Xiuquan himself, lived a luxurious and carnivalesque life in Nanjing. The economy was hugely damaged, and regions under the control of the Taiping army had a dark period.[7]

At the early stage of the Taiping Rebellion, the Qing government's reaction was slow and very weak partly because the Qing army lost its military capacity and local bureaucrats lacked competence. The fiscal weakness of the Qing government, which had existed since the sixteenth century, resulted in a paucity of public services and inability to cope with exigent events (He 2004), like the Taiping Rebellion. The Qing army was confronted with a series of military defeats in southern China. The Qing rulers were so anxious that they allowed local governors to organise private troops to fight against the Taiping army. In this process, many local bureaucrats arose, such as Zeng Guofan (1811–1872), Zuo Zongtang (1812–1885) and Li Hongzhang, etc. Although they were all ethnically Han people, the Manchurian rulers gave them large independence. Facing the extremely dangerous attacks from the Taiping army, they gradually accepted the opinion that foreign weaponry did work much better. While they organised regional forces to fight against the Taiping army, they launched the self-strengthening movement in which military factories were established to strengthen their troops' armoury. In the Yangtze Delta, Fujian Province, and Tianjin, etc., industrialised factories which utilised foreign technology and workers were established.

[6] In the book, *Tianchao Tianmu Zhidu*, Hong Xiuquan abolished the landlord class and the peasant class as well. Private ownership was also abolished. All lands and assets belonged to "the sacred treasury". People cultivated together, and harvest was submitted to "the sacred treasury". People were then allocated basic consumption goods. The arrangement was so full of impractical utopian characteristics that many historians doubted whether it had ever been adopted in practice.

[7] Some historians estimated that around one hundred million people died due to warfare and famine during the Taiping Rebellion. About the evaluation on the Taiping Rebellion, see Deng (2012: Chap. 4).

In 1864, Nanjing was reclaimed by troops led by Zeng Guofan, and Hong Xiuquan died in his palace. Most of the generals and governors on the Qing government's side, who contributed to the fall of the Taiping Kingdom, were promoted and gained powerful positions in central and provincial governments. They continued to carry forward the self-strengthening movement and to extend its scope. In the 1870s and 1880s, modernised fleets were established by Zuo Zongtang and Li Hongzhang; In 1890, Zhang Zhidong (1837–1909) launched construction of a steel factory in Hanyang, which was the biggest steel factory in the Far East for a quite long time; Li Hongzhang established commercial enterprises in Shanghai and Tianjin. Unlike their stubbornly conservative colleagues who refused any changes and insisted in the value of the traditional society, advocates for the self-strengthening movement recognised the necessity of "learning from foreigners". Among them Feng Guifen (1809–1874) was the most radical.[8] While Feng agreed with Lin Zexu, who proposed that China should learn from foreigners and would then be able to outcompete them, Feng went further. He argued that westerners' superiority came not only from military power, but also from more efficient institutions. Thus, Feng proposed to reform the country comprehensively, including reforms in education (the state examination system), the economy, science and the bureaucratic system (Mühlhahn 2019: 159). On the other hand, Feng insisted in the value of Confucian ethic and preaching. Such a standpoint typically represented most advocates for the self-strengthening movement. They recognised the advantage of foreign technology but refused to acknowledge the disadvantages of Chinese culture, as well as China's societal structure and political system.

During the self-strengthening movement and the process of repressing the Taiping Rebellion, the trend of regional decentralisation unanticipated by the Qing government developed overwhelmingly. Due to chaos in the fiscal system, the Qing government did not have sufficient financial resources to support military actions. Between 1851 and 1868, total state expenses in coping with the Taiping Rebellion, the Nian Rebellion, and other smaller uprisings in the northwest and the southwest ran

[8] Feng's ideas were collected in his comprehensive book, *Jiaobinlu Kangyi*. In Wright's monograph (1962), there is a detailed introduction about Feng's opinions in military, agricultural, educational and political issues in different chapters. Wright considered Feng the most radical member of his peers partly because Feng stepped in the field of political reform.

as high as 300 million tael of silver (Peng 1983: 136). But the Qing government could only achieve an annual income of some 40 million tael (He 2013: 131). Fatally threatened by the Taiping army, the Qing government began to take a more flexible and tolerant attitude towards competent governors. More political power was granted to them. Firstly, local bureaucrats were encouraged to organise troops in order to fight against the Taiping army. For example, Zeng Guofan recruited an army consisting mainly of peasants in Hunan Province and the adjacent regions; Zuo Zongtang and Li Hongzhang also organised their independently commanded troops. Apart from organising troops, provincial governors also gained the power to appoint more civil positions. Gradually, local bureaucrats eroded the central power. Secondly, local revenues of provincial governments in the war zones were directly transported in the hands of generals. "Funds from other provincial governments were often sent to the military stations instead of going through the provincial treasury as in normal times" (He 2013: 143). The Taiping Rebellion swept across southern China, which was the most important source of fiscal revenues. It resulted in the situation that most revenues of the Qing government flowed towards the general-governors. Thirdly, local governors also gained the power to collect lijin duties. Lijin duties were levied on consumptions goods, such as tobacco and salt, etc., and were targeted at big wholesalers or guilds.[9] Since the Taiping Rebellion necessitated the lijin collection, which provided financial resources for front troops, it persisted through the war. Afterwards, because it was able to offer enormous revenues, the lijin collection became a long-term practice until the founding of Communist China.[10]

On the whole, fiscal and political decentralisation was necessitated by military operations (He 2013: 150). The central government had suffered so much from fiscal deficits, that it could not provide sufficient supports for generals in war zones. It allowed generals to create new financial sources, which strengthened their military capacity. Gradually local general-governors organised locally controlled treasuries, i.e.,

[9] The lijin collection was often practised in three cases: (1) when a large amount of a given commodity was packaged and ready for transportation; (2) when the package passed certain pivotal nodes in the transportation networks; and (3) when the package arrived in a new market before it was dispatched to small retailers. See He (2013: 167).

[10] After the collapse of the Qing dynasty, local warlords continued this practice, and the exploitation became fiercer.

"waixiao". These sorts of revenues were not reported to the central government, but it was not completely equal to corruption involving local officials. Local governments were responsible for its collection, utilisation, auditing and supervision. During the uprisings through the 1850s to the 1870s, "waixiao" was mainly used to repress rebellions. After the uprisings, it was used for the maintenance of local infrastructure, disaster relief and other public affairs which local governors aimed to do (Chen 2020). By the end of the nineteenth century, the lijin duties, which were the main component of "waixiao", made up 15–19% of all revenues of the Qing government (Mühlhahn 2019: 163). Local governments did not only get fiscal autonomy, but also partial political independence in some way. General-governors received vast power to appoint their own acquaintances as officials. For example, many disciples and staff of Zeng Guofan got influential positions, such as governorship of rich provinces in southern China. The regional cliques grew so strong that Zeng Guofan was asked whether he would replace the Qing government after the Taiping Rebellion was repressed.[11] Although the main regional troops were dismantled after the Taiping Rebellion, Han bureaucrats kept almost unassailable control over military forces in the Qing empire. More importantly, for instance, Li Hongzhang started to organise modernised fleets. From another perspective, in this political decentralisation, Han bureaucrats overpowered Manchurian bureaucrats. This trend eroded legitimacy of the Qing government.

The political and economic trends which originated during the uprisings in the 1850s and developed thereafter vitally affected the fate of imperial China in the second half of the nineteenth century and the beginning years of the twentieth century. For the Qing government, the principal–agent problem worsened continuously. The central court could no longer control those local governors efficiently, and their interests were no longer mutually compatible. The conflict of interests heated up in the final years of the Qing dynasty. Eventually, Yuan Shikai, a local governor and the founder of Qing's modernised troops, forced the baby emperor to abdicate so he could become the head of China in 1911. From this perspective, the self-strengthening movement launched by a

[11] After repressing the Taiping Rebellion, Zuo Zongtang asked surreptitiously Zeng Guofan whether he might replace the Qing government since Han bureaucrats controlled the most powerful military forces. Zeng refused to do so and dismantled his army.

few bureaucrats facilitated political decentralisation. Additionally, the self-strengthening movement introduced western technology and a wealth of new knowledge. New intellectual institutes were erected. Also, with the establishment of several industrial enterprises, managerial methods and new organisational structures such as the joint-stock company was adopted, which had a beneficial impact on economic growth (Wang 2005). All of these factors contributed to the search for modernisation in China, although bureaucrats subjectively aimed to sustain their conservative society. In brief, the self-strengthening movement was an effort full of mixed influences.

> The Chinese efforts were ambitious, but effectively limited by an unwillingness to fundamentally change political processes and institutions. There was no effort to overhaul the empire's political system. There was no initiative to draft a modern constitution or commercial law, and no reform of the currency system. … Most limiting was the Qing restoration's inability to raise sufficient funds for the defence industry and for other modernisation programs such as the building of railroads.
>
> ……
>
> While falling short of its initial grand plans and high hopes of restoring the dynasty to prosperity and power, self-strengthening in the late Qing nonetheless created early experiences of industrialisation and limited examples of gradual institutional innovation, above all in business, upon which later generations could build. (Mühlhahn 2019: 169)

The self-strengthening movement lasting from the 1860s to the 1890s was an intentional effort to promote industrialisation in China. Although attacked by other conservative officials for deteriorating Confucian ethic and value, those active proponents for this movement did not intend to do so. Acemoglu and Robinson (2013: 56–60) held that cultural values cannot compose obstacles for industrialisation and the adoption of new technologies. However, cultural insistence of the conservative officials in the late Qing dynasty indeed hindered the adoption of new technologies coming mainly from the West. Even those open-minded bureaucrats had to confront fierce criticism from the conservative officials who often occupied top positions in the central government. Many industrial proposals were rejected with hatred and animosity in the court because they were considered inimical to traditional and harmonious lifestyle. Furthermore, the proudness of Chinese traditional values prevented those proponents from taking more actions to reform institutions which hindered industrialisation and modernisation. They superficially believed that western material forces would be able to make China regain its prosperity and strength. However, without progress in the corresponding institutions, even industrialisation could not go further.

The formal failure of the self-strengthening movement was symbolised by the Sino-Japan war in 1894. During the Meiji Reform starting in 1868, Japan had lots of progress in industrialization and modernisation. Gradually Japan began to expand its influence in the Korean Peninsula, which was the tributary of the Qing empire. In 1894, Japan and the Qing empire had battles in Korea, and soon Japan enlarged battles into a large-scale war against the Qing empire. The modernised fleet of the Qing empire, which was controlled by Li Hongzhang, were confronted with a devastating defeat. After Li's fleet was destroyed, the Qing empire lost its power to fight.[12] In the second year, Japan forced the Qing empire to sign the Treaty of Shimonoseki. Most influential were two terms: Taiwan was ceded to Japan, and foreigners were allowed to invest in China. Introduction of foreign investment hugely influenced industrialisation in China. On the one hand, it pushed forward industrialisation especially in coastal zones and treaty ports. New technology and organisations were constantly introduced. Economic prosperity in treaty ports which had independent legal status from the Chinese government was eye-catching in the beginning decades of the twentieth century.[13] On the other hand, the new factors functioned to decompose the traditional structure of Chinese society.[14] Autarky agricultural economy was slowly

[12] There are many academic works about the reasons why the Qing empire lost this war since the Qing empire was much stronger than Japan in terms of aggregate capacity. Traditional explanations include corruption of the Qing empire, demoralisation of Qing troops and the technical disadvantage of Li's fleet. In recent years, research attributed it to the nonexistence of a fiscal state in the Qing empire. While Japan succeeded to establish a fiscal state which could centralise financial resources and thus enhance state capacity, the Qing empire failed to collect enough revenues. See He (2013: Chapters 3, 4 and 6).

[13] The industrial economy prospered in treaty ports and adjacent regions, such as the Yangtze Delta, Canton and Shandong. See So and Myers (2011).

[14] According to China's Marxists, the foreign investment, made possible by the Treaty of Shimonoseki, contributed to the growth of capitalist factors in China. More factories, operated by either foreigners or the Chinese, increased the number of proletarians. According to this historical interpretation, while foreign investment brought pain to the

influenced, and more farmers were pulled into markets. The economic base of the Imperial Mode was gradually eroded, although the peasant economy was never totally disintegrated by industrialisation at this stage.

Nevertheless, Chinese felt shamed and angry about the loss of territory and sovereignty. The intellectual circle, within which Kang Youwei (1858–1927) was the most outstanding one, felt it urgent to reform Chinese society. In 1898, Kang formed a team of young bureaucrats in the central court and advised the young emperor to launch a comprehensive and speedy reform. The reformatory content was unprecedentedly wholescale, including the drastic reduction of bureaucrats and departments, fiscal reform, educational reform, etc. The final goal was to transform the Qing empire into a constitutional monarchy.[15] However, their actions were politically naïve. The reform did not last for over one hundred days. It was abruptly terminated by the Empress Cixi (1835–1908) in a coup d'état. Then, the young emperor was put into house detention and the Empress Cixi stepped ahead into the central stage again. Although the political reform was ended, the urgency of reform could not be denied. The Empress Cixi and top officials close to her launched a political reform in the 1900s. Many measures aiming to create a constitutional monarchy were taken. The most drastic was the abolition of the state examination system in 1905. As the key to sustaining the bureaucratic system, the state examination system was a vital component of the imperial structure. Moreover, a Cabinet was organised to replace the old administrative system. Nonetheless, the Manchurian royal family was never truehearted about the political reform. The Cabinet was full of royal members and conservative bureaucrats. Briefly speaking, the political reform did not intend to reach its goals.

In 1911, a small-scale rebellion of a modernised army erupted in Wuchang, an industrialised town in middle China. Very soon many provincial governors announced independence and detachment from the Qing government. In just a few months, the reign of the Manchurian empire collapsed. Threatened by Yuan Shikai, the head of the Beiyang army, which was the most powerful troop of the Qing government, the Qing royal family announced abdication. The last imperial dynasty was

Chinese, it contributed to historical progress from feudalism to capitalism. This kind of Marxist history was debated heatedly.

[15] As an intellectual strategy, Kang resorted to Confucian ideals and the Meiji Reform. About Kang's ideas, see Mühlhahn (2019: 189–190).

formally ended. Its collapse was directly caused by political decentralisation and intractable bureaucrats, such as Yuan Shikai. In-depth reasons include its inability to cope with external shocks and the weakening state capacity (Wang 2022: Chap. 8). Even before the mid-nineteenth century, the Qing government incapable of maintaining public good provision in local communities and rural areas had to delegate some responsibilities to local elites. The situation got worse after the Qing empire confronted more crises. As Wang (2022: 195–197) suggests, local elites tended to claim independence since the central government had not been able to protect their interests and sustain social order. Conversely, Local elites tended to take collective actions to defend themselves under the circumstance that the state as a whole was weak. Like many precedents in Chinese history, bureaucrats/elites who did not listen to the central emperorship again overthrew the dynasty. As illustrated before, political decentralisation had grown since the 1850s. After the Qing dynasty ended, regional warlordism became the de facto situation in China, although the Republic of China kept nominal reign.

2 Nation-Building Efforts in the Republic of China

The Qing dynasty was replaced by the Republic of China (RC) in 1912. Sun Yet-sen was nominated as the president of the RC, although he did not factually lead this revolutionary process in 1911.[16] According to Sun's designation, the newborn nation was a constitutional republic. In his mind, the model was based on the United States of America, and indeed the RC was praised as the "first republic in Asia" (Mühlhahn 2019: 209). Sun's ideas could be described as the "Three Principles of the People" consisting of nationalism ("minzu"), democrac y("minquan") and welfare ("minsheng"). Firstly, China had to fight back against the negative influence of imperialism. It had been extensively known that the impoverishment and bitterness of the Chinese people in the second half of the nineteenth century were caused mainly by several invasions from foreigner powers. Sun believed that in order to cure such sick phenomena as cultural degradation, economic depression and social

[16] When the uprising erupted in Wuchang, Sun was still overseas. He and his close clique did not plan the uprising. It was directly led by a group of enthusiasts who followed Sun's preaching and tenets.

ruptures, China must supress imperialism. Secondly, Sun recognised the backwardness of Chinese societal mechanisms and thus acknowledged the necessity of learning western institutions. Rejecting the constitutional monarchy proposed by Kang Youwei and his comrades, Sun believed that China should have a top-down monarchical reform but a bottom-up republican revolution. Through establishing a national parliament and granting citizens political rights such as election and referendum, etc., China would become strong and well-administered (Mühlhahn 2019: 222–223). Thirdly, the Principle of "minsheng" was mainly related to economic policies. But this component was the least clear and the least accurately defined. Sun vaguely pursued the optimisation of economic conditions, such as infrastructure (railways, harbours, domestic transportation networks and so on) and a commercial environment with the aim of improving the living standard. Simultaneously, Sun mentioned the equality issue. He clearly objected to big landownership and commercial monopolies. On the whole, Sun's "Three Principles of the People" was an eclectic ideology which combined western political theories and Chinese traditions. After the Kuomintang, who were headed by Sun in the 1910s and 1920s, established a national regime in the 1930s, Sun's doctrines were worshipped as the constitutional foundation of the RC.

However, in the 1910s, Sun Yat-sen and his party, i.e., the Kuomintang, were militarily weak. After negotiating with Yuan Shikai, Sun transferred presidency to Yuan. Thereafter, Yuan established the Beiyang government (1912–1928), with the RC as the nominal national government. The Beiyang government ushered in an era characterised by regional warlordism, chaos and political fragmentation. While Yuan Shikai kept his power through his Beiyang troops, provinces were controlled by regional warlords. Sun and the Kuomintang controlled Guangdong; Some of Yuan's opponents controlled Yunnan and Guizhou; Even some of Yuan's subordinates, such as Duan Qirui and Feng Guozhang, controlled some northern provinces and they did not completely abide by Yuan's commands. Domestic social order almost collapsed, except in treaty ports.[17] Regional warlords took advantage of terrorism to exploit farmers and merchants in their controlled areas. In order to satisfy demand of troops and their own rapacity, warlords exerted unprecedentedly high taxes upon residents, and the tax collection was often informal.

[17] About how treaty ports sustained their internal social order and legal independence, Ma (2011: 33–46) provided a case study in the Yangtze Delta.

They printed regional money which persistently devalued in order to extract wealth. Their armies pillaged villages and robbed merchants in cities. In most cases, warlords' armies were nothing different from bandits and pirates (Sheridan 1983: 318). In this period, the imperial structure collapsed, and the Imperial Mode disintegrated again, in line with historical precedents, thus failing to offer essential public goods, including social order and national defence.

The era of the Beiyang warlords did not terminate until the Kuomintang launched a war against them from Guangdong and eventually achieved nominal unification in 1928. With assistance from the Soviet Union, Sun Yat-sen revolutionised the Kuomintang with Leninist creeds and organised an army in Guangdong. In 1926, Chiang Kai-shek, one of Sun's successors, launched northward wars against Beiyang warlords. In two years, Chiang achieved nominal political unification since most Beiyang warlords either surrendered or quitted from the political stage. "For the first time since 1911, the country was governed again by a single centre" (Mühlhahn 2019: 264). While regional warlordism continued to exist especially in peripheral regions, such as Sichuan, Gansu, Yunnan and Xinjiang, etc., Chiang could exert relatively effective control in most urban areas. In the 1930s, the Kuomintang started diverse nation-building efforts aiming to accomplish Sun Yat-sen's ideas, i.e., transforming China into a modernised republican nation. It built a set of new political institutions full of republican colours. As a copy of the US political structure in which the Presidency, the Parliament and the Supreme Court sustained impartiality and balance, the Kuomintang established five branches: a Legislative House, an Executive House, a Judicial House, a Supervisory House and an Examination House.[18] It also built institutions which strived to develop an industrialised economy. The economic departments led by Soong Tse-ven took sweeping steps to push forward economic growth. Soong envisioned an industrialisation in which state-controlled enterprises dominated and private enterprises also prospered. In 1935, Soong led a currency reform significant for a

[18] The former three were copied from US politics. The last two stemmed from traditional Confucian bureaucracy. The Supervisory House was in charge of overseeing officials with the power of auditing, impeachment, and censure. The Examination House was in charge of examining government's candidates and appointing new staff. See Mühlhahn (2019: 269).

nationalist economy. In this currency reform, the Kuomintang government succeeded to abolish the silver standard and to issue its fiat paper money which was pegged to the US dollar (Shiroyama 2008: Chap. 7).

The Kuomintang government led by Chiang Kai-shek filled many Americans into its departments and offices as advisors. For example, Arthur Young participated deeply in the nation-building efforts as a top advisor, and he wrote a systematic book about such efforts in the 1930s (Young 1971). In some respects, the Kuomintang government achieved economic growth: from 1931 to 1936, industry grew at an annual rate of 6.7% (Mühlhahn 2019: 282). Also, the Kuomintang government marched forward to build a nationalist republican nation. Although those efforts were definitely not fruitless, it failed to achieve China's modernisation. There are multiple reasons for this. The primary one was the Kuomintang per se. It did not actually establish effective dominance over the whole nation. Many Beiyang warlords transmuted into Kuomintang warlords, and Kuomintang generals became new warlords. Within the Kuomintang, the party was always teared by cliques so that the central leadership could not command bureaucrats and troops efficiently.[19] Economic growth was only restricted to a few urban areas in which the central government could exert effective influence. Rural areas suffered severely from banditry, warlordism, natural disasters and discretionary economic exploitation. Economic growth was highly uneven. The Kuomintang government basically gave up its existence in rural areas, which gave space to the rise of the Chinese Communist Party (CCP) in the late 1930s.

From the mid-1930s, the nation-building efforts were to a large extent interrupted by the Second Sino-Japan war. The whole of China was dragged into the Anti-Japan war. Regional warlordism and party factions harmed military actions against Japanese army. Many eastern and southern territories were occupied by Japan until it was defeated in 1945. When the Kuomintang prepared to harvest the fruits of defeating Japan, it found surprisedly that the CCP had strengthened its power through attracting peasants and tenants in rural areas. In 1946, the Kuomintang and the CCP started a civil war which lasted for three years. Finally, the Kuomintang government was banished to Taiwan which was returned to the RC from Japan in 1945. The communist era would ensue. On the

[19] About the internal divisions of the Kuomintang after 1928, see Mühlhahn (2019: 264–268).

whole, from 1912 to 1949, the RC was not a successful government. It upended the Qing dynasty, which marked the nominal end of the imperial system. The Imperial Mode disintegrated, and then it ushered in an era of disorder. The Kuomintang introduced much more factors of modernity than the late Qing government, but it lacked the fundamental capacity to push forward modernisation. It failed in its nationalist goals combined with modernisation.

3 Disintegration of the Imperial Mode

Since the middle nineteenth century, the Imperial Mode started its formal disintegration. Decades before the advent of foreign colonialists, the Qing empire had declined economically and societally. The Qing government had been unable to cope with those social issues, such as infrastructure maintenance and disaster relief. The central government basically left those tasks to local elites and the gentry class, while it only shouldered the task to sustain social order. Accordingly, the Qing government extracted much less taxes from different economic sectors than its western counterparts.[20] When commercial sectors grew, the Qing government failed to treat and support them seriously. Conversely, it also lacked either the desire or the ability to sustain the peasant economy which had been harmed by rugged economic conditions, including frequent deflation and inflation, deteriorated infrastructure and the corrupted bureaucracy. While many negative signals emerged, the Qing empire had not been driven to the edge of collapse. The central authority and the bureaucratic system showed flexibility and pragmatism after the 1850s (Ni 2021). With the introduction of western experiences, in its final fifty years the Qing government actively reformed its institutions with the aim to save its conservative structure. New economic factors were introduced, including industrialisation efforts in the self-strengthening movement and the growth of private enterprises after the 1890s. The central authority even made some experiments with political reforms. Institutional changes happened in a visible and gradual way, thus leading to the slow disintegration of the Imperial Mode and the move towards modernisation.

[20] It has been widely acknowledged by scholars in recent years that taxation in the Qing dynasty was not as heavy as in west European states, even much lighter. The fiscal income of the Qing government was also less than European counterparts. See He (2021).

The most noticeable changes happened in treaty ports. Since occidental and Japanese colonists occupied urban zones in treaty ports, those cities had been changed so much that they looked like what Max Weber defined as autonomous associations in European history.[21] When the Chinese government lost its sovereignty in treaty ports, the autonomous order grew very fast there. Self-independent institutes were organised to sustain legal and social order, thus creating precious oasis for industrial and commercial economy. Thus, mechanised factories and financial organisations developed fast, which were invested in by Chinese individuals and foreign capital. The support from foreign powers kept destruction away during chaotic periods, such as the Taiping Rebellion and Beiyang warlordism. Shanghai and adjacent areas in particular became prosperous and free economic zones (Ma 2011). After the end of the Qing dynasty, treaty ports kept their special status until 1949 when the CCP abolished all privileges of foreign colonialists. In the development process of treaty ports, they showed the many colours of modernisation: an autonomous society in which the free capitalist market economy prevailed, and the positive governance in which public institutions provided essential public goods including social order and juridical justice with minimum costs.

The modernisation effort pushed by the RC was mixed. The most important public goods offered by the Imperial Mode were social order and national defence, but the RC, including the Beiyang government and the Kuomintang government, never accomplished the minimum of an orderly and peaceful society. During the RC, China was always plagued by internal political fragmentation, warlordism and foreign invasions. Meanwhile, the RC had taken actions towards economic and political modernisation. Announcing the RC as a republic, at least some institutional reforms were tried. The capitalist economy grew in urban areas relatively fast. From 1914 to 1936, Chinese economy achieved the highest growth since the 1870s.[22] The widespread introduction of capitalist institutions paved the way for this growth. Nevertheless, there were also apparent signals that the Kuomintang government leaned towards the

[21] Weber described many European cities in the late Medieval Age and early Modern Age as autonomous associations in which urban dwellers held relatively large political power and independence. Such characteristics contributed to the rise of capitalism in Western Europe. Weber presented his thinking in *Wirtschaft und Gesellschaft* (English: *Economy and Society*). See Weber (1983).

[22] Wang (2005) has calculated the economic data from the 1870s to the late 1940s.

Table 1 China's National Income (1850–1949)

In 1936 Chinese Currency: 100,000,000					
Year	*1850*	*1887*	*1914*	*1936*	*1949*
Agriculture		99.87	128.01	166.41	98.00
Industry and transportation		14.49	24.80	40.06	23.20
Services		29.07	34.72	51.51	68.28
Total	181.64	143.43	187.64	257.98	189.48
Period	1850–1887		1887–1914	1914–1936	1936–1949
Growth rate %	−0.64		1.00	1.45	−2.40

Imperial Mode in the 1930s. Chiang Kai-shek strived for a political central authority with efforts to clamp down on regional warlords and the CCP, in which he used some non-upright strategies. In addition, once the Kuomintang government established nationwide dominance in urban areas after the mid-1930s, it changed to interventionist and exploitative policies (Ma 2011). Since the Anti-Japan war and the civil war with the CCP happened continuously in the late 1930s and the 1940s, the Kuomintang government did not have the opportunity to experiment with its ideas. In short, the RC played a widely changing role in China's modernisation period.

On the whole, the economy during the one hundred years was a bitter fruit. As illustrated in Tables 1 and 2,[23] the economy was locked into ups and downs. There was not any stable long-run growth. The Qing government was lukewarm at best regarding industrialisation and modernisation. After the Taiping Rebellion which had already caused astronomical destruction in the wealthiest regions, the Qing government gradually lost the power to adopt national policies. In the RC period, domestic economy suffered from rapacious warlords and fickle politics. While the Kuomintang government intended to make China prosperous and strong, it was not able to do so. To conclude, plagued by disorder and chronic wars, while stimulated by new capitalist factors, China's economy at this time walked on a zigzag pathway (Table 3).

In some respects, the change that occurred when the RC replaced the Qing dynasty was very similar to any dynastic supersedure in Chinese history, in regard to the rupture of a national government. Alternatively,

[23] Source: Wang (2005: 466).

Table 2 China's National Income *per capita* (1850–1949)

In 1936 Chinese Currency					
Year	*1850*	*1887*	*1914*	*1936*	*1949*
NI[a]	181.64	143.43	187.64	257.98	189.48
Population[b]	414,699	377,636	455,243	510,789	541,670
NI *per capita*	43.8	38.0	41.22	50.51	34.98
Period	1850–1887		1887–1914	1914–1936	1936–1949
Growth Rate %	−0.38		0.30	0.92	−2.87

[a]In 100,000,000
[b]In 1000

Table 3 *Per capita* Production of Agricultural Products

	1955–57	*1964–66*	*1977–79*	*1983–85*
(kilograms *per capita*)				
Grain	303	274	318	376
Edible oil	7.5	4.9[a]	5.4	12.3
Meat	6.2[b]	7.6[c]	9.3	15.1
Cotton	2.4	2.8	2.2	4.8

Source Naughton (1995: 53)
[a]1964–65 only
[b]1957 only
[c]1965 only

concerning the perspective that the Imperial Mode disintegrated and could therefore no longer play its role in Chinese society, the RC could be described as a bridge period between two nationally unified regimes, which was characterised by the absence of social order and effective governance. Then, as previously described, during the RC, the Imperial Mode of the former regime, i.e., the Qing dynasty, fell apart, and the Imperial Mode was reestablished by the following regime after the RC, i.e., the PRC. But what was quite different from previous historical precedents was that the collapse of the Imperial Mode in this period was accompanied with the formal transformation towards modernity. Indeed, the collapse of the Qing empire was primarily caused by internal factors

(Ni 2021),[24] among which the intractable bureaucracy was one of its spearheads. However, the influence of foreign capitalism had a disintegrating effect on the Imperial Mode and ushered in a movement towards modernity.

As demonstrated before, the Imperial Mode was a set of institutions suitable for an agricultural society in which the central authority and the tamed bureaucracy administered the peasant economy. Its incompatibility to a commercial and industrial economy had slowly loomed since the early Ming dynasty. During the late Qing dynasty, the crises caused by domestic and foreign pressure made the disintegration of the Imperial Mode unavoidable. Nevertheless, although the Imperial Mode declined during the late Qing dynasty and finally disintegrated during the RC, its components did not disappear completely. The peasant economy was still predominant, while urban areas experienced fast and widespread industrialisation. The aim to reestablish the despotic political structure came again and again. The Imperial Mode never stopped existing and functioning. After 1949, working on the legacy, the CCP launched its unique path towards modernisation.

4 Maoist Socialism: A Mixture of the Planned Economy and the Imperial Mode

After domestic wars against the Kuomintang, the CCP succeeded in establishing a nationwide regime. Due to serious economic crises, weaknesses of the military troops and strategic mistakes, Chiang Kai-shek and his followers failed disastrously and were banished to Taiwan, the former Japanese colony, which was returned to China in 1945 after the end of the Second World War. The victory of the CCP was so overwhelming and revolutionary that this communist party did not need to serve the vested interests of capitalists and old bureaucrats. Nonetheless, Mao Zedong and his cadres chose to move slowly at first. The CCP integrated those representatives of bourgeoisie into the government, who organised several small parties. The CCP declared itself to be the successor of Sun Yetsen and that it would construct "New Democracy" in China, which was announced as the updated version of the "Three Principles of the People".

[24] Although many Chinese communist scholars still insist that China's backwardness was predominantly caused by foreign intervention and invasions, it is arguable that foreign influence was not so extensive.

With the consideration, the CCP implemented many republican policies at the beginning of its rule.

An important part of these policies was the land reform in rural areas. Before 1949, the CCP has conducted land reforms in northern rural areas which it occupied (Mühlhahn 2019: 402–403). With the nation-wide regime the CCP extended its land reforms southwards in the 1950s. The core part of this land reform was to confiscate lands off landlords and to redistribute these lands among peasants and tenants. As envisioned by communist cadres, the landlord class was eliminated, although many villages had no prominent landholding class (Mühlhahn 2019: 402–403). Criminal acts against rich peasants and landlords were committed in order to fulfil the task of "cleaning up landlords". Through the land reform, many tenants gained lands and peasants amassed productive materials by "legally" robbing landlords. The peasant economy was strengthened in rural areas. Peasants who were individual private-property owners dominated between 1950 and 1955 (Mühlhahn 2019: 417). However, after the elimination of the landlord class, the traditional structure in rural areas was destroyed because in the past rich residents, i.e., the gentry class, acted as communal elites. As illustrated in previous chapters, the gentry class offered necessary public goods to local communities. In the Ming and Qing dynasties, the central government almost made rural areas be run autonomously (Deng 2015). However, the CCP decided to exert direct control in rural areas. It established party committees in every village. As Mühlhahn (2019: 368, 371) wrote,

> It penetrated society far more deeply, however, as its bureaucratic apparatus reached into even the most remote villages. This new state was thus able to wield far greater power than its republican predecessor or its late imperial counterpart in the nineteenth century.
>
> ……
>
> Party committees also existed in every rural commune, every university, every factory, and every residential neighbourhood. This nationwide network of party committees exercised supervision and control over administrative processes at each level and, in short, extended across all social institutions and economic enterprises.

In cities, the CCP did not immediately nationalise bourgeoisie enterprises within the first several years. By confiscating some big enterprises possessed by the Kuomintang, the CCP established state-owned companies in manufacturing and the financial industries, while the CCP allowed bourgeois enterprises to exist and operate. In 1949 Mao declared that "China must utilise all the factors of urban and rural capitalism that are beneficial and not harmful to the national economy and the people's livelihood, and we must unite with the national bourgeoisie in common struggle. Our present policy is to regulate capitalism, not to destroy it" (Mao 1967: 411–421). Thus, a mixed economy emerged in which state-owned enterprises dominated in key sectors and private small enterprises operated in trading and handicraft industries. From many angles, the domestic economic policies of the CCP at this stage were relatively similar to Lenin's New Economic Policy model (Mühlhahn 2019: 418). Moreover, the living standard in rural areas rose remarkably, and industrial and commercial growth was equally impressive, thanks to the restored social order after decades of political chaos and warfare (Mühlhahn 2019: 404).

Things changed very soon. Around 1953 or 1954, Mao decided to hasten the process of a socialist transition. Repudiating suggestions of Chinese and Soviet colleagues, Mao made up his mind to increase the speed of collectivisation in rural areas and of nationalisation in urban areas (Bernstein and Li 2010: 1–24). Mao's ambition betrayed his promise to the business community and his more modest communist colleagues, such as Liu Shaoqi and Zhang Wentian who had closer ties to the Soviet Union. To some degree, Mao's ambition to transform China into a socialist nation more quickly was sparked by the change of political atmosphere in the Soviet Union. After Stalin's death, Mao aspired to replace Stalin as the top leader in the communist world. This would make China a more prominent socialist model to the world.[25] Starting from 1954, the socialist transition was accelerated, although Mao's plan confronted some covert resistance from bureaucrats.[26] Eventually, Mao's plan overwhelmed other potential opponents through means of various political strategies.

Since the mid-1950s, collectivisation in rural areas sped up. Peasants who had gained lands and productive tools several years ago took part

[25] There could be a couple of reasons why Mao changed so dramatically. About a detailed analysis of the possible reasons, see Mühlhahn (2019: 418–420).

[26] Collectivisation in rural areas did not develop as fast as Mao wanted. Mao criticised several times those cadres responsible for specific tasks, including Zhou Enlai and Deng Zihui. See Macfarquhar (1974: 15–38).

in collective units which had the ownership of land, livestock and other property. The private ownership of land was abolished, and the peasant economy was effectively terminated in this process. In urban areas, private entrepreneurs "voluntarily" devoted their business to the government so that all enterprises were nationalised. Individual entrepreneurs became the only stakeholders who received dividends annually.[27] Simultaneously, with the help of Soviet engineers, many factories for heavy industry were established. Moreover, like the Soviet Union, China utilised "price scissors" to accumulate capital for the sake of more investment in heavy industry.[28] The unified purchase system ("tonggou tongxiao") was established on the basis of collectivisation in rural areas, in which agricultural products were uniformly handed up with meagre financial repayment. A Soviet-style planned economy was fundamentally established by the end of 1956.

It is worth mentioning some key figures in the establishment process of China's planned economy because the ideas which they had profoundly influenced China until the burst of the Cultural Revolution. Outstanding politicians, such as Liu Shaoqi (1898–1969) and Chen Yun (1905–1995), were enthusiastic for establishing a planned economy in China. They were ideologically quite close to the Stalinist mode. Both of them had the belief not only in the Stalinist economic mode, but also in the Leninist organisational structure. Liu Shaoqi was a stubborn proponent for the hierarchical structure within a communist party. Liu and Chen were responsible for making the CCP a centralised and tightly controlled party in earlier years.[29] In other words, they wanted to implant the Soviet-style political and economic modes in China. On the other hand, they represented those members in the CCP who were also relatively flexible and pragmatic. They were prepared to compromise principles if the facts did not match

[27] In most cases, the right to receiving dividends annually was also "voluntarily" abolished after a couple of years, with the reasoning that everyone should be independent and work for their own existence according to communist ideals.

[28] The "price scissors" were commonly used in the Stalinist economy. The government purposefully lowered the prices of agricultural products, while it heightened the prices of industrial products, so that profits of industrial products could be higher. Thereafter, the government could gain more capital to reinvest in industry. Sometimes, the government directly exported agricultural products in order to accumulate capital. It is obvious that such an act could be possible only if the government has absolute authority upon the agricultural sectors.

[29] Vogel (2011: 717–720) has written a brief introduction about Chen Yun's efforts in organising the CCP in the 1930s.

with their own principles. However, Mao Zedong did not always agree with them. In the process of collectivisation in the mid-1950s, conflicts had emerged. The fissures between Mao and other pragmatic politicians would gradually enlarge in the following 1860s.

The turning point came when Khrushchev's fierce criticism of Stalin precipitated crises in the socialist world after 1956. Unlike Liu Shaoqi or Chen Yun, Mao Zedong did not have personal affection for Stalin or the Soviet Union. In the past, during the CCP's path to power in China, Stalin often gave wrong and ill-willed advice. In the late 1930s, Stalin did not support Mao to become the top leader of the CCP because Stalin preferred those cadres who had personal connections in Moscow and professional training in Marxism and Leninism.[30] Moreover, during the Sino-Japan war and the war between the Kuomintang and the CCP, Stalin always put more support behind the Kuomintang, in that it promised to guarantee the interests of the Soviet Union in China. Mao had always been unsatisfied with Stalin. With Khrushchev attacking Stalin, Mao also got the chance to get rid of Stalinism. Mao also saw Khrushchev as a weak man incapable to lead the socialist world. Mao's ambition grew further. His speech "On the Ten Major Relationships" in 1956 manifested his thinking about how to find a way out of the standard Stalinist Mode.[31] By the end of 1957, China's first five-year plan achieved huge industrial growth. Mao's confidence as a result bloated so that he decided to use his way to push China's socialism forward.

The result was the "Great Leap Forward" movement. Agitated partly by the planning bureaucrats and partly by his own brainchild, Mao started to infuse unconventional thinking about economy and society into the Soviet-style planned economy.[32] In 1958, Mao decided to launch a large-scale mass movement to improve the economy. Since the Stalinist

[30] Mao launched political campaigns (the "zhengfeng" movement) to politically banish those cadres supported by Stalin in Yan'an. Liu Shaoqi and Chen Yun helped a lot in these campaigns. Only after this did Mao become the undisputed leader of the CCP. See Gao (2019).

[31] In this speech, Mao (1977: 284–307) talked about the economic balance between such fields as agriculture and industry, coastal zones and inland zones, etc. He preached to find China's own path of socialism and not to follow any foreign model blindly.

[32] According to Bachman (1991), the "Great Leap Forward" movement was a combined product on a whim from Mao and the purposes of a couple of top planning bureaucrats, among whom Bo Yibo and Deng Zihui were most involved. Bo and Deng were representatives of heavy industry and supported stringent planning, while Chen Yun

Mode was characterised by a highly centralised planning system, Mao turned to establish a relatively decentralised economic system. However, unlike economic reforms launched by Malenkov and Khrushchev contemporarily, Mao's decentralisation was more "casual". Local political units gained much more power in designing economic goals than before. The central planning agency no longer played a role in the coordination of the economy (Perkins 2010: 122–123). Simultaneously, large-scale mobilisation of labour was encouraged. Farmers in rural areas and residents in urban areas were mobilised to participate in various campaigns aimed to enhance production. The most catastrophic event was to mobilise farmers to produce steel at the price of giving up agricultural work. Farmers' techniques were not sufficient to produce qualified steel, while agricultural work was severely harmed. In addition, without coordination and supervision of a central agency, provincial and municipal units bragged too much about their "achievements", thus resulting in unreasonable extraction of grain. Subsequently, economic chaos emerged, and severe famine swept China.[33] The "Great Leap Forward" movement turned out to be a total catastrophe. It was evident that Mao used mass campaigns as the main motor for economic growth. On the one hand, it was because Mao did not trust the bureaucratic apparatus established by his doctrinaire colleagues. According to his experience, "people" were always the reliable force and also the most powerful. He chose to directly motivate local cadres and low labourers to achieve his aspiration. On the other hand, the mass campaigns were just like the corvée labour in ancient China. "People" were moved to work on national grand projects. Highlighting the power of the masses, Mao transformed Marxist doctrines into real actions.

The economic disasters and widespread famine forced Mao to retreat, both actively and passively. His pragmatic colleagues, including Liu Shaoqi and Zhou Enlai (1898–1976), etc., stood out to cure the damaged economy since the early 1960s. They abandoned Mao's acts in the "Great Leap Forward" movement and partly restored the Stalinist Mode

and others were representatives of light industry and supported a gradual and slow transition to a planned economy. Since the eighth National Congress of the CCP, the interest group represented by Bo and Deng did not get preferential treatment. The "Great Leap Forward" was also a strategy from them in order to obtain political capital.

[33] The number of people who died during this famine remains a mystery. The CCP itself will never reveal it. Scholars' calculations vary significantly, ranging from a few million to thirty million.

(Macfarquhar 1999: 184–233). The centralised planning system regained authority upon economic affairs. Collectivisation in rural areas was loosened so that farmers could get tiny plots to plant some vegetables. For just a few years in the early 1960s, the Stalinist bureaucrats gained legitimacy and power in the CCP, while Mao Zedong partly lost his position as the head of the party. Consequently, in the fear of being sidelined, Mao could not tolerate the actions that brought the economy back to Stalinism.[34] Again, Mao moved mass campaigns to remove colleagues with whom he was unsatisfied with in 1966, including Liu Shaoqi and Deng Xiaoping (1904–1997), etc. Mao launched the Cultural Revolution to keep the nation under his control. Annoyed by the Stalinist Mode, Mao's ideal was alternative. "The Cultural Revolution was an onslaught on bureaucratic structures. The idea of a hierarchical, centrally-planned economy was under attack" (Weber 2019). In the following ten years, Chinese society was characterised by a mixture of the Stalinist planned economy and Maoist ideas. Compared to the evident centralisation in the Soviet Union, China's planned economy had more decentralisation (Naughton 1995: 41–44). During the Cultural Revolution between 1966 and 1976, the whole society was always plagued by frequent political campaigns directed by Mao. A stable social environment barely existed. "The economy was locked into persistent stop-and-go cycles" (Naughton 1995: 51).

During the Cultural Revolution, economic development was never an important affair, while palace intrigues within the CCP and the class struggle in the society became popular. The efforts to restore the Stalinist socialism since the early 1960s failed, and Mao continued to rule over China with his own understanding of socialism. At best it was an awkward combination of the Imperial Mode of China and a planned economy. On the one hand, the planned economy was undoubtedly erected. Collectivisation in rural areas existed until the end of 1970s. Nationalisation dominated in urban areas. The unified purchase system bridged the two areas, while the absolute demarcation, i.e., the household registration system ("hukou"), kept migration very difficult, if not

[34] Mao was always afraid that he would be severely criticised after his death, like Khrushchev did to Stalin. Indeed, the efforts of those pragmatic colleagues to restore economy always reminded him of this threat. When Mao was still alive, his policies were toppled in the early 1960s. He could not help imagining what could happen after his death.

impossible (Piketty 2020: 611). Consumption and distribution of products were controlled by the rationing system. Clearly, at this stage the Chinese economy possessed most of the essential elements of a planned economy. On the other hand, the planned economy in China was rarely as centralised as it in the Soviet Union. In China, local administrative units had more power, thus resulting in more chaos (Naughton 1995: 46–51). Partly due to personal hatred towards Stalin and the Chinese colleagues who got education in the Soviet Union in the 1930s and 1940s,[35] Mao Zedong looked down on those bureaucrats who insisted on the Soviet-style system. He had never seriously talked about any "plan" since the late 1950s, although he allowed those colleagues to carry out five-year plans.[36] His attention turned more to political affairs.

To some extent, Mao's understanding about Marxism and socialism was dubious. "There is no evidence that Mao ever seriously studied Marx beyond the basic texts that were translated into Chinese in his youth" (Westad 2012: 286). It is difficult to judge what intellectual sources were more influential upon Mao.[37] In comparison with the Marxian works which he had undoubtedly read, he showed a strong preference for reading Chinese historical books. He was quite familiar with how ancient rulers administered Chinese society. It is also clear that Mao relied more on ideas and inspirations obtained from his reading on Chinese classics in the final decade of his life.[38] Under this influence, the path dependence took effect. The Imperial Mode functioned subconsciously. The socialist transformation abolished the peasant economy, but the CCP replaced the bureaucratic system with its own communist bureaucracy which was more

[35] Mao's hatred was mainly caused by two factors. Firstly, Stalin and other communist leaders in Europe did approve Mao's practice which took farmers, rather than industrial workers, as the pillar of a communist revolution. Mao personally thought that the instructions from the Soviet Union were misleading China's revolution. Secondly, the Soviet Union always wanted to erect the leadership of the Chinese communists who had educational backgrounds in the Soviet Union, rather than Mao Zedong who had never gone overseas before 1949. Mao did not establish his absolute leadership until 1945.

[36] For example, from 1966 to 1970 no party meeting was ever held to discuss annual or multiyear economic plans. See Vogel (2011: 732).

[37] Wakeman (1973) has traced the formation of Mao's thought. There were both Marxist and Chinese traditional influences in his mind. And some scholars suspect that Chinese classics had more influence on Mao than Marxism.

[38] Every writer of Mao's biography must notice that how much Mao loved reading Chinese classics especially in the final years of his life. See Terrill (1999).

powerful and pervasive. Nationalisation in the planned economy could be easily accomplished, in that the domination from the government in economic fields was never strange to China, which was characterised by the state monopoly of key industries in its imperial dynasties, such as iron and salt. More importantly, the operational methods of political power in Maoist China were inherited from the Imperial Mode. In ancient dynasties, governments had responsibility on such public goods as social order and public projects. In Maoist China, the government became omnipotent for taking responsibility everywhere. Even the consumption of products became a public field which the government controlled for decades.

So, in terms of the nature of the society in Maoist China between the early 1950s and the late 1970s, the planned economy was constructed on the base of the Imperial Mode. Before the CCP, the Kuomintang government tried to adopt nationalist economic policies, while the market economy dominated. The CCP, as a communist party, declared to establish a socialist economy. In the 1950s, to a large degree socialist transformation copied Stalinism. Soon thereafter the CCP adopted socialist ideals with local circumstances. Path dependence was imprinted in Maoist socialism such that Maoism had a mixed relation to China's past. Although the CCP abolished the peasant economy through socialist collectivisation, so that the Imperial Mode was partly demolished, the bureaucratic system and the central authority continued to exist and were even strengthened, only under the cloak of communism. In short, Maoist socialism left an ambivalent legacy for the following era.

5 A Consideration on the Socialist Planned Economy

The extensive introduction of a planned economy was a distinctive economic phenomenon in the twentieth century. Led by Stalin, the Soviet Union was the spearhead. After the Second World War, a planned economy was practised not only in those satellite nations of the Soviet Union in Eastern Europe and communist nations in Asia, but also in many developing countries in South Asia, Latin America and Africa. However, in around five decades from the 1930s to the late 1980s, its failure was equally eye-catching. In popular impression, the socialist planned economy was characterised by low living levels, strict central planning, bureaucrats' institutional venality and a persistent pressure of potential inflation in many cases. Almost without exception, economic plight was accompanied by a repressive political structure consisting often of a police state, extensive gulags and forced labour. On the whole, the planned economy had appallingly failed what it promised to achieve. Then, as the spiritual father of scientific socialism and communism which subsequent revolutionaries announced as their sacred ideology, Karl Marx's ideas were put into the whirlpool of controversies, criticism and smears.

However, the connection between Marx and a planned economy, on which I mean the real planned economy which had already been practised by communist statesmen, is kept highly blurred, especially so in comparison with regard to the technical details of the Stalinist planned economy, in which every single detail was prescribed in government's codes and edicts. Marx's occasional description on socialism and communism was a sketchy image at best. In fact, most of such description scattered on variegated works, including *The Poverty of Philosophy* and *Anti-Dühring*. And the description was not based on what a socialist society can be but based on what a socialist society cannot be—Marx and Engels repudiated Rodbertus's and Proudhon's blueprints partly or in certain cases completely (Hollander 2008: 398–400). This situation left a big stage for followers of communism to play. Nonetheless, in order to probe into Marx's envisage about socialism and communism, we have to delve into his totality of historical materialism.

It is widely known that Marx offers "a coherent sequence of models which represent different phases of development and indicate[s] the forces which lead from one stage of development to the next" (Schefold 2014: 14). Marx envisioned an evolutionary path of human civilisation, from the primitive society to the feudal society, then to the capitalist society and further on. While the specific categorisation is arguable, it reveals that Marx thought of capitalism from a historical perspective. Between the supersedure functioned the mode of production predominantly, including the dynamic between the relations of production and the productive forces. There was also the role of class struggle. Recognising Marx's totality, we could say that a post-capitalist society would rely on many preconditions which Marx set as the driving forces behind history. Clearly, the bulk of Marx's economic work was concentrated on capitalism, more precisely on how the capitalist mode of production succeeded and where it would fail.[39] Marx and Engels spoke highly of capitalism because of its economic power. Nevertheless, socialism would in their eyes supersede capitalism.

> It will arrive once the capitalist system has fully developed and become not just mature but overripe. The replacement will occur in places where the capitalist system of production had become an obstacle to the development of the forces of production but had also paved the way for a more highly developed system of production than itself by providing the material conditions for socialism. It will have made these preparations by causing the bulk of production to be undertaken on a large industrial scale. With modern technology and a high degree of organisation within the company. This high degree of organisation and concentration of production will leave only a handful of capitalist proprietors, who will be swept aside so that the proletariat can take over the running of production. (Kornai 1992: 18–19)

In line with his historical materialism, Marx deduced that capitalism would certainly be replaced by next-stage social types, i.e., socialism and then communism. The next-stage order was not an ideal to be realised, but "a natural outgrowth of the existing capitalist order" (Arnold 1989: 160). It would be the externalisation of the inner dynamics governing human civilisation. But Marx had little to say on the details about a post-capitalist society. This situation resulted in profound ambiguity which bore everlasting academic struggles and practical confusions. Whether Marx's tenets led to the central planning is full of controversy.[40] It is also unclear whether central planning is a logically necessary condition for socialism as Marx conceived it. But one thing is for sure with Marx: it was for him self-evident that the socialist order would take power first in the most highly developed of the capitalist countries. Marx wrote in 1870,

[39] Marx's arguments on why the capitalist mode of production must fail are another big issue, which cannot be adequately discussed here. To be succinct, capitalism persistently creates crises through its own inner dynamics which is the motor of capitalism.

[40] I reserve my own opinions for now. I offer further reading materials. About the positive association between Marx and the central planning, see Arnold (1989). About Marx's appreciation of the role of markets as the allocation system, see Hollander (2008: 396–401). Sowell (1980: 218) wrote that "Marx and Engels were unsparing in their criticisms of their fellow socialists and fellow communists who wanted to replace price competition with central planning".

> England alone can serve as the lever for a serious economic revolution. It is the only country where the capitalist form, that is to say combined labour on a large scale under capitalist masters, now embraces virtually the whole of production. It is the only country where the great majority of the population consists of wage labourers. It is the only country where the class struggle and the organisation of the working class by the trade unions have acquired a certain degree of maturity. … If landlordism and capitalism are classical features in England, on the other hand, the material conditions for their destruction are the most mature here. (Marx 1870: 118)

And Engels continued. He argued that "countries which are only just turning over to capitalist production now might arrive at socialism, but the indispensable condition for that is the example and active assistance of the hitherto capitalist West". The more backward countries could only set themselves out on the road to socialism "if there has been an advance beyond the capitalist economic system in its own native land and in the countries where it has flourished".[41] In addition, although Engels imagined that the solution to the allocation question within a socialist system could be based on some standards related with labour and free of "third product" (i.e., sorts of currency), he did not come to the conclusion of a planned economy.[42] Therefore, neither Marx nor Engels imagined socialism as a panacea to problems in backward countries, which became clear as the planned economy developed in the twentieth century.

In the 1920s, the rise of a socialist nation in Russia had become unstoppable in the eyes of westerners. How a socialist economy could work became a very imminent and realistic question. Whether a planned economy could work was a mathematical issue for some economists, while some others argued that the economic system was a comprehensive and sophisticated structure which cannot function without free pricing mechanism (Lavoie 1981). Hereafter, the famous "Debate on Socialist Calculation" ensued. On the one side stood the Austrian School. As a core figure, Ludwig von Mises insisted on the impossibility of "socialist calculation" and to some degree alluded to the destined doom of the socialist economy earlier than Friedrich von Hayek. The key point of von

[41] Original quotation: Engels (1894: 428). Secondary quotation: Kornai (1992: 19 the footnote).

[42] Arguably, Hollander (2008: 398–401) wrote that Engels was actually supporting some sorts of central planning.

Mises was that without markets and free pricing mechanisms no economy could work. On the other side stood the "neoclassicals", among whom Oskar Lange was distinguished. Lange believed in the efficacy of one or some other sort of the Walrasian simultaneous-equation formulation. More scholars from both sides participated in this debate, but it seemed that no one could win the theoretical argument. Later the Austrian School developed into an unshaken opponent against government's interference in any case. Ludwig von Mises (1932, 1936) extended his criticism upon socialism into a comprehensive and voluminous monograph, ranging from economic issues, political structure, cultural phenomena (ethic and religion), and international relations.[43]

After the 1950s, more socialist regimes were founded in less economically developed countries than Russia itself, including those in Asia, Africa and Latin America. What Marx might feel about that will never be known. In 1881, in a letter to a Russian follower, Vera Zasulich, Marx expressed flexibility about historical development. Negating determinate predictive implications of his theory, Marx alluded to an alternative pathway towards socialism. Marx also acknowledged that new conditions could be created to influence future development.[44] However, the "Marxist" practices in the Third World were full of radical idealism, deranged Nazism and lunatic authoritarianism, such as what happened in North Korea, Cambodia and Africa. No one could welcome such a "victory". To a large degree, Marxist ideological tools became weapons of those idealists and revolutionaries. What would Marx think of when he saw socialism founding in many places where agricultural economy occupied a predominant status and peasants composed primarily most of the population, while none of the highly developed countries chose the socialist pathway, as he formulated? This will certainly continue to trigger more debates among Marxists in the future.

China's planned economy was beyond what Marx conceivably could have imagined. Even before the PRC was founded, Marxism had been transformed into merely ideological weapons used for the CCP's revolutionary activities. The CCP used those ideas of Marxism which preached economic egalitarianism and redistribution of material richness to expand

[43] This monograph is *Die Gemeinwirtschaft: Untersuchungen über den Sozialismus* published in 1932. It was translated into English 1936—*Socialism: An Economic and Sociological Analysis*.

[44] Both Vera Zasulich's letter and Marx's reply are available online: marxists.org.

its influence. In practice, what inspired early Chinese Communists was Leninism rather than Marxism, and "it was the organisational ideals of the Soviet revolution rather than Marx's predictions about world capitalism that fired their minds" (Westad 2012: 285). Before Mao gained practical influence, the CCP aimed to activate proletariats in urban zones, as standard communism taught. However, it turned out to be a fiasco in the 1930s. Mao Zedong turned to the peasant class. Indeed, right from the beginning of his revolutionary career he did not bet on a proletarian revolution in China. Relying on the impoverished in rural areas, the CCP became stronger than its rival, the Kuomintang. After taking over China, the CCP leaders decided to exercise the Stalinist planned economy which had proven its effectiveness during the Second World War and its ability to direct rapid industrialisation. Nevertheless, not all CCP leaders had a stubborn belief in the Soviet Union. Mao Zedong was one of them. Except the first five-year plan, China did not fully implement the other five-year plans with much care or ambition. Political campaigns always interrupted the process. Certainly, however, Maoist China established the fundamental structure of a planned economy. Furthermore, most illnesses of a planned economy diagnosed by Kornai (1992, 2014) also appeared: soft budget constraints, potential unemployment, potential inflation and lack of innovation, etc. While Mao Zedong was also unsatisfied with the Stalinist Mode, he was not able to completely move on from it. It was other more enlightened leaders within the CCP that opened the door for economic reforms towards free market economy. Did Chinese communist leaders finally acknowledge that China, a poor agricultural society, could not skip a capitalist stage, as Marx and Engels originally thought? Not one of them would be able to bluntly admit this. It is also a question about how one defined capitalism, market economy, and the connection between them.

Economic Reforms Out of a Planned Economy

Mao Zedong died in 1976. The economy had been plagued for decades by political campaigns. After a few years of palace intrigues, Deng Xiaoping started to gain policymaking power since 1979. He and his colleagues launched a reformatory process aiming to abolish the planned economy and to achieve marketisation and modernisation in China.[45] In contrast to the propaganda of the CCP in which the economic reforms were designated intentionally, policymakers in the late 1970s and 1980s had no idea about how to act in the long run or what China would become later. The reforms were "not a result of a carefully plotted reform strategy", and "many of the most successful reform measures were introduced with little forethought or awareness of the consequences" (Naughton 1995: 309–310). The reforms unfolded more like a step-by-step experiment, which turned out to eventually demolish the planned economy and to introduce a marketisation process.

Changes happened at first in rural areas. After decades of collectivisation, not only agricultural productivity but also living standards did not get improved. By the late 1970s, the production of some agricultural products remained the same as in the mid-1950s. Some indicators, such as edible oil and cotton, were even lower (See Table 1). Some poor areas consistently faced the danger of famine and extreme poverty. In 1978, forced by poverty, farmers in a small village in Anhui Province decided to give up collectivisation and to allocate lands (right to use) to households secretly. Later the action was legalised and encouraged by the government—a bottom-up reform. By 1983, 98% of rural collective units had adopted this decollectivisation, and households again became independent economic units, while households did not own lands as the constitution formulates that all lands belong to the nation, i.e., the government. The effectiveness of the rural reform was large. According

[45] Speaking of why Deng Xiaoping started the reformatory process, no answer could be convincing without talking about Deng's individuality. By 1976, the Chinese economy was dangerously driven close to bankruptcy, but policymakers, such as Hua Guofeng and Li Xiannian, chose to strengthen the planned economy and to launch another small "Great Leap Forward". Subsequently, the government confronted a fiscal crisis. It would be hard to say that Deng's reform was destined. Many cadres were still alert to marketisation and capitalism. Deng was flexible and open-minded enough to embrace opportunities which might improve people's living standards and China's economy. On the one hand, Deng had been to Europe in the 1920s to witness how market mechanisms worked. On the other hand, Deng spent years in a poor province meditating quietly on the problems which China were confronted with when he was demoted by Mao Zedong during the Cultural Revolution. He already had new ideas after coming back to Beijing. "By the time Deng left Jiangxi, he had no illusions about the seriousness of China's problems and about the depth of change that was needed". See Vogel (2011: 18–25, 51–57).

to the calculation of the production-function approach, the institutional change contributed to almost half of the output growth during 1978–1984 (Lin 1992).

Moreover, many township and village enterprises (TVEs) mushroomed in rural areas. Entrepreneurs in towns and villages, many of whom were relatives of communist cadres or cadres themselves, took advantage of locally specific resources, such as agricultural products and mines, to do business. In official documents of the government in the late 1970s and the early 1980s, attitudes turned from toleration to encouragement (Naughton 1995: 144–148). Although TVEs were often plagued by the ambiguity of ownership and thus corruption, it was clear by the early 1980s that TVEs brought obvious economic improvement to these regions.[46] The emergence of TVEs was a part of the decentralisation policy starting from the late 1970s. In rural areas, households became independently self-sufficient units, and TVEs arose as profit-oriented entities.

In urban areas, reforms began in mainly three aspects. First, the government relaxed restrictions in some industries, including the sale of consumption goods and light industry. In the Maoist era, private commercial entities were criticised vehemently as the evilness of capitalism, while only public (state-owned or community-owned) entities were allowed to operate enterprises. Since 1979, state monopoly over some commercial sectors was relaxed. Consequently, the demand for goods resulted in the distortion of prices, in that in a planned economy there was always potential inflation which had been repressed by the rationing system (Kornai 1992: Chapters 11 and 12). Very soon the distortion of prices attracted many individuals and households to do business. The entry cost declined substantially, and such change introduced the market mechanism in a relatively stable way. Decreasing the market entry cost became a valuable experience for the government when introducing reforms (Naughton 1995: 311–315). Small private firms eroded the market share of state-run firms. Gradually, the economy became driven by private firms who had

[46] About the details of the emergence of TVEs and their role in China's rural industrialisation, see Naughton (2007: 271–291).

formed self-sufficient dynamics. In the reformatory process, the private sector has become one of the most energetic sectors.[47]

Secondly, for state-owned enterprises (SOEs), bureaucrats in the government began to require them to become revenue maximisers (Naughton 1995: 315–317). In a planned economy, the soft budget constraint always existed. Excess expenditure could always be compensated by some other institution, which was typically the government. Such a mechanism resulted in the low economic efficiency of state-owned enterprises (Kornai 1979, 1986). In the 1980s, bureaucrats took more and more non-interventionist attitudes. Measures had been taken to dissolve many enterprises from the government. Given these actions, even state-run enterprises became profit-seekers. A creation to facilitate the marketisation of SOEs was the dual-track system since the early 1980s. Launched by Zhao Ziyang, the contemporary primer, the dual-track system introduced marketisation into the industrial sector relatively smoothly (Naughton 1995: 177–187, 315). The products of SOEs were separated into two parts: one part was still controlled by the government via its plans, while the other part was controlled by the enterprises themselves (in fact, the officials running the enterprises). The former was used to sustain the planning mechanism, while the latter circulated in markets (Weber 2019). The planning part was subject to state-set prices, which were in most cases very low in order to guarantee the subsistence of most people, while the market part was subject to the free price mechanism. Demand for goods, which had been kept low before in the planning period, consistently pushed prices in markets up. Due to the difference in prices between the two parts, there were more profits to be made in the market part and hence the percent of marketisation became increasingly large. Although the system led to more space for bureaucratic venality and especially rent-seeking, it avoided the negative effect created by the shock therapy which Russia experienced in the 1990s.

Last but not the least, since the late 1970s, the central government set four special economic zones (SEZs) in the southeast coast. A set of special institutions were applied in the SEZs in order to attract foreign investment: Advantageous taxation for foreign businesses was introduced; Law and regulations different from the rest of China were implemented; new

[47] Nee and Opper (2012) described this process as capitalism from below. Indeed, capitalist dynamics emerged in the grassroot stratification, rather than as the consequence of any top-down command.

economic organisations, including foreigner-invested firms, were allowed, etc. (Wall 1991). In the 1980s and 1990s, more economic zones were set along coastal provinces, most of which contributed to rapid economic growth (Park 1997). Shenzhen especially arose from a scarcely populated fishing village to an economically energetic industrial and commercial metropolis harbouring over twelve million residents (2020).[48] In addition, the economic impact of SEZs expanded gradually to neighbouring regions. Commercial behaviours and domestic investment grew exponentially even in non-SEZs continually (Wang 2013). In sum, the market mechanism and the accompanying economic growth grew rapidly in SEZs and coastal provinces.

Meanwhile, within the CCP opinions were not uniform. Most reforms were launched by Deng Xiaoping and some of his colleagues, such as Zhao Ziyang and Ren Zhongyi,[49] etc. While the strong leadership of the CCP created a friendly environment, many conservative cadres raised more and more doubts about economic reforms in the 1980s, among whom Chen Yun was the key figure.[50] As illustrated before, in the Maoist era, Chen helped to establish the planned economy, although he was sidelined by Mao for a long time in the 1960s and 1970s. "As a founding father of Chinese economic planning who spent years putting the details in place, Chen Yun had an understandable attachment to the system that had once worked and a determination not to let anyone ruin his painstaking handiwork, which had already been destroyed once" (Vogel 2011: 721). While Chen did not agree with Mao Zedong who abolished planning and radically exterminated the private economy, he believed in "the bird in the cage", which meant that the private economy, including household farming in the agricultural sector and small bourgeois firms, could be allowed to exist only if the economy was controlled by state-level

[48] About the specific process of economic growth, see Wu (1999).

[49] Vogel (2011: 734–738, 743–745) has written a brief but well-organised introduction about these figures.

[50] While I. M. Weber (2021) provides a cogent analysis about how past experiences and foreign experts helped China not to choose the shock therapy which liberalises prices overnight, she might neglect the most important factor that slowed down radical reformers—the powerful conservatives, including Chen Yun and Li Xiannian, etc. In my view, radical reformers, e.g., Zhao Ziyang, had tried several times in the 1980s to have something similar to a shock therapy, but none of them led to complete liberalisation when facing momentous hindrance of the conservatives.

planning and big state-owned enterprises.[51] In short, Chen allowed the market mechanism to run under the limits of government's plans. Since 1978, Chen and Deng were the most politically powerful statesmen. Their opposition to radical Maoism led to their cooperation in the late 1970s. Nonetheless, they did not share common ideas.

> Chen was less willing to take risks, more determined to prevent inflation, more sympathetic to the Soviet Union, less ready to form deep ties with the capitalist countries, less willing to expand the role of markets, and more determined to follow regular party procedures. Deng was more prepared to experiment, to work outside the party framework, to open widely to the West, and to move boldly (Vogel 2011: 717).

After the mid-1980s, conservative members gradually converged around Chen Yun. Especially when mistakes in newly introduced reforms led to disastrous inflation multiple times in the 1980s (Naughton 1995: 247–253),[52] and rocketing corruption instigated widespread unsatisfaction among people, the conservative wing started to attack the reformers. In 1989, partly due to the sudden death of Hu Yaobang, the former general secretary of the CCP, large-scale protests happened in Beijing. The protests led to a strong and radical reaction of the conservative wing, even including Deng himself. After military suppression, the reformatory process seemed discontinued because most reformers were demoted, and the West punished China severely in terms of trade and foreign investment. The younger generation of the CCP leaders hesitated about moving ahead (Kuhn 2004: Chapter 12). Once more, Deng showed his strategic flexibility and also determination for further reforms. In 1992, Deng travelled in several southern cities, especially those SEZs. His talking with local cadres in this southern journey warned those conservative leaders who were prepared to topple marketisation. Because Deng still controlled troops very tightly, the CCP was quickly forced to conduct more reforms. Very soon in 1992, the CCP announced that the aim of economic reforms would be to establish "the socialist market economy". The marketisation reforms were driven to the fast lane.

[51] About works of Chen Yun, see Chen (1997).

[52] In the 1980s, a few instances of high inflation agitated people's unsatisfaction against the marketisation mechanism which was said to be responsible for such inflation. It was said that inflation was a unique phenomenon of capitalism.

In the 1990s, reforms developed rapidly in more sectors and deeper mechanisms, including the SOEs and the financial sector. Firstly, the state monopoly in many more industries was halted. The shareholding system was introduced in many key industrial sectors. Private and foreign capital were allowed to operate in such sectors which were forbidden for them to step in before. In addition, the bankruptcy mechanism was introduced in SOEs. The government no longer took responsibility for SOEs. It resulted in much bankruptcy and unemployment, which in turn instilled more labour into the market mechanism.[53] Economic efficiency was further heightened. Secondly, the banking system started to act as an independent commercial institution, rather than the provisioner of free loans to SOEs like before. The stock exchange was also established in the late 1990s in Shenzhen and Shanghai. Thus, the market mechanism was also partly introduced to the financial sector.

Ever since then, hastening marketisation did not stop until the mid-2000s. The share of public capital in the economy declined to approximately 30% in 2005 and rarely changed since then.[54] The mixed economy was sustained when SOEs controlled key industries and private small firms grew in less important industries. Financial liberalisation was fundamentally halted after the 2010s, although China was accepted to the World Trade Organisation in 2001. Political reforms on the bureaucratic structure, which were once considered seriously in the first decade of the twenty-first century, were no longer mentioned in the second decade. In the 2010s, the CCP aimed to tame bureaucracy and to strengthen the central authority through communist doctrines and ethical preaching. Although private firms still developed fast, thereby encouraging economic growth which strengthened legitimacy of the private sectors in the eyes of the CCP, the government's control upon the economy was also consolidated through manipulating the banking system and public licences, etc. Industrial policies become increasingly important as communist cadres aim to compete with western economic hegemons (Naughton 2021). The CCP is now satisfied with such a structure—an unchallengeable central

[53] Sarah Schefold (2008) did a detailed investigation about the unemployment ("Xiagang") caused by the bankruptcy of SOEs. In Northeast China in which SOEs were densely located, the unemployment problem was quite serious.

[54] From 2005 to 2018, the share of public capital was roughly sustained at around 30%. In 2007 and 2008, the number rose to 35%. Then it returned to around 31%. The number in 1978 was 70%. See Piketty (2020: 607).

authority, a domesticated and able bureaucracy and a mixed economy consisting of state-owned capital and private capital.

During the four decades, trends of economic reforms experienced noticeable fluctuations (See Fig. 1). Economic sectors were deregulated in the 1980s and most years of the 1990s. During a few years after the Tiananmen Square Event in 1989 and the twenty-first century, the level of regulation was rising. On the whole, China's rapid growth was generated by two factors: First of all, enterprises that had more freedom to do business had wider access to the vast mass of domestic and international markets, thus making valuable assets and cheap labour that China has; Secondly, introduction and extensive application of more efficient technologies from the West and Japan enhanced productivity and aggregate output. Both factors contributed profoundly to higher efficiency within the Chinese economy. In other words, China was transiting from extractive economic institutions to inclusive ones.[55] However, there were always "critical junctures" leading back to the conservative pathway when political considerations carried more weights.

6 "Oriental Capitalism" in Contemporary China

In many ways, Marxism arrived in China more like a religion. According to Marx, the communist revolution was to be based on the class consciousness of the proletariat class. However, the Chinese communist revolution took place in a predominantly agricultural country. In the early stage of this revolution, after the proletarian unrest broke out in urban areas, the communist movement reinvented itself as a peasant revolution. Land distribution replaced worker control over factories as the top priority (Mühlhahn 2019: 249). The practical change made the Chinese revolution distant from standard Marxism or Stalinism. Then, it followed that communism had to be preached and imposed.[56] It was, however, opposed in China not only by rich capitalists and by landowners, but also by large

[55] Acemoglu and Robinson (2013) devised relevant conceptions, but they did not give definitive answers to what extractive/inclusive institutions are. They just gave narratives and characteristic descriptions. See also Lu and Zhu (2021: Chapter 12).

[56] Dirlik (1989) has a succinct analysis about how Marxism was introduced and gradually accepted in China in the early stage of the communist revolution.

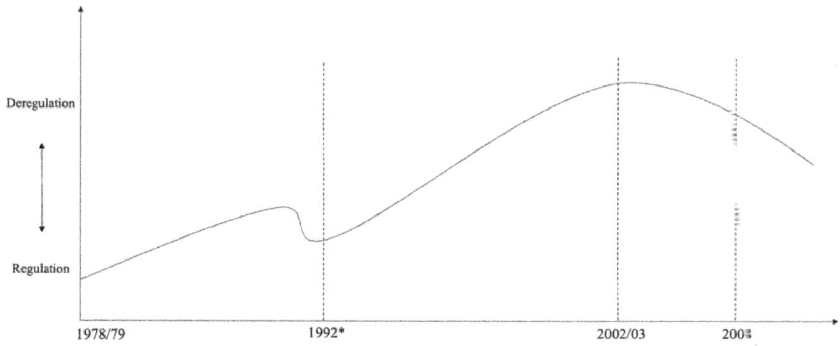

Fig. 1 Sketch of China's Liberalisation Process. *In Walter's original graph, the year is 1990. However, I believe that the authentic reverse of the conservative/back-to-planning trends after 1989 happened only after Deng Xiaoping had his southern travel in 1992. Threatened by Deng's power, communist cadres returned to economic reforms, including the General Secretary, Jiang Zemin (*Source* Walter and Howie 2012: 4)

sections of the peasants.[57] The party, far from representing the people in the sense of forming a unity with them, hence unable to rule by democratic means, had to become the ruling elite. The party introduced the planned economy and later the market economy to transform China, but members of the CCP acted more and more like those bureaucrats under the Imperial Mode of China.

In the first thirty years of the communist regime, the planned economy was implanted. The planned economy had high compatibility with China's traditional institutional structures, i.e., the Imperial Mode. The Stalinist planned economy abolished private ownership. Chinese imperial governments never treated property rights seriously, although peasants and landlords developed very sophisticated transaction systems for lands.[58] The control upon the people of the state apparatus in communist China was conceivably unprecedented. Implantation of the planned economy in the traditional structure was quite easy, since they were

[57] As illustrated before, in the mid-1950s, a large part of the peasant population opposed collectivisation which would confiscate their lands and most of their assets and would restrict most of their private life.

[58] Long (2018) has detailed research on the transaction system of lands in ancient China.

similar in many ways. Firstly, the Imperial Mode felt never estranged to economic nationalisation, in that it had practised a state monopoly in key industries for thousands of years. A planned economy extended the scope and scale of such a state monopoly. Secondly, confiscation was relatively common under the Imperial Mode. Ancient China never developed a strict awareness of ownership protection. When the society and economy was running smoothly, the government hardly intervened into private assets; when there economic or social troubles, the government could easily confiscate private assets. The biggest problem within the fiscal system of the Imperial Mode was its uncertainty.[59] Thirdly, the two societal types were both ruled through hierarchical bureaucracy. The central authority issued commands, and the bureaucratic system implemented them. Bureaucrats were always held accountable by the top of the pyramid structure, rather than citizens below. Fourthly, but most importantly, cultural inertia under the Imperial Mode was completely utilised in China's planned economy. Traditionally, individuals devoted surpluses and labour in exchange for public goods offered by the bureaucracy and the top authority. The existence of the Imperial Mode relied on the extinction of other competing power forces. The government became people's sole provider. The government and the people were never equal. Such an ideology was inherited in the communist era.

Path dependence has been a key concept in the comparative analysis of societal transitions. The institutional environment, whether formal or informal, always continues in the process of transitions (DiMaggio and Powell 1983). Both Maoist policies had a strong association with traditional socio-economic structures. As illustrated before, Mao had a subjective hatred to the planned economy. His approach to economy and society revealed a lot of continuity with China's imperial structures, for example, through the tight control over the masses and the regulation of economic activities (Acemoglu and Robinson 2019: 229). After the 1980s, China abandoned the planned economy and autarkic policies that had been pursued under the Maoist era that had resulted in economic recession and poverty in vast areas (Mühlhahn 2019: 607). Economic growth relied on injecting so-called capitalist elements into the planned economy: market liberalisation, opening up to the international market and foreign investment, creation of a functionable financial system, less

[59] Thanks to a lecture given by Debin Ma on 29th January 2021 in Tsinghua University, Beijing.

interventionist public policies, and fair implementation of law (Mühlhahn 2019: 610). In China's economic reforms the CCP did establish relatively more inclusive institutions than in the Maoist era. Nevertheless, these economic reforms echoed a lasting necessity: modernisation since the late Qing dynasty. The CCP's program that China would utilise Western technology and market mechanisms to develop the economy while keeping the one-party state resonated with China's late nineteenth-century self-strengthening movement that sought to adopt Western technology and economic methods while still maintaining the traditional Confucian state and values (Fairbank and Goldman 2006: 408).

Since Deng's economic reforms, China achieved unprecedented economic growth, which made China the world's largest trading economy and the current second-largest economy in terms of GDP (2021). However, the CCP keeps alert to avoid a completely liberalist capitalism. After the mid-2000s, the bureaucratic system of the CCP was not weakened but rather strengthened. The CCP began to form a quasi-imperial structure, in which private firms replaced peasants in the Imperial Mode, and the bureaucratic system and the central authority successfully attempted to strengthen this pyramid structure. The path dependence would play a central role in China in the foreseeable future (Nee and Cao 1999). Marxist ideology almost completely collapsed in China. The CCP distanced itself from radical communism and utopian goals. "It became, perhaps, no longer communist except in name" (Mühlhahn 2019: 611–612). It has defined its legitimacy around continued economic growth and its moral leadership (Acemoglu and Robinson 2019: 233). What those leaders of the CCP now care about is nothing different from what ancient rulers had cared about under the Imperial Mode—social stability, economic welfare and a functional bureaucracy. Now, China is leaning towards a mixture of the Imperial Mode and the capitalist market economy: "Oriental Capitalism".

The main argument of this chapter is concise: on the base of the Imperial Mode of China, the RC and PRC tried to introduce western elements to achieve modernisation; The CCP implanted a planned economy and market economy sequentially; the practice of a planned economy led to Maoist socialism, an economic mode carrying historical legacy of the Imperial Mode of China; the practice of reforms led to "Oriental Capitalism", a societal type which combined the capitalist market economy and the Imperial Mode of China. From the late 1970s to the mid-2000s, capitalist components consistently increased. Through accommodating more inclusive economic institutions, China achieved huge economic growth. From the mid-2000s, China leaned forwards more to the Imperial Mode of China. Whether consciously or unconsciously, the CCP, as the ruling force in the one-party state, began to strengthen a quasi-imperial structure. Today, the party tries to educate young party members as successors in an aristocratic stratum of society. The question is how long they will be able to reproduce as an aristocracy dedicated to economic growth and poor relief, and whether they will become oligarchs who lose self-control and are unable to provide efficient leadership.[60] Whether China's economy will have sustained relies to a large degree on how politics interacts with the economy.

References

Acemoglu, D., and J. A. Robinson. 2013. *Why Nations Fail: The Origins of Power*. Prosperity and Poverty: Profile Books Ltd.

Acemoglu, D., and J. A. Robinson 2019. *The Narrow Corridor: States, Societies and the Fate of Liberty*. GB: Viking.

Arnold, N. S. 1989. Marx, Central Planning, and Utopian Socialism. *Social Philosophy and Policy* 6 (2): 160–199.

Bachman, David. 1991. *Bureaucracy, Economy, and Leadership in China: The Institutional Origins of the Great Leap Forward*. Cambridge: Cambridge University Press.

Bernstein, Thomas P., and Li, Hua-Yu (eds.). 2010. *China Learns from the Soviet Union, 1949-Present*. Lanham: Rowman and Littlefield.

Chen, Yong. 2020. Waixiao: Another Aspect of Finance in the Late Qing Dynasty. *Researches in Chinese Economic History* 6: 59–68. (in Chinese).

Chen, Yun. 1997. *Selected Works of Chen Yun: 1956–1994*. Beijing: Foreign Language Press.

Deng, Kent Gang. 2012. *China's Political Economy in Modern Times: Changes and Economic Consequences, 1800–2000*. London: Routledge.

[60] Here I want to express my gratitude to intellectual exchange with Bertram Schefold. The prediction is becoming increasingly true from the mid-2010s. From the 1990s to the 2010s, communist cadres who hold key positions in the Chinese government take economic growth as their priority, slightly neglecting ideology and social control. Under the circumstance, cadres carried out a tournament aiming to achieve economic growth. See Zhou (2014). However, as social control and ideological education become increasingly tight after the mid-2010s, the communist regime devalues economic growth and emphasises political cult. The leadership is confronting challenges of legitimacy.

Deng, Kent Gang. 2015. Imperial China under the Song and Late Qing. In *Fiscal Regimes and the Political Economy of Premodern States*, ed. Andrew Monson and Walter Scheidel, 308–342. Cambridge: Cambridge University Press.

DiMaggio, Paul J., and Walter W. Powell. 1983. The Iron Cage Revisited: Institutional Isomorphism and Collective Rationality in Organizational Fields. *American Sociological Review* 48 (2): 147–160.

Dirlik, Arif. 1989. *The Origins of Chinese Communism*. Oxford: Oxford University Press.

Elvin, Mark, Cuirong Liu, et al. (eds.). 1998. *Sediments of Time: Environment and Society in Chinese History*. New York: Cambridge University Press.

Engels, Friedrich. 1963[1894]. Nachwort (1894) [zu Soziales aus Russland]. *Karl Marx, Friedrich Engels Werke* 22: 421–435.

Fairbank, John K. and Goldman, M. 2006. *China: A New History*. Cambridge: The Belknap Press of Harvard University Press.

Gao, Hua. 2019. *How the Red Sun Rose: The origin and Development of the Yan'an Rectification Movement, 1930–1945*. Trans. Stacy Mosher and Guo Jian. Hong Kong: The Chinese University of Hong Kong Press.

He, Ping. 2004. On Un-completed Financial System: Its Mechanism of Damaging the Society of the Qing Dynasty. *Academic Research* 6: 89–94.

He, Wenkai. 2013. *Paths toward the Modern Fiscal State: England, Japan, and China*. Cambridge, MA: Harvard University Press.

He, Wenkai. 2021. Fiscal System, State Legitimation, and State Capacity: A Re-evaluation of the State Capacity in Qing China. *Researches in Chinese Economic History* 1: 18–31. (in Chinese).

Hollander, Samuel. 2008. *The Economics of Karl Marx: Analysis and Application*. Cambridge: Cambridge University Press.

Huang, Yasheng. 2008. *Capitalism with Chinese Characteristics: Entrepreneurship and the State*. Cambridge: Cambridge University Press.

Kornai, János. 1979. *Economics of Shortage*. Amsterdam: North-Holland Publishing Company.

Kornai, János. 1986. The Soft Budget Constraint. *Kyklos* 39 (1): 3–30.

Kornai, János. 1992. *The Socialist System: The Political Economy of Communism*. Oxford: Oxford University Press.

Kornai, János. 2014. *Dynamism, Rivalry, and the Surplus Economy: Two Essays on the Nature of Capitalism*. Oxford: Oxford University Press.

Kuhn, Robert L. 2004. *The Man Who Changed China: The Life and Legacy of Jiang Zemin*. New York: Crown Publishers.

Lavoie, Don. 1981. A Critique of the Standard Account of the Socialist Calculation Debate. *Journal of Libertarian Studies* 5: 41–87.

Lin, Justin Yifu. 1992. Rural Reforms and Agricultural Growth in China. *The American Economic Review* 38 (1): 34–51.

Lin, Man-houng. 2006. *China Upside Down: Currency, Society, and Ideologies, 1801–1856*. Cambridge, MA: Harvard University Press.

Long, Denggao. 2018. *The Evolution of Traditional Institutions of Land Property Rights in China*. Beijing: China Social Sciences Press. (in Chinese).

Lu, Xianxiang, and Zhu, Qiaoling. 2021. *New Institutional Economics*. Beijing: Peking University Press. (in Chinese).

Ma, Debin. 2011. The Rise of Modern Shanghai, 1900–1936: An Institutional Perspective. In *The Treaty Port Economy in Modern China: Empirical Studies of Institutional Change and Economics Performance*, ed. K. L. So Billy et al. Berkeley: Institute of East Asian Studies, University of California.

Macfarquhar, Roderick. 1974. *The Origins of the Cultural Revolution, Volume 1: Contradictions among the People, 1956–1957*. New York: Columbia University Press.

Macfarquhar, Roderick. 1999. *The Origins of the Cultural Revolution, Volume 3: The Coming of the Cataclysm, 1961–1966*. New York: Columbia University Press.

Mao, Zedong. 1967. *On the People's Democratic Dictatorship, in Selected Works of Mao Tse-Tung*, vol. 4. Peking: Foreign Languages Press.

Mao, Zedong. 1977. *On the Ten Major Relationships, in Selected Works of Mao Tse-Tung*, vol. 5. Peking: Foreign Languages Press.

Marx, Karl. 1975[1870]. Confidential Talk. *Marx/Engels Collected Works*, vol. 21, 112–125. New York: International Publishers.

Mühlhahn, Klaus. 2019. *Making China Modern: from the great Qing to Xi Jinping*. Cambridge: The Belknap Press of Harvard University Press.

Naughton, Barry. 1995. *Growing Out of the Plan: Chinese Economic Reform, 1978–1993*. Cambridge: Cambridge University Press.

Naughton, Barry. 2007. *The Chinese Economy: Transitions and Growth*. Cambridge, Massachusetts: The MIT Press.

Naughton, Barry. 2021. *The Rise of China's Industrial Policy, 1978–2020*. México: Universidad Nacional Autónoma de México.

Nee, Victor, and Yang Cao. 1999. Path Dependent Societal Transformation: Stratification in Hybrid Mixed Economies. *Theory and Society* 28: 799–834.

Nee, Victor and Opper, Sonja. 2012. *Capitalism from below: Markets and Institutional Change in China*. Cambridge: Harvard University Press.

Ni, Yuping. 2021. Rethinking the Ability of Financial Management in Qing Dynasty from the Perspective of "Great Divergence." *Researches in Chinese Economic History* 1: 32–39. (in Chinese).

Park, Chong-dong. 1997. *The Special Economic Zones of China and Their Impact on Its Economic Development*. Westport: Praeger.

Peng, Zeyi. 1983. *Shijiu shiji houbanqi de Zhongguo caizheng yu jingji [Public Finance and Economy in China in the Second Half of the Nineteenth Century]*. Beijing: People's Press. (in Chinese).

Perkins, Dwight H. 2010. China's Prereform Economy in World Perspective. In *China's Rise in Historical Perspective*, ed. Brantly Womack. Lanham MD: Rowman and Littlefield.

Piketty, Thomas. 2020. *Capital and Ideology*. Trans. Arthur Goldhammer. Cambridge: The Belknap Press of Harvard University Press.

Schefold, Bertram. 2014. Marx, Sombart, Weber and the Debate about the Genesis of Modern Capitalism. *Journal of Institutional Studies* 6 (2): 10–26.

Schefold, Sarah. 2008. *Arbeitslosigkeit, neue Märkte und soziale Differenzierung im urbanen China*, 46. Nr: Arbeitsblätter des Instituts für Sozialanthropologie der Universität Bern.

Sheridan, James. 1983. The Warlord Era: Politics and Militarism under the Peking Government, 1916–1928. In *The Cambridge History of China*, ed. Denis Twitchett and J. K. Fairbank, vol. 12, 284–321. Cambridge: Cambridge University Press.

Shiroyama, Tomoko. 2008. *China during the Great Depression: Market, State, and the World Economy, 1929–1937*. Cambridge, MA: the Harvard University Asia Centre.

Billy K. L. So, and R. H. Myers (eds.). 2013[2011]. *The Treaty Port Economy in Modern China: Empirical Studies of Institutional Change and Economic Performance*. Trans. Yinong Cheng and Huan Tian. Zhejiang: Zhejiang University Press. (in Chinese).

Sowell, Thomas. 1980. *Knowledge and Decisions*. New York: Basic Books.

Terrill, Ross. 1999. *Mao: A Biography*. Stanford: Stanford University Press.

Vogel, Erza F. 1969. *Canton under Communism: Program and Politics in a Provincial Capital, 1949–1968*. Cambridge: Harvard University Press.

Vogel, Erza F. 2011. *Deng Xiaoping and the Transformation of China*. Cambridge, MA: The Belknap Press of Harvard University Press.

von Mises, Ludwig. 1932. *Die Gemeinwirtschaft: Untersuchungen über den Sozialismus*. Jena: Gustav Fischer.

von Mises, Ludwig. 1936. *Socialism: An Economic and Sociological Analysis*. Trans. J. Kahane. London: Jonathan Cape.

Wakeman, Frederic E. 1973. *History and Will: Philosophical Perspectives of Mao Tse-tung's Thoughts*. California: University of California press.

Wall, David. 1991. *Special Economic Zones in China: The Administrative and Regulatory Framework*. Canberra: Economic Division, National Centre for Development Studies, Australian National University.

Walter, Carl E. and Howie, Fraser J. T. 2012. *Red Capitalism: The Fragile Financial Foundation of China's Extraordinary Rise*. New York: Wiley.

Wang, Jin. 2013. The Economic Impact of Special Economic Zones: Evidence from Chinese Municipalities. *Journal of Development Economics* 101: 133–147.

Wang, Yuhua. 2022. *The Rise of Fall of Imperial China: The Social Origins of State Development*. Princeton: Princeton University Press.

Wang, Yuru. 2005. Economic Growth and the Medium-long Cycles in Modern China. *Chinese Economic Quarterly* 4 (2): 461–490. (in Chinese).

Weber, Isabella M. 2019. Escaping Shock Therapy: An Interview on the Development of the Chinese Economic Model. *IPPR Progressive Review* 26 (1): 99–106.

Weber, Isabella M. 2021. *How China Escaped Shock Therapy: The Market Reform Debate*. London: Routledge.

Weber, Max. 1983. *Max Weber on Capitalism, Bureaucracy, and Religion, edited by Stanislav Andreski*. London: George Allen and Unwin.

Westad, Odd Arne. 2012. *Restless Empire: China and the World since 1750*. London: Vintage Books.

Will, Pierre-Etienne., and R. Bin. Wong. 1991. *Nourish the People: The State Civilian Granary System in China: 1650–1850*. Ann Arbor: University of Michigan Press.

Wright, Mary C. 1962. *The Last Stand of Chinese Conservatism: The T'ung-Chih Restoration, 1862–1874*. Stanford University Press.

Wu, Weiping. 1999. *Pioneering Economic Reform in China's Special Economic Zones: The Promotion of Foreign Investment and Technology Transfer in Shenzhen*. Aldershot: Ashgate.

Young, Arthur N. 1971. *China's Nation-building Effort, 1927–1937*. Hoover: Hoover Press.

Zhou, Li'an. 2014. Administrative Subcontract. *Chinese Journal of Sociology* 34 (6): 1–38. (in Chinese).

CHAPTER 10

To Understand China: Past and Future

China is full of conundrums that outsiders find difficult to understand. The Chinese civilisation is famous for its early formation and long-lasting "invariability". In the agricultural era, Chinese people created unparalleled material wealth and technological advancement. However, its relative backwardness in the early modern time was almost equally eye-catching. From the 1980s, it is also perplexing that communist China achieved spectacular economic growth with little progress of democratisation which westerners consider as important for economic growth. While some scholars propose to classify China as another vivid example of the developmental state to which three of the four Asian Tigers belong,[1] and some scholars predict that without democratisation China cannot sustain economic growth (Acemoglu and Robinson 2013: 437–446), China has its own uniqueness. While uniqueness is not equal to exceptionalism, the uniqueness has historical particularity. History has important meaning. "Once society gets organised in a particular way, this tends to

[1] The "developmental state" is a conception proposed to explain the pattern of development in South Korea, Singapore, and Taiwan after the Second World War. Basically, it is a mixed economy in which a free-market mechanism exists while the government adopts strong interventionist policies to direct economic growth. It is arguable whether China is such a "developmental state". See: Birdsall and Campos (1993); Knight (2014); Chang (2007).

G. H. Jiang, *The Imperial Mode of China*, Palgrave Studies in Economic History, https://doi.org/10.1007/978-3-031-27015-4_10

persist" (Acemoglu and Robinson 2013: 44). With previous chapters, a conceptual framework is proposed to understand China's past, present and future.

1 The Historical Trajectory of China

In the Pre-Qin period, economic, political and social revolutions occurred concurrently. In the "first economic revolution", new agricultural tools were put into widespread use, which resulted in higher agricultural productivity. As necessitated by natural conditions, demand for public good provision grew accordingly. Simultaneously, the feudalistic society collapsed gradually as military and economic capacity of the central court declined. As a result, interstate competition became fierce. Rivalry motivated kingdoms to create innovative institutions for the sake of pursuing hegemony.[2] Through autocratic rule and commoners' obedience which massive building of infrastructure necessitated, states competed to create an efficient state apparatus to mobilise resources—mainly labour force and land—more intensively than rivals (van Leeuwen and van Zanden 2018: 1–3). In the process, different schools handed out diverse thought, among which Legalism was the most successful one. In several waves of Legalist reforms, bloodline-based aristocracy was abolished, and merit-based bureaucracy was established; the politically feudal decentralised system was also abolished, and a centralised authority was established; Household-based peasantry and private ownership of land were legalised as the predominant economic form. Thereafter, a pyramid-structured Imperial Mode took shape. The peasant economy provided economic surpluses and labour; The bureaucratic system and the central authority collaborated to mobilise resources and achieve public good provision. However, the structure was by no means perfect or balanced by itself. Its inherent drawbacks, such as the principal–agent problems between the three layers, led to its recurring instability. The fate of the Imperial Mode determined the dynastic cycles in Chinese history.

In the Qin (221–206 BCE) and Han (202 BC–9 AD, 25–220 AD) dynasties, many fundamental components of the Imperial Mode further took shape. The government introduced monopoly on key economic industries, such as the salt and iron industries, was formulated and

[2] The need for warfare was highlighted. A "military-physiocratic state" emerged. See: von Glahn (2016: 85).

fixed as a state policy. In subsequent dynasties, its scope continued to extend. Moreover, a combination of Confucianism and Legalism began to predominate as the official ideology (Zhao 2015). The Imperial Mode formed fundamentally. However, the bureaucratic system slowly degraded into a puppet of aristocracy in the Han dynasty. Magnates coming from local celebrities and consort kinsmen gradually formed untamed powers. They and their heir monopolised the government's offices; They annexed peasants' assets and integrated them into the manorial economy, which meant a kind of serfdom. In the final decades of the Han dynasty, the central court had no ability to change this trend. Finally, with the rise of regional warlords and the invasion of northern nomadic tribes, the Imperial Mode collapsed. The "Age of Disunion" lasted for hundreds of years. It once appeared that feudalistic systems came back, which were characterised by aristocracy, absence of centralised power and the manorial economy.

However, efficacy of the Imperial Mode was deeply rooted in economic, political and ideological conditions, so that it rebounded soon. Fragmentation was ended, and the Imperial Mode was restored in the Sui and Tang dynasties. Aristocracy was gradually demolished through establishing and improving the state examination system, in which theoretically every single man could get a position in bureaucracy through succeeding in the examinations. Thereafter, the state examination system became "an effective instrument in recruiting and 'reproducing' the ruling elite" (van Leeuwen and van Zanden 2018: 9). Private ownership of land was reconfirmed in the Tang dynasty and further strengthened in the Song dynasty by the development of the transaction system of lands. In sum, the Imperial Mode became respectably mature in the Tang and Song dynasties. Suitability between the base and the superstructure stimulated further economic growth. Especially in the Song dynasty, international trade, urban commerce, marketisation and monetarisation developed fast. Proto-industrialisation developed under stimuli of technological progress. In cultural fields, some literati became more intellectually open-minded and more tolerant towards commerce which was initially criticised by the main ideology. Social atmosphere also appeared more friendly towards profit-oriented activities (Lin 2011: 284–327). In one word, changes were comprehensive and multiple (Hartwell 1982). The changes were so outstanding that some scholars called them the Tang-Song transition, a potential possibility towards modernisation.

In the Tang-Song transition, imperial China had prepared many preconditions for the next-stage mode of production descending from the Imperial Mode. The economy appeared more commercialised and marketised. A fiscal state was also looming. In the Tang dynasty (618–907 AD) and the following chaotic period, soldiery had achieved to some degree professionalisation. In the Song dynasty (960–1279 AD), fierce conflicts with northern nomadic rivals which rose continuously posed enormous fiscal pressure upon the Song government. It devised unprecedented innovative methods to increase fiscal revenues, including expanding indirect taxation, issuing state bonds and monopolistic operation in profitable commercial sectors, such as tea, alcohol, and salt. Annually, indirect taxes had composed over two-thirds of the total revenues of the Song government. Correspondingly, the Song government also had a well-organised bureaucracy to manage and operate the fiscal system (Liu and Guan 2021). Schumpeter (1954) and Tilly (1992) had described the rise of fiscal states in Western Europe as a key component of the transition from feudalism to capitalism. Conceivably, in the Song dynasty, China had possessed most characters of a transition to a fiscal state, which were not so dissimilar to those defined by European scholars.

Seemingly, China could have started a different track when the Imperial Mode had been ripe in the Tang-Song transition, and it had successfully pushed productive forces to the entrance towards the next mode of production. Although it is still arguable whether we have overestimated the possibility of industrialisation and then modernisation during the Song dynasty (van Leeuwen and van Zanden 2018; Li 2010), it was disrupted by the administration of the subsequent Yuan (1271–1368 AD) and Ming (1368–1644 AD) dynasties. As Mongolians, Yuan rulers practised ethnic discrimination and strict social control. Ming emperors decided to concentrate on agriculture and ban international trade at the wrong point when westerners started sea expeditions (Acemoglu and Robinson 2013: 117–118). Later, Qing (1644–1911 AD) emperors continued to ossify the Imperial Mode regarding the bureaucratic system, agriculture and social culture. In sum, the possibility of a holistic transformation was smothered in the Ming-Qing era. As Anderson (1974: 540–541) wrote,

> For the growth in the forces of production in Imperial China appears, in effect, to have taken a curiously spiral form after the great socio-economic revolutions of the Song age in the 10–13th centuries. It repeated

> its motions on ascending levels, without ever twisting away into a new figure altogether, until finally this dynamic recurrence was broken and overwhelmed by forces external to the traditional social formation. The paradox of this peculiar movement of Chinese history in the early modern epoch is that most of the purely technical preconditions for a capitalist industrialisation were achieved far earlier in China than they were in Europe. China possessed a comprehensive and decisive technological lead over the Occident by the later Middle Ages, anticipating by centuries virtually every one of the key inventions in material production whose conjugation was to release the economic dynamism of Renaissance Europe.

It was in the Ming-Qing era that the Great Divergence started (Broadberry 2021). While "this deep disproportion can doubtless be traced to the whole structure of Chinese state and society itself" (Anderson 1974: 542), the roots of the failures lied in the combination of institutional path dependence and historical contingency. Just like the Black Death which was certainly not historically preordained but posed an uncountable influence on European history (Acemoglu and Robinson 2013: 96–117), many events in the Yuan, Ming and Qing dynasties were contingent but reversed the historical direction. Absolutist practices were blocking industrialisation and marketisation in China. In contrast, in the same period, although in Western Europe the wane of feudalism was accompanied by the rise of absolutism, which was also a sort of political centralisation, the rise of absolutism was nevertheless accompanied by the development of the capitalist mode of production. European monarchs aspired to take political power from feudal lords and manorial masters, but "unfortunately" they confronted the adolescent bourgeoisie class. The bourgeoisie class cannot live with an unlimited monarchy. They had inner dynamic conflicts with each other.[3] Therefore, we see again that the European absolutist monarchy played as the unconscious tool of history. Absolutism intentionally wanted to destroy the feudal mode of production, but unintentionally facilitated development of the capitalist mode of production which harboured inner dynamics to destroy absolutist centralisation.

[3] With the help of existent constraints on the monarchy, the British bourgeoisie arose and continued to tame political centralisation. Gradually, political centralisation in England facilitated the establishment of inclusive institutions. See Acemoglu and Robinson (2013: 191–197, 208–212).

Let us recall the sentences of Anderson (1974: 40–41), which had been mentioned before:

> The apparent paradox of Absolutism in Western Europe was that it fundamentally represented an apparatus for the protection of aristocratic property and privileges, yet at the same time, the means whereby this protection was promoted could *simultaneously* ensure the basic interests of the nascent mercantile and manufacturing classes. The Absolutist State increasingly centralised political power and worked towards more uniform legal systems: ... It did away with a large number of internal barriers to trade, and sponsored external tariffs against foreign competitors. ... It provided lucrative if risky investments in public finance for usury capital. ... It mobilised rural property by seizure of ecclesiastical lands. ... It offered rentier sinecures in the bureaucracy. ... It sponsored colonial enterprises and trading companies. ... In other words, it accomplished certain partial functions in the primitive accumulation necessary for the eventual triumph of the capitalist mode of production itself. ... There was, however, always a potential field of compatibility at this stage between the nature and programme of the Absolutist State and the operations of mercantile and manufacturing capital.

However, when the feudal mode of production (although not completely in the same meaning as the European one) fell into the waning stage during the Pre-Qin period in China, the agricultural economy was on the rise. An autocratic pyramid-like structure was not only necessary but also advantageous, in that the agricultural economy in China necessitated public good provision including such large-scale projects as the Great Wall and the Great Canal, national defence and relevant arrangements to sustain social order. The rise of a centralised structure reduced transaction costs and contributed to collective actions, leading to the growth of the agricultural economy. The agricultural economy required different productive factors from the commercial and industrial economy. As a result, the Imperial Mode formed in China, a sort of societal mode which never existed in Europe.[4]

In the first place, the Imperial Mode was not only a result of historical contingency but also the necessary development of economic, political and social factors. Its inherent structure led to an "old fashioned" idea,

[4] Thanks to the lecture by Prof.Yue Shen on 17th, March 2021 in Peking University.

i.e., the dynastic cycles. The Imperial Mode had its inner utility and instability, both of which came from the same sources. On the one hand, it was a relatively efficient mechanism to achieve public good provision. On the other hand, monarchical despotism and the principal–agent problems in most cases corrupted the whole structure. As van Leeuwen and van Zanden (2018: 6) argue, “the state-centred ideology, combined with an education system geared towards supplying the bureaucracy with new members, and an infrastructure able to extract revenue from all parts of the Empire, facilitated the phoenix-like character of the Chinese state re-emerging each time after a dynasty was toppled”. As Marx hinted in his economics that the particular mechanism of capitalism to create prosperity contained self-destructive seeds, the Imperial Mode of China also possessed a similar duality.

A successful economy depends on certain institutions capable of creating the right incentives for economic growth. As circumstances change, institutions need to adjust. What matters therefore is for institutions to have the capacity to adapt as circumstances change (Mokyr 2009: 8–9). Capable of mobilising resources to provide public goods through a centralised structure with higher institutional efficiency and lower transaction costs than other decentralised structure, the Imperial Mode of China reached a peak in the era of the agricultural economy. However, it not only was unconducive to a commercial and industrial economy, but also thwarted the possibility of a holistic transformation due to its inherent conservativeness in politics, economy and ideology. When the real challenges came, China had to start modernisation based on the Imperial Mode.

2 Path Dependence and Present China

One of the main arguments of the book is that China’s ambition towards modernisation carries many historical legacies that derived from the Imperial Mode. As detailed before, Chinese governments did not create a proper institutional environment which could have provided sufficient incentives for industrialisation and modernisation. Before the mid-nineteenth century, focusing on stabilising the imperial rule, China’s emperors did not accept any pathbreaking reformatory proposals. They refused to take into consideration what was happening in the West (Peyrefitte 1992). Western Europe was experiencing the rise of market-based capitalism and sweeping industrialisation. As Marx (1848: Bourgeois and

Proletarians) depicted, "the bourgeoisie, during its rule of scarce one hundred years, has created more massive and more colossal productive forces than have all preceding generations together". When the West came with its military supremacy and economic superiority, China had to face the challenges presented by a capitalised, industrialised and modernised occidental civilisational mode.

Since the advent of westerners in the nineteenth century, which was accompanied with China's political humiliation and declining international status, China tried to strike a unique way to achieve modernisation. Whether actively or passively, almost all reformatory or revolutionary actions were conducted based on existent institutional settings. "Since the set of organisations present at any moment is determined by the inherited structure of institutions, the process of change is mainly incremental and path dependent: institutions tend to be long-lived and difficult to reform" (Murrell 2005: 668). Path dependence was an apparent element which influenced China's intellectual choices and practical pathways regarding changes towards modernisation. Path dependence could be caused by sunk costs, or an existent cognitive system (North 2005: 45–46). It is highlighted that structural inertia makes organisations slow to adjust to changes in the institutional environment (Hannan and Freeman 1984). The vested interests in existent institutions also resulted in oppositional norms which manifested themselves in subconscious ways and in informal rules (Nee and Ingram 1998). Consequently, path dependence hindered a smooth transition towards institutions with higher efficiency.

Path dependence manifested itself very clearly in the reformatory actions of the Qing government between the mid-nineteenth century and its collapse in 1911. Rulers recognised certain political risks which new institutions would bring about, and then feared possible creative destruction (Acemoglu and Robinson 2013: 231–234). They appeared very hesitant to stay a step ahead. Like other absolutist rulers in Eurasia at the same period, including sultans in the Ottoman Empire, tsars in Russia, and emperors in Habsburg-Austria and in Spain, the primary goal of their concern was political stability. When the Qing dynasty ended, the Republic of China (1912–1949 AD) tried to find a feasible pathway towards modernisation with legacies of the Imperial Mode in a chaotic period. However, efforts hardly succeeded. The Kuomintang government (1928–1949 AD) not only was unable to completely extinguish warlordism and domestic chaos, but also appeared lukewarm at best towards authentic modernisation. Finally, in 1949, the Chinese Communist Party seized political power.

While many Leninist and Stalinist practices were implemented in communist China, path dependence of the Imperial Mode was still ever-present and exerting influence. As Greif (2005: xxiv) wrote about path dependence,

> Even if a particular institution is no longer self-enforcing – its past institutional elements no longer generating a particular behaviour – its constituting institutional elements still influence the direction of institutional change. Institutional elements inherited from the past, such as shared beliefs, communities, political and economic organisations, internalised norms, and cognitive systems embodied in rules transcend the situations that led to their emergence. … Past institutional elements provide the foundation for, and influence the process leading to, new institutions.

Communist China was barely an exception. In the Maoist era, China's governmental pattern was to a large degree a mixture of the Imperial Mode and communism/Stalinism. After the 1980s, China began reforms with its own uniqueness. Unlike other communist countries in Eastern Europe and the Soviet Union, China began its economic reforms without having experienced systematic collapse. China's reforms were marked with the consideration of gradualism. The limits of acceptable change advanced as previous changes led to success (Murrell 2005: 688). As a result, potency of path dependence was more salient. By introducing elements of inclusive institutions, China succeeded to generate remarkable economic growth. However, with the political structure going back to a sort of quasi-Imperial Mode, present China is in the process of forming "Oriental Capitalism", a mode in which the market economy takes effect in some economic sectors while imperial despotism still functions prominently. Therefore, whether communist China can get rid of the Imperial Mode and truly achieve modernisation is not yet clear.

> A new cycle only began with the victory of the Chinese communist party under the leadership of Mao in 1949. In a way, it followed classic patterns – flawed practices at first (with the Great Leap Forward (1958–1962) as the most extreme experiment in this respect), followed, after 1978, by radical market-oriented reforms, which unleashed underlying forces of economic growth to produce a growth miracle unheard of in history. The succession

> of central planning (copied after the example of the USSR) and market reforms fits nicely into the classical pattern of the dynastic cycle, in which the 'mandate from heaven' is now replaced by a contract with Marxist ideology. What was different from previous cycles is that this resulted in massive changes in the structure and productivity of the economy. (van Leeuwen and van Zanden 2018: 13)

Without little doubt, the introduction of economic inclusive institutions since the 1980s is unprecedented. But sustained economic growth requires more. Loaded by path dependence, China experienced a zigzag pathway in the last one hundred and eighty years. All three players during this stage, i.e., the Qing government, the Republic of China and the People's Republic of China, made efforts almost for the same aim, although their specific actions in most cases appeared diagonally different. At least for now, China seems to be on a similar track (see Fig. 1). Modernisation entails industrialisation and marketisation in economic spheres, democratisation and bureaucracy in political spheres, and other inclusive institutions in societal spheres (Qian 2010: Sects. 1 and 2). Since the CCP also nominally aspires to achieve modernisation in China, China has to strike a way of new birth, not always in the old fashion.

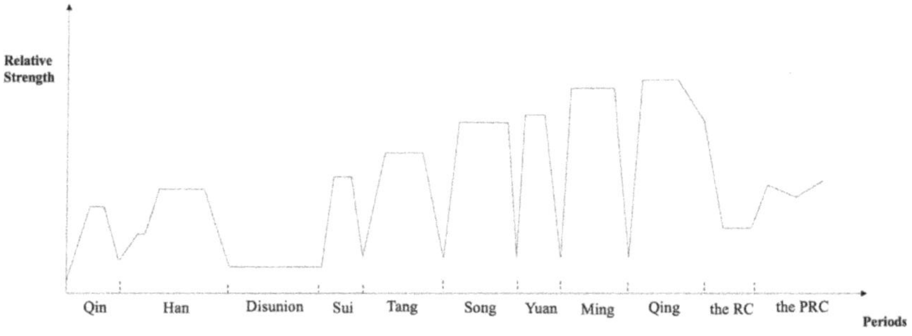

Fig. 1 Relative strength of the imperial mode of China[5]

[5] The estimates of "relative strength" of the Imperial Mode are highly sketchy. Variants may include basic characters of the Imperial Mode, such as political despotism, economic control, and cultural repression, etc. The figure is mainly for illustrating its rudimentary evolutionary pathway. I do not mean to measure the "relative strength" accurately or quantitatively.

Roughly speaking, China has experienced three waves of economic revolutions from the Pre-Qin period to the present. The "first economic revolution" in the Pre-Qin period contributed to the emergence of the Imperial Mode, as planting agriculture required a centralised mechanism to achieve public good provision. The formation of the imperial structure was a successful reaction to economic changes and further facilitated socio-economic development. The "second economic revolution" in the Tang-Song era contributed to huge material prosperity and maturity of the Imperial Mode. The imperial structure reached a zenith regarding its capacity to facilitate socio-economic development and institutional changes in the Tang-Song era. Driven by autonomous technological progress, the first two economic revolutions were mostly internal events, while the "third economic revolution" was sparked by external shocks, namely the advent of the West which has more advanced technology and institutions. From the mid-nineteenth century, China has been struggling to find a feasible way to cope with challenges that the West brings and carry out modernisation with its own characteristics. China is still trying to complete this process.

3 Ordoliberalism and Future China

As Joel Mokyr (2009: 11) puts it, "each continental country has its own specific constraints and obstacles that needs to be removed or overcome before it could do what Britain did, and follow its own variation on the theme of industrialisation and the modernisation of production". What Britain did for forging modernity has deep historical roots,[6] contingency and conscious actions. Anglo-Saxon liberalist practices were mainly copied in Britain's colonies, while other countries which achieved modernisation, such as France, Germany, Nordic countries, and Japan, have a wide variety of modern capitalism. Even in those British colonies, variants are injected into specific practices. Likewise, it might be unwise to believe that China will simply copy any liberalist practices, including direct democracy

[6] Macfarlane (1978: Chapter 8) argues that at least English individualism is not a recent product. It may date back to the very early period of the Middle Ages. If less-developed countries need to imitate what England had done, it may be necessary to consider whether the holistic tradition can be copied or whether it is proper to copy such a holistic societal structure.

and neoliberalist policies. Especially considering that the Chinese government is basing its legitimacy upon economic growth and rising welfare of the majority, it would be unrealistic to expect a straightforward transition towards liberalism. Once the West expected that through integrating China into international trade, China could be changed politically and economically, but the result is mixed at best (Tan 2021). As Acemoglu and Robinson (2006: 1) said, "[…], democracy is never created because society is relatively egalitarian and prosperous, which makes the nondemocratic political status quo stable. The system is not challenged because people are sufficiently satisfied under the existing political institutions".

In global economic history, it is widely concluded that to achieve modernisation and sustained economic growth, inclusive institutions are necessary. In the Chinese case, China will have to establish its own inclusive institutions under the influence of path dependence. While there are universal rules, there are local circumstances. The future of China can only emerge in between. China had introduced market mechanisms since the 1980s, while one-party leadership was not undermined but strengthened. It is natural to require more liberalist reforms in China. But it is hardly reasonable to take for granted a neoliberalist democratic transition. China must strike its own unique pathway. No scholars are so prescient as to be able to predict what will occur in future China. Meanwhile, in my view, German Ordoliberalism would be suggestive for finding a "Third Way" between an Anglo-Saxon market economy and a state-controlled economy.

German Ordoliberalism was precisely founded in searching for a "Third Way" between the laissez-faire economy and planned economy between the 1930s and 1950s. In Germany, market mechanisms and relevant ideologies were never as prevalent as in Great Britain and North America. Since the early nineteenth century, Friedrich List had underscored the positive role of governments in developing the economy; Later, viewing government's intervention as a positive and necessary force, the German historical school had little favour towards Anglo-Saxon neoclassics which preached laissez-faire policies. In the 1930s, German economists tried to rescue Germany's economy which was suffering from fiscal bankruptcy and recurring inflation and deflation. Soon, the Nazi Party's economic practices brought interventionist policies to a peak.

Within a series of complex social events, Walter Eucken proposed "economic order" and then Ordoliberalism in the late 1930s and early 1940s.[7] In the late 1940s, after Alfred Müller-Armack further explored the "Ordnungspolitik", Ordoliberalism gained its famous name, the Social Market Economy (Tribe 1995: 214–215; Müller-Armack 1947). In the 1950s, through Ludwig Erhard's plans of economic recovery, the concept became Germany's "economic constitution" on which today Germany's economic policies are still based (Erhard 1957).

Ordoliberalism/Social Market Economy is a sophisticated but straightforward economic philosophy. The primary principle is that the price mechanism, i.e., the market mechanism, plays a fundamental role. Without doubt, it is an economic order dominated by elements of the market economy. But it is "a consciously guided, indeed a socially guided market economy" (Müller-Armack 1947: 88). Accordingly, there is a distinctive menu of social measures to achieve social goals. This menu includes: the creation of a new participatory enterprise organisations[8]; proceeding though a publicly regulated competition order and the pursuit of anti-monopoly policy in order to forestall possible misuse of power in the economy; provision for the extension of social insurance; minimum wages and the securing of individual wages through free wage agreements (Tribe 1995: 236). In general, the goal of the Social Market Economy is to sustain "economic order" in which the market economy can be guided by governmental interventions for the sake of social goals, and in turn social harmony could drive sustained economic growth in a win–win situation.

It appears that the Chinese Socialist Market Economy initiated by the CCP resembled the German Social Market Economy. In 1992, the CCP decided to combine Chinese characteristics, socialist practices, and the market economy together in order to achieve modernisation (Wu 2018: Chapter 2). On the one hand, China needs to push forwards marketisation reforms to accommodate more market-oriented mechanisms. While Ordoliberalism emphasises the role of governmental interventions, markets are unconditionally respected. In China, the government still

[7] "Ordnung der Wirtschaft". See Eucken (1940).

[8] Thomas Piketty (2020: Chapter 17) proposed a "participatory socialism" to replace capitalism. This system is supposed to gradually abolish capitalist mechanisms which make exploitation possible. As a solution, a series of institutional arrangements may redistribute wealth and power to workers and citizens.

directly participates in economic activities, as embodied in omnipotent state-owned enterprises, licenced monopoly in key industries and discretionary economic interference. The policymaking process is still short of checks and balances. Thus, in order for sustained economic growth, further reforms are inevitable. On the other hand, due to multiple factors, legacies of the Imperial Mode cannot be expected to be removed very soon. Communist ideologies still take effect in many spheres. Comparatively speaking, a sort of modernisation with Chinese characteristics is a more feasible option.

In recent years, China seems to have halted those changes which the West expects to occur in China. In international relations, China appears increasingly aggressive since conflicts between China and the West are growing fast in areas concerning economy, politics and ideology (Rudd 2021, 2022; Brown 2018). China's behaviours seem to be difficult to grasp for many observers in the West or seem to be exactly in alignment with the sensational predictions that radical liberalists make. To some degree, China seems to be happy with the situation that the "Chinese Mode" is contrasted with the "Occidental Mode". No future is destined, though. The past emerged from a combination of historical necessity and contingency, so will be the future. The choice that China will make in ensuing days will be of significance not only for China's vast masses and the Chinese government itself, but also for the whole of mankind.

References

Acemoglu, Daron, and James A. Robinson. 2006. *Economic Origins of Dictatorship and Democracy*. Cambridge University Press.

Acemoglu, D., and J.A. Robinson. 2013. *Why Nations Fail: The Origins of Power Prosperity and Poverty*. Profile Books Ltd.

Anderson, Perry. 1974. *Lineages of the Absolutist State*. Verso.

Birdsall, Nacy M., and Jose E. Campos, et al. 1993. *The East Asian Miracle: Economic Growth and Public Policy: Main Report*. A World Bank Research Report: World Bank Group.

Broadberry, Stephen. 2021. Accounting for the Great Divergence: Recent Findings from Historical National Accounting. CEPR Discussion Paper No. DP15936 (March 2021).

Brown, Kerry. 2018. *The World According to Xi: Everything You Need to Know about the New China*. I. T. Tauris.

Chang, Ha-Joon. 2007. *The East Asian Development Experience: The Miracle, the Crisis and the Future*. Zed Books.

Erhard, Ludwig. 1957. *Wohlstand für Alle*. Düsseldorf: Econ Verlag.
Eucken, Walter. 1940. *Die Grundlagen der Nationalökonomie*. Jena: Gustav Fischer.
Greif, Avner. 2005. Institutions, Markets, and Games. In *The Economic Sociology of Capitalism*, ed. Victor Nee and Richard Swedberg. Princeton University Press.
Hannan, Michael T., and John Freeman. 1984. Structural Inertia and Organisational Change. *American Sociological Review* 49: 149–164.
Hartwell, Robert M. 1982. Demographic, Political and Social Transformations of China, 750–1550. *Harvard Journal of Asiatic Studies* 42 (2): 365–442.
Knight, John B. 2014. China as a Developmental State. *The World Economy* 37 (10): 1335–1347.
Li, Huarui (ed.). 2010. *Tangsong Biange Lun de Youlai yu Fazhan* [The Origin and Development of the Theory of the Tang-Song Transition]. Tianjin: Tianjin Ancient Books Publishing House (in Chinese).
Lin, Wenxun. 2011. *Tangsong Shehui Biange Lungang* [The Synopsis of Social Transitions in Tang and Song]. Beijing: People's Press (in Chinese).
Liu, Guanglin, and Qiyun Guan. 2021. Warfare and the Fiscal State during the Tang-Song Transition. *Researches on Chinese Economic History* 2: 39–56 (in Chinese).
Macfarlane, Alan. 1978. *Origins of English Individualism: The Family Property and Social Transition*. Wiley.
Marx, Karl. 1848. *The Manifesto of the Communist Party*. Online Archive.
Mokyr, Joel. 2009. *The Enlightened Economy: Britain and the Industrial Revolution, 1700–1850*. Penguin Books.
Müller-Armack, Alfred. 1947. *Wirtschaftslenkung und Marktwirtschaft*. Hamburg: Verlag für Wirtschaft und Sozialpolitik.
Murrell, Peter. 2005. Institutions and Firms in Transition Economics. In *Handbook of New Institutional Economics*, ed. C. Menard and M.M. Shirley, 667–699. The Netherlands: Springer.
Nee, Victor, and Paul Ingram. 1998. Embeddedness and Beyond: Institutions, Exchange, and Social Structure. In *The New Institutionalism in Sociology*, ed. Mary C. Brinton and Victor Nee, 19–45. New York: Russell Sage.
North, Douglas. 2005. Capitalism and Economic Growth. In *The Economic Sociology of Capitalism*, ed. Victor Nee and Richard Swedberg, 41–52. Princeton University Press.
Peyrefitte, Alain. (1992). *The Immobile Empire*, trans. Jon Rothschild. New York: Knopf.
Piketty, Thomas. 2020. *Capital and Ideology*, trans. Arthur Goldhammer. The Belknap Press of Harvard University Press.

Qian, Chengdan. 2010. *Shijie Xiandaihua Licheng* [The Course of the World's Modernisation], vol. I. Nanjing: Jiangsu People's Publishing House. (in Chinese).

Rudd, Kevin. 2021. How to Keep U.S.-Chinese Confrontation from Ending in Calamity. *Foreign Affairs*, March/April: 58–72.

Rudd, Kevin. 2022. *The Avoidable War: The Dangers of a Catastrophic Conflict between the US and Xi Jinping's China*. Public Affairs.

Schumpeter, Joseph A. 1954. The Crisis of the Tax State. *International Economic Papers* 4: 99–140.

Tan, Yeling. 2021. How the WTO Changed China: The Mixed Legacy of Economic Engagement. *Foreign Affairs*, March/April: 90–102.

Tilly, Charles. 1992. *Coercion, Capital, and European States, AD 990 – 1992*. Blackwell Publishing.

Tribe, Keith. 1995. *Strategies of Economic Order: German Economic Discourse 1750–1950*. Cambridge University Press.

van Leeuwen, Bas, and van Zanden, Jan Luiten. 2018. China as a Nation. In *China in the Local and Global Economy*, ed. Steven Brakman, et al., 1–17. London: Routledge.

von Glahn, Richard. 2016. *The Economic History of China: From Antiquity to the Nineteenth Century*. Cambridge University Press.

Wu, Jinglian. 2018. *China's Economic Reform Process*. Beijing: Encyclopedia of China Publishing House (in Chinese).

Zhao, Dingxin. 2015. *The Confucian-Legalist State: A New Theory of Chinese History*. Oxford University Press.

Index

A
Aberdeen, 221
absolute spirit, 150
absolutism, 104, 309
accountability, 24
Africa, 162, 206, 284, 288
Age of Disunion, 100, 120, 123, 126, 127, 129, 130, 133, 138, 141, 170, 180, 182, 186
Age of Glory, 248, 249
agnosticism, 87
agricultural economy, 17, 21, 22, 24, 34, 73, 74, 98, 163, 165, 171, 178, 179, 191, 193, 196, 198, 227, 231, 243, 244, 246, 248, 266, 288, 310
agricultural revolution, 43
altruism, 78
America, 206, 219, 256, 268, 316
Amsterdam, 206, 237
Analects, 51, 68, 76, 80, 81, 150
anarchy, 23, 78, 141
animism, 69
An Lushan, 133, 140, 144
anti-commercialism, 163, 183
Arabic World, 2, 155
aristocracy, 20, 23, 58, 65–67, 92, 98, 99, 107, 108, 118–123, 126, 129, 130, 137–139, 141, 143, 170, 179, 186, 214, 300, 305, 307
aristocratic groups, 119, 120, 122, 129, 130, 133, 136–138
Aristotle, 63
Arrow, Kenneth J., 16
Asia, 2, 7, 29, 31, 117, 126, 153, 155, 159, 161, 162, 206, 249, 268, 284, 288
Asian Tigers, 305
Asiatic mode of production, 7–10
Asiatic society(ies), 3, 8
Austrian School, 287
autarky economy, 163, 167
authoritarianism, 288
axial age, 63

B
Bacon, Francis, 221

G. H. Jiang, *The Imperial Mode of China*, Palgrave Studies in Economic History, https://doi.org/10.1007/978-3-031-27015-4

ba-gu-wen, 169
Ban Gu, 49, 110
Banliang, 49
Beijing, xvii, 152, 158, 159, 164, 237, 290, 294, 298
Beiyang, 256, 267, 269–271, 273
bookkeeping, 146
Book of Lord Shang, 54, 55, 68, 89
bourgeois, 8, 215, 247, 278, 293
bourgeoisie, 211, 214, 276, 277, 309, 312
British Isles, 19, 210, 211, 221
bronze economy, 35
Buddha, 63
Buddhism, 126, 127
bureaucracy, 12, 23, 52, 76, 90, 92, 101, 107, 108, 119, 120, 122, 123, 129, 134, 140, 142, 143, 157, 170, 171, 184, 187, 215, 231, 241, 242, 270, 272, 276, 283, 295, 298, 299, 306–308, 310, 311, 314
bureaucratic state, 51, 53, 55, 58, 75, 116
Burma, 157

C

California School, 168, 195, 235–238, 246, 247
Calvin, 233, 234
Calvinism, 5, 204, 214, 216, 233, 234, 245
Cambodia, 288
Cao Can, 109
Cao Cao, 118, 120, 123
Cao, Pi, 118
capitalism, xv, 3, 8, 11, 20, 38, 198, 216, 218, 233–235, 245, 258, 267, 273, 276, 278, 285–287, 289–292, 294, 299, 308, 311, 315, 317
capitalist economy, 216, 220, 273
capitalist society, 8, 216, 233, 285, 286
Carta, Magna, 204, 209
Caucasus, 152
central planning, 17, 22, 191, 281, 284, 286, 287, 314
Cha-Ju, 107, 121
Cheng, Hao, 150
Cheng, Yi, 150
Chen, Yun, 279, 280, 293, 294
Christianity, 12, 233
Chushuimu, 51
city-states, 50
civil administration, 92
Classical economics, 77, 82
collective action, 17
collectivisation, 257, 278, 280, 282, 284, 290, 297
colonialism, 160, 215
colonisation, 159
commercial economy, 148, 183, 198, 204, 273
commercialisation, 19, 49, 147, 156, 161, 167, 206, 207, 248, 250
communism, xiv, xv, 8, 22, 284–286, 289, 296, 299, 313
Confucian culture, 18
Confucianism, 12, 40, 64, 65, 68, 69, 71, 73, 75–77, 80, 82, 83, 86, 90–92, 99, 108, 114–116, 126–128, 130, 133, 149–151, 168, 183, 189, 191, 234, 235, 245, 307
Confucians, 70, 71, 79, 84, 92, 126, 150, 163
Confucius, 51, 63–65, 68–72, 74–77, 79–82, 90, 116, 150, 234
conscription, 113, 125, 140
consort kinsmen, 99, 106, 110, 117, 129, 307
constitutionalism, 211
Continental Europe, 211

copper coins, 111, 147, 164
corruption, xiii, 23, 40, 107, 148, 154, 158, 159, 164, 166, 213, 232, 259, 264, 266, 291, 294
corvée labour, 22, 44, 46, 48, 102, 128, 144, 148, 163, 164, 178, 180, 185, 191, 281
cronyism, 23

D

Dao De Jing, 68, 77, 79–82
Daoism, 2, 12, 64, 65, 68, 69, 71, 77, 80, 83, 86, 88, 90–92, 98, 108, 110, 114, 115, 126
decentralisation, 161, 166, 240, 256, 262, 263, 265, 281, 282, 291
democratisation, 305, 314
demonetarisation, 164
Deng Tong, 111
Deng, Xiaoping, xiii, 282, 289, 290, 293, 297
Descartes, René, 221, 222
despotism, 153, 156, 204, 211, 227, 311, 313, 314
determinism, 4, 5, 232
developmental state, 305
dialectics, 82, 110
disaster relief system, 15, 72, 90, 92, 168, 191
disenchantment, 217
division of labour, 4, 23, 146, 170, 191, 236
Dong, Zhongshu, 115, 116
dual-track system, 292
Duanmu, Ci, 65
dynastic cycles, 29, 158, 177, 179, 193, 194, 197, 306

E

early modern times, 42, 59, 222, 228
Eastern Europe, xv, 127, 313
economic base, 4–6, 10, 11, 20, 89, 108, 128, 134, 182, 198, 216, 250, 267
economic growth, xiii, 2, 12, 17, 21, 23, 33, 59, 84, 100, 137, 171, 179, 180, 192, 194, 196, 198, 203, 204, 208, 210, 212, 213, 217, 218, 223, 228, 234, 236, 238–241, 243, 245–247, 249, 257, 258, 265, 270, 271, 281, 293, 295, 299, 300, 305, 307, 311, 313, 314, 316–318
economic knowledge, 217, 220
Edinburgh, 221
egalitarianism, 288
Egypt, 1, 9, 32
eight-legged essay, 169
Emperor Gaodi of Han, 98, 108
Emperor Gaozong, 139
Emperor Huidi, 109, 110
Emperor Jingdi, 105, 106, 115
Emperor of Xiaowendi, 122
emperorship, 22, 157, 160, 163, 169, 171, 178, 185, 187, 189, 190, 227, 231, 242, 268
Emperor Wendi, 99, 100, 105, 106, 110, 111, 115, 119, 136–138
Emperor Wendi of Sui, 99, 100, 119, 136, 138
Emperor Wudi, 76, 99, 105–108, 110–116, 128, 185, 190
Emperor Wudi of Han, 76, 99, 190
Emperor Xiaowendi, 99, 121, 124
Emperor Xuanzong, 140
Emperor Yangdi, 137, 138, 146
empiricism, 221
Empress Cixi, 267
Empress Lü, 105, 110, 111
Empress Wu, 138–140, 142
enforcement, 17, 22, 23, 188, 255
Engels, Friedrich, xv, 3–7, 9, 179, 216, 247, 285–287, 289

England, 163, 187, 208–210, 214, 216, 218, 219, 221, 222, 227, 229, 236, 239, 242, 287, 309, 315
Enlightenment Movement, 2
entrepreneurship, 213, 245
entry cost, 214, 291
equal-field system, 99, 124, 125, 134, 140, 144, 181
Erhard, Ludwig, 317
Eucken, Walter, 317
eunuchs, 117, 133, 141, 158, 160
Eurasia, 19, 22, 152, 153, 155, 195, 204, 312
Eurocentrism, 19, 237
European Marriage Pattern, 217
externality, 15, 188, 192, 196

F
factionalism, 133, 140, 154, 158, 160
factor markets, 19, 192, 220, 236
Fairbank, John K., 18, 63, 69, 74, 82, 101, 127, 134, 138, 139, 141, 153, 159, 162, 164, 184, 231, 232, 238, 245, 299
Fan, Li, 48
Far East, 63, 262
Feng, Guifen, 262
Feng-jian, 38–41, 50
feudalism, 3, 8, 20, 38, 104, 153, 182, 212, 239, 267, 308, 309
first economic revolution, 20, 42, 48, 57, 64, 143, 149, 171, 179, 247, 306
fiscal state, 147–149, 266, 308
fiscal system, 112, 125, 164, 165, 171, 183, 185, 227, 262, 298
five-year plan, 280, 289
flood control, 14, 43, 45, 57, 238
flying cash, 147
forcible apparatus, 14
France, 2, 77, 221, 222, 255, 315
freemen, 204, 208, 220
free-rider problem, 13, 14, 44, 188, 196
Friedrich List, 316
Friesland, 206
frontier regions, 140, 230
fu-bing, 124, 140
Fujian, 230, 261

G
Gansu, 161, 270
general equivalent, 36, 37
general-governors, 240, 263
Genghis Khan, 152
gentry, 40, 84, 151, 167, 178, 189, 227, 241, 244, 257, 272, 277
German historical school, 316
Germany, xv, 233, 315, 316
Glasgow, 221
global economy, 18, 165, 168, 204, 211
Glorious Revolution, 204, 210–212
Golden Age, 205–207
governance, 13, 17, 19, 29, 58, 114, 159, 192, 205, 210, 212, 227, 241, 242, 255, 256, 273, 275
governor-lords, 161
gradualism, 313
granary system, 15, 192, 240, 255, 259
Great Britain, 23, 203, 204, 208–213, 215, 237, 239, 255, 259, 316
Great Leap Forward, 280, 281, 290, 313
Greece, 63
Groningen, 206
Guangdong, 259
Guangzhou, 227, 260
Guan-Long aristocratic groups, 121, 136, 138, 139
Guan Zhong, 48, 50, 51, 56, 58, 84–86, 183

Guan Zi, 68, 84–86
Guizhou, 269

H
Habsburg-Austria, 312
Han Fei, 63, 68, 75, 77, 79, 82, 84, 87–89
Hangzhou, 146
Hayek, Friedrich A., 77, 81, 82, 91, 111, 211, 287
Hegel, G.W.F., 7, 69, 150
He, Jin, 106
Heyday of China, 248
High-level Equilibrium Trap, 18, 136, 161, 232
Hintze, Otto, 6
historical-comparative sociology, 3, 11
historical materialism, xiv, xv, 3–5, 8, 10, 128, 134, 160, 179, 246, 247, 285, 286
historical school, 12
historical stages, xvi, 8, 11, 20
Holland, 205, 206
Hongwu, 135, 155–157, 162–164, 185
Hong, Xiuquan, 260–262
household registration, 54, 102, 125, 137, 282
huang-ce, 167
Huang-Lao, 83, 91, 98, 108–111, 114, 115, 128
Hubei, 230
hu-diao, 125
hui-zi, 147
Hume, David, 221
Hunan, 230, 263
hunter-gatherer civilisation, 151, 172, 223
huo-mai, 181
Hu Weiyong, 156
Hu, Yaobang, 294
hydraulic projects, 7, 9, 14, 20, 30, 32, 34, 43–46, 48, 53, 125, 144, 154, 168, 232, 239, 241, 255

I
Ideal types, xvi
ideal types, 11, 177
Imperial Confucianism, 73, 115, 116
imperialism, 268
imperial structure, 17, 19, 75–77, 89–92, 97, 116, 135, 160, 161, 178, 184, 185, 190, 194, 238, 241, 255, 267, 270, 299, 300
India, xiv, 2, 7, 63, 206, 210
Indian Ocean, 155, 157
individualism, 218, 220, 315
industrialisation, 3, 21, 143, 156, 208, 211, 231, 232, 236, 237, 250, 256, 265, 266, 270, 272, 274, 276, 289, 291, 307–309, 311, 314, 315
Industrial Revolution, 3, 17, 21, 203, 208, 211, 214, 219, 220, 222, 223, 229, 233, 236–238, 245
Industrious Revolution, 219
information asymmetry, 13, 16, 23, 241
Inner Court, 106, 185
institutional efficiency, 13, 17, 58, 130, 178, 196, 245
institutionalism, 13, 17, 187
institutional settings, 18, 312
internationalisation, 147, 256
interventionism, 85, 86, 148, 152
invisible hand, 77, 91
Iran, 152
irrigation, 9, 14, 30–32, 34, 43–45, 57, 104, 125, 182, 186
Islamic world, 135, 162

J
James II, 210
Japan, 38, 162, 165, 168, 219, 255, 256, 266, 271, 274, 280, 296, 315
Jiangnan, 19, 126, 136, 140, 144, 146, 151, 163, 164, 167, 171, 183, 191, 192, 235, 238
Jiankang, 126
jiao-zi, 147
jin-shi, 142
jin-yi-wei, 156
joint-stock company, 265
Jones, Richard, 7
jue-mai, 181
jun-ji-chu, 160
jun-tian, 124
Jurchen, 135, 151, 153, 158
Jurchen", 159
Juxtaposition of Commandery and State, 104, 105, 119

K
Kafka, 1, 22
Kaifeng, 146
Kai-shek, Chiang, 256, 270, 271, 274, 276
Kangxi, 159, 160, 165, 166
Kang, Youwei, 267, 269
ke-ju, 186
Keynes, John Maynard, 63, 85
Khitan, 135, 151, 153
Khrushchev, 280–282
King Charles I, 209
King Hui of Liang, 72
King John, 209
King Wuling of Zhao, 51
Kissinger, Henry, 76
Korea, 168, 266, 288, 305
Korean Peninsula, 137, 158, 266
Kornai, 287
Kornai, János, 286, 289, 291, 292
Kublai Khan, 154
Kuomintang, 256, 257, 269–271, 273, 274, 276, 278, 280, 284, 289, 312

L
laissez-faire, 49, 77, 98, 108, 110, 111, 238, 316
landlord, 261, 277
Lange, Oskar, 288
Laozi, 63, 68, 77–82, 87, 88, 91, 109
large-scale public projects, 17, 56, 104, 196, 240
Latin America, 165, 259, 284, 288
Legalism, 49, 58, 64, 65, 68, 75, 77, 82–84, 86–89, 91, 92, 104, 114, 115, 148, 188, 306, 307
legitimacy, 101, 113, 119, 151, 169, 189, 196, 264, 282, 295, 299, 316
Leiden, 205
Leipzig, 237
Lenin, 65, 278
Leninism, 280, 289
liang-shui fa, 144
Liao, 151
Liao, Boyuan, 107
liberalisation, xiii, 258, 295, 298
liberalism, 79, 81, 83, 209, 316
Lie Zi, 78
Li, Hongzhang, 161, 260–264, 266
li-jia, 163
lijin, 240, 263, 264
Li, Kui, 47, 51–53, 56, 58, 85, 88
Lingqu Canal, 101
Lin, Zexu, 259, 262
Li, Si, 75, 84, 87, 100, 188
literacy rate, 211
literary inquisition, 169
literati, 12, 72, 76, 133, 138, 142, 152, 159, 160, 184, 245, 307

Liu, Bang, 103–105
Liu, Shaoqi, 278–281
Liu, Xiu, 117
Liu, Yan, 183
Li, Xiannian, 290, 293
Li-Xue, 150
Li, Yuan, 138
Locke, John, 221
lordship, 75, 98, 100, 183
Lü Buwei, 49, 68
Luther, 233
Lutheranism, 245
Lu, Xiangshan, 169

M
magnates, 98, 99, 105, 108, 114, 117–127, 129, 180, 307
Malenkov, 281
Malthusian Trap, 228, 229
Manchuria, 151, 158, 165
Manchus, 159
manorial economy, 20, 97, 99, 114, 122, 179, 180
Maoist socialism, 257, 284
Mao, Zedong, xiv, 197, 257, 276, 278, 280–283, 289, 290, 293, 298, 313
market economy, 114, 136, 149, 152, 163, 167, 171, 235, 258, 260, 273, 284, 289, 294, 297, 299, 313, 316, 317
marketisation, 147, 149, 162, 167, 170, 184, 218, 235, 236, 247, 290, 292, 294, 295, 307, 314, 317
Marxism, xv, 3, 9, 258, 280, 283, 288, 296
Marxists, 3, 5, 7–9, 266, 288
Marx, Karl, xiv, xv, 3–10, 12, 20, 24, 37, 58, 65, 171, 198, 216, 218, 222, 233, 235, 238, 243, 283, 285–288, 296, 311, 312
Material forces, 11
mausoleum, 102, 110, 189
mechanisation, 207, 211
Mencius, 40, 41, 49, 63, 68, 72–74, 76, 78, 90, 116, 150
Meng Zi, 71, 72, 74, 78
Mesopotamia, 1, 9, 32
microeconomics, 13
military groups, 121, 130, 133
Ministry of Personnel, 138
Ministry of Rites, 138
mixed economy, 278, 295, 305
mode of production, 4–10, 20, 204, 207, 215, 216, 223, 247, 249, 285, 286, 308–310
modernisation, 3, 19, 22, 151, 161, 171, 187, 223, 231, 250, 256, 258, 265, 266, 271–274, 276, 290, 299, 307, 308, 311–317
modernities, 11
monarchical constitutionalism, 22
monarchy, 135, 156, 160, 190, 204, 205, 207, 209, 212–215, 257, 269, 309
monastery, 127, 128
monetarisation, 149, 161–164, 170, 307
Mongol, 135, 152, 153, 155, 162, 230
Mongolia, 159, 249
monsoon, 29–33, 43
Montesquieu, 7
moral hazard, 13, 16, 178, 185
Moscow, 280
mu-bing, 140
Müller-Armack, Alfred, 317

N
Nanjing, 164, 255, 259, 260, 262
national defence, 14, 15, 20, 56, 103, 119, 120, 178, 188, 196, 256, 270, 273, 310

Nationalisation, 282, 284
nationalism, 268
natural order, 82, 83, 91
Nazism, 288
Needham, Joseph, 45, 233, 246
neoclassical economics, 12, 13, 18, 196
Neo-Confucianism, 133, 150, 151, 168, 189
Nepal, 126
New Democracy, 276
New Economic Policy, 278
new institutional economics, 12
Newton, Isaac, 221
Nian, 161, 262
nine-rank system, 118–120, 126, 129, 186
Nordic countries, 315
Northern Africa, 127

O
official ideology, 64, 68, 70, 74, 76, 83, 90, 91, 99, 104, 108, 114, 128, 133, 151, 189, 307
one-party state, 299, 300
Ordoliberalism, 315–317
Oriental Despotism, 9, 30
Ostrom, Elinor, 15

P
palace examination, 139, 142
paper money, 147, 154, 162, 164, 240, 245, 271
Pareto, 17, 78
Pareto Optimal, 17
parliament, 204, 209, 210, 214, 242, 269
partible inheritance, 54, 66, 91
patent system, 213
path dependence, 21, 184, 258, 283, 284, 299, 312–314, 316
patterned action, 11
peasantry economy, 20, 84, 89–92, 98, 99, 103, 108, 111, 114, 118, 122, 128–130, 134, 141, 145, 158, 162, 163, 170, 178, 180–182, 184, 185, 190, 191, 193, 204, 227, 242, 243, 257, 272, 276, 277, 279, 283, 284, 306
peasants, 20, 22–24, 40, 48, 54, 57, 76, 83–85, 88, 91, 103, 108, 110, 113, 114, 116, 120, 122, 127–129, 134, 135, 138, 140, 143–145, 148, 158, 163, 164, 178, 180–182, 187, 188, 191, 193, 241, 259, 263, 271, 277, 278, 288, 297, 299, 307
perfect information, 13, 16
perfect market, 16
Persia, 162
Physiocracy, 77
planned economy, 257, 279–282, 284, 285, 287, 288, 290–293, 297–299, 316
planting agriculture, 33, 34, 36, 153
Plato, 63
Polo, Marco, 2, 135
Predestination, 234
price scissors, 279
primitive accumulation, 208, 215, 310
primogeniture, 54, 154, 190
principal-agent problem, 16, 23, 76, 98, 99, 108, 122, 128, 133, 135, 143, 158, 170, 171, 178, 184, 185, 187, 188, 190, 241, 256, 264, 306, 311
private economy, 293
private ownership, 30, 41, 47, 48, 51, 52, 54, 55, 58, 83, 99, 102, 108, 134, 140, 143–145, 167, 170, 180–182, 279, 297, 306, 307
privatisation, 15

productive forces, 3–5, 8, 9, 21, 23, 24, 57, 134, 135, 156, 168, 171, 172, 179, 198, 223, 285, 308, 312
property relations, 4, 6
property rights, 17, 47, 59, 143, 145, 172, 196, 206, 209–211, 213, 218, 231, 240, 242–245, 297
Protestantism, 11, 209, 216, 234
Proudhon, 285
public good, 10, 13–17, 20, 22–24, 30, 48, 56–58, 64, 72–74, 76, 90, 92, 98, 99, 101, 103, 120, 123, 128, 129, 137, 167, 168, 178, 179, 182, 183, 187, 188, 191, 193, 238, 239, 242, 244, 248, 270, 273, 277, 284, 298, 306, 310, 311
public good provision, 10, 13–17, 20, 22–24, 30, 48, 56–58, 73, 74, 76, 92, 98, 99, 101, 103, 120, 123, 128, 129, 178, 179, 182, 183, 187, 188, 191, 193, 239, 244, 248, 306, 310, 311
public ownership, 47, 51, 57, 103, 123, 125, 134, 140, 144, 180, 181

Q

Qianlong, 159, 160, 191, 241, 259
Qin Emperor the First, 49, 54, 87
qing-miao, 148
Quanzhou, 146
Quesnay, 2, 77

R

rationalisation, 23, 216, 217, 219
rationalism, 12, 221
rationality, 12, 13, 207
rational thinking, 58
recession, 18, 231, 298
relations of production, 4–6, 24, 57, 135, 156, 171, 198, 223, 285
rent-seeking, 213, 259, 292
Ren, Zhongyi, 293
republicanism, 22, 258
Rodbertus, 285
Roman Empire, 101, 118, 222
Rome, 117, 179
Rousseau, Jean-Jacques, 222
rural economy, 146, 164
Russia, xiv, 7, 152, 156, 161, 255, 287, 288, 292, 312

S

salvation, 12, 127, 216, 234
samurai, 162
Sang Hongyang, 112, 113, 148, 183, 190
san-zhang, 124
Saudi Arab, 190
Scotland, 221
sea-ban, 135, 162, 164, 195
second economic revolution, 21, 143, 149, 243
Second World War, 276, 284, 289, 305
SEZs, 292, 294
Shaanxi, 161
Shanghai, 237, 260, 262, 273, 295
Shang, Yang, 47, 51, 53–56, 58, 66, 86, 88, 89, 91, 100, 102, 180, 184
Shaoxing, 126
Shen Buhai, 51, 88
Shenzhen, 293, 295
Shuihudi, 55, 103
Sichuan, 115, 147, 230, 256, 270
Sima, Qian, 32, 54, 77, 79, 82, 87, 110, 113
Sinicisation, 99
slavery, 7, 9, 20

small peasantry, 41, 46, 48, 51, 53, 56, 58, 99, 103, 108, 125, 128, 130, 134, 141, 149, 168, 170, 185
Smith, Adam, xiv, 7, 91, 243
Smithian dynamics, 236
Smithian growth, 170, 192, 196
socialism, 8, 257, 258, 280, 282–288, 317
socialist calculation, 287
socialist transition, 278
SOEs, 292, 295
soft budget constraint, 292
Sombart, 238
South Asia, 284
South China Sea, 155
Spain, 205, 312
spontaneous order, 77, 82, 91
Stalin, 278, 280, 282, 284
Stalinism, 257, 280, 282, 284, 296, 313
Stalinist Mode, 280, 281, 289
Stalinists, 8, 20
St. Andrews, 222
state apparatus, 204, 205, 214, 215, 222, 297, 306
state capacity, 214, 215, 227, 239, 240, 242, 247, 266
state examination system, 100, 119, 122, 130, 133, 134, 136, 138, 139, 142, 149, 151, 153, 156, 159, 168–170, 179, 184, 186, 189, 227, 246, 262, 267, 307
state monopoly, 284, 291, 295, 298
succession problem, 101, 189
Sun, Yet-sen, 256, 268, 276
superstructure, 4–6, 10, 11, 21, 57, 64, 134, 156, 168, 171, 172, 179, 182, 198, 216, 235, 242–244, 247–249, 307
surveillance, 157, 185

T
Taiping, 161, 256, 260–262, 264, 273, 274
Taiping Movement, 161
Taiwan, 159, 266, 271, 276, 305
Tang-Song transition, 21, 134, 144, 149, 155, 170, 171, 179, 198, 307, 308
taxation system, 125, 144, 148, 157, 165, 243
the Bill of Rights, 210
the Black Death, 217, 236, 309
the British East India Company, 210
the CCP, 257, 258, 271, 273, 274, 276, 277, 279–284, 288, 290, 293–295, 297, 299, 300, 314, 317
the central plain, 30–35, 39, 43, 49, 53, 57, 90, 99, 102, 119, 120, 123, 129, 140
the common law, 211
the Cultural Revolution, 279, 282, 290
the Dongting Lake, 230
the Dutch East India Company, 206
the Dutch Republic, 205
the Dutch West India Company, 206
the Enlightenment movement, 220, 221, 223, 245
the Great Canal, 14, 137, 240, 310
the Great Divergence, 18, 196, 223, 228, 233, 236, 237, 246, 309
the Great Wall, 1, 14, 56, 58, 98, 101, 310
the loess plateau, 31, 33, 35, 43, 57, 140
the Low Countries, 218, 227
the Meiji Reform, 266, 267
the Middle Ages, 20, 50, 219, 315
the Middle East, 7
the Needham Puzzle, 246
the Neolithic era, 36

the Netherlands, 203, 205–208, 210–212, 237
the New World, 2, 19, 163, 168, 205, 236, 237
the Norman Conquest, 211
the Orange Dynasty, 212
the Pacific Ocean, 31
the People's Republic of China, 197, 314
the Reformation movement, 216, 233, 234
the Renaissance, 134, 211
the Republic of China, 256, 268, 312, 314
the Roman law, 211
the Royal Society, 221
the self-strengthening movement, 256, 261, 262, 264, 266, 272
the Soviet Union, xv, 270, 278–280, 282–284, 289, 294, 313
The Tang-Song transition, 21
the Treaty of Shimonoseki, 266
the United Provinces, 212
the United States, 213, 255, 268
the West, 2, 12, 20, 21, 135, 157, 172, 195, 214, 215, 218, 233, 237, 238, 246, 247, 250, 255, 260, 265, 294, 296, 311, 315, 316, 318
the Yangtze Delta, 19, 42, 45, 99, 120, 124, 125, 137, 192, 261, 266, 269
the Yangtze River, 29, 34, 45, 101
the Yellow River, 29, 34, 47, 164
Third Way, 316
Three Principles of the People, 268, 276
Tiananmen Square Event, 296
Tiangong Kaiwu, 246
Tianjin, 261, 262
Tibet, 159, 249
tonggou tongxiao, 279
Tong-Guang Restoration, 256
traditionalism, 12, 216, 233
tragedy of the commons, 13, 14
transaction costs, 13, 16, 17, 22, 30, 44, 57, 76, 146, 149, 178, 182, 183, 188, 191, 206, 207, 210, 217
treaty ports, 266, 269, 273
Tulip Mania, 207
tun-tian, 118, 123
Turgot, 2, 77
TVEs, 291
two-tax system, 144, 147

U
Uighurs, 155
unified purchase system, 279, 282
unilinear evolutionism, 11
urbanisation, 19, 146, 149, 161, 170, 206, 207, 232, 235
Utrecht, xvii, 205, 206
Uygur, 161

V
Vera Zasulich, 288
Vietnam, 157
von Mises, Ludwig, 287

W
waixiao, 264
Wang, Anshi, 148, 183
Wang, Mang, 106, 116
Wang, Yangming, 169
warlordism, 133, 135, 141, 142, 148, 152, 256, 268–271, 273, 312
Warlords, 141
water control, 33, 35, 43, 44, 242
water erosion, 33
water supply, 32, 34, 43, 44
Watt, James, 211

weathering processes, 33
Weber, Max, xiv–xvi, 3, 5, 10, 12, 23, 64, 71, 216, 218, 233, 273
well-field system, 38, 40, 41, 47, 48, 50, 54, 57, 66, 180
wen-zi-yu, 169
Western Europe, 2, 3, 7, 11, 18–21, 23, 58, 130, 179, 187, 194, 197, 203, 204, 212, 214–219, 221–223, 227–229, 233, 236–239, 243–245, 247–249, 273, 308–311
westernisation, 258
West Pacific Ocean, 157
Wittfogel, Karl, xiv, 9, 30, 44
World Trade Organisation, 295
wu-bao, 180
Wuchang, 267, 268
Wu, Qi, 51
Wuwei, 64, 81–83
Wuzhu coin, 112

X
Xianbei, 120, 121
Ximen Bao, 52
Xinjiang, 230, 249, 256, 270
Xin-xue, 169
Xiongnu, 106, 110, 112, 120
Xuanxue, 126
Xunzi, 68, 74, 75, 87, 90

Y
Yang, Jian, 121
Yangshao, 34
Yang, Yan, 144
Yangzhou, 126
Yang Zhu, 77, 78
Yantie Lun, 113
Yan Ying, 50
Yi Jing, 68
yi-tiao-bian-fa, 165
Yongle, 157, 162
Yongzheng, 159, 160, 165, 166, 185, 190
Yuan, Shikai, 256, 264, 267, 269
Yunnan, 230, 269, 270
Yu the Great, 32, 35

Z
Zasulich, Vera, 288
Zeng, Guofan, 161, 261–264
Zhang Wentian, 278
Zhang, Zhidong, 262
zhan-tian ke-tian, 124
Zhao, Kuangyin, 141, 142
Zhao, Ziyang, 292, 293
Zheng, He, 157, 162
Zhou Enlai, 278, 281
Zhuangzi, 63, 82
Zhujiang River, 101
Zhu, Xi, 150, 168
Zichan, 49
zou-zhe, 160
Zuo, Zongtang, 261–264

Ingram Content Group UK Ltd.
Milton Keynes UK
UKHW010826270623
424112UK00001B/33

9 783031 270161